America's Achilles' Heel

BCSIA Studies in International Security

Michael E. Brown, Sean M. Lynn-Jones, & Steven E. Miller, series editors
Karen Motley, executive editor
Belfer Center for Science and International Affairs (BCSIA)
John F. Kennedy School of Government, Harvard University

Published by the MIT Press:

Allison, Graham T., Owen R. Coté, Jr., Richard A. Falkenrath, & Steven E. Miller, *Avoiding Nuclear Anarchy: Containing the Threat of Loose Russian Nuclear Weapons and Fissile Material* (1996)

Allison, Graham T., and Kalypso Nicolaïdis, eds., *The Greek Paradox: Promise vs. Performance* (1996)

Arbatov, Alexei, Abram Chayes, Antonia Handler Chayes, and Lara Olson, eds., *Managing Conflict in the Former Soviet Union: Russian and American Perspectives* (1997)

Blackwill, Robert D., and Michael Stürmer, eds., *Allies Divided: Transatlantic Policies for the Greater Middle East* (1997)

Brown, Michael E., ed., *The International Dimensions of Internal Conflict* (1996)

Brown, Michael E., and Šumit Ganguly, eds., *Government Policies and Ethnic Relations in Asia and the Pacific* (1997)

Elman, Miriam Fendius, ed., *Paths to Peace: Is Democracy the Answer?* (1997)

Falkenrath, Richard A., *Shaping Europe's Military Order: The Origins and Consequences of the CFE Treaty* (1994)

Falkenrath, Richard A., Robert D. Newman, and Bradley A. Thayer, *America's Achilles' Heel: Nuclear, Biological, and Chemical Terrorism and Covert Attack* (1998)

Feldman, Shai, *Nuclear Weapons and Arms Control in the Middle East* (1996)

Forsberg, Randall, ed., *The Arms Production Dilemma: Contraction and Restraint in the World Combat Aircraft Industry* (1994)

Hagerty, Devin T., *The Consequences of Nuclear Proliferation: Lessons from South Asia* (1998)

Heymann, Philip B., *Terrorism and America: A Common Sense Strategy for a Democratic Society* (1998)

Kokoshin, Andrei A., *Soviet Strategic Thought, 1917–91* (1998)

Shields, John M., and William C. Potter, eds., *Dismantling the Cold War: U.S. and NIS Perspectives on the Nunn-Lugar Cooperative Threat Reduction Program* (1997)

America's Achilles' Heel
Nuclear, Biological, and Chemical Terrorism and Covert Attack

Richard A. Falkenrath, Robert D. Newman,
and Bradley A. Thayer

BCSIA Studies in International Security

The MIT Press
Cambridge, Massachusetts
London, England

Library of Congress Cataloging-in-Publication Data

Falkenrath, Richard A.
America's Achilles' heel: nuclear, biological, and chemical terrorism and covert attack / Richard A. Falkenrath, Robert D. Newman, and Bradley A. Thayer.
    p.   cm.—(BCSIA studies in international security)
    Includes bibliographical references and index.
    ISBN 0-262-56118-2 (pbk.: alk. paper)
    1. Terrorism—United States. 2. Weapons of mass destruction. I. Newman, Robert D., 1966–   . II. Thayer, Bradley A. III. Title. IV. Series.
HV6432.F35   1998
363.3'2'0973—dc21   98-17401
                                                                                        CIP

Printed in the United States of America

Edited, designed, and typeset by
Teresa J. Lawson Editorial Consulting, Stow, Massachusetts

Cover photo:
Scanning electron micrograph of *Bacillus anthracis* by Kathy Kuehl, courtesy of the U.S. Army Medical Research Institute of Infectious Diseases. Previously published in the *Journal of the American Medical Association*, Vol. 278, No. 5 (August 6, 1997), p. 438. The cylindrical bacteria are 3–5 microns long.

10 9 8 7 6

Contents

Boxes

Figures

Tables

Recommendations

About the Authors

Richard A. Falkenrath is the Executive Director of the Belfer Center for Science and International Affairs at Harvard University's Kennedy School of Government. He was previously a Research Fellow in the Center's International Security Program, and a visiting research fellow at the German Society of Foreign Affairs (DGAP) in Bonn. He is a co-author of *Avoiding Nuclear Anarchy: Containing the Threat of Loose Russian Nuclear Weapons and Fissile Material* (MIT Press, 1996), and the author of *Shaping Europe's Military Order: The Origins and Consequences of the CFE Treaty* (MIT Press, 1995). He has served as a consultant to the RAND Corporation and the Defense Science Board, and is a member of the International Institute for Strategic Studies, the American Economic Association, the Council on Foreign Relations, and the American Council on Germany. He holds a Ph.D from the Department of War Studies, King's College London, where he was a British Marshall Scholar.

Robert D. Newman is an arms control specialist working in Washington. He was a fellow at the Center for Science and International Affairs from 1995 to 1997. He holds a master's degree in international politics from the London School of Economics, where he was a British Marshall Scholar, and an undergraduate degree in physics from MIT.

Bradley A. Thayer is a Visiting Assistant Professor of Government at Dartmouth College. From 1995 to 1997, he was a fellow at the Center for Science and International Affairs. He holds a Ph.D from the University of Chicago.

Preface

Homer's *Iliad* tells of Achilles, mightiest of all the warriors of the Trojan War. When Achilles was an infant, his mother, the sea-goddess Thetis, plunged his body into the River Styx to make him invulnerable to bodily harm. The heel by which she held him, though, was untouched by the waters, and thus remained his small, mortal vulnerability.

Achilles' heel is a fitting metaphor for the threat of covert or terrorist attack involving weapons of mass destruction — nuclear, biological, or chemical. The level of security and prosperity enjoyed by today's advanced democracies is virtually unprecedented in history. Internally, the basic political order of these states is not seriously contested. There are only a handful of external military threats, none yet global in reach. The world's many civil wars and internal conflicts are largely confined to specific regions, and their effects can be prevented from spilling over into the protected nations of the West. There are of course many serious long-term challenges to the West — China's rise, Russia's decline, energy, environmental problems, and widening economic inequality come to mind — but great vulnerabilities are few.

Nevertheless, all open societies are vulnerable to massive loss of life from the covert or terrorist delivery of nuclear, biological, or chemical weapons. A score of potential aggressors already possess these immensely lethal weapons, and the technologies that lie behind them grow inexorably more accessible with time. A free and open society cannot construct a perfect defense against covert attacks and terrorism, and even trying to do so may make it significantly less free and open. As a result, virtually all potential aggressors could employ covert or terrorist means of delivery with good chances of success. Accessible, extremely destructive weapons that can be delivered by clandestine means represent a significant vulnerability, one which can be regarded as "small" only in the sense that few aggressors have chosen to exploit it. We hope this threat continues to lie dormant, but believe it is imprudent to assume that it will.

How This Book Began

This book began to take form while one of the authors was engaged in writing an earlier volume in the CSIA (now BCSIA) Studies in International Security. That book, *Avoiding Nuclear Anarchy*, argued that the United States has a vital national interest in improving the ability of Russia and the other states of the former Soviet Union to secure and account for their nuclear weapons and fissile material. The collapse of the Soviet Union left vast quantities of weapons-usable nuclear materials vulnerable to theft and diversion, which opened a new and potentially quite attractive route by which a hostile state could acquire a basic nuclear weapons capability. This possibility also threatened to eliminate the most important technical barrier that has held down the risk of nuclear weapons acquisition by terrorist groups in the past. Given the grave consequences of nuclear weapons acquisition by hostile states or terrorists, it seemed clear to us that the United States, and indeed the international community as a whole, should be investing heavily in reversing the alarming trend toward insecure nuclear stockpiles in the former Soviet Union.

We were reminded, however, that what seems self-evident at Harvard often has little to do with Washington's political realities. A handful of small U.S. government programs were struggling to gain the funding and high-level political support they needed to make serious headway in the complicated, secretive, and impoverished Russian nuclear complex. The innovative Nunn-Lugar program, begun in 1991 to help the Soviet Union implement its arms control commitments, scored a major success in ensuring that Russia became the sole nuclear successor state of the Soviet Union, but the problem of providing security for the consolidated remnants of the Soviet nuclear arsenal has proved less tractable. The priorities of the Clinton administration's national security and foreign policies were directed elsewhere, and these issues did not enjoy high-level political attention. Several important initiatives emerged from the legislative branch, but the general attitude of the U.S. Congress toward nuclear security programs in the former Soviet Union was dubious at best, hostile at worst. Critical national security initiatives, tarred as "foreign aid," were sorely constrained by the Congress's grudging financial support, and continually jeopardized by amendments proposing complete excision.

Avoiding Nuclear Anarchy highlighted the potential connection between insecure nuclear stockpiles in Russia and nuclear terrorism in America, helping make the case for nuclear security programs in the former Soviet Union more politically compelling. In the aftermath of the World Trade

Center and Oklahoma City bombings, this argument seemed to resonate, and we were certainly not alone in making it. Gradually, the importance of securing vulnerable fissile material stockpiles began to seep into the consciousness of Americans outside of the narrow community of professional nonproliferation analysts and officials, and the funding base for a few key programs has become somewhat more solid. Far more remains to be done, but the trend is in the right direction.

Many questions about the risk of nuclear terrorism remained unanswered, however. What could motivate an act of nuclear terrorism? Just how likely was such an event? Why be concerned only with nuclear weapons? Shouldn't we also worry about less destructive, but more accessible, chemical and biological weapons, especially in the aftermath of the March 1995 nerve gas attack in the Tokyo subway? If the United States were to take the threat of nuclear terrorism seriously by investing in the security of Russian nuclear materials, should it not also invest in preparing itself for domestic threats of nuclear, biological, or chemical (NBC) weapons attack? How well prepared is the United States for these contingencies? Does the concept of "terrorism" adequately encompass the problem? Shouldn't we also worry about covert attack by hostile states?

These issues also raised broader questions about U.S. national security strategy, and the priorities that flow from it. In the second half of the twentieth century, no national security objective has ranked higher than preventing nuclear detonations in American cities. In 1940, Albert Einstein warned President Franklin D. Roosevelt that a "single [nuclear] bomb ..., carried by boat and exploded in a port, might very well destroy the whole port together with some of the surrounding territory."[1] During the Cold War, the nuclear threat to the United States emanated from the Soviet Union, and a vast complex was erected to deter, and defend against, Soviet strategic nuclear capabilities. But the passing of the Soviet threat has fundamentally changed the nature of the mass-destruction threat to U.S. cities, making it necessary to update the strategic assumptions of U.S. defense policy.

There are several different means by which weapons of mass destruction might be delivered to targets in the United States, but one — ballistic

---

1. For the full text of Einstein's letter to Roosevelt, see Spencer R. Weart and Gertrud Weiss Szilard, eds., *Leo Szilard: His Version of the Facts: Selected Recollections and Correspondence* (Cambridge, Mass.: MIT Press, 1978), pp. 94–96. At the time, Einstein was unsure about whether nuclear weapons would ever be compact enough for aircraft delivery.

missiles — holds a position of unique priority in the allocation of U.S. defense dollars. National and theater ballistic missile defense budgets have decreased more slowly than overall U.S. defense expenditures, and the Congress regularly votes funds over and above the administration's requests. There is, however, no program for addressing the U.S. vulnerability to covert NBC attack that is even remotely comparable in size or scope to the ballistic missile defense program. Many officials and experts underestimate how poorly prepared the United States is for this form of attack. In 1993, the director of the Ballistic Missile Defense Organization told the Congress:

I think we have mechanisms in place to detect and counter things like bombs in suitcases, bombs in airline terminals, and bombs in ships of various kinds. These things can be tracked and looked at, and there are ways to counter them. I can't think of anything except a strategic missile today that we don't have a counter-measure in-hand for.[2]

We believe this statement is inaccurate, as was President Clinton's in 1996, when he formally certified to the Congress that "the United States has the capability to prevent the illegal importation of nuclear, biological, and chemical weapons into the United States and its possessions."[3] Both indicate the lack of attention given to the simplest forms of NBC delivery, the broad category of covert delivery options first suggested by Einstein. This is an imbalance in U.S. defense policy, and one that we believe is irrational and imprudent.

There are several explanations for why U.S. defense policy emphasizes defenses against the most technologically sophisticated delivery systems. For one, although aspects of the covert NBC threat have existed for years, it has really come to the fore only with the passing of the Soviet strategic

---

2.   Testimony by then Major General Malcolm R. O'Neill, Acting Director of the Ballistic Missile Defense Organization, *Hearings on Procurement of Aircraft, Missiles, Weapons, and Tracked Vehicles*, Subcommittee on Military Acquisition, Research, and Technology of the House Armed Services Committee, 103rd Cong., 1st Sess., June 10, 1993 (Washington, D.C.: U.S. Government Printing Office [U.S. GPO], 1993), p. 184.

3.   Letter from the President to the Speaker of the House and the President of the Senate, dated November 4, 1996, released by the Office of the White House Press Secretary November 6, 1996. This document is available on the White House web page at <library.whitehouse.gov/Search/Query-PressReleases.html>. Internet references given in this book were current in autumn 1997.

nuclear threat. Second, there is a tendency to assume — wrongly — that the threat is so hard to counter that trying is futile. Third, the covert NBC threat straddles the divide between national security, law enforcement, and emergency management, allowing the Department of Defense to dodge responsibility. Fourth, there are no politically powerful government institutions dedicated to national preparedness against covert NBC threats. Fifth, vigorous support for ballistic missile defense is an enduring element of the Republican Party platform. Sixth, the tight fiscal climate of the 1990s discourages new national security initiatives. And finally, the end of the Cold War has turned the defense budget into less an instrument of national strategy and more a program for distributing federal largess and jobs.

We do believe that defense against ballistic missile attack is a critically important mission for the U.S. military, one that should be pursued with vigor and determination. However, there should also be comparable efforts aimed at reducing U.S. vulnerability to covert NBC threats. This view, more than anything else, motivated us to write this book.

The Nature of the Problem

The danger of covert attack with nuclear, biological, or chemical weapons is growing, but it is not new. Chemical warfare agents have existed since before World War I, and have grown increasingly accessible as a result of the diffusion of knowledge and technology. Nuclear weapons and modern biological weapons were developed during World War II, and refined in the decades after, bringing the possibility of covert attack into the realm of strategic importance for the first time. Even before the first nuclear test, the possibility of devastating covert attacks by states was apparent. In March 1945, the physicist Leo Szilard wrote:

Clearly, if such [nuclear] bombs are available, it is not necessary to bomb our cities from the air in order to destroy them. All that is necessary is to place a comparatively small number of such bombs in each of our major cities and to detonate them at some later time.... The United States has a very long coastline which will make it possible to smuggle in such bombs in peacetime and to carry them by truck into our cities. The long coastline, the structure of our society, and our very heterogeneous population may make an effective control of such "traffic" virtually impossible.... So far it has not been possible to devise any methods which would enable us to detect hidden atomic bombs buried in the ground or otherwise efficiently protected against detection.[4]

Less attention has traditionally been given to the risk of covert biological and chemical attack, but the Tokyo nerve gas attack in March 1995 (see Box 1, Aum Shinrikyo, p. 19) has revived interest in this subject, leading to a number of important recent studies with good policy recommendations.[5] The contribution of this book to the literature comes from its systematic examination of the threat presented by all three weapon types, its attention to the motivations of state and non-state actors, and its detailed prescriptive agenda for the U.S. government.

This book focuses on U.S. vulnerability to covert NBC attack, and we direct our recommendations principally to American policymakers and analysts. We did this to make the study more manageable, and to allow us to concentrate on the strategic challenges that are unique to the world's only remaining military superpower. We believe, however, that most of our analysis of the covert NBC threat applies broadly to all advanced democracies, and that the recommendations made in Chapter 5 could be readily adapted to other countries. We also recognize that no country can implement an effective response against the covert NBC threat on a purely unilateral basis. The threat is fundamentally a transnational one, and it must be met with a combination of national and international measures.

Some may question the wisdom of publishing a detailed analysis of the threat of NBC terrorism and covert attack. There are two key risks: giving potential aggressors new ideas; and making it easier to obtain or employ NBC weapons. We take these possibilities seriously, but believe they are often exaggerated and must be balanced against the problems associated

---

4.   Leo Szilard, "Atomic Bombs and the Postwar Position of the United States in the World," memorandum for President Franklin D. Roosevelt, March 1945; reprinted in Morton Grodzins and Eugene Rabinowitch, eds., *The Atomic Age: Scientists in National and World Affairs, Articles from the* Bulletin of the Atomic Scientists *1945–1962* (New York: Basic Books, 1963), pp. 13–14.

5.   For a broad literature review, see Ron Purver, *Chemical and Biological Terrorism: The Threat according to the Open Literature*, Canadian Security Intelligence Service (unclassified), June 1995. We are indebted to Purver for this review, which has led us to a number of other useful sources. For an overview of the nuclear terrorism debate in the 1970s, see the compilation of articles in Augustus R. Norton and Martin H. Greenberg, eds., *Studies in Nuclear Terrorism* (Boston, Mass.: G.K. Hall, 1979).

with an incomplete understanding of the threat and the severity of current vulnerabilities. We suspect that the states and non-state actors capable of carrying out covert NBC attacks are likely to be able, without help from us, to identify existing vulnerabilities and appropriate attack options. Nevertheless, we have refrained from providing technical details or primary references on how to acquire or use NBC weapons, and do not describe scenarios for catastrophic NBC weapons use. We believe that those who think this book will make it significantly easier for a terrorist group to build and use a weapon of mass destruction are underestimating just how much detailed technical information on nuclear, biological, and chemical weapons is easily available to a determined and moderately well-educated researcher.

Acknowledgments

Work on this book began with the preparations for a major national conference on NBC proliferation and terrorism jointly sponsored by the Center for Science and International Affairs (CSIA, now the Belfer Center for Science and International Affairs) and the Los Alamos National Laboratory in May 1996. This conference was convened at the request of Senator Pete Domenici, and was supported and attended by Senators John Glenn, Richard Lugar, Sam Nunn, and Ted Stevens. It anticipated some of the policy ideas contained in the important Defense against Weapons of Mass Destruction Act of 1996, better known as the Nunn-Lugar-Domenici amendment (see Box 11, Nunn-Lugar-Domenici, p. 262). In February 1997, a smaller conference was convened in Santa Fe, New Mexico, co-sponsored by CSIA, Los Alamos, and the Monterey Institute of International Studies. These two conferences brought together many of the nation's leading technical and policy experts on nuclear, biological, and chemical weapons, terrorism, and U.S. national strategy, and provided invaluable opportunities to discuss the early ideas that lay behind this study.

While researching and writing this book, we have benefited from the support and advice of a truly exceptional group of colleagues and institutions. At Harvard, Graham Allison's encouragement and insight have been essential to this project. We are deeply grateful to him for his generosity and for supporting the research demands on his Executive Director's time. Steven Miller has been a mentor to us, and our debt to him has only grown from his encouragement and astute advice as we were completing this study. It was also our great fortune that Ash Carter returned from the Pentagon to the Center while this project was in midcourse; his support and insight have been invaluable. Robert Blackwill has helped in many ways, all greatly appreciated. We are also grateful to Matthew Meselson, who has taught us much about chemical and biological weapons, and has helped remind us of the subtle role of human morality in the subject at hand. Shai Feldman raised the level of collegiality at the Center to new heights, and was a resource for us on a variety of topics, particularly the Middle East and terrorism. Sean Lynn-Jones provided extremely useful detailed comments on the manuscript on several occasions. We have benefited from exchanges with many other Harvard colleagues as well, including most importantly Harvey Brooks, Matthew Bunn, Marie Chevrier, Owen R. Coté, Jr. (now at MIT), Paul Doty, Jason Ellis, Amy Gordon, Philip Heymann, Fiona Hill, John Holdren, Celeste Johnson, Gregory Koblentz, Doug MacEachin, Dean Joseph Nye, Lieutenant General Terry Scott, Jennifer Weeks, Richard Weitz, Philip Zelikow, and Dorothy Zinberg.

Beyond Harvard, the list of associations from which we have profited is even longer. We thank Walt Kirchner, Don Cobb, Sig Hecker, Joe Pilat, Steve Marannen, and Ann Kaufman of Los Alamos National Laboratory. We also thank Senator Pete Domenici, Senator Richard Lugar, Senator Sam Nunn, and Senate staff members Alex Flint, Ken Myers, Jr., Ken Myers III, John Sopko, Dan Gelber, and John Roots. We are grateful to Bill Potter, Amy Sands, Jonathan Tucker, and Dick Combs of the Monterey Institute of International Studies, and to Brad Roberts, Victor Utgoff, and Karl Lowe of the Institute for Defense Analyses. We thank members of the Defense Science Board Summer Study on Transnational Threats, including Bob Hermann, General Larry Welch, Zoë Baird, Steve Friedman, Craig Fields, General Michael Carns, Bert Fowler, David Heebner, George Whitesides, Nina Stewart, Richard Wagner, and especially Regina Dugan, whose comments on the manuscript were singularly helpful. We thank David Grienke, Julie Evans, and Brad Smith of SAI; Seth Carus of the Center for Naval Analyses; and John Deutch of the Massachusetts Institute of Technology; at Rockefeller University, Joshua Lederberg; at the Center for Strategic and International Studies, Fred Iklé; at the Fletcher School of Law and Diplomacy, Greg Rattray; at St. Andrew's University, Bruce Hoffman and William Walker; at the Chemical and Biological Arms Control Institute, Michael Moodie; at the Carnegie Endowment for International Peace, Leonard Spector; at the Nixon Center for Peace and Freedom, Geoffrey Kemp; at Tel Aviv University, Ariel Merari; at the German Society for Foreign Affairs, Karl Kaiser and Joachim Krause; at IABG, Uwe Nerlich; at Wesleyan University, Martha Crenshaw; at the University of Maryland,

Michael Nacht and Milton Leitenberg; at Kissinger Associates, L. Paul Bremer III; at the University of California at Los Angeles, David Rapoport; at SAIC, Lewis Dunn and David Kay; E.J. Hogendoorn of Human Rights Watch; Richard L. Garwin of IBM; Sandy Bogucki at Yale University; Ruth Kempf at Brookhaven National Laboratory; and recently departed from government service, Jessica Stern, General Wayne Downing, and Admiral Frank Young. We have also benefited from conversations with various executive branch officials, officials of several state and local governments, and a number of federal contractors, all of whom, because of their continuing service, are best acknowledged anonymously.

A few others deserve special mention for the work they did to help us complete this project. John Ellis van Courtland Moon read the entire manuscript, and we are grateful for his detailed comments, particularly on the historical sections. Jonathan Tucker also provided detailed comments, and earned an equal share of gratitude. In the fall of 1997, we were assisted by three distinguished military officers in residence at Harvard as National Security Fellows: Lieutenant Colonel William DeCamp, USMC; Commander Michael Mulcahy, USN; and Lieutenant Colonel Robin Swan, USA. Brett Neely of Occidental College provided extremely valuable research assistance during the summer of 1997, supported by a Ford Foundation grant. Wyeth Touey also provided important research assistance in 1996–97. Caroline Levine graciously helped us with our prose, as she has done in the past.

At the Center, the authors were supported in a variety of ways by Anne Cushing, Libby Fellinger, Jess Hobart, Harold Johnson, Ted Lantaff, Dawn Opstad, Pawel Swiatek, Graceann Todaro, and Meara Keegan Zaheer. Without Patricia Walsh's arrival at the Center, this book would probably never have been finished. Karen Motley and Sean Lynn-Jones managed the arduous process of turning a manuscript into a book. Lynne Meyer-Gay helped edit several chapters. We thank them all.

And finally, Teresa Lawson, no longer at the Center but still a colleague, proved again her worth as editor of the entire volume, demanding clarity and smoothing our prose. We owe her special thanks.

Financial support for this project came from the Carnegie Corporation of New York, CSIA's Ford Foundation endowment for science and international security, and Robert and Renée Belfer, whose gift to Harvard greatly enhanced CSIA's endowment, resulting in the Center's renaming as the Robert and Renée Belfer Center for Science and International Affairs (BCSIA) in May 1997. We are grateful for their generosity.

Of course, responsibility for the views expressed here lies with the authors alone.

— Richard A. Falkenrath
— Robert D. Newman
— Bradley A. Thayer
Cambridge, Mass., November 1997

Introduction

Nuclear, biological, and chemical (NBC) weapons share three terrible characteristics. The first is immense lethality: a single weapon can kill thousands of people. The second is portability, which allows them to be easily delivered against civilian populations and unprepared military forces. And the third is accessibility, which means that they may fall into hostile hands, despite the best efforts at prevention. These three characteristics combine to make NBC weapons the single most serious long-term security threat facing the advanced democracies of the West.

This book is a study of one form of NBC attack — covert delivery — and its threat to one advanced democracy, the United States. A covert nuclear, biological, or chemical attack could be carried out in peacetime or during war, and could target civilians, military forces, or infrastructure. The purpose of this book is to demonstrate that the risk of such attacks is significantly higher than is commonly assumed. Every reader can imagine gruesome attacks, which have been depicted in Hollywood films and classified briefings for years. But these graphic scenarios have been more illustrative than persuasive, and the United States has never mounted a serious effort to reduce its own vulnerability to covert NBC attack. We argue that this effort deserves higher priority in U.S. national security strategy, and we describe a balanced set of policy initiatives to achieve this objective without compromising core American values or weakening civil liberties.

Covert delivery goes by many names: unconventional, paramilitary, surreptitious, clandestine, and terrorist, among others. The defining element of a covert attack is that the weapon is delivered against its target in a manner that cannot readily be distinguished from normal background traffic and activity. Covert NBC delivery methods range from the simple to the sophisticated, and can be employed by anyone with access to an appropriate weapon. The threat therefore encompasses both states and non-state actors (including terrorist organizations), since either can obtain NBC weapons, and both have done so. The covert threat is often described as "NBC terrorism," since it involves techniques that are typically used by terrorist groups, but it is really a more inclusive concept, defined by the method of attack, not by the type of attacker.

A covert nuclear, biological, or chemical attack against the United States is a quintessential low-probability, high-consequence event. The severity of the consequences is easily demonstrated. But how low is the probability? Until recently, one might reasonably have said that the historical record contained not a single case of a covert attack involving a weapon of mass destruction, whether by a state or a non-state actor.[1] All that changed in June 1994, when an apocalyptic Buddhist cult, Aum Shinrikyo, carried out a covert nerve gas attack in the town of Matsumoto, Japan, followed by a second attack in the Tokyo subway in March 1995 (see Box 1, Aum Shinrikyo, p. 19). Still, the Aum case may have been unique, and the two attacks only killed a few people. If history were our only guide, we might conclude that modern societies have little to fear from the prospect of covert NBC aggression.

We argue that the likelihood of covert NBC attacks against the United States, its military forces, and its allies may still be low today, but it is not zero, and it is growing greater with time, for three key reasons. First, NBC weapons are becoming more accessible to a wider range of groups. Second, the predominance of U.S. military forces and the virtual invulnerability of the U.S. homeland to direct military attack leave America's international adversaries with few options other than unconventional threats, including covert attacks with weapons of mass destruction. And third, the nature of

---

1.   Older articles and studies that have drawn attention to these problems include: Brock Chisholm, "Biological Warfare: Demand for Answers," in Morton Grodzins and Eugene Rabinowitch, eds., *The Atomic Age: Scientists in National and World Affairs, Articles from the* Bulletin of the Atomic Scientists *1945–1962* (New York, Basic Books, 1963), pp. 178–182; Mason Willrich and Theodore B. Taylor, *Nuclear Theft: Risks and Safeguards* (Cambridge, Mass.: Ballinger, 1974); Brian M. Jenkins, "Will Terrorists Go Nuclear?" RAND Report P-5541, November 1975; National Committee on Criminal Justice Standards and Goals, *Disorders and Terrorism: Report of the Task Force on Disorders and Terrorism* (Washington, D.C.: U.S. Department of Justice, 1976); Paul Leventhal and Yonah Alexander, eds., *Preventing Nuclear Terrorism: The Report and Papers of the International Task Force on Prevention of Nuclear Terrorism* (Lexington, Mass.: Lexington Books, 1987); Jeffrey D. Simon, *Terrorists and the Potential Use of Biological Weapons: A Discussion of Possibilities*, R-3771-AFMIC (Santa Monica, Calif.: RAND, 1989); Brad Roberts, ed., *Biological Weapons: Weapons of the Future?* (Washington, D.C.: Center for Strategic and International Studies, 1993); and Jessica Stern, "Will Terrorists Turn to Poison?" *Orbis*, Vol. 37, No. 3 (Summer 1993), pp. 393–410.

non-state violence is changing in a way that strongly suggests rising NBC risks. In short, covert NBC attacks have been rare in the past, but the reasons for this infrequency are eroding.

These worrisome trends have not gone wholly unnoticed. Several important recent studies have drawn attention to the problem, and have made cogent recommendations.[2] The number of national security officials and analysts who have expressed concern in public with the possibility of covert NBC attack and terrorism has risen markedly in the 1990s. To quote a few:

- Secretary of Defense William Cohen, April 1997: "An emerging and significant threat is represented by improvised biological, chemical, and nuclear devices that exploit technologies that were once the sole preserve of world and regional powers. The potential to decimate large population centers and wreak havoc on an unprecedented scale has devolved from nation states to groups and even individuals."[3]

---

2.   More recent studies include: Brad Roberts, ed., *Terrorism with Chemical and Biological Weapons: Calibrating Risks and Responses* (Alexandria, Va.: Chemical and Biological Arms Control Institute, 1997); Jonathan B. Tucker, "Chemical/Biological Terrorism: Coping with a New Threat," *Politics and the Life Sciences*, Vol. 15, No. 2 (September 1996), pp. 167–183; Defense Science Board 1997 Summer Study Task Force, *DoD Responses to Transnational Threats*, Vol. I (Washington, D.C.: Office of the Undersecretary of Defense for Acquisition and Technology, October 1997); National Defense Panel, *Transforming Defense: National Security in the 21st Century* (Washington, D.C.: U.S. Department of Defense, 1997); John Deutch, "Terrorism," *Foreign Policy*, No. 108 (Fall 1997), pp. 10–21; Bruce Hoffmann, "Terrorism and WMD: Some Preliminary Hypotheses," *Nonproliferation Review*, Vol. 4, No. 3 (Spring–Summer 1997), pp. 45–53; Jessica Stern, *Risk and Dread: Preempting the New Terrorists* (Cambridge, Mass.: Harvard University Press, forthcoming); and the forthcoming report of the Universities Faculty Study Group on Grand Terrorism, led by Ashton B. Carter and John Deutch.

3.   William S. Cohen, *Annual Report to the President and the Congress* (Washington, D.C.: U.S. Department of Defense, April 1997), p. 76. See also Office of the Secretary of Defense, *Proliferation: Threat and Response* (Washington, D.C.: U.S. Department of Defense, 1997), pp. 43–45, available at <www.defenselink.mil/pubs/prolif97>; and Counterproliferation Program Review Committee, *Report on Activities and Programs for Countering Proliferation* (Washington, D.C.: U.S. Department of Defense, May 1996), pp. 10–14.

- FBI Director Louis Freeh, May 1997: "The acquisition, proliferation, threatened or actual use of weapons of mass destruction by a terrorist group or individuals constitutes one of the gravest threats to the United States. The government's policy recognizes that there is no higher priority than preventing the acquisition of this capability or removing this capability from terrorist groups potentially opposed to the United States."[4]

- Former Under Secretary of Defense for Policy Fred Iklé, March 1997: "Alas, America's future enemies may not fight according to these Marquess of Queensberry rules. They might use nuclear, biological, or chemical weapons, not only on the 'regional' battlefield that Pentagon planners assign to them, but also in that unanticipated region of warfare — the United States itself."[5]

- Former Director of Central Intelligence R. James Woolsey and former Assistant Secretary of Defense Joseph Nye, June 1997: "We should not wait for another Pearl Harbor to awaken us to the fact that there is no greater threat to our security than terrorism involving weapons of mass destruction."[6]

- Ambassador Richard Burt, February 1996: "Terrorist use of a nuclear device remains the only real possibility and, indeed, the only plausible scenario for nuclear use."[7]

These are not the alarmist voices of the past, not the lunatic fringe for whom the sky has always been falling. These are respected mainstream national security officials and experts. Some may dismiss their concern, claiming that they are simply seeking new perils to justify their livelihoods now that the

---

4. Louis J. Freeh, "Counterterrorism," Statement before the Senate Appropriations Committee, U.S. Senate, May 13, 1997, available at <www.fbi.gov/congress/counter/terror.htm>.

5. Fred C. Iklé, "Naked to Our Enemies," *Wall Street Journal*, March 10, 1997, p. A18.

6. Joseph S. Nye, Jr., and R. James Woolsey, "Defend Against the Stealth Enemy," *Los Angeles Times* (Washington Edition), June 1, 1997, p. 4.

7. Richard Burt, "Nuclear Fear and Loathing," *Wall Street Journal*, February 8, 1996, p. 15.

Soviet Union is gone, but the conclusion that they are acting only out of self-interest is uncharitable and incorrect. The concern they express is valid. The question is what to do.

This book argues that covert NBC attack should be treated as a significant threat in U.S. national security policy. It also outlines our recommendations for a U.S. government that should — but currently does not — take the problem seriously.

Consequences of Covert NBC Attacks and Terrorism

Understanding the covert NBC threat requires some idea of what a nuclear, biological, or chemical weapons attack on an unprepared civilian target could do. The consequences of a major NBC attack would not all be immediate. The first effect would be physical damage, but covert NBC attacks would also have broad repercussions for the economy, for the nation's strategic position in world affairs, and perhaps even for its ability to sustain itself as a strong and democratic polity. These effects would be compounded by an organized campaign of multiple attacks, or if more than one weapon type were used. The severity of the effects would vary greatly with the type and scale of the attack. At least seven general types of consequences are likely: massive casualties, contamination, panic, degraded response capabilities, economic damage, loss of strategic position, and social-psychological damage and political change.

MASSIVE CASUALTIES

The first and most obvious effect of an NBC attack would be its destruction of human life. The Tokyo subway attack killed 12 and injured about 5,000; this is low on the scale of NBC weapons effects. If Aum Shinrikyo had been more proficient in its delivery of the nerve gas, fatalities would have climbed into the thousands. A well-executed chemical weapon attack against a crowded civilian target could kill several thousand people. Biological weapons effects are also widely variable, but fatalities in the low tens of thousands are feasible even with unsophisticated weapons. A single nuclear weapon could easily kill over a hundred thousand people if detonated in a densely populated urban area. Only wars, plagues, natural disasters, and a few extraordinary accidents have produced casualties on such a scale — never a single attack from within.

CONTAMINATION

NBC attack could cause enormous contamination. Depending on the weapon type, the area immediately affected by the attack could be rendered uninhabitable for extended periods of time, requiring a costly and perhaps dangerous clean-up operation. A nuclear weapon would also spew radioactive waste into the atmosphere, killing and sickening people downwind. NBC contamination could raise the disease rates and reduce the quality of life for a much larger population than that which suffered the immediate effects of the weapon.

PANIC

An NBC attack against a civilian population would, in all likelihood, trigger a panic far in excess of the real effects of the weapons. After the World Trade Center bombing, many more people reported to hospitals claiming ill effects than were actually injured in the incident. After a chemical, biological, or nuclear attack, hospitals are likely to be overwhelmed not only by the sick and injured, but by people fearing contamination or infection. A nuclear attack — or even a limited radiological incident — is also likely to stimulate movement away from the affected area, given the public's deep-seated fear of all things radioactive.

DEGRADED RESPONSE CAPABILITIES

The government personnel needed to conduct an effective operational response to a real NBC threat may themselves be injured, panic, flee, or refuse to carry out their responsibilities as required, compounding the effects of any attack. Active-duty military personnel will generally have the training and discipline needed to conduct operations in an extremely hazardous environment. But without appropriate equipment and training, emergency response personnel such as police, firefighters, and paramedics may well end up among the first casualties of an NBC incident. Those who arrive at the scene later might decide that the risks to themselves are too high. Congested roads and airspace are also likely to complicate whatever operational response the government is able to mount.

ECONOMIC DAMAGE

An NBC attack could cause major economic damage to the affected area. A large attack or a series of attacks could damage the national economy. Likely effects include the death and injury of workers, the destruction of physical plant, and the contamination of workplaces. An attack could also trigger a run on international financial and equity markets, especially if the target has unusual economic significance. The loss of plant and productivity from even a single, moderately damaging NBC attack could easily climb into the hundreds of millions or billions of dollars.

LOSS OF STRATEGIC POSITION

An NBC attack or campaign of attacks could do great damage to the strategic position of the United States. The United States might be deterred from entering a regional crisis in which its national interests are threatened. Key U.S. institutions and political leaders might be attacked directly, or U.S. forces and force-projection capabilities might be damaged, in an effort to prevent effective U.S. military action. Under threat of NBC attack, a U.S.-led coalition might collapse, or an essential ally might request the withdrawal of U.S. forces from its territory. The precise nature of these strategic effects is impossible to predict, but they could seriously complicate U.S. efforts to deal with a foreign adversary or crisis.

SOCIAL-PSYCHOLOGICAL DAMAGE AND POLITICAL CHANGE

Mass casualties, and the prospect of continued attacks, could have a profound psychological effect on the target population, and an equally profound effect on the nation's politics and law. Public terror in the aftermath of a domestic NBC incident would likely be more intense than the abstract Cold War fear of nuclear war. Xenophobia, isolationism, vengeful fury, and other powerful forces would struggle for control of foreign policy. Domestically, the inability to prevent covert NBC attacks, or to respond to them effectively, could cause the citizenry to lose confidence in its government, and initiate a chain of political and legal reactions leading to a fundamental shift in the relationship between citizen and state. A society that comes to fear massively destructive terrorist attacks is likely to demand action from its government. In the case of the covert NBC threat, such action may lead to a significant curtailment of the civil liberties that lie at the core of the American system of limited, democratic governance.

Calibrating the Response and Preserving Civil Liberties

The U.S. response to the covert nuclear, biological, and chemical threat should be vigorous, coherent, and purposeful, but it should also be measured, balanced, and respectful of core American values. It is clearly impossible to protect all potential targets from covert NBC attacks all the time, and this should not be attempted. But a purely reactive posture is equally unsatisfactory. The United States should instead put in place a package of measures that make covert NBC threats less likely to emerge, and that create operational capabilities that give the U.S. government a reasonable chance of detecting, defeating, and minimizing the consequences of specific covert NBC threats. These measures should be viewed as a prudent investment in the long-term security of U.S. citizens and interests, not as an emergency campaign. Therefore, our prescriptive agenda seeks not only to be effective against the covert NBC threat, but also to safeguard the personal freedoms and civil liberties that have made the U.S. political system so successful, so durable, and so worth fighting for.

Any discussion of how to respond to the covert NBC threat will almost inevitably raise uncomfortable questions about the relationship between the state and its citizens. Many of the measures that could be taken to combat covert NBC threats would tend to increase the power of the state, at the expense of the freedom and privacy of individuals or groups. U.S. law regulates the ways the state can monitor, investigate, search, detain, and punish individuals within its jurisdiction, but there is an inevitable temptation to encroach on these legal restrictions when the security of the nation appears to be at risk. This has been true in the past of many domestic measures taken in the name of national security: the Alien and Sedition Acts of the 1790s; the Red Scare after World War I; the internment of Japanese-Americans during World War II; the hunt for Communists in the 1950s; and the domestic spying directed at anti-war activists during the Vietnam years. Today, some argue that terrorism and transnational organized crime, particularly drug trafficking, are problems that could be combated more effectively if the government were able to operate with less regard for the rights and freedoms of its citizens. The United States has addressed both problems primarily through law enforcement, which restricts when and how the government can gather information on, and apprehend, suspected criminals.[8] These constraints limit the effectiveness of the government in some respects, and may occasionally be the cause of failure. But the American system of governance was not conceived to maximize the operational efficiency of its law enforcement and national security agencies.[9] In situations short of national emergency, American democracy has no higher purpose than to protect citizens from the arbitrary power of the state.

8.   For example, information gathered in ways that do not comply with these limitations will generally be inadmissible as evidence in court, a key judicial check on the power of the executive in the American political system.

9.   We are indebted to Brent Scowcroft for this formulation.

The covert NBC threat straddles the traditional domains of law enforcement and national security. The monitoring and suppression of hostile, violent groups, including foreign agents and terrorists, within the United States is a task that the U.S. political system prefers to give to law enforcement, since its agencies are used to respecting the rights of citizens.[10] But weapons of mass destruction are usually regarded as a matter for national security policy, which is concerned most fundamentally with protecting the people and institutions of the state from attack. The distinction is important, since the national security approach is very different from the law enforcement approach. U.S. law enforcement agencies are geared toward satisfying the requirements of a successful criminal prosecution, and their culture is case-driven, fastidious, reactive, and compartmentalized. National security agencies, on the other hand, are mission-driven, and are concerned mainly with building capability, gathering intelligence on known adversaries as well as potential threats, and preempting threats as soon as they are identified. The deep dilemma of the covert NBC threat is that while the severity of its potential consequences calls for preventive efforts and preparedness that are characteristic of a national security response, its latency and domestic character suggest that the more restrained law enforcement approach is in order.

The United States should avoid making any changes in the rules that currently govern the monitoring, investigation, and detention of individuals subject to U.S. law. Limited defensive measures, within existing constraints, can greatly reduce U.S. vulnerability to covert NBC attack. Nevertheless, the intelligence, planning, and response capabilities of U.S. national security agencies make them indispensable to any effort to design and implement a government-wide response to the covert NBC threat. These agencies should be given greater responsibility for managing the consequences of domestic NBC attacks, and should be intimate partners in the effort to detect and assess possible threats. They should therefore also play a larger role in making government policy on responses to the covert NBC threat, but they need not and should not be asked to take on a law enforcement role.

As long as the U.S. vulnerability to covert NBC attack goes unexploited, this approach should remain viable. But if weapons of mass destruction were used against American cities, political pressure would mount for invasive and potentially repressive measures. Such measures might or

---

10. Indeed, intelligence agencies are largely prohibited from gathering information on domestic threats.

might not help prevent attacks, but either way, individual citizens would become less free of the heavy hand of the state. This is one reason for acting now to reduce the long-term risk of covert NBC aggression.

Outline of the Study

This study has five main chapters and a conclusion. About a dozen boxes explain particular subjects of interest, such as the Aum Shinrikyo attack, the Iraqi NBC weapons programs, Japan's World War II biological warfare program, and several less well-known cases involving non-state actors and chemical or biological warfare agents. Chapter 5 also displays thirteen boxes summarizing our specific recommendations.

Chapter 1 analyzes the history of involvement by states and non-state actors with weapons of mass destruction. For each of the two types of actors, the chapter first describes the record of known attempts to acquire and use nuclear, biological, and chemical weapons, and then identifies the factors that explain the character and frequency of these past patterns. With respect to states, there is a clear historical pattern of extensive NBC proliferation coupled with quite infrequent NBC use. The most powerful explanation for this pattern is that weapons of mass destruction are attractive possessions principally because they are extremely effective as instruments of deterrence, and tend to be effective as weapons of war only when the other side cannot retaliate in kind or escalate to even more destructive weapons types. Explaining the nuclear, biological, and chemical weapons activities of non-state actors is more difficult, in part because there is so little to explain. There is almost no evidence that any traditional terrorist organization has attempted to acquire or use NBC weapons. There have been a few marginal incidents involving lone individuals, religious cults, and disorganized extremist groups, but the Japanese cult Aum Shinrikyo remains the singular example of a non-state actor that has acquired and used a weapon of mass destruction. A combination of motivational constraints and technological barriers explains why non-state actors have only rarely crossed the threshold to the acquisition and use of real NBC weapons. Understanding these reasons is the first step toward finding means of prevention.

Chapter 2 provides an assessment of the vulnerability of open societies to covert NBC attack, leading to three discomfiting conclusions. First, improvised NBC weapons can be acquired by many states and some capable non-state actors, and some of the key technical barriers to NBC acquisition are eroding. Second, weapons of all three types could be delivered by covert means against a variety of civilian targets, and against some military or political targets, with good chances of success and limited risk of detection and attribution. And third, the effects of even a single successful covert NBC attack on a concentrated, unprotected population would be severe. Taken together, these three arguments substantiate our basic conclusion that open societies are acutely vulnerable to covert NBC attack.[11]

Chapters 3 and 4 complete our threat assessment by analyzing the factors that may motivate states or non-state actors to carry out a covert NBC attack. Chapter 3 focuses on non-state actors. It argues that the threat of NBC terrorism is growing more serious because large-scale societal trends are gradually expanding the number of groups that are both capable of acquiring weapons of mass destruction and interested in inflicting mass casualties. Although there is minimal evidence of rising non-state interest in NBC weapons *per se*, these two trends suggest that the number of violent non-state actors in a position to make an effective foray into the largely uncharted territory of NBC terrorism is increasing.

Chapter 4 focuses on the covert NBC threat from states. It argues that the risk that an international adversary of the United States will conduct a covert NBC attack against U.S. territory, forces, or allies is significant and growing. An array of motives might drive states to acquire and to use nuclear, biological, or chemical weapons: compensation for the loss of superpower patronage; deterrence of a much more powerful adversary, such as the United States, or of its coalition partners; victory over a more powerful adversary on the battlefield; the temptation to "decapitate" an opposing government by killing its senior officials, thus weakening its ability to respond; the desire to weaken an adversary's economic strength or political will; or simply the urge to exact revenge. Nuclear, biological,

---

11. Perhaps more than any other contemporary national security problem, the covert NBC threat focuses attention on the difference between a vulnerability and a threat. A vulnerability is a situation of being open to harm; a threat is the known or suspected presence of an actor with the ability, will, and motive to inflict harm. All real threats involve a vulnerability, since one cannot be threatened by something to which one is invulnerable. But in general, vulnerabilities make poor proxies for threats. For example, even though a massive British nuclear strike could devastate every major city in the United States, no sane American worries about a British nuclear threat. The reason is the absence of hostile British intent. Sound national security policy lies between the paranoia that sees in every vulnerability a significant threat, and the complacency that sees threats only where they have already been demonstrated.

and chemical weapons are the likely tools of any state that opts for an "asymmetric strategy" against the superior military might of the United States, seeking to deter its more powerful opponent with the threat of limited numbers of mass-destruction attacks. Moreover, for many states, and especially for states in conflict with the United States, covert attacks could have important advantages over military use of NBC weapons, offering the possibility of deterring and harming the United States while evading identification and retaliation. There is no reason to believe that the threat of unconventional NBC delivery is less serious than the threat of NBC delivery by ballistic missiles.

Chapter 5 contains our prescriptive agenda for the U.S. government. There is no technical "fix" that can end U.S. vulnerability to covert nuclear, biological, and chemical attack: the government will never be able to protect all potential targets, all the time, from all possible forms of attack. But there are many measures that, singly or in combination, can make U.S. citizens and interests substantially less vulnerable to the most devastating forms of aggression. There are five key areas in which increased funding and effort could substantially improve the ability of the United States to contain and respond to the unconventional NBC threat. These areas are: (1) national strategy, planning, and coordination; (2) intelligence and threat identification; (3) operational preparedness; (4) fissile material security; and (5) declaratory policy and law. In each area, we assess current U.S. policy, capabilities, and preparedness, and make detailed recommendations.

Chapter 6 briefly describes some of the political issues that are likely to affect how much the U.S. government will do about the covert NBC threat in advance of an actual attack. Bureaucratic and political tendencies toward complacency and lethargy will be difficult to overcome until the first NBC attack against the United States has occurred. Far-sighted leadership will be needed to put in place appropriate preventive measures before the need for them is demonstrated in practice. After a significant attack, the danger is more likely to be overreaction.

Scope of the Study

This study looks at three types of weapons, two types of actors, and one form of delivery. Nuclear, biological, and chemical weapons are technically dissimilar, but are appropriate to treat as a group for broad policy purposes because of their shared characteristics of lethality, portability, and accessibility.[12] Since the techniques that a terrorist group would use to deliver a weapon are really not that different from the techniques a state adversary might use, many elements of the covert NBC threat from states and non-state actors can be analyzed together. All overt forms of NBC delivery — such as ballistic missiles, cruise missiles, strike aircraft, and artillery — are excluded from the scope of this study. These delivery methods have received extensive attention from other analysts, and are discussed here only for purposes of comparison to the covert NBC threat.[13] Although much of our analysis is focused on the covert NBC threat to domestic targets, overseas targets share similar vulnerabilities.

TYPES OF ACTORS

The covert NBC threat is an operationally distinct form of attack that can be employed by two fundamentally different types of attackers: states and non-state actors. The target of a covert NBC attack may not know whether the perpetrator is a state or a non-state actor, and the issue will not make much difference to the immediate operational response to the incident. However, significant differences between states and non-state actors — territory, sovereignty, resources, people, technical infrastructure, objectives, strategic personality, history, etc. — make the covert NBC threat considerably more complex both to assess and to address, since the two types of potential attackers are likely to be quite differently motivated. These differences are discussed in detail in Chapter 1, which explains the historical rarity of covert NBC attack, and in Chapters 3 and 4, which explore the motives that might prompt non-state actors or states, respectively, to carry out nuclear, biological, or chemical covert attacks in the future. State-sponsored terrorist groups, which in most ways occupy an intermediate position between states and non-state actors, are also discussed.

---

12. We use the terms "NBC weapons" and "weapons of mass destruction" (WMD) interchangeably. Note, however, that the U.S. government's definition of WMD also encompasses ballistic missile delivery systems.

13. Standard military means of delivery are usually readily identifiable, if sometimes difficult to defend against. This difference between overt and covert means of NBC delivery implies that in a covert NBC attack, the attacker might be able to maintain anonymity, reducing a potential attacker's fear of reprisal and therefore also the expected effectiveness of deterrence.

WEAPON TYPES

Few people have ever actually laid eyes upon a nuclear, biological, or chemical weapon, much less built one, and few have actually seen their effects on human beings. However, knowledge of some basic facts about the three weapon types is important for understanding the nature of the covert NBC threat, and for fashioning an appropriate strategy against it.

NUCLEAR WEAPONS. Nuclear weapons release vast amounts of energy either through nuclear fission, splitting the nuclei of elements such as plutonium, or through a combination of fission and fusion, combining hydrogen nuclei to create helium. Fusion weapons are far more destructive than fission weapons, but can be produced only by technologically advanced states at great cost. Fission weapons are much less powerful than fusion weapons, but are still highly destructive, and are considerably easier to build. A first-generation fission weapon, like those the United States used on Hiroshima and Nagasaki, would have an explosive yield of about 10,000 tons (10 kilotons) of TNT.[14] Such a weapon, detonated in a city, could kill over one hundred thousand people and devastate an area extending a mile or more from ground zero. The physical, economic, social, and political consequences of such a catastrophe would be profoundly disruptive to the lives of all people living nearby, and to the target state as a whole. Post-detonation consequence management could aid the survivors and eventually rebuild the city, but most of the damage to life and property would be immediate. The only real possibility for damage limitation, unless the weapon can be found and disabled, is evacuation prior to the detonation of the weapon, an option that a surprise attack would preclude.

Nuclear weapons are presently found in the arsenals of only eight states. The five declared nuclear powers — the United States, Russia, Great Britain, France, and China — all possess a range of fission and fusion weapons coupled with a variety of delivery systems, from demolition charges that a single person can carry, to artillery projectiles, to bombs and ICBMs. In addition, India, Pakistan, and Israel are believed to possess fission weapons, and the latter may possess enhanced-yield weapons, but all three maintain an official ambiguity on the subject. The white minority government of South Africa built six fission weapons. Before the transfer of power to the ANC-led government, however, South Africa dismantled the weapons and, in 1991, acceded to the Nuclear Non-Proliferation Treaty (NPT). Iraq sought to obtain nuclear weapons, but its program was frozen

---

14. For comparison, the Oklahoma City bomb was equal to about two tons of TNT, about one five-thousandth as powerful as a small nuclear weapon.

by the inspection and disarmament measures imposed by the United Nations after the 1990–91 Gulf War. North Korea is believed to have produced and separated a small amount of plutonium, perhaps enough for one or two weapons, but further production appears to have been suspended and the weapons program is being rolled back under a negotiated agreement. Iran is believed to be seeking nuclear weapons, but is thought to be at least several years from developing them. Other states, including several in Europe, plus Japan, South Korea, Taiwan, Brazil, and Argentina, have a well-developed scientific and industrial base that would allow them to build nuclear weapons relatively easily if they chose to do so.

Commonly confused with nuclear weapons are radiological weapons, which disperse radioactive substances but do not produce a nuclear explosion. The simplest radiological weapon would consist of a conventional explosive surrounded by a quantity of any radioactive material. Crude radiological weapons are far more accessible than nuclear weapons, and are therefore more likely to be used by non-state actors. However, although a radiological weapon could contaminate an area and be costly to clean up, building and using such a weapon is not an easy way to produce mass casualties. Large quantities of highly radioactive material would generally be needed to produce strong effects over even a moderate area. Obtaining and working with large amounts of such materials would be challenging because of the high radiation levels involved. Due to widespread public fear of radiation, however, a radiological attack might trigger panic and social and economic disruption out of proportion with its real destructiveness. Some of our recommendations concerning the covert NBC threat are also relevant to radiological threats, but because of the low lethality of radiological weapons, they are not a focus of this study.

BIOLOGICAL WEAPONS. Biological weapons disseminate pathogenic microorganisms or biologically produced toxins to cause illness or death in human, animal, or plant populations.[15] Whereas normal diseases begin in small pockets and spread through natural processes of contagion, biological weapons using microbial agents deliberately release large quantities of infectious organisms against a target population, generally as an aerosol — a cloud of small particles or droplets suspended in the air. If enough victims breathe in enough of the agent, the result is a massive, largely simultaneous outbreak of disease after an incubation period of half a day to several days, depending on the agent and the dose inhaled. Because of their ability to

---

15. Living biological warfare agents include bacteria, viruses, rickettsia, and fungi. See Chapter 2 for a full discussion.

multiply inside the host, pathogenic microorganisms can be lethal in minute quantities: a few kilograms of effectively disseminated concentrated agent can cause tens to hundreds of thousands of casualties. Biological warfare agents without a system for aerosol dissemination cannot easily cause casualties on this scale, and should therefore be considered potentially dangerous contaminants rather than weapons of mass destruction.

Toxin weapons disseminate poisonous substances produced by living organisms, and are therefore often classified as biological weapons. Like biological agents, toxins generally need to be delivered as an aerosol to be effective as anything more than a contaminant or an assassination weapon. Toxins differ from microbial biological warfare agents, such as bacteria, in that they are non-living, like man-made chemical poisons. Indeed, a number of toxins can now be chemically synthesized. Lacking the potential for reproduction and contagion, toxins are less deadly, gram for gram, than certain living pathogens, and cannot spread beyond the population directly attacked. The majority of the U.S. criminal cases involving biological weapons actually involve small-scale poisonings with ricin, a lethal toxin produced from castor beans. These incidents are only peripherally related to the risk of mass destruction attacks.

Aerosols of toxins and pathogenic microorganisms in low concentrations are generally odorless, tasteless, and invisible. Unless the agent-dissemination device (e.g., an aerosol sprayer) is noticed and identified, a covert biological weapons attack might go undetected until the affected population began to show symptoms of disease or poisoning. Depending on the type of agent used and the nature of the disease outbreak, a surreptitious biological attack on a civilian population could initially be mistaken for a natural epidemic. Detection time, therefore, would depend on the nature of the attack and the quality of the public health system. By the time a surreptitious biological attack is identified, it may be too late to limit its geographic extent or control its medical consequences. In addition, dispersal devices could be gone, perpetrators could be nowhere near the scene of the attack, and responsibility for the attack could be very difficult to attribute to a particular state or non-state actor. This combination of factors makes biological weapons especially suitable for covert delivery.

Biological weapons have come to be regarded with almost unique opprobrium by the international community. Despite the minimal technical obstacles to biological weapons acquisition, actual use of biological weapons has been exceedingly rare. The United States officially ended its offensive biological weapons program in 1969, and biological weapons are formally banned by the 1972 Biological Weapons Convention (BWC), an unverified agreement that has been ratified by 140 nations. However, it is now known that both the Soviet Union and Iraq, both signatories of the BWC, had large-scale illegal biological weapons programs, and that Russia continued the program for some time after the collapse of the Soviet Union. The U.S. government and outside experts further suspect another eight countries — Libya, North Korea, Taiwan, Syria, Israel, Iran, China, and Egypt — of possessing offensive biological weapons programs.[16]

CHEMICAL WEAPONS. Chemical weapons are extremely lethal man-made poisons that can be disseminated as gases, liquids, or aerosols. There are four basic types of chemical weapons: choking agents, such as chlorine and phosgene, which damage lung tissue; blood gases, such as hydrogen cyanide, which block the transport or use of oxygen; vesicants, such as mustard gas, which cause burns and damage to body tissues, especially the skin, the eyes, and inside the lungs; and nerve agents, such as tabun, sarin, and VX, which kill by disabling a crucial enzyme in the nervous system. Chemical warfare agents are highly toxic, but must be delivered in large doses to affect large areas. The mass of agent required for effective attacks on open-air targets can easily be hundreds or thousands of kilograms per square kilometer, even for a highly toxic agent such as sarin, and even if the agent is efficiently dispersed. A relatively simple outdoor attack, involving no more planning and execution than a large truck-bomb attack, is thus likely to kill a few hundred people. An attack on a crowded indoor area might kill a few thousand people. Some chemical warfare agents are highly persistent, however, and could render an attack site uninhabitable for weeks or months, requiring costly decontamination and cleanup.

Chemical weapons have been used or stockpiled by many militaries for most of this century, beginning with their first large-scale use in World War I. Immense quantities of chemical weapons were produced by the United States and the Soviet Union during World War II and Cold War. The United States stockpiled some 30,000 tons of chemical agent, which it is now in the process of incinerating at eight sites in the United States as well as on Johnston Atoll in the Pacific. Russia has declared a chemical weapons stockpile of 40,000 tons, but some estimates of the true size of the stockpile range as high as 200,000 tons. Russia has pledged to destroy the chemical weapons stockpile it inherited from the Soviet Union, but its program to do

---

16. U.S. Congress, Office of Technology Assessment (OTA), *Proliferation of Weapons of Mass Destruction: Assessing the Risks* (Washington, D.C.: U.S. Government Printing Office [U.S. GPO], August 1993), p. 83.

so has been delayed by financial difficulties.[17] Most other major states with chemical weapons arsenals have pledged to destroy these stocks under the Chemical Weapons Convention (CWC), but several states have either boycotted the CWC or have joined but are still suspected of harboring clandestine chemical warfare programs. These states include Libya, Iran, Syria, Egypt, Israel, China, North Korea, Taiwan, Myanmar (Burma), and Vietnam.[18] No non-state actor is currently known to possess chemical weapons, though the Japanese cult Aum Shinrikyo did succeed in manufacturing significant quantities of the nerve gas sarin in 1994–95 (see Box 1, Aum Shinrikyo).

---

17. See Amy Smithson, *Chemical Weapons Disarmament in Russia: Problems and Prospects*, Stimson Center Report No. 17 (Washington, D.C.: Henry L. Stimson Center, October 1995).

18. OTA, *Proliferation of Weapons of Mass Destruction*, p. 65.

Box 1
Aum Shinrikyo

On the morning of March 20, 1995, five members of the Japanese cult Aum Shinrikyo boarded subway trains at five stations around Tokyo.[1] Each of them carried two sealed plastic pouches of dilute sarin nerve gas, and a sharpened umbrella to puncture the pouches. As the trains converged near the center of Tokyo, the five men placed the bags on the floors of their train cars, punctured them, and fled. As the strong-smelling liquid leaked out and began to evaporate, commuters on the crowded trains started to sweat. Their noses ran, they coughed, they had difficulty breathing, and they felt weak and giddy. Some vomited, had seizures, or developed pulmonary edema. As people began to feel sick, and to observe other passengers getting sick, some began to leave the trains, which continued from station to station, leaving havoc in their wake, for a few minutes before evacuation warnings cleared the stations. One train continued on its way for an hour and a half. In all, 12 people died; more than 5,000 were injured, and some suffered permanent neurological damage.

Aum Shinrikyo was led by Shoko Asahara, a charismatic former acupuncturist, herbalist, and yoga instructor, nearly blind since birth. From its founding in 1984 to the time of the Tokyo attack, the cult grew into a large organization with thousands of members and branches in several countries, wealthy from the savings that new members turned over to the cult, from tax-exempt businesses staffed by cult members at low wages, and from fraud and extortion. Aum's assets have been estimated at $300 million to $1 billion.[2] The cult succeeded in recruiting a variety of highly trained scientists, including graduate students in physics, chemists, electrical engineers, doctors, and biologists, several of whom had been educated at top Japanese universities. To expand its membership, Aum used a wide range of standard brainwashing techniques, such as sleep deprivation and forced isolation. The cult also enhanced meditation and indoctrination with psychotropic drugs such as LSD. It manufactured these in its own labs and sold some on the side.[3] To retain members, the cult had taken to threatening, imprisoning, kidnaping, and even killing those who tried to leave. Several outside critics were also silenced by kidnaping and murder.[4]

Asahara apparently had ambitions beyond cult leadership: he launched the cult into a bizarre campaign in the Japanese general elections of February 1990, in which he and other cult members contested 25 seats in the lower house of parliament.[5] In a campaign that cost Aum $7 million, Asahara received only 1,783 votes out of half a million cast in his district, despite the presence there of 1,800 of his own followers. Aum also lost a number of members, sent into the outside world as campaign workers, who left their

Box 1, Aum Shinrikyo, *cont.*

communes and returned to more or less normal lives. The costly defeat was contrary to Asahara's prophesies of a brilliant victory, and apparently triggered a turn toward a darker and more violent path for the cult.[6] Asahara began to prophesy the approach of Armageddon in the form of world war. The cult sought to acquire a wide range of weapons, including biological, chemical, and nuclear weapons, as well as fanciful laser weapons and earthquake generators.

On a number of occasions in the early 1990s, Asahara reportedly ordered the use of these weapons to strike out at enemies, real and perceived, and to try to create disasters that would confirm his prophesies. According to one account, in April 1990, Aum attempted to attack the Japanese parliament with botulinum toxin aerosol. In June 1993, the cult made a similar effort, this time targeting the wedding of the crown prince. Later that month, Aum reportedly also attempted to spray anthrax spores from the roof of a building in Tokyo. All three attacks failed to produce casualties.[7]

Aum's chemical weapons acquisition efforts apparently began in earnest in the spring of 1993, and bore fruit less than a year later, with the first production of sarin in November of 1993.[8] Aum produced sarin on at least five occasions, including production of 30 kilograms in February 1994.[9] Twenty kilograms of this batch were reportedly used in a June 27, 1994, attack on the lodgings of three judges in the town of Matsumoto, who were hearing a land-fraud suit brought against the cult by a local man.[10] The attack injured 150 and killed four. Production efforts were eventually halted following accidental chemical releases at the facility in July 1994,[11] and the cult apparently never came close to producing the tens of tons of sarin Asahara intended to spray on Japan's cities. The cult also experimented with making mustard gas, cyanide, and VX.

For air delivery of chemical weapons, Aum Shinrikyo procured a Russian military helicopter. It also sought to mass-produce in a cult factory copies of a Russian military automatic rifle.[12] In addition, it at least considered trying to buy nuclear weapons in Russia, as well as enriching uranium on its own.[13] Even more fanciful was the search for a laser powerful enough to destroy the Tokyo police headquarters,[14] and for a means of triggering earthquakes.[15]

For several years, Aum's nefarious activities went unpunished, despite substantial press attention and some official investigations. The decentralized nature of Japan's law enforcement system made investigating a far-flung organization like Aum difficult.[16] Furthermore, in 1989, Aum was officially recognized as a religious organization, gaining it a tax exemption and a significant degree of protection from official interference. The Japanese

Box 1, Aum Shinrikyo, *cont.*

constitution, imposed by the United States after World War II, was designed to restrain the power of the central government. Article 20 of the Constitution, a reaction to the use of religion by the state to further the cult of the Emperor before and during World War II, banned state involvement in religious activity. That provision and associated laws have given the government and the police a hands-off approach to religious organizations.[17] Eventually, however, the cult's history of kidnaping, murder, land fraud, and other abuses, culminating in the Matsumoto attack, finally began to draw sustained law enforcement attention. By early 1995, the Tokyo Metropolitan Police — Japan's closest analogue to a national investigative agency — had begun to investigate Aum Shinrikyo seriously.

When the police finally began to close in on the group, Aum Shinrikyo tried to use its weapons of mass destruction, first biological and then chemical, to forestall a raid on its headquarters planned for March 22. Aum learned in advance of the raid from its members in the Japanese military, which had been called in by the police for its chemical weapons expertise.[18] In response, on March 15, 1995, Aum reportedly attempted an aerosol botulinum toxin attack in the Tokyo subway. This attack failed, reportedly due to an attack of conscience that led the person filling the delivery devices — briefcases fitted with sprayers — to use water instead of the toxin solution, though the earlier failures call into question whether the weapons would have worked in any case.[19] Finally, a small batch of low-grade sarin was made and used in the March 20 subway attack. Planned and executed at short notice, this attack used no sprayers. The impurity of the sarin, combined with the improvised delivery method used (the plastic bags and sharpened umbrellas described above), were all that saved hundreds or thousands of people from death.[20]

After the March 20 attack, police raids against the cult's facilities nationwide began to dismantle the organization. But only on May 16 was Asahara himself arrested. In the intervening weeks, the cult had carried out further attacks, including the shooting of the Tokyo police commissioner (who survived), and a failed attack with an improvised cyanide gas generator in a Tokyo train station.[21]

Lessons

Aum Shinrikyo's sarin attacks in the Tokyo subway and the town of Matsumoto marked the first times a non-state actor is known to have developed and used a chemical weapon, or any other weapon of mass destruction, in a terrorist attack. As the only case of its kind, it holds important lessons for the future. Some of these lessons are clear, but others are more tentative.[22]

Box 1, Aum Shinrikyo, *cont.*

One clear and crucial lesson of the events in Japan is that intelligence cannot be relied upon to provide early warning of weapons acquisition by non-state actors, at least if the groups in question are not under surveillance for other reasons. This is best illustrated by the total failure of U.S. intelligence to detect Aum, much less to monitor its activities, in advance of the Tokyo attack. This occurred despite the cult's large size; its great wealth; its international operations, including training and weapons-buying in Russia as well as efforts in the United States to buy export-controlled equipment relevant to nuclear proliferation; its extensive public discussions — on the radio in Russia, on the Internet, and in various publications — of sarin, of coming war between Japan and the United States, and of the end of the world; and its use of sarin in Matsumoto nine months before the Tokyo subway attack. The Matsumoto attack was widely discussed in Japan, and an American researcher who traveled to Japan to investigate the attack warned afterwards that Matsumoto was a practice run, indicating the presence of a serious chemical terrorist threat in Japan.[23] Despite all this, the Central Intelligence Agency, as it admitted in later testimony, did not know about Aum before the Tokyo attack.[24] U.S. intelligence agencies cannot watch every odd religious group in the world, and naturally focus less on friendly states such as Japan, but the failure to catch the many international indicators of the cult's activities is a worthwhile reminder of the great difficulty of the intelligence task.

A second lesson is that lack of knowledge, training, and coordination among law enforcement agencies can cause fatal delays and errors in investigating weapons acquisition and use. Japan's decentralized police system left investigations in the hands of local police forces ill-prepared to deal with weapons of mass destruction. The Matsumoto police apparently did not have access to experts who could have debunked their theory that a local man had made sarin by accident, a theory that presumably delayed a real investigation. Later, after chemical tests showed the presence of sarin's breakdown products outside the cult's compound, nearly three months of inexplicable official hesitation allowed Aum time to partially sanitize its facilities, and to carry out both a failed biological aerosol attack and the fatal Tokyo sarin attack, before investigators searched the compound.[25]

A third lesson is that cities are unprepared to manage man-made disasters such as chemical attacks. It would be a grave mistake to assume that the limited damage caused by the Tokyo and Matsumoto attacks is representative of the effects of future attacks. The consequences would have been far more severe if the agent had been dispersed more efficiently. Even with the relative ineffectiveness of the Tokyo attack, many of the fire, police, and ambulance personnel who responded to the incident were injured, and

Box 1, Aum Shinrikyo, *cont.*

hospitals were flooded with victims. The injuries to rescuers occurred despite the fact that most victims were able to flee to street level under their own power, and despite the low level of secondary contamination resulting from agent that leaked onto the floor rather than being sprayed. An effective response to a more carefully executed attack would require rescue personnel with protective equipment, who would be able to haul victims out of contaminated stations, decontaminate them, and administer antidotes.

A fourth set of lessons about the accessibility or inaccessibility of weapons of mass destruction is less obvious and less certain, given the limitations of the available sources. Most clearly, Aum demonstrated that a large, wealthy organization with several members who were well-trained scientists can make and use chemical weapons on a small scale. What the affair demonstrates about the resources needed to produce chemical or biological weapons, however, or about the likely effects of terrorist chemical weapons attacks, is far less clear. In this case, a group with large resources was surprisingly ineffective. The chemical attacks Aum carried out were less deadly than some single-person shooting sprees, and required considerably more effort to prepare for and carry out. Furthermore, despite substantial effort, the group completely failed to produce effective biological weapons.

On the one hand, Aum Shinrikyo's failures illustrate the level of uncertainty faced by a would-be attacker, particularly with biological weapons. The cult's weapons were built under the guidance of reasonably well-trained biologists and chemists. The failures of the cult's attacks could be taken to mean that biological weapons, and chemical weapons capable of killing more than a few people, are beyond the reach even of wealthy groups with good scientists, but the real lessons are probably somewhat different. Aum Shinrikyo's erratic leadership and its scientists' lack of common sense and technical skill substantially hampered its quest for weapons of mass destruction. Even so, simple delivery devices like those reportedly used for the failed March 15, 1995, biological attack would have changed the nature of the March 20 attack by dispersing the sarin far more effectively. It was only the last-minute, improvised nature of the Tokyo attack that saved many people from death that day.

The guru's grandiose ambitions led Aum Shinrikyo to seek an extraordinarily wide range of weapons, thus diluting the technical resources available for each project. Furthermore, elements of fantasy appear to have entered into at least some projects. Some of the projects Aum pursued, including research into high-power laser weapons and a search for a way to induce earthquakes by means of electromagnetic fields, show either that the cult's technical efforts were driven primarily by the guru's wild imagination, or that the cult's scientists felt unconstrained by physical laws and the limitations of current technology.

Box 1, Aum Shinrikyo, *cont.*

Within a given area of effort, if the reports are to be believed, the cult unnecessarily complicated its acquisition efforts, seeking not a single, simple, effective weapon, but a host of complex and exotic ones. Alongside botulinum toxin and anthrax bacteria, the cult apparently sought Ebola virus for its biological weapons; this would have been a difficult and costly elaboration of a program that had failed to produce a working weapon even with well-known agents that are relatively easy to culture.[26] In the chemical area, instead of the relatively easy approach of making simple chemical agents in a batch process in a laboratory, the cult went to great effort and expense to build a specialized production facility to produce sarin on a larger scale. Not only is sarin harder to make than several other highly effective chemical agents, but running a production facility safely is not an easy task, as the cult discovered when repeated accidents finally forced the closure of the plant. It is remarkable that Aum succeeded in producing significant quantities of agent even by this difficult route.

Some of Aum Shinrikyo's other actions also seem to indicate that many of the cult's scientific personnel were not as good as their resumes would suggest. For example, if the description given in the one available source is at all accurate, the cult used a very primitive method to disseminate sarin in the Matsumoto attack, putting its delivery personnel in great danger.[27] Similarly, mistakes occurred in the biological weapons program that would probably have killed the production and delivery personnel if Aum had actually produced a lethal agent or an effective delivery device. At the least, these events demonstrate a lack of practical competence and good sense.

Perhaps what made Aum's scientists want to build weapons of mass destruction also made them unlikely to do it well. This could be true for several reasons. First, isolated from the outside world within an environment governed by an erratic autocrat like Asahara, constantly faced with the reminder that in this organization failure could be punished with death, it must have been easy to lose touch with reality. Second, a self-selection bias may exist in people who join cults. Those alienated enough from their work and from the larger society to seek such an escape may be too prone to fantasy to make good judgments in the lab. Those who stay with the cult, and are willing to build chemical and biological weapons meant to bring about the doomsday prophesies of the cult's leader, may be in a mental state unlikely to be compatible with good scientific work, and especially with the practical planning and engineering that go into making workable delivery devices. Finally, the cult's own practices, from sleep deprivation to poor nutrition to widespread use of hallucinogens, may have made it hard for members to think clearly. If forces such as these are indeed at work under such circumstances, nihilistic religious movements may pose less of a threat than they otherwise appear to.

Box 1, Aum Shinrikyo, *cont.*

NOTES

1. The cult's name, literally translated, means Aum Supreme Truth; Aum is the Buddhist mantra. We are aware of three main English language sources on Aum Shinrikyo. This account draws heavily on all of them. They are: a report by U.S. Senate investigators, "Staff Statement, Global Proliferation of Weapons of Mass Destruction: A Case Study on the Aum Shinrikyo" (hereafter cited as "Senate Staff Statement"), in *Global Proliferation of Weapons of Mass Destruction*, Part I, Hearings before the Permanent Subcommittee on Investigations of the Committee on Governmental Affairs, U.S. Senate, 104th Cong., 1st Sess. (Washington, D.C.: U.S. Government Printing Office [U.S. GPO], 1996), Chap. 22, pp. 47–102 (these hearings are hereafter cited as *Global Proliferation of Weapons of Mass Destruction*, Part I); Murray Sayle, "Nerve Gas and the Four Noble Truths," *The New Yorker*, April 1, 1996, pp. 56–71; and David E. Kaplan and Andrew Marshall, *The Cult at the End of the World: The Incredible Story of Aum* (London: Arrow Books, 1996). Each of these sources has its strengths: the Senate report is an excellent early effort to describe the facts on Aum Shinrikyo and the attacks; Sayle provides a well-written overview of the story and some of its implications; and Kaplan and Marshall provide a host of interesting vignettes. But the three are neither detailed histories of the cult and its activities, nor particularly reliable on technical questions. Kaplan and Marshall offer the most information on some aspects of the story, scattered in the many tales they tell, but there are some notable technical errors, and the gaps and inconsistencies in what is there make it hard to judge whether their sources were truthful, lying, or confused, or when the authors are mistaken.

2. "Senate Staff Statement," Chap. 22, pp. 48, 57; compare Kevin Sullivan, "Japan Cult Survives While Guru is Jailed: Group Worships Leader on Trial in Gas Attack," *Washington Post*, September 28, 1997, p. A21.

3. Sayle, "Nerve Gas and the Four Noble Truths," p. 64; and Kaplan and Marshall, *The Cult at the End of the World*, pp. 60–63.

4. See, for example, Sayle, "Nerve Gas and the Four Noble Truths," p. 61, and Kaplan and Marshall, *The Cult at the End of the World*, pp. 37–43, on the disappearance and murder, along with his wife and baby, of a lawyer planning to sue the cult on behalf of the parents of members — only one of a number of murders the cult carried out.

5. Sayle, "Nerve Gas and the Four Noble Truths," p. 62; and Kaplan and Marshall, *The Cult at the End of the World*, pp. 46–48.

6. "Senate Staff Statement," Chap. 22, p. 51.

7. See Kaplan and Marshall, *The Cult at the End of the World*, pp. 57–58, and 93–96. This is the only English-language source we know of that reports the attempted anthrax attack, or that provides much detail on the botulinum toxin attempts, so there is some reason to be cautious in interpreting these elements of the case. The Japanese police have released very little official information on Aum Shinrikyo's

Box 1, Aum Shinrikyo, *cont.*

biological warfare activities, and it is probably too early to judge which elements of the available press accounts are accurate.

8. Ibid., pp. 84–86, 125.

9. "Senate Staff Statement," Chap. 22, p. 60.

10. The attack is described in Sayle, "Nerve Gas and the Four Noble Truths," pp. 67–68; and Kaplan and Marshall, *The Cult at the End of the World*, pp. 137–146.

11. Kaplan and Marshall, *The Cult at the End of the World*, pp. 147–148.

12. Ibid., p. 88; and "Senate Staff Statement," Chap. 22, pp. 58–59.

13. Ibid., pp. 208; and hints in "Senate Staff Statement," Chap. 22, pp. 47–102.

14. Kaplan and Marshall, *The Cult at the End of the World*, p. 230.

15. Sayle, "Nerve Gas and the Four Noble Truths," p. 61.

16. Ibid., p. 68.

17. Ibid., pp. 61–62.

18. "Senate Staff Statement," Chap. 22, p. 56; Sayle, "Nerve Gas and the Four Noble Truths," p. 69.

19. Kaplan and Marshall, *The Cult at the End of the World*, pp. 235–236.

20. Testimony on the Tokyo attack before the U.S. Senate Committee on Governmental Affairs includes estimates that tens of thousands of people could have been killed. "Senate Staff Statement," Chap. 22, p. 67.

21. Sayle, "Nerve Gas and the Four Noble Truths," p. 70.

22. The limitations of the available English-language sources are one reason the story is hard to interpret with confidence.

23. Testimony of Kyle B. Olsen, *Global Proliferation of Weapons of Mass Destruction*, Part I, pp. 103–104.

24. *Global Proliferation of Weapons of Mass Destruction*, Part I, p. 273.

25. By January 1, 1995, the Japanese press was reporting that soil sampling had shown the presence in the soil outside the cult's compound of breakdown products of sarin. Given that the mystery of the Matsumoto sarin attack remained unsolved, and that Aum Shinrikyo's possible involvement in that event had been widely discussed, this piece of evidence should have led to immediate raids. Instead, the cult had time to gut its sophisticated chemical production facility and disguise it as a temple. Tons of sarin precursors were destroyed, dumped down a well, but three pounds of a key precursor were saved. This material was later used to make the sarin used in Tokyo. Kaplan and Marshall, *The Cult at the End of the World*, p. 215–216.

26. Aum Shinrikyo reportedly sent a "medical mission" to Zaire during the 1992 Ebola outbreak, presumably intending to bring back a sample of the virus. See Sayle, "Nerve Gas and the Four Noble Truths," p. 67.

27. Kaplan and Marshall, *The Cult at the End of the World*, pp. 139–141.

Chapter 1

The Covert NBC Threat in Historical Perspective

For decades, public discourse on nuclear, biological, and chemical (NBC) terrorism and covert attack has been dominated by two opposing schools of thought. At one extreme is the alarmist view, which considers future terrorist use of weapons of mass destruction a virtual certainty.[1] Complacency characterizes the other extreme, a conviction grounded in assumptions about terrorist motivations and the technical difficulty of acquiring NBC weapons.[2] Each school of thought contains grains of truth, but the correct view lies somewhere between the two extremes.

A sound judgment on the seriousness of the modern threat of NBC terrorism and unconventional delivery depends on an understanding of what has and has not happened in the past. This chapter reviews the historical record of NBC acquisition and use, and explains its intrinsic patterns. The record is relatively brief: while numerous attempts have been made to acquire NBC weapons — by states more than by non-state actors (individuals and groups) — serious attempts to use them are rare. This chapter explains this infrequency.

Almost no evidence has surfaced of any traditional terrorist organization, such as Hezbollah (Party of God) or the Irish Republican Army (IRA), attempting to acquire or use NBC weapons. A number of lone individuals,

---

1. See Alvin Toffler, "Third Wave Terrorism Rides the Tokyo Subway," *New Perspectives Quarterly*, Vol. 12, No. 3 (Summer 1995), pp. 4–76; Joseph D. Douglass, Jr., and Neil C. Livingstone, *America the Vulnerable: The Threat of Chemical and Biological Warfare* (Lexington, Mass.: Lexington Books, 1987); and Robert H. Kupperman and David M. Smith, "Coping with Biological Terrorism," in Brad Roberts, ed., *Biological Weapons: Weapons of the Future?* (Washington, D.C.: Center for Strategic and International Studies, 1993), pp. 35–46.

2. See Karl-Heinz Kamp, "An Overrated Nightmare," *Bulletin of the Atomic Scientists*, Vol. 52, No. 4 (July/August 1996), pp. 30–34; K. Scott McMahon, "Unconventional Nuclear, Biological, and Chemical Weapons Delivery Methods: Whither the 'Smuggled Bomb,'" *Comparative Strategy*, Vol. 15, No. 2 (April–June 1996), pp. 123–134; Wayne Biddle, "It Must Be Simple and Reliable; Weapons and Bombs Used by Terrorists," *Discover*, June 1986.

religious cults, and extremist groups have sought to acquire and use biological and chemical warfare agents, common poisons, and radioactive materials, but these incidents generally have not involved true weapons of mass destruction because the quantities of agent were either too small or not linked to an effective mass-dissemination delivery system. The principal exception is the 1995 nerve gas attack in the Tokyo subway by the apocalyptic cult Aum Shinrikyo (see Box 1, Aum Shinrikyo, p. 19). The attack killed twelve people and injured thousands of others, but the cult's weapons lacked the effective system of agent dispersal needed to cause extensive fatalities. The most common delivery methods in other cases have been product tampering (e.g., the 1978 Tylenol product-tampering case, which killed seven people), contamination of municipal water supplies, and other forms of poisoning, none of which is very effective compared to modern biological and chemical weapons, which disseminate lethal aerosols, vapors, or liquids absorbed through the lungs or skin. A combination of motivational constraints and technological barriers explains why the thresholds to acquisition and use of real NBC weapons by non-state actors have almost never been crossed.

States have a different historical pattern, one of extensive NBC proliferation but infrequent NBC use. The most powerful explanation for this pattern is that weapons of mass destruction are more useful as instruments of deterrence than as weapons of war. Because NBC weapons are so destructive, states have powerful incentives against initiating NBC weapons use in war against similarly armed adversaries. The risks of retaliation in kind, hostile international reaction, domestic political backlash, and moral opprobrium serve as effective brakes on such highly destructive acts. Since World War I, a few states have used weapons of mass destruction despite these risks, most often against adversaries that were unable to retaliate in kind. These disincentives apply not only to overt military use of NBC weapons by states, but also to state sponsorship of NBC terrorism. No case is publicly known of a state assisting a terrorist organization to acquire NBC weapons, a circumstance explained not least by the great risks to the sponsor of arming a potentially unreliable group.

Because of the basic differences in their motivations, technological constraints, and past behavior, states and non-state actors must be analyzed separately. Accordingly, the first section of this chapter focuses on non-state actors, while the second focuses on states. Each section answers the same basic questions: (1) what is the known record of attempts to acquire or use nuclear, biological, and chemical weapons? and (2) what factors explain the character and frequency of past NBC weapons acquisition and use?

The answers to these questions are central to any evaluation of the threat of covert NBC attack, but they do not in themselves constitute a comprehensive assessment of the threat that states or non-state actors pose. A threat assessment must concern itself principally with the likelihood of future events, not the realities of past ones, so it must, in addition, weigh the changes in technology and in the motivations of potential attackers that are occurring or can be expected in the future. These are the subjects of Chapters 2, 3, and 4. A more comprehensive threat assessment is important in determining how the United States can better prepare for potential covert NBC attacks, and how high a priority should be attached to these preparations, issues taken up in Chapter 5.

Non-state Actors

An assessment of the covert NBC threat to U.S. territory, military forces, and allies cannot ignore the possibility that the aggressor will be some entity other than a state. Acquiring a nuclear, biological, or chemical weapons capability is possible for many non-state actors, and those who succeed and decide to attack are likely to employ covert means of delivery, especially if they wish to attack a powerful target such as the United States. Unfortunately, relatively little is known about the involvement of non-state actors with weapons of mass destruction. Only a few cases have been reported that connect non-state actors with nuclear, biological, or chemical weapons. Most of these cases have not been carefully investigated or analyzed; by contrast, a small industry has grown up around the monitoring of NBC proliferation among states. Generalizations about state behavior are difficult and often misleading, but at least there is a relatively large set of generally accurate data on which to base them. In the case of non-state actors, data are scarce, their accuracy is often questionable, and the great diversity of groups and individuals involved make generalizations suspect.

The term "non-state actors" includes the traditional terrorist organizations that provide a regular stream of newsworthy violence. Other pertinent non-state actors include paramilitary guerrilla groups fighting for the control of territory; cults and other religious organizations; militias or other geographically fixed paramilitary groups; organized crime syndicates; mercenary groups; breakaway units of a state's military, intelligence, or security services; corrupt multinational corporations; and lone individuals. This is, of course, a heterogeneous category, but all the types of non-state actors have at least one common element that is relevant to an assessment of the covert NBC threat and to the design and implementation of countermeasures: unlike states, non-state actors lack sovereignty over a piece of territory. Whereas states can freely develop, produce, and stockpile weapons of mass destruction on their own territory (albeit against the efforts of the international community), non-state actors operate in a much less permissive environment, one in which the slightest mistake or indiscretion can result in the termination of the specific NBC acquisition program and even in the elimination of the group itself.

This section addresses two basic questions. First, what patterns can be discerned in the history of non-state actors' involvement with nuclear, biological, and chemical weapons? The strongest lesson of the historical record is that non-state actors that become involved with weapons of mass destruction are extremely rare, and rarer still are those that possess both the intent and the technical capacity to inflict massive human casualties with an NBC weapon. Why this is the case is the second question addressed in this section.

The most basic reason for the historical rarity of NBC terrorism is that, except for Aum Shinrikyo, no non-state actor has yet emerged with both the technical ability and the will to acquire and to use nuclear, biological, or chemical weapons. Clearly, there are non-state actors — including many of unambiguous hostility, such as terrorist organizations — that possess the technical ability to acquire and use such weapons, but the historical evidence suggests that virtually none of these groups has entertained a serious interest in carrying out NBC attacks. Conversely, with the exception of Aum Shinrikyo, non-state actors that have wanted to commit acts of NBC terrorism have not, so far, been able to bring it off. Because both phenomena are directly relevant to an assessment of the covert NBC threat, we analyze them in turn below.

PATTERNS OF PAST NBC ACQUISITION AND USE

A review of the history of non-state actor involvement with weapons of mass destruction yields five basic conclusions. First, with the important exception of the Aum Shinrikyo nerve gas attacks, no non-state actor has ever conducted, or attempted to conduct, an attack with a functional nuclear, biological, or chemical weapon — by which we mean a device that can produce a nuclear yield or disseminate significant quantities of biological or chemical agent over a wide area in effective form. Second, dozens of cases have been documented in which a non-state actor is known to have used, or attempted to use, lethal chemicals or harmful biological agents in mass poisonings, and there have also been countless individual assassinations and assassination attempts involving poisons. These incidents should not be confused with mass destruction attacks, which require effective means for wide-area airborne dissemination and generally far more lethal agents.

Third, many cases have been reported — including several in the mid-1990s — in which non-state actors have been caught in possession of lethal chemicals, dangerous biological agents, or radioactive material, but, with the exception of the Aum Shinrikyo case, all of these lack evidence of serious intent or technical capacity to use the agent as an effective weapon of mass destruction. Fourth, non-state actors have made countless threats and extortion attempts involving nuclear, biological, or chemical weapons attack, but virtually all of these have been hoaxes — often perpetrated by mentally unstable individuals — and most have been easy to dismiss as not credible. Finally, there is little evidence that any established terrorist organization is or has been interested in acquiring, much less using, weapons of mass destruction.

NO NBC WEAPONS USE, WITH ONE EXCEPTION. No non-state actor has ever used a nuclear weapon or aerosol-based biological weapon, and only Aum Shinrikyo has carried out attacks involving modern chemical weapons. Aum reportedly also attempted anthrax and botulinum toxin attacks in Tokyo using an aerosol delivery system, but these attempts failed. Moreover, its nerve gas attacks fell far short of their destructive potential because of the crude dissemination method and poor quality of nerve gas used in the attacks (see Box 1, Aum Shinrikyo, p. 19). Other than Aum, there is little evidence that any non-state actor has ever mounted a serious effort to acquire nuclear, biological, or chemical weapons capability, with just one suspicious case in 1980 involving the Red Army Faction in Paris and a few vague allegations about the Palestine Liberation Organization (PLO),[3]

---

3. "Abu Tayyib, the commander of Fatah's Force 17, stated in an interview that the Palestine Liberation Organization (PLO) has chemical and biological weapons and would not hesitate to use them in future wars." Foreign Broadcast Information Service (FBIS), January 13, 1988, p. 47, cited in Jeffrey D. Simon, "Terrorists and the Potential Use of Biological Weapons: A Discussion of Possibilities," R-3771-AFMIC (Santa Monica, Calif.: RAND, 1989), p. 2, n. 3. A few other reports suggest some PLO interest in weapons of mass destruction, but none appears particularly reliable. See William H. Thornton, *Modern Terrorism: The Potential for Increased Lethality* (Langley Air Force Base, Va.: Center for Low Intensity·Conflict, 1987), p. 7; Robert H. Kupperman and R. James Woolsey, Testimony before the Subcommittee on Technology and Law, Committee on the Judiciary, U.S. Senate, May 19, 1988, in U.S. Department of Justice, Federal Bureau of Investigations, *Terrorism and Technology*, May 19, 1988, p. 5; Ron Purver, *Chemical and Biological Terrorism: The Threat*

Hezbollah,[4] Kurdish Workers' Party (PKK), and German neo-Nazis.[5] The Red Army Faction (Baader-Meinhof Gang) is reported to have attacked a U.S. Army base in Germany in January 1977 in an effort to steal nuclear weapons, and Armenian rebels are reported to have attacked a Soviet base in Azerbaijan in January 1990 with the same goal.[6] None of these incidents can be confirmed with publicly available evidence. The World Trade Center bombing has sometimes been mentioned as a chemical weapons attack, but this claim does not appear plausible.[7]

According to the Open Literature, Canadian Security Intelligence Service (unclassified), June 1995, p. 86; Walter Laqueur, *The Age of Terrorism* (Boston: Little, Brown, 1987), p. 317; and Leonard S. Spector, "Clandestine Nuclear Trade and the Threat of Nuclear Terrorism," in Paul Leventhal and Yonah Alexander, eds., *Preventing Nuclear Terrorism: The Report and Papers of the International Task Force on Prevention of Nuclear Terrorism* (Lexington, Mass.: Lexington Books, 1987), pp. 82–84.

4. FBIS, June 23, 1987, p. L2, cited in Simon, "Terrorists and the Potential Use of Biological Weapons," p. 19, n. 8.

5. According to the U.S. Department of Defense, "in February 1996, German police confiscated from a neo-Nazi group a coded diskette that contained information on how to produce the chemical agent mustard gas. German police have stated that there are no indications yet of intent or effort to manufacture the agent." Counterproliferation Program Review Committee, *Report on Activities and Programs for Countering Proliferation* (Washington, D.C.: U.S. Department of Defense, May 1996), p. 13.

6. Stories of these events are recounted in Andrew Cockburn and Leslie Cockburn, *One Point Safe* (New York: Doubleday, 1997), pp. 1–12. Many experts question the accuracy of these reports.

7. In sentencing Ramzi Yousef, the leading terrorist convicted of the crime, the presiding judge stated: "You had sodium cyanide around, and I'm sure it was in the bomb. Thank God the sodium cyanide burned instead of vaporizing. If the sodium cyanide had vaporized, it is clear what would have happened is the cyanide gas would have been sucked into the north tower and everybody in the north tower would have been killed. That to my mind is exactly what was intended." Quoted in the prepared statement of John F. Sopko and Alan Edelman, Permanent Subcommittee on Investigations, in Senate Hearings 104-422, *Global Proliferation of Weapons of Mass Destruction,* Part III, Hearings before the Permanent Subcommittee on Investigations of the Committee on Governmental Affairs, U.S. Senate, 104th Cong., 2nd Sess. (Washington, D.C.: U.S. Government Printing Office [U.S. GPO], 1996), p. 23. The judge's claim does not appear to be based on a reliable technical analysis: even if the sodium cyanide could have been disseminated effectively by the bomb's

POISONING, PRODUCT CONTAMINATION, AND ASSASSINATION. Poisoning is an age-old means of doing in a foe: in both history and literature, countless characters have been killed off by deliberate exposure to a lethal chemical of some kind. Most often, the poison used is a readily available lethal chemical, such as cyanide or strychnine, that kills only if ingested in sufficient quantities. Occasionally, poisoning can affect a large number of people, usually through the successful contamination of a food product, but more often the intended victim is a single individual who has been targeted for murder or assassination. Murdering a few people with poison is a relatively simple matter, but there are logistical limits to the number of people who can be killed through product tampering. This fact gives non-respirable poisons, toxins, and pathogens a far lower casualty potential than chemical or biological weapons of mass destruction. Product tampering cases do, however, affect the producers of the product in question, who suffer commercially.

Poisonings and individual assassinations should not be equated with attacks involving modern nuclear, biological, or chemical weapons. Small incidents involving some ingredient of a potential weapon of mass destruction are fundamentally different from mass-destruction attacks. Biological and chemical agents are not weapons of mass destruction unless they can be effectively delivered, and the mere possession of even large quantities of harmful agent does not necessarily imply a high potential for effective mass dissemination. Some radioactive materials present health hazards, but nuclear weapon materials, unless they can be made into a working atomic bomb, are less dangerous than many chemical poisons. Simple attempts to poison individuals or small groups, contaminate water supplies, tamper with consumable products, or kill people with radioactive material have far less lethal potential than modern chemical, biological, or nuclear weapons.

The most lethal chemical poisoning ever, outside of the Nazi gas chambers, appears to be the arsenic poisoning of several thousand captive German SS soldiers in April 1946 by the Jewish reprisal organization Nakam.[8] Other incidents have been considerably less dramatic. In 1978,

---

explosion, which it could not, the amount present was too small to be lethal except in a tightly confined space, which the World Trade Center is not.

8.   This attack was carried out by a group of European Jews, many of whom had survived the war as guerrilla fighters, who banded together after the war to carry out vengeance attacks against Germans. They called their group "Nakam," after the Hebrew word for vengeance. In addition to tracking down and killing individual

Palestinian terrorists injected mercury into Israeli oranges destined for export; a handful of Europeans became sick.[9] In 1978, seven people in the United States died from ingesting cyanide-laced Tylenol capsules.[10] On November 18, 1978, more than 900 members of the People's Temple, followers of the cult leader Jim Jones, committed mass suicide in Jonestown, Guyana, by drinking cyanide-laced Kool-Aid.[11] On New Year's Eve 1994, nine Russian soldiers and six civilians in Tajikistan are reported to have died after drinking cyanide-laced champagne, and another 53 were hospitalized.[12] There are also reports that terrorists in the Philippines tried to poison pineapples destined for export,[13] and that Kurdish terrorists tried to poison the water supply of a Turkish military base with potassium

---

Nazis, Nakam planned but did not carry out an operation to poison the water supplies of some German cities. The group's most successful operation was made against German prisoners in a U.S. prisoner-of-war camp outside Nuremberg in April 1946. Members of the group infiltrated the bakery that supplied bread to the camp, and spread an arsenic-based poison on the loaves. Although forced to flee before they had finished, the group is estimated to have killed hundreds of prisoners, and made thousands ill. See Michael Bar-Zohar, *The Avengers*, trans. Len Ortzen (London: Arthur Barker, 1968), pp. 43–58. We are indebted to Benjamin Frankel for bringing this incident to our attention.

9. There is some disagreement in the literature about when this incident occurred, how many people were affected, and in which countries. See Simon, "Terrorists and the Potential Use of Biological Weapons," p. 9; Douglass and Livingstone, *America the Vulnerable*, p. 30; Brian M. Jenkins, "The Threat of Product Contamination," *TVI Report*, Vol. 8, No. 3 (1989), p. 2; and Purver, *Chemical and Biological Terrorism*, pp. 88–89.

10. Purver, *Chemical and Biological Terrorism*, p. 90. We draw heavily on Purver in this listing of small-scale chemical and biological incidents.

11. Leonard Downie, Jr., "Jonestown Story Grew Uglier with Each Chapter," *Washington Post*, November 26, 1978, p. A20.

12. "Poisoned Champagne Kills 10 in Tajikistan," Reuters North American Wire, January 2, 1995; "Champagne au Cyanure: 15 Morts et 53 Hospitalisé, Selon un Nouveau Bilan"; both cited in Purver, *Chemical and Biological Terrorism*, p. 89.

13. Neil C. Livingstone, *The War against Terrorism* (Lexington, Mass.: Lexington Books, 1982), p. 113; Douglass and Livingstone, *America the Vulnerable*, p. 30; and Purver, *Chemical and Biological Terrorism*, p. 86.

cyanide in 1992.[14] Members of Aum Shinrikyo reportedly killed one person and injured two others in 1994 and 1995 by spraying VX nerve gas on them from a hypodermic needle.[15]

Fewer cases have been documented in which non-state actors used harmful biological agents to various ends.[16] In October 1996, twelve hospital employees in Dallas, Texas, became ill when their cafeteria food was contaminated with *Shigella dysenteriae* type 2 — a type of bacteria that causes diarrhea — apparently by a disaffected worker.[17] In August and September 1995, an oncologist from Kansas City, Missouri, attempted three times to poison her husband with ricin she had extracted from castor beans.[18] In June 1990, nine people in Edinburgh, Scotland, were infected with *Giardia lamblia* — which causes severe diarrhea — when the water supply tank of their apartment building was intentionally contaminated.[19] In September 1984, two members of an Oregon cult led by the Bhagwan Shree Rajneesh cultivated *Salmonella* bacteria and used them to contaminate salad bars in restaurants to influence a local election; an estimated 750 people became

---

14. Alexander Chelyshev, "Terrorists Poison the Water Supply in Turkish Army Cantonment," TASS, March 29, 1992; and Purver, *Chemical and Biological Terrorism*, pp. 86–87.

15. See "Hearings on Global Proliferation of Weapons of Mass Destruction: A Case Study of Aum Shinrikyo," Senate Hearings 104-422, *Global Proliferation of Weapons of Mass Destruction*, Part I, Hearings before the Permanent Subcommittee on Investigations of the Committee on Governmental Affairs, U.S. Senate, 104th Cong., 2nd Sess. (Washington, D.C.: U.S. GPO, October 31, 1995), pp. 87–88.

16. For a summary, see Purver, *Chemical and Biological Terrorism*, pp. 34–35; and Simon, "Terrorists and the Potential Use of Biological Weapons."

17. Shellie A. Kolavic et al., "An Outbreak of *Shigella dysenteriae* Type 2 among Laboratory Workers Due to Intentional Food Contamination," *Journal of the American Medical Association (JAMA)*, Vol. 278, No. 5 (August 6, 1997), pp. 396–398.

18. Tony Rizzo, "Fire Inquiry Examined Possible Poisoning," *Kansas City Star*, November 9, 1995; Alan Bavley, "Castor-Oil Plant Packs Toxic Punch," *Kansas City Star*, December 12, 1995; and Tony Rizzo, "Green Gets Life Sentence," *Kansas City Star*, May 31, 1996.

19. C.N. Ramsey and J. Marsh, "Giardiasis Due to Deliberate Contamination of Water Supply," *The Lancet*, Vol. 336 (October 6, 1990), pp. 880–881; Robert S. Root-Bernstein, "Infectious Terrorism," *The Atlantic* (May 1991), p. 48.

ill.[20] In Canada in February 1970, a postdoctoral student in parasitology contaminated the food of four of his roommates with *Ascaris suum*, a pig parasite, causing them to become seriously ill.[21] In 1966, a Japanese doctor confessed to causing a series of typhoid and dysentery outbreaks by contaminating foodstuffs, reportedly affecting over 100 people and resulting in four deaths.[22] More remotely, there are reports that in 1915, a German-American doctor in the United States, with the support of the Imperial German government, produced a quantity of *Bacillus anthracis* (anthrax) and *Pseudomonas mallei* (glanders) that was used to infect 3,000 horses, mules, and cattle being sent to the Allies in Europe.[23]

Although some of these incidents resulted in more than one death, none should be considered to involve a weapon of mass destruction. Poisoning, product tampering, and assassination — whether by chemical or biological means — is a separate and altogether less worrisome phenomenon than the threat of covert attack involving biological or chemical weapons of mass destruction, or nuclear weapons, simply because the number of possible casualties is far more limited. Moreover, most of the individuals involved in these cases do not appear to have been interested in causing massive, indiscriminate human casualties, nor were most capable of fabricating an effective mass-dissemination system for the chemical or biological agent in their possession.

---

20.   See Thomas J. Török et al., "A Large Community Outbreak of Salmonellosis Caused by Intentional Contamination of Restaurant Salad Bars," *JAMA*, Vol. 278, No. 5 (August 6, 1997), pp. 389–395.

21.   "Four Treated for Parasitic Worm as Trail of Student Leads to U.S.," *The Globe and Mail* (Toronto), February 27, 1970, p. 1.

22.   "Deliberate Spreading of Typhoid in Japan," *Science Journal*, Vol. 2 (1966), pp. 2.11–2.76; "Suzuki Confesses to Spreading Typhoid," *Japan Times*, April 14, 1966, p. 1; and "Suzuki Says He Fed Kin with Germs," *Japan Times*, April 21, 1966, p. 3.

23.   Imperial Germany supported other covert activities involving biological agents (generally non-lethal ones) in World War I. See George W. Christopher, Theodore J. Cieslak, Julie A. Pavlin, et al., "Biological Warfare: A Historical Perspective," *JAMA*, Vol. 278, No. 5 (August 6, 1997), pp. 412–417; Harvey J. McGeorge, "Chemical and Biological Terrorism: Analyzing the Problem," *ASA* (*Applied Science and Analysis, Inc.*) *Newsletter*, No. 42 (June 16, 1994), p. 12, cited in Purver, *Chemical and Biological Terrorism*, p. 39; and Jules Witcover, *Sabotage at Black Tom: Imperial Germany's Secret War in America, 1914–1917* (Chapel Hill, N.C.: Algonquin Books, 1989), p. 92.

POSSESSION OF CHEMICAL AND BIOLOGICAL AGENTS AND RADIOACTIVE MATERIAL. There have been countless reports of individuals and groups possessing poisonous chemicals, harmful biological organisms, or radioactive material.[24] Although the information available about most of these cases is sketchy, it is clear that the majority have not presented any sort of mass-destruction threat, either because the materials in question preclude such a threat, or the people involved lacked the capacity to make effective weapons of mass destruction, or both.

Among the innumerable low-level criminal cases involving poison, a handful of incidents have been cited as evidence of rising chemical terrorism risks. In 1975, 53 canisters of mustard gas were reported stolen from a U.S. army base in West Germany; the Red Army Faction subsequently threatened to use the gas against the citizens of Stuttgart unless their imprisoned colleagues were freed, but it is not clear that these terrorists even possessed the gas canisters (many of which were recovered later).[25] There are hazy reports of an underground group in Vienna in the mid-1970s that had a nerve agent manufacturing facility (for sarin, tabun, or both); the group apparently hoped to sell nerve gas to criminal groups for profit.[26] There is also a report that anti-Castro Cubans in the United States tried but failed to acquire sarin from the Chilean intelligence

---

24. For a summary of cases in the mid-1990s, see David E. Kaplan, "Terrorism's Next Wave," *U.S. News and World Report*, November 17, 1997, pp. 26–31.

25. Yonah Alexander, "Will Terrorists Use Chemical Weapons?" *JINSA Security Affairs* (June–July 1990), p. 10; Brian M. Jenkins and Alfred P. Rubin, "New Vulnerabilities and the Acquisition of New Weapons by Nongovernmental Groups," in Alona E. Evans and John F. Murphy, eds., *Legal Aspects of International Terrorism* (Lexington, Mass.: Lexington Books, 1978), p. 228; Robert H. Kupperman and Jeff Kamen, *Final Warning: Averting Disaster in the New Age of Terrorism* (New York: Doubleday, 1989), p. 102; Wayman C. Mullins, "An Overview and Analysis of Nuclear, Biological, and Chemical Terrorism: The Weapons, Strategies, and Solutions to a Growing Problem," *American Journal of Criminal Justice*, Vol. 16, No. 2 (1992), p. 107; and Purver, *Chemical and Biological Terrorism*, pp. 84–85.

26. Kupperman and Kamen, *Final Warning*, p. 101; Douglass and Livingstone, *America the Vulnerable*, p. 87; Jenkins and Rubin, "New Vulnerabilities and the Acquisition of New Weapons by Nongovernmental Groups," p. 228; Robert K. Mullen, "Mass Destruction and Terrorism," *Journal of International Affairs*, Vol. 31, No. 1 (Spring–Summer 1978), pp. 69, 88; James H. Jackson, "When Terrorists Turn to Chemical Weapons," *Jane's Intelligence Review* (November 1992), p. 520; Thornton, *Modern Terrorism*, p. 7; and Purver, *Chemical and Biological Terrorism*, pp. 83–84.

agency.[27] In 1986, the FBI reportedly found large quantities of potassium cyanide in the Arkansas compound of a right-wing group called the Covenant, Sword, and Arm of the Lord.[28] Even if all of these reports are accurate, none of them presented anything close to the threat of Aum Shinrikyo, which created a secret nerve gas production facility in the Japanese countryside and managed to produce several tens of kilograms of sarin in 1993–95.

A handful of incidents have also involved harmful biological organisms and toxins. In 1972, members of the Order of the Rising Sun, an American fascist organization, were found in possession of 30–40 kilograms of typhoid bacteria culture, which they reportedly planned to introduce into the water supplies of Chicago, St. Louis, and other cities.[29] In October 1980, a cell of the Red Army Faction was discovered in Paris with cultured

---

27. Douglass and Livingstone, *America the Vulnerable*, p. 30; and Purver, *Chemical and Biological Terrorism*, p. 83.

28. See James K. Campbell, "Weapons of Mass Destruction and Terrorism: Proliferation by Non-state Actors," Thesis, Naval Postgraduate School, Monterey, California, December 1996, pp. 217–262; Mullins, "An Overview and Analysis of Nuclear, Biological, and Chemical Terrorism," p. 95; and Purver, *Chemical and Biological Terrorism*, p. 86.

29. Yonah Alexander, "Terrorism and High-Technology Weapons," in Lawrence Z. Freedman and Yonah Alexander, eds., *Perspectives on Terrorism* (Wilmington, Del.: Scholarly Resources, 1983), p. 230; Robert H. Kupperman and Darrell M. Trent, *Terrorism: Threat, Reality, and Response* (Stanford, Calif.: Hoover Institution Press, 1979), p. 46; Kupperman and Kamen, *Final Warning*, p. 105; B.J. Berkowitz et al., *Superviolence: The Civil Threat of Mass Destruction Weapons*, Report A72-034-10 (Santa Barbara, Calif.: Advanced Concepts Research Corporation, September 29, 1972), p. VI-6; R.W. Mengel, "Terrorism and New Technologies of Destruction: An Overview of the Potential Risk," in *Disorders and Terrorism*, Report of the Task Force on Disorders and Terrorism (Washington, D.C.: National Advisory Committee on Criminal Justice, Standards, and Goals, 1976), p. 450; Jenkins and Rubin, "New Vulnerabilities and the Acquisition of New Weapons by Nongovernmental Groups," p. 228; Jonathan B. Tucker, "Chemical/Biological Terrorism: Coping with a New Threat," *Politics and the Life Sciences*, Vol. 15, No. 2 (September 1996), p. 169; Office of Technology Assessment (OTA), *Technology against Terrorism: Structuring Security* (Washington, D.C.: U.S. GPO, 1992), p. 40; Purver, *Chemical and Biological Terrorism*, p. 37.

Clostridium botulinum, the bacterium that produces botulinum toxin.[30] In 1984, two Canadians were arrested by the FBI when they tried to order *Clostridium botulinum* from the American Type Culture Collection, a biological supply house.[31] In April 1993, Canadian border police confiscated 130 grams of ricin from Thomas Lewis Lavy, an Arkansas resident with reported links to survivalist groups, as he tried to enter Canada from Alaska.[32] After a two-year investigation by the FBI, Lavy was arrested and charged under the 1989 Biological Weapons Anti-Terrorism Act with possession of a biological toxin with intent to kill. He was never tried, because he hanged himself in his cell shortly after arraignment.[33] In August 1994, Douglas Allen Baker and Leroy Charles Wheeler — both associated with the Minnesota Patriots Council, a right-wing militia group — were arrested for possession of ricin and planning to murder law enforcement personnel; their intended delivery technique was to smear the toxin on the doorknobs of their intended victims.[34] In 1995, Larry Wayne Harris, a

---

30. "W. German Terrorists Said to Test Bacteria," *International Herald Tribune,* November 8–9, 1980, p. 2; Kupperman and Smith, "Coping with Biological Terrorism," pp. 36–37; OTA, *Technology against Terrorism,* p. 40; Mullins, "An Overview and Analysis of Nuclear, Biological, and Chemical Terrorism," p. 102; Kupperman and Kamen, *Final Warning,* p. 102; Tucker, "Chemical/Biological Terrorism," p. 169; Purver, *Chemical and Biological Terrorism,* pp. 36–37; and FBIS, December 19, 1980, p. 8, cited in Simon, "Terrorists and the Potential Use of Biological Weapons," p. 8, n. 4.

31. "Two Canadians Held in U.S. over Bacteria," *The Sun* (Vancouver), November 24, 1984, p. A7.

32. "A search of Lavy's car by Canadian customs agents revealed that he was carrying four guns, 20,000 rounds of ammunition, a belt-buckle knife, $89,000 in cash, neo-Nazi literature and a handbook on use of poisons," as well as a "white, powdery substance" that was confiscated and later identified as ricin. Michael Dorman, "Deadly Poison, Fatal Mystery; Toxic Terror or Overkill? Probers Seek Answers, Suicide Blocks Way," *Newsday,* January 7, 1996, p. A10.

33. See also John Kifner, "Man Arrested in Poison Case Kills Himself in Jail Cell," *New York Times,* December 24, 1995, p. 11; and Tucker, "Chemical/Biological Terrorism," pp. 169–170.

34. The two had 0.7 grams of ricin in their possession. See Purver, *Chemical and Biological Terrorism,* pp. 37–38; Conrad DeFiebre, "Two Convicted of Possessing Deadly Poison," *Chicago Star Tribune,* March 1, 1995; and Marie Cocco, "We Underestimate Militias at Our Peril," *The Times Union,* June 16, 1996. In February 1995, they were convicted under the Biological Weapons Antiterrorism Act of 1989.

Box 2
The Larry Wayne Harris Case; 1995–98

In May 1995, Larry Wayne Harris, a resident of Lancaster, Ohio, ordered three vials of freeze-dried *Yersinia pestis*, the bacterium that causes bubonic plague, from the American Type Culture Collection (ATCC) in Maryland. The ATCC routinely supplies thousands of biological cultures each year to laboratories around the world and rarely has reason to question an order. Alerted, however, by Harris's repeated calls asking about the status of his order, the company examined their files and realized that the laboratory he claimed to represent did not exist. The plague bacteria had already been shipped by that time, and Harris received the vials several days later.

Harris does not appear to have had any plans to use the vials of plague bacteria on humans. Instead, he said that he feared an "imminent invasion from Iraq of super-germ-carrying mice."[1] He planned to do "research" with the bacteria to discover a "plague antidote" (although treatments already exist). As a lab technician and a member of the American Society for Microbiology, Harris had the basic knowledge required to cultivate the plague samples, but there is no direct evidence that his use of the bacteria would have been inappropriate.

Despite Harris's association with extremist groups like the Aryan Nations and the Christian Identity Church, there was little authorities could do to prevent the samples from coming into his possession. Possession of plague and other potentially lethal bacteria was not illegal at the time. However, by lying to the ATCC over the telephone about the laboratory he claimed to represent, Harris committed wire fraud. Federal agents recovered the unopened culture samples from Harris. He was convicted of wire fraud, and received a six-month suspended sentence.

---

member of the white supremacist organization Aryan Nations, was arrested for mail fraud after ordering three vials of freeze-dried bubonic plague bacteria from the American Type Culture Collection (see Box 2, Larry Wayne Harris Case). These are not the only cases in which non-state actors have acquired some quantity of biological warfare agents, but they are the best-known. Even so, information about them is spotty and inconsistent.

In addition to a few dozen terrorist or radical activist attacks against commercial nuclear facilities,[35] many cases have been documented of individuals or small groups caught with illegal radioactive materials in their

---

35. See "Appendix: Nuclear-Related Terrorist Activities by Political Terrorists," in Leventhal and Alexander, *Preventing Nuclear Terrorism*, pp. 123–133.

Box 2, Larry Wayne Harris Case, *cont.*

As a result of this case, the U.S. Congress passed a law, now implemented in regulations issued by the federal Centers for Disease Control (CDC), that restricts the transport of pathogens such as bubonic plague to registered laboratories only.[2]

Harris was arrested again at the end of February 1998, on the basis of reports that he possessed cultures of anthrax bacteria for use as a biological weapon. Laboratory tests showed that the material in his possession was veterinary anthrax vaccine, made from a non-pathogenic anthrax strain.[3]

NOTES

1. See Jim Woods, "Plague Case is Federal Matter; Prosecutor to Drop State Counts," *Columbus Dispatch*, June 28, 1995.

2. See "CDC Urges Rule to Track Killer Germs: Terrorism Fears Spark Shipping Crackdown," *Atlanta Journal and Constitution*, June 19, 1996, p. A5. For an overview of the new regulations, and of legislation aimed at preventing biological terrorism, see James R. Ferguson, "Biological Weapons and U.S. Law," *Journal of the American Medical Association*, Vol. 278, No. 5 (August 6, 1997), pp. 359–360. For the regulations themselves, see "Additional requirements for facilities transferring or receiving select agents: Final rule," *Federal Register*, October 24, 1996, 61, p. 55190.

3. Todd S. Purdum, "Tests Indicate Seized Material is Non-Lethal Form of Anthrax," *New York Times*, February 22, 1998, Section 1, p. 1.

---

possession. In June 1994, New York police uncovered a plot by three members of the "Long Island UFO Network" to use radium, a radioactive material, to assassinate three Long Island Republican Party officials for allegedly covering up a UFO landing. The group had enough radium "to fill several coffee cups," and allegedly planned to contaminate their targets' food, toothpaste, and cars with the material — a farfetched murder technique given radium's relatively mild radioactivity.[36] Moreover, in the 1990s, dozens if not hundreds of incidents of "nuclear smuggling" have occurred in the former Soviet Union, including six incidents involving material that could be used to build a nuclear weapon if gathered in

---

36. John T. McQuiston, "Plot against L.I. Leaders Is Tied to Fear of UFOs," *New York Times*, June 22, 1996, p. 24; Larry Sutton and Frank Lombardi, "Third Man Held in L.I. Plot," *New York Daily News*, June 15, 1996, p. 9; and "Two Accused of Radioactive Murder Plot," *Associated Press*, June 14, 1996.

sufficient quantities.[37] By and large, however, little evidence links individuals caught in possession of radioactive materials to any conspiracy to conduct a serious radiological, much less a nuclear, attack. In November 1995, Chechen separatists left about a gram of Cesium-137 in a Moscow park, an amount that posed no threat to the population, although it attracted considerable media attention.[38] In general, most thieves and smugglers caught trying to remove radioactive material from the former Soviet Union have been amateurs, motivated by misplaced hope for quick financial gain. These incidents have revealed major deficiencies in the post-Soviet nuclear custodial system — an issue of highest international importance — but they have not revealed a hostile "demand side" of the problem, such as a terrorist group seeking to carry out a nuclear or radiological attack.

THREATS, HOAXES, AND EXTORTION ATTEMPTS. Threats, hoaxes, and extortion attempts involving claims about the potential use of nuclear, biological, and chemical weapons are common. Perhaps the most famous case was the May 1974 extortion threat made by "Captain Midnight" to detonate an improvised nuclear device in Boston, an incident that turned out to be a hoax but was deemed credible enough to mobilize a major deployment of nuclear experts from the national weapon laboratories.[39] The Boston incident led to the creation of the U.S. Nuclear Emergency Search Team (NEST), which was next activated in November 1975 to deal with a nuclear terrorism threat in Spokane, Washington. In the years since, the FBI has continued to receive and evaluate nuclear terrorist threats, although most of these threats have been readily identified as hoaxes. NEST was deployed to possible nuclear-terrorism sites approximately 30 times between 1975 and 1993.[40]

---

37. For a summary of these incidents, see Graham T. Allison, Owen R. Coté, Jr., Richard A. Falkenrath, and Steven E. Miller, *Avoiding Nuclear Anarchy: Containing the Threat of Loose Russian Nuclear Weapons and Fissile Material*, CSIA Studies in International Security (Cambridge, Mass.: MIT Press, 1996), pp. 23–28.

38. Mark Hibbs, "Chechen Separatists Take Credit for Moscow Cesium-137 Threat," *Nuclear Fuel*, Vol. 20, No. 25 (December 4, 1995), p. 5.

39. See Mahlon E. Gates, "The Nuclear Emergency Search Team," in Leventhal and Alexander, *Preventing Nuclear Terrorism*, p. 400.

40. Stephen Green, "Secretive Unit Awaits Call to Battle Nuclear Terrorism," *San Diego Union-Tribune*, December 12, 1993, p. A-1; see also John G. Roos, "The Ultimate Nightmare," *Armed Forces Journal International*, October 1995, p. 66.

An even greater number of threats involving chemical poisons and biological weapons have taken place, including countless threats to municipal water supplies.[41] In 1973, a German biologist threatened to contaminate water supplies with anthrax and botulinum unless he was paid $8.5 million,[42] and in 1980, the Red Army Faction reportedly threatened to spread anthrax through the German mail system.[43] In 1980, someone tried to extort $10 million from two hotels on Lake Tahoe with a note threatening to poison their water supplies.[44] In 1986, Tamil guerrillas in Sri Lanka sent letters to the embassies of several Western countries, claiming that they had laced Sri Lankan export tea with potassium cyanide.[45] Four individuals were arrested in London in 1987 after seeking to extort $15 million from the Cypriot government by threatening to attack Nicosia with airborne dioxin.[46] In 1988, two Chilean grapes were found to contain minute traces of cyanide, leading to quarantine and recall in the United States of all Chilean fruit.[47] In 1992, reportedly, a neo-Nazi group's plan to pump hydrogen cyanide into a synagogue was thwarted by German officials.[48] In April 1995, just a month after the Tokyo subway attack, an unknown person or group threatened a

---

41. See Purver, *Chemical and Biological Terrorism*, pp. 31–40, 80–90.

42. Jenkins and Rubin, "New Vulnerabilities and the Acquisition of New Weapons by Nongovernmental Groups," p. 228; Kupperman and Trent, *Terrorism*, p. 46; and Purver, *Chemical and Biological Terrorism*, p. 35.

43. Richard C. Clark, *Technological Terrorism* (Old Greenwich, Conn.: Devin-Alder, 1980), p. 137, cited in Purver, *Chemical and Biological Terrorism*, p. 34.

44. Simon, "Terrorists and the Potential Use of Biological Weapons," p. 6.

45. Jessica Stern, "Will Terrorists Turn to Poison?" *Orbis*, Vol. 37, No. 3 (Summer 1993), p. 396; Simon, "Terrorists and the Potential Use of Biological Weapons," p. 9; and Purver, *Chemical and Biological Terrorism*, p. 83.

46. Jackson, "When Terrorists Turn to Chemical Weapons," p. 520; Simon, "Terrorists and the Potential Use of Biological Weapons," p. 6; and Purver, *Chemical and Biological Terrorism*, p. 81.

47. Stern, "Will Terrorists Turn to Poison?" pp. 395–396; Simon, "Terrorists and the Potential Use of Biological Weapons," p. 9; and Purver, *Chemical and Biological Terrorism*, p. 89.

48. Kupperman and Smith, "Coping with Biological Terrorism," p. 37; and Purver, *Chemical and Biological Terrorism*, p. 80.

sarin attack against Disneyland in California over Easter weekend.[49] This threat prompted a major deployment of U.S. emergency response personnel and chemical defense forces, but the attack never occurred. Early press reports said that the plot was foiled when Tokyo police alerted the FBI, which arrested two Aum Shinrikyo members at Los Angeles International Airport; these reports were denied by the Justice Department. On April 24, 1997, the world headquarters of B'nai B'rith in Washington, D.C., received a foul-smelling package reportedly marked "anthrachs." Emergency personnel sealed off the building and held some of its occupants for observation, only to discover that the package contained harmless bacteria.[50] These incidents represent only a small sample of the total number of nuclear, biological, and chemical threats made around the world every year. The vast majority are easily dismissed as not credible by authorities, and many are perpetrated by individuals of questionable mental health.

ESTABLISHED TERRORIST ORGANIZATIONS SEEM UNINTERESTED. Established terrorist organizations appear consistently uninterested in acquiring a nuclear, biological, or chemical weapons capability. There are virtually no reports, much less solid evidence, linking established terrorist groups — the Irish Republican Army, the Basque ETA, the Fatah faction of the PLO, Hezbollah, Jewish extremists, the Italian Red Brigade, the many different Latin American terrorist and revolutionary groups, the Japanese United Red Army, or the various Turkish and Armenian terrorist organizations — to any serious interest in weapons of mass destruction. A possible exception is West Germany's Red Army Faction (RAF), which may have tried to produce botulinum toxin in Paris in 1980, but it is not at all certain that the RAF had a clear delivery concept in mind for the toxin, much less the determination to use it.[51]

---

49. Tucker, "Chemical/Biological Terrorism," p. 169.

50. See Matthew L. Wald, "Suspicious Package Prompts 8-Hour Vigil at B'nai B'rith," *New York Times*, April 25, 1997, p. A12; and "Jewish Center Package Causes Alert," *Facts on File News Digest*, May 29, 1997.

51. "W. German Terrorists Said to Test Bacteria," *International Herald Tribune*, November 8–9, 1980, p. 2; Kupperman and Smith, "Coping with Biological Terrorism," pp. 36–37; OTA, *Technology against Terrorism*, p. 40; Mullins, "An Overview and Analysis of Nuclear, Biological, and Chemical Terrorism," p. 102; Kupperman and Kamen, *Final Warning*, p. 102; Tucker, "Chemical/Biological Terrorism," p. 169; Purver, *Chemical and Biological Terrorism*, pp. 36–37; and FBIS, December 19, 1980, p. 8, cited in Simon, "Terrorists and the Potential Use of Biological Weapons," p. 8, n. 4.

REASONS FOR LACK OF INTEREST AMONG CAPABLE NON-STATE ACTORS

As we explain in the next chapter, chemical weapons suitable for terrorist use could be acquired by a wide variety of organizations, biological weapons could be acquired by a smaller number of groups, and even nuclear weapons might be accessible to a few, if they could obtain enough fissile material to construct a weapon. However, the vast majority of capable non-state actors — Aum Shinrikyo being the principal exception — appear completely uninterested in either acquiring or using nuclear, biological, or chemical weapons. What factors account for this?

Among the different non-state actors under consideration here, terrorists have been the most extensively described and analyzed. Considerable thought has gone into assessing the probability that a terrorist organization would turn to nuclear, biological, or chemical weapons to inflict massive human casualties.[52] One strand of the "terrorism studies" community concerns itself almost exclusively with explaining perceived trends toward greater casualties and higher technology weaponry, and mainstream terrorism analysts have reached a loose consensus on the reasons why established political terrorist organizations are unlikely to add weapons of mass destruction to their arsenals. Less progress has been made, however, in understanding whether other types of non-state actors — such as guerrilla movements, fanatical religious organizations, criminal syndicates, constituent parts of collapsing states, or lone individuals — might be drawn toward NBC weapons. These non-state actors have generally fallen outside the scope, or languished in the margins, of the terrorism studies literature, and therefore little is known about the nuclear, biological, and chemical risks they pose.

There are at least five reasons why capable non-state actors have not been interested in NBC weapons. First and most important, inflicting massive human casualties does not serve the objectives of most non-state actors, and would indeed often be highly counterproductive. Second, alternative, conventional means of attack are more easily available to those groups that do wish to cause mass casualties. Third, the acquisition and use

---

52. This intense interest in the prospect of NBC terrorism dates from the mid-1970s, when a marked rise in the frequency and lethality of conventional terrorism coincided with a heightened awareness that fabricating nuclear weapons (once fissile material was on hand) would not be an insurmountable task for a well-organized and trained terrorist group. Nuclear terrorism has traditionally received more analytical attention than biological or chemical terrorism, but the latter began to attract heightened attention in the mid-1990s.

of NBC weapons would bring additional risks and challenges to a terrorist organization beyond those associated with conventional weapons. Fourth, the absence of precedent may make NBC weapons appear out of reach or ineffective. Relatively few instances of NBC use by states in war have been successful, and no cases of successful large-scale nuclear, biological, or chemical terrorism by non-state actors have occurred, the Tokyo nerve gas attack notwithstanding. And finally, there appears to be a special moral reservation against killing people with poison, disease, or the atom: a norm against nuclear, biological, or chemical weapons use against human beings. Taken together, these five factors provide a persuasive explanation for why NBC terrorism has been so rare.

MASS CASUALTIES DO NOT SERVE THE PURPOSES OF MOST NON-STATE ACTORS. The fundamental purpose of acquiring weapons of mass destruction is to kill large numbers of people. To the extent that non-state actors are averse to inflicting mass casualties, the covert NBC risks they represent will remain small. Indeed, most terrorist incidents do not kill anyone. According to the best publicly available database on international terrorism, only 17 percent of terrorist incidents in the 1970s, and only 19 percent in the 1980s, resulted in even a single human casualty.[53] "Mass casualty" terrorist events with 100 or more dead are quite rare: in modern times, there are only about a dozen known incidents of this kind (summarized in Table 1). Undoubtedly, other terrorist attempts to inflict mass casualties have been made — the World Trade Center bombing and the Tokyo subway attack are examples — but even so, the available data strongly suggest a general aversion to mass casualties among most non-state actors. (The principal exceptions to this general rule are ruthless guerrilla groups animated by a particular ethnic hatred or extreme ideology, such as the Bosnian Serbs, Algerian Islamic radicals, Rwandan militias, and Khmer Rouge, whose mass casualty attacks are not included in Table 1.) Moreover, this aversion does not appear to result from a technical incapacity or lack of opportunity to kill large numbers of people. Thus, it appears that non-state actors and particularly terrorist organizations have made conscious decisions to kill fewer people than they could. The most compelling explanations for this phenomenon are discussed next.

---

53. These data are from the RAND–St. Andrews University Chronology of International Terrorist Incidents. See Bruce Hoffman, "Terrorism and WMD: Some Preliminary Hypotheses," *Nonproliferation Review*, Vol. 4, No. 3 (Spring–Summer 1997), p. 47.

Table 1. Mass-casualty Attacks by Terrorists in the Twentieth Century (100 or more fatalities).

Year	Event	Deaths
1925	Bombing of cathedral in Sofia, Bulgaria	160
1946	Nakam attack in Germany	100s (?)
1979	Arson attack on a cinema in Abadan, Iran	477
1983	Bombing of the U.S. Marine barracks in Lebanon	241
1985	Bombing of Air India passenger airliner over the Irish Sea	328
1987	Bombing of South Korean airliner near the Thai-Burmese border	117
1987	Car bomb in Sri Lanka bus station	113
1988	Bombing of Pan Am Flight 103 over Lockerbie, Scotland	278
1989	Bombing of French UTA airliner over Niger	171
1989	Bombing of Colombian Avianca aircraft near Bogota	107
1993	Bombings in Bombay (10 bombs in less than 3 hours)	235
1995	Bombing of federal building in Oklahoma City	168

NOTE: This table includes only conventional terrorist attacks. It does not include the many large-scale massacres, such as those in Cambodia, Rwanda, or Algeria, carried out by militaries or guerrilla groups using guns, machetes, or other small arms.

SOURCES: Bruce Hoffman, "Responding to Terrorism across the Technological Spectrum," *Terrorism and Political Violence*, Vol. 6, No. 3 (Autumn 1994), p. 385, n. 13; A.D. Harvey, "Research Note: The Attempt to Assassinate the Bulgarian Cabinet," *Terrorism and Political Violence*, Vol. 4, No. 1 (Spring 1992), p. 104; Jo Thomas, "Letter by McVeigh Told of Attitude," *New York Times*, May 9, 1997, p. A1; Associated Press, "Car Bomb Kills Close to 150 at Crowded Sri Lanka Bus Depot," *Los Angeles Times*, June 21, 1987, p. 2; Kenneth J. Cooper, "Sri Lankan Rebels on a Rebound," *Washington Post*, July 27, 1996, p. A18; and Sanjoy Hazarika, "Focus Is on Tamils in Bombay Blasts," *New York Times*, March 16, 1993, p. 7.

The first explanation is that mass casualties undermine political support. Most established terrorist organizations pursue political objectives, such as creating a separate national homeland or advancing a particular ideology (e.g., Marxism-Leninism, fascism, anarchy).[54] These strategic-minded terrorist organizations recognize that limited political ends cannot be achieved by unlimited violent means. When they kill, it is not for the sake of killing, but as a means of achieving political objectives, and they do it carefully. Groups like this tend to use violence to draw attention to themselves and their causes, to create the conditions for revolution by undermining social stability, and to erode the resolve of oppressive governments. In so doing, they must strike a delicate balance between attracting too little attention and being ignored, and attracting so much attention that public hatred affects their cause. In implementing such a strategy, the media — especially television in the modern era — offers vital support to terrorists, since the images of brutal acts of terrorism can be beamed directly to millions, while only a few are harmed. For such terrorists, the true targets are the people watching and reading about the act; the victims are a means, not an end.

---

54. The largest nationalist-separatist terrorist organizations are well known and well established; examples include the Irish Republican Army (IRA), the Palestine Liberation Organization (PLO), the Abu Nidal Organization (ANO), Hamas (Islamic Resistance Movement), the Basque ETA (Euzkadi Ta Askatasun, or Fatherland and Liberty), the Secret Army for the Liberation of Armenia, the Liberation Tigers of Tamil Eelam (LTTE) in Sri Lanka, the Palestine Islamic Jihad (PIJ), and various Sikh groups in India. Ideologically motivated groups tend to be more ephemeral; these include the anarchists of the late nineteenth century, the People's Will of pre-revolutionary Russia, the right-wing terrorists of the 1930s, the Red Army Faction (RAF) and other left-wing German groups, the Italian Red Brigades, the Japanese Red Army (JRA), the Tupamaros of Uruguay, the right-wing Jewish group Kach, various Turkish groups on the left and right, the Revolutionary Armed Forces of Columbia (FARC), and Peru's Shining Path (Sendero Luminoso, SL) and Tupac Amaru Revolutionary Movement (MRTA). Groups often exhibit signs of both national-separatist and ideological character, as in the case of the Islamic Jihad, which seeks to establish a Palestinian homeland that is both independent and Islamic, and the Turkish Workers' Party (PKK), which to seeks to establish a Marxist-Leninist Kurdish state in southeastern Turkey. For good surveys of terrorist organizations, see *Patterns of Global Terrorism 1996* (Washington, D.C.: U.S. Department of State, 1997), available at <www.state.gov/www/global/terrorism>; and Martha Crenshaw, ed., *Terrorism in Context* (University Park: Pennsylvania State University Press, 1995).

Groups that knowingly kill large numbers of innocents are likely to be perceived as crazed mass murderers, not the righteous crusaders that traditional terrorists present themselves to be. National separatist movements, for example, must avoid actions that permanently alienate international opinion, since their ultimate objective is to create a state with respect and standing in the international community, and not to bring the wrath of the larger community down upon their ethnic brethren. Likewise, ideological groups at the margins of society that hope to stimulate the dormant revolutionary impulses of "the people" must avoid shedding so much blood as to permanently destroy whatever popular support they may have. Political goals tend not to be achieved through measures that intensify existing opposition and erode latent support.

This interpretation of political terrorism is fairly widespread in the literature.[55] Among modern analysts, Brian Jenkins has had considerable influence with his analysis of terrorism as a strategic and political phenomenon. He writes that "terrorists fear alienating the perceived constituents on whose behalf they claim to fight."[56] Jenkins also penned the oft-cited summation: "Terrorists want a lot of people watching, not a lot of people

---

55. Martha Crenshaw argues that by "exploiting the publicity their acts receive, terrorist organizations reach large numbers of people vicariously while causing a relatively small number of physical victims." Martha Crenshaw, "Transnational Terrorism and World Politics," *Jerusalem Journal of International Relations*, Vol. 1, No. 2 (Winter 1975), p. 127; see also Martha Crenshaw, "The Causes of Terrorism," *Comparative Politics*, Vol. 13, No. 4 (July 1981), pp. 379–399. Jerrold M. Post argues that an "action which produces mass casualties would, by definition, disaffect the general population, the very population whose support the terrorists require, and whom the terrorists are seeking to influence positively to support their cause." Jerrold M. Post, "Superterrorism: Biological, Chemical, and Nuclear," *Terrorism*, Vol. 13, No. 2 (1990), p. 166. See also L. John Martin, "The Media's Role in International Terrorism," in Charles W. Kegley, Jr., ed., *International Terrorism: Characteristics, Causes, Controls* (New York: St. Martin's, 1990), pp. 158–162; Bruce Hoffman, "Terrorist Targeting," *Terrorism and Political Violence*, Vol. 5, No. 2 (Summer 1993), pp. 12–29; Laqueur, *The Age of Terrorism*, pp. 312–321; Mullen, "Mass Destruction and Terrorism"; Elliott Hurwitz, "Terrorists and Chemical/Biological Weapons," *Naval War College Review*, Vol. 35, No. 3 (May–June 1982), pp. 36–40; and Donald J. Hanle, *Terrorism: The Newest Face of Warfare* (Washington, D.C.: Pergamon-Brassey's, 1989), pp. 103–120.

56. Brian M. Jenkins, *International Terrorism: The Other World War*, RAND Report R-3302-AF (Santa Monica, Calif.: RAND, November 1985), p. 23.

dead."[57] A similar formulation was also used by J. Bowyer Bell who, in discussing the possibility of terrorist attacks against nuclear reactors, wrote that "there is no evidence that terrorists have any interest in killing large numbers of people with a meltdown. The new transnational television terrorist wants media exposure, not exposure of the masses to radioactive fallout."[58] The essence of this view dates back to the early terrorist doctrines articulated by nineteenth-century writers such as Karl Heinzen, Peter Kropotkin, and Johann Most.[59] In 1880, for instance, Kropotkin argued that the masses could only be moved to revolution through "propaganda by deed," since theoretical speeches and pamphlets bored most men. Action, on the other hand, especially violent action, would capture the attention of the people and, it was hoped, move them to unite against their oppressors.[60] These revolutionary theories have had few successes, but much of the terrorist activity of the last century has been animated by the basic notion that violent action produces political results by working through the media to influence the attitudes of the people watching.[61] Indeed, in the era of

---

57. Brian M. Jenkins, "Will Terrorists Go Nuclear?" RAND Report P-5541 (Santa Monica, Calif.: RAND, November 1975), p. 4.

58. J. Bowyer Bell, *A Time of Terror: How Democratic Societies Respond to Revolutionary Violence* (New York: Basic Books, 1978), p. 121.

59. For good surveys, see Martin A. Miller, "The Intellectual Origins of Terrorism in Europe," in Crenshaw, *Terrorism in Context*, pp. 27–62; Laqueur, *The Age of Terrorism*, pp. 24–71; and Marie Fleming, "Propaganda by the Deed: Terrorism and Anarchist Theory in Late Nineteenth Century Europe," in Yonah Alexander and Kenneth A. Meyers, eds., *Terrorism in Europe* (New York: St. Martin's, 1982), pp. 8–28.

60. "The Spirit of Revolt" is reprinted in Roger N. Baldwin, ed., *Kropotkin's Revolutionary Pamphlets: A Collection of Writings by Peter Kropotkin* (New York: Dover, 1970), pp. 35–43. Later in life, Kropotkin came to doubt the effectiveness of "propaganda by deed" and other forms of terrorist violence.

61. This strategic concept makes clear the difference between terrorism and traditional warfare: in war, violent action produces political results through the military defeat of the opponent's forces or the occupation of the opponent's territory.

CNN (Cable News Network), the mechanism for transmitting terrorist imagery to the target audience has become more efficient than ever.[62]

Of course, this explanation for mass-casualty aversion applies mainly to terrorist organizations that adopt rational strategies to achieve political aims, not to the full gamut of potentially violent non-state actors. Apolitical or religious terrorists may not be bound by this logic, nor may a guerrilla organization that seeks to establish control over some population and piece of territory,[63] nor may a genocidal, ethnic-cleansing mob. Finally, an exceptionally ruthless and intelligent revolutionary — the "next Lenin," in the evocative phase of Fred Iklé — might find a way to use the terror of casualties on a truly massive scale to topple a democratic government and assume power.[64]

A second and related reason why terrorist organizations and other hostile non-state actors have been reluctant to inflict mass casualties is that they do not want to risk stronger government countermeasures. Terrorism experts generally believe that "terrorists fear provoking widespread public revulsion because that can be exploited by the government and used against them."[65] Many terrorist organizations believe that they can withstand the

---

62. For a strong critique of the media's role in propagating terrorist messages, see Laqueur, *The Age of Terrorism*, pp. 121–127. For a more optimistic view, see Patrick Clawson, "Why We Need More But Better Coverage of Terrorism," in Kegley, *International Terrorism*, pp. 241–244.

63. The Viet Cong, for instance, are estimated to have killed 10,000 village leaders in South Vietnam in the late 1950s and early 1960s. Bernard B. Fall, *Last Reflections on a War* (New York: Doubleday, 1967), p. 219. In the Algerian civil war, at least 60,000 people are believed to have been killed between 1992 and 1996. See "Middle East Overview" in U.S. State Department, *Patterns of Global Terrorism 1996*, <www.state.gov/www/global/terrorism/1996report/middle.html>.

64. Fred Iklé, "The Next Lenin," *The National Interest*, No. 47 (Spring 1997), pp. 9–19.

65. The quotation is from Jenkins, *International Terrorism*, p. 24. See also B. David, "The Capability and Motivation of Terrorist Organizations to Use Mass-Destruction Weapons," in Ariel Merari, ed., *On Terrorism and Combating Terrorism* (Frederick, Md.: University Publications of America, 1985), pp. 150–151; Hoffman, "Terrorist Targetting," p. 23; Hurwitz, "Terrorists and Chemical/Biological Weapons," p. 39; Kupperman and Trent, *Terrorism*, p. 49; Kupperman and Woolsey, Testimony before the Subcommittee on Technology and Law, May 19, 1988, pp. 2–3; Mullen, "Mass Destruction and Terrorism," pp. 84–85; Simon, "Terrorists and the Potential Use of Biological Weapons," p. 9; and Stanley L. Wiener, "Terrorist Use of Biological

repression, reprisals, and investigations that "normal" terrorism provokes from their adversaries, but they would be challenged by the heightened level of scrutiny and persecution that would follow an especially ghastly attack. Indeed, this concern should apply to all non-state actors — not just terrorist organizations — that are rational, concerned with their own survival, and operating against governments that exhibit self-restraint. A good example of the sort of state response that a terrorist organization might fear if it goes too far is that of Israel after the Palestinian terrorist attack against Israeli athletes at the 1972 Munich Olympics. Israeli agents systematically hunted down and killed all of the terrorists involved in the incident (and at least one innocent victim of mistaken identity) in a secret operation known as the "Wrath of God."[66] If the level of terrorist threat is deemed high enough, even liberal democracies can restrict civil liberties, loosen the rules of engagement, and prosecute counterterrorism in ways that would seem uncivilized in a safer society.

In the past, some terrorist groups (particularly those on the left) have deliberately tried to provoke their governmental adversaries into more repressive behavior in order to anger the public and foment revolution.[67] However, this strategy does not appear ever to have succeeded, not least because mass casualties tend to undermine whatever latent popular support

---

Weapons," *Terrorism*, Vol. 14, No. 2 (1991), p. 130.

66. Most or all terrorists involved in the Munich massacre were eventually assassinated by the Israelis. But the operation was exposed when six Israeli agents killed an innocent Moroccan waiter in Lillehammer, Norway; they were captured by Norwegian police, tried for murder, convicted, and sentenced to jail terms. See Ian Black and Benny Morris, *Israel's Secret Wars: A History of Israel's Intelligence Services* (New York: Grove Weidenfeld, 1991), pp. 272–277; Dan Raviv and Yossi Melman, *Every Spy a Prince: The Complete History of Israel's Intelligence Community* (Boston: Houghton Mifflin, 1990), pp. 184–194; and Victor Ostrovsky and Claire Hoy, *By Way of Deception* (New York: St. Martin's, 1990), pp. 178–179.

67. The Tupamaros of Uruguay exemplified this terrorist strategy, as did the West German RAF. See Paul Wilkinson, *Political Terrorism* (London: Macmillan, 1974), pp. 113–114. This particular terrorist strategy is also mentioned in Jenkins, *International Terrorism*, p. 10; Brad Roberts, "Has the Taboo Been Broken?" in Brad Roberts, ed., *Terrorism with Chemical and Biological Weapons: Calibrating Risks and Responses* (Alexandria, Va.: Chemical and Biological Arms Control Institute, 1997), p. 129; Kupperman and Trent, *Terrorism*, p. 51; and Thornton, *Modern Terrorism*, p. 2.

there may be for the terrorists' cause, and encourage people to look to government authorities to restore order.[68]

The third reason is that increasing casualties does not reduce the difficulty of terrorist coercion. One popularly held belief is that a terrorist with a weapon of mass destruction would *ipso facto* possess great coercive power. A terrorist with a nuclear weapon could, in theory, dictate terms to the targeted government, leaving authorities little choice but to capitulate. In fact, coercion by terrorism is anything but easy, and an ability to inflict higher levels of casualties does not appear to be a particularly important determinant of terrorists' success rate.

Terrorist coercion is rarely successful: "Acts of terrorism almost never appear to accomplish anything politically significant."[69] The reason for this lies not primarily in any limitations on the terrorists' power to inflict casualties but instead in the nature of coercion. If it were true that the success rate of terrorist coercion could be improved by increasing casualty levels — a quite simple matter — then political terrorism should be much more frequent, more extensive, and more deadly than it has in fact been. Coercion involves an attempt to compel the adversary to take specific action by inflicting harm or making a threat to inflict harm. It is an uncertain proposition even for states, but for non-state actors it is particularly challenging. The logistics of implementing the coercive strategy will often reveal the identity of the perpetrator, inviting reprisals or countermeasures.[70] Governments, moreover, rarely make major political concessions, such as self-dissolution or the evacuation of contested territory, in response

---

68. "Society will tolerate terrorism as long as it is no more than a nuisance. Once insecurity spreads and terror becomes a real danger, the authorities are no longer blamed for disregarding human rights." Walter Laqueur, "The Futility of Terrorism," in Kegley, *International Terrorism*, p. 70.

69. Thomas C. Schelling, "What Purposes Can 'International Terrorism' Serve?" in R.G. Frey and Christopher W. Morris, eds., *Violence, Terrorism, and Justice* (Cambridge: Cambridge University Press, 1991), p. 21. See also Laqueur, "The Futility of Terrorism," in Kegley, *International Terrorism*, pp. 69–73. This view is controversial within the "terrorism studies" community, but we believe it is basically correct. For arguments that terrorism has been politically successful, see Paul Johnson, "The Seven Deadly Sins of Terrorism," in Kegley, *International Terrorism*, pp. 63–68.

70. This is most clear in the case of extortion, where money changes hands, or political concessions, such as the freeing of prisoners or the loosening of political controls in a given area.

to terrorist threats, and even carefully orchestrated terrorist campaigns are much more likely to elicit vigorous reprisals than capitulation.[71] The point is not that terrorist coercion is never successful; indeed, there are instances of minor concessions being made to terrorists (e.g., the freeing of prisoners), and even a few arguable cases in which major concessions appear to have been made (e.g., Israeli negotiations with the PLO; British willingness to negotiate over the political status of Northern Ireland; U.S. withdrawal from Lebanon in 1983; British withdrawal from Palestine). The point is that the level of human casualties threatened or inflicted by the terrorist does not appear to be a significant factor in determining whether the coercive strategy succeeds or fails. More significant factors include the tenacity and savvy of the terrorists, the political and social context of their coercive gambit, and the level of government interest in retaining whatever the terrorists are demanding.

Of course, non-state actors can and do use violence for purposes other than coercion. For instance, instead of demanding some specific concession, violence can be used to trigger predictable, reflexive reactions within the target population. The Hamas-sponsored campaign of suicide bombings in Israel after the assassination of Prime Minister Yitzhak Rabin and prior to the Israeli elections is widely credited with tipping the electoral balance toward the Likud Party, resulting in the narrow election of Benjamin Netanyahu as Israeli prime minister and, shortly thereafter, in the disruption of the Middle East peace process, a key Hamas objective. Alternatively, the threat of violence can be used for deterrence, which is in general a less demanding strategy than coercion.[72] The ability to inflict mass casualties is more useful in preventing an action from being taken, but deterrent threats associated with non-state violence are uncommon. Non-state actors, unlike states, are more likely to rely on secrecy rather than deterrence for their survival. The limited coercive utility of mass casualties will also not be a factor for non-state actors that employ violence for apolitical reasons, such as religion, revenge, or nihilism.

Finally, heightened violence tends to increase internal dissension. Many terrorist groups and violent non-state actors behave like other political

---

71. As Schelling has noted, "the threat that compels rather than deters often takes the form of administering the punishment until the other acts, rather than *if* he acts." Thomas C. Schelling, *The Strategy of Conflict* (Cambridge, Mass.: Harvard University Press, 1960), p. 196 (emphasis in original).

72. See Schelling, *The Strategy of Conflict*, pp. 195–199; and Schelling, "What Purposes Can 'International Terrorism' Serve?" pp. 25–26.

organizations, which means among other things that they are fundamentally concerned with their own survival.[73] Group survival is, of course, subject to both external and internal threats. Some analysts argue that terrorist organizations debate the level and types of violence that they should employ to meet their aims, and that they eventually reach a consensus that governs (perhaps temporarily) how far they will go.[74] The issue of mass casualties has the potential to divide the organization, separating those who take a dimmer view of mass murder from the more bloodthirsty. Terrorist groups have considerable ability to enforce conformity within their ranks, but all secret organizations are susceptible to the risks of factionalism and betrayal. Internal dissension increases the risks that one or more members of the group will leave the organization, form a splinter group, or even go to the authorities with information leading to the demise of the group. Inflicting mass casualties is therefore likely to be seen as harmful to the survival of the group, so the idea that the group should seek to kill in vast numbers is likely to be discouraged or suppressed by the organization's leaders or instinctively avoided by the rank and file. Not all non-state actors possess this fundamental concern with their own survival, but many do, especially the "traditional" terrorist organizations, and those that do are likely to shy away from activities with a high potential to kill large numbers of people.

MASS DESTRUCTION IS POSSIBLE WITHOUT WEAPONS OF MASS DESTRUCTION. The potential drawbacks of large-scale killing have not stopped some non-state groups from seeking to inflict casualties on a massive scale, and more than a few such efforts have succeeded. Indeed, the number of high-lethality terrorist attacks appears to have risen since the late 1980s and, as we argue in Chapter 3, there is reason to fear that the incidence of such attacks will continue to grow in the future. Likewise, insurgents and guerrilla groups, such as the Viet Cong, Khmer Rouge, and Algeria's Armed Islamic Group (GIA), have killed innocent civilians by the thousands to achieve their political, military, religious, or ideological objectives. In 1994,

---

73. Martha Crenshaw, "An Organizational Approach to the Analysis of Political Terrorism," *Orbis*, Vol. 29, No. 3 (Fall 1985), pp. 473–487. In developing this argument, Crenshaw makes good use of James Q. Wilson, *Political Organizations* (New York: Basic Books, 1973). See also Laqueur, *The Age of Terrorism*, pp. 93–96.

74. Jenkins, *International Terrorism*, p. 24; and Jenkins, "Understanding the Link between Motives and Methods," in Roberts, *Terrorism with Chemical and Biological Weapons*, pp. 46–47.

for example, an estimated 800,000 Rwandans were killed in two months.[75] These vicious non-state actors, like many before them, have managed to kill large numbers of people without resorting to nuclear, biological, or chemical weapons, and the casualty levels they were able to inflict were not strongly dependent on their access to weaponry.[76] Thus, to the extent that non-state actors have wanted to frighten or kill more than a few, they have generally been able to achieve their desired casualty levels by employing knives, small arms, chemical explosives, and other types of conventional weapons. This is the second main reason why non-state actors that possess the theoretical capacity to acquire and use nuclear, biological, or chemical weapons have generally been uninterested in doing so.

The overwhelming majority of organized, violent acts carried out by terrorist groups and other hostile non-state actors involve only conventional weapons and military equipment, such as guns and chemical explosives. Chemical explosives — ranging from the simplest, such as ammonium nitrate mixed with fuel oil, to the most advanced military high explosives, such as C-4 and Semtex — can be used to kill up to a few hundred people in a shocking, highly destructive manner. The other tactics commonly employed by terrorist groups — such as hostage-taking, aircraft hijacking, and the occasional machine-gunning of a crowd — generally cause fewer casualties than a single, well-placed conventional bomb. (The relative frequency with which terrorist groups employ these low-lethality tactics is further evidence of their aversion to mass casualties.) Conventional weapons and forms of attack also appear to suffice for the other types of non-state actors that occasionally attempt to kill in large numbers. Roving bands in Rwanda massacred hundreds of thousands of their countrymen with machetes in 1994. In Algeria, militant Islamic insurgents kill with knives, guns, and occasionally bombs. In Bosnia, the tools were guns and death camps; in Chechnya, guns and mortars. Members of fanatical religious movements have managed to kill themselves by the dozens, and

---

75. Stephen John Stedman, "Conflict and Conciliation in Sub-Saharan Africa," in Michael E. Brown, ed., *The International Dimensions of Internal Conflict*, CSIA Studies in International Security (Cambridge, Mass.: MIT Press, 1996), p. 235.

76. Jenkins notes that "there is no substantial technical ceiling on the killing of large numbers of people with the traditional instruments of terror, which implies that technical constraints have not been the primary barrier to the use of massively destructive weapons by terrorists." Jenkins, "Understanding the Link between Motives and Methods," pp. 45–46. See also Jenkins and Rubin, "New Vulnerabilities and the Acquisition of New Weapons by Nongovernmental Groups," pp. 221–276.

sometimes hundreds, with common poisons. In sum, mass killing has not required exotic weapons and has created no particular demand for NBC weapons among murderous non-state actors.

NBC ACQUISITION, WHILE POSSIBLE, ENTAILS ADDITIONAL RISKS AND CHALLENGES. While theoretically possible for many groups, the acquisition and use of NBC weapons by a non-state actor poses risks and challenges well beyond those associated with conventional weapons and explosives. With respect to acquisition, NBC weapons are more technologically challenging than conventional weapons, and also generally more expensive. Work on weapons of mass destruction inevitably involves a certain heightened hazard to health: fissile material is radioactive (albeit less so than most people think, especially if it is weapons-grade); biological warfare agents are pathogenic microorganisms or toxins that can kill human beings in extremely small doses; and chemical weapons are extremely lethal substances and also generally volatile. These hazards can be reduced to acceptable levels if the materials are handled by trained personnel using proper equipment, but non-state actors may lack such facilities and expertise. Attempts to acquire NBC weapons also raise the risk that the group will be found out and crushed by authorities, especially if individuals with special expertise must be recruited for the NBC acquisition effort. For the terrorist group planning a covert NBC attack, the risk of betrayal and discovery increases with every new member that must be recruited in order to assemble a team capable of fabricating a functional weapon of mass destruction. The risk of detection also increases with the general complexity and distinctiveness of the covert undertaking: the more discrete and unusual the steps involved (e.g., the acquisition of fissile material, which would be highly suggestive of the intent of the operation), the greater the chance of accidental detection. There are costs, risks, and challenges associated with acquiring conventional weapons as well, but these are on the whole less severe than those associated with weapons of mass destruction.

With respect to the actual use of the device, NBC weapons again present risks and challenges beyond those of their conventional counterparts. The effects of a nuclear, biological, or chemical weapon will generally be less predictable than those of a conventional weapon, and terrorists in particular are believed to prefer highly predictable and reliable forms of attack.[77] In some cases, NBC weapons may also be somewhat easier for authorities to detect, even if they are not specifically looking for them. And NBC weapons may have a harmful physical or psychological effect on the human operatives charged with handling or delivering them: these individuals may, for instance, be contaminated by the weapon's emissions, or simply "spooked" by holding the device in their hands. Holding other factors constant, a rational attacker will employ the simplest, least costly, and most reliable means of attack available to it. The fact that nuclear, biological, and chemical weapons are often inferior to conventional weapons in these respects, especially for attackers not seeking mass casualties, is another key explanation for the historical infrequency of non-state actor aggression involving weapons of mass destruction.

ABSENCE OF PRECEDENT. No non-state actor had successfully used a weapon of mass destruction until Aum Shinrikyo's nerve gas attacks in Matsumoto and Tokyo. This absence of precedent gives special weight to any decision about NBC use, and probably accounts in part for the rarity of non-state NBC aggression.

Setting off a conventional bomb in a major city is far from unusual, and is perhaps even routine for some terrorist groups. Setting off a nuclear, chemical, or biological weapon in a city would be anything but routine. Potential aggressors contemplating a covert NBC attack have no historical basis for predicting the immediate effects and long-term consequences of the event, compounding the uncertainties attendant to the plan. These uncertainties probably have a dissuasive effect on groups sophisticated enough to conceive and implement a covert NBC attack. The absence of precedent also implies that some potential aggressors may be unaware of the ease, and even the possibility, of conducting a covert NBC attack against their opponents.[78] This latter point is not particularly persuasive, however, because it would be a rare non-state actor indeed that is intelligent enough to carry out a covert NBC attack successfully, yet stupid enough not to have thought of the possibility on its own.

---

77. Jenkins and Rubin, "New Vulnerabilities and the Acquisition of New Weapons by Nongovernmental Groups," p. 225; Simon, "Terrorists and the Potential Use of Biological Weapons," p. 12; Mullins, "An Overview and Analysis of Nuclear, Biological, and Chemical Terrorism," pp. 103–107; Mengel, "Terrorism and New Technologies of Destruction," p. 446; and Purver, *Chemical and Biological Terrorism*, pp. 40–41.

78. Wiener, "Terrorist Use of Biological Weapons," p. 130; and Purver, *Chemical and Biological Terrorism*, p. 45.

MORAL CONSIDERATIONS. The final and most controversial explanation for the lack of interest in NBC weapons evident among groups capable of acquiring and using them is that group leaders and members may hold moral objections to their use.[79] This may seem counterintuitive, given the willingness of most terrorist groups and many states to kill innocent people in order to achieve their political goals. NBC weapons, however, have a special stigma, and to be willing to use them against innocents is clearly to possess an uncommon level of wickedness.[80] The norm against non-use probably is strongest in the case of biological weapons. In a species that has spent its existence battling against the predations of microbial disease,[81] it is certainly possible that a norm against biological weapons — which, after all, amount to the deliberate use of disease to kill or harm an adversary — has taken hold. While it will never be possible to separate the causal impact of self-interest (including group preservation) from that of morality on decisions not to launch NBC weapons attacks, neither should the notion be ignored. In understanding the rarity of NBC terrorism, the absence of precedent and the immorality of using NBC weapons do not have the explanatory power of other reasons noted above, but they should not be dismissed altogether.

REASONS FOR INABILITY AMONG THE INTERESTED

The majority of groups capable of acquiring and using NBC weapons have shown no interest in doing so, with Aum Shinrikyo the signal exception. Yet, it stands to reason that there are some groups and individuals that are, in fact, interested. Among these, most are incapable of obtaining functional weapons of mass destruction. Very few groups and individuals that have been caught with radioactive materials or with chemical or biological

---

79. See Jenkins, "Understanding the Link between Motives and Methods," p. 46. Hoffman argues that this observation applies mainly to "secular political" terrorists, not "religious political" ones. Bruce Hoffman, "The Contrasting Ethical Foundations of Terrorism in the 1980s," *Terrorism and Political Violence*, Vol. 1, No. 3 (July 1989), p. 363.

80. To the extent that there exists an international norm against the use of NBC weapons, it has been reinforced by a variety of international conventions and treaties, including the Hague Conventions of 1899 and 1907, the 1925 Geneva Protocol, the 1968 Nuclear Non-Proliferation Treaty, the 1972 Biological Weapons Convention, and the 1993 Chemical Weapons Convention.

81. For the seminal work on the role of disease in human development, see William H. McNeill, *Plagues and Peoples* (New York: Doubleday, 1977).

warfare agents appear capable of building an effective weapon of mass destruction, even if they wanted to. This lack of ability among the interested is the second general explanation for the rarity of all forms of non-state NBC violence.

Explaining the constraints on "interested" groups is more difficult than explaining the lack of interest of "capable" groups. It is possible to know with some certainty which types of groups are theoretically capable of overcoming the technical and operational barriers to NBC weapons acquisition and use, allowing one to argue persuasively that the absence of NBC "events" among these groups results principally from motivational restraints. The other category of non-state actor, however, presents a far murkier picture, since it is virtually impossible to untangle technical inability from genuine lack of motive. How many groups or individuals would employ NBC weapons if they only had the ability to do so? How many would not, even if they suddenly became able to? These questions are unanswerable. The full range of individuals and groups that possess a latent interest in using weapons of mass destruction or otherwise inflicting mass casualties cannot be definitively known. The best one can do is to look for clues in the handful of known, failed, or flawed attempts by non-state actors to acquire NBC weapons.

The known cases demonstrate that non-state actors with an interest in NBC weapons have trouble acquiring or using them successfully. Two reasons appear to explain this. The first is that the psychological makeup of an individual or group that wishes to conduct mass casualty attacks is likely to be incompatible with the technical and organizational requirements for acquiring and using nuclear, biological, or chemical weapons. This powerful argument applies most obviously to deranged individuals who are motivated to kill not by a clear, rational purpose but by mental illness. The second argument has a far narrower scope, applying only to terrorist groups that benefit from the sponsorship of a state. In the unlikely event that a state-sponsored terrorist organization decided to obtain or use a weapon of mass destruction, it is quite likely that the state sponsor would actively oppose its efforts because of the extreme risks involved. These two arguments are examined next.

PSYCHOLOGICAL INCOMPATIBILITY. A desire to kill large numbers of people says something about one's psychological makeup. Much blood has been shed for clear, calculated political purposes by tyrants, insurgents, and even terrorists, but most mass murderers in history have suffered from some form of mental imbalance, and most have preferred to kill their victims personally by ones and twos. These mentally unbalanced individuals are occasionally capable, but more often than not their blood lust is a manifestation of an underlying inability to function effectively in society. As Jerrold Post has put it: "On the one hand, to be motivated to carry out an act of mass destruction suggests profound psychological distortions usually found only in severely disabled individuals, such as paranoid psychotics. On the other hand, to implement an act of nuclear terrorism requires not only organizational skills but also the ability to work cooperatively with a small team. To be suffering from major psychopathology, such as paranoid psychotic states, is incompatible with being able to work effectively with a small group."[82] Normal people simply do not have an urge to kill in vast numbers; abnormal ones occasionally do. And it is precisely this abnormality — be it nihilistic misanthropy, extreme social alienation, religious fanaticism, or any number of clinical mental illnesses — that tends to make the people most likely to want to inflict mass casualties the least able to do so with a weapon of mass destruction.

It is easy to understand how a psychologically dysfunctional person, or group of persons, would find it difficult to acquire or use a nuclear, biological, or chemical weapon. As explained in detail in Chapter 2, the technical, operational, and financial demands of acquiring an NBC weapon are serious. Building an NBC weapon is a complex operation requiring specialized equipment, materials, and skills, most importantly the capacity and mental state to undertake careful library research, technical experimentation, and meticulous planning. Most clandestine NBC weapons programs — even small ones — will require a team of committed individuals, as well as substantial sums of money, to buy materials and equipment. Leading a clandestine conspiracy of this kind is no small matter and is clearly beyond the abilities of casual killers and most mentally unstable individuals. Crazy people usually make poor leaders of complex technical processes, and even worse financiers.

SPONSORS' CAUTION CONSTRAINS STATE-SPONSORED GROUPS. Although major international terrorist organizations that benefit from some form of state sponsorship (e.g., financial support, arms, sanctuary) face many disincentives to acquire or use NBC weapons, it is nonetheless possible that one may develop such an interest. A terrorist organization that fell into this category, however, would almost certainly face an additional difficulty in

---

82. Jerrold M. Post, "Prospects for Nuclear Terrorism: Psychological Motivations and Constraints," in Leventhal and Alexander, *Preventing Nuclear Terrorism*, pp. 92–93.

its clandestine NBC acquisition plans: the active opposition of its state sponsor.

Even when a state has absolute confidence in and perfect political control over its NBC weapons handlers, a covert NBC weapon attack plan would be an extremely risky undertaking. States would probably regard these risks as even more severe if the individuals responsible for implementing the covert NBC attack were considered unreliable or possessed an independent political agenda. The group would probably be less controllable, and therefore more likely to fail, than an official team, and there is no guarantee that the group, once in possession of such a powerful weapon, would follow through on the agreed attack plan rather than pursuing some other objective — a *coup d'état*, for instance. For these reasons, states are unlikely to supply NBC weapons to, or facilitate NBC acquisition by, groups they do not hold in extremely high confidence.

Even if a group is able to acquire an NBC weapon without the direct assistance of its sponsoring state, the state sponsor is extremely likely to oppose the group's acquisition of NBC weapons, not to mention any covert NBC attack plans the group may harbor. The state will fear bearing the brunt of the consequences of the attack, becoming the target of military reprisals, economic sanctions, and international outrage for a covert NBC attack that it did not even authorize. Even if the state's tie to the group responsible for the attack is not found out, the state would still become vulnerable to blackmail from individuals possessing incriminating evidence. In short, the sponsoring state's calculus will likely be governed by the principles discussed in the next section.

States

To understand the threat of covert nuclear, biological, and chemical attack posed by states, one must start by considering their NBC activities in a broader context — how states have acquired these weapons, how they have planned to employ them, and how they have used them in practice. The first part of this section summarizes the historical record of cases in which states have acquired, threatened to use, or used NBC weapons. The second part briefly describes why states have and have not acquired NBC weapons. The final part analyzes why all forms of NBC use, especially covert attacks, have occurred so rarely since World War I.

PATTERNS OF PAST NBC ACQUISITION AND USE

Five empirical observations emerge from a review of states' involvement with weapons of mass destruction. First, there have been dozens of known attempts by states to acquire NBC weapons in the twentieth century, most of them successful. Second, states that possess NBC weapons have issued many implicit and explicit threats to use them against adversaries, if challenged; threats such as these are taken more seriously when backed up by genuine NBC capabilities. Third, while chemical weapons were used extensively on the battlefields of World War I, they have rarely been used since; nuclear weapons have been used only twice, although they have been tested many times; and modern biological weapons remain essentially untested in war. Fourth, since the end of World War II, there is no unambiguous evidence of a state attempting to deliver nuclear, biological, or chemical weapons against an adversary by covert means. Finally, no documented cases exist of a state assisting a non-state actor to acquire an NBC weapons capability.

ATTEMPTED AND SUCCESSFUL NBC ACQUISITION. Many states have attempted to acquire NBC weapons in the twentieth century; most have succeeded.[83] There are, of course, many stages of NBC weapons acquisition, ranging from the first vague ambition of a nation's leader, to an industrialized society's inherent but unrealized capacity to fabricate NBC weapons given sufficient time and determination, to a superpower's possession of fully operational and deployed weapons systems. Table 2 lists these states and their stages of involvement in NBC weapons acquisition, categorized by states believed to possess operational NBC weapons, states believed to be seeking to acquire NBC weapons, and states known to have relinquished an NBC weapons program (some of them involuntarily).

---

83. The information presented here should be reviewed with caution. Detailed information about most states' NBC activities is difficult for intelligence agencies to acquire, and what they acquire is usually kept secret, so complete and reliable information is not publicly available. Moreover, NBC acquisition programs are generally conducted on a clandestine basis, so their existence must be inferred from their externally observed features. As revealed in Iraq after the 1990–91 Gulf War, the true extent of even a large program can be successfully concealed.

Table 2. Declared and Suspected NBC Possession by States.

Nuclear Weapons	Biological Weapons	Chemical Weapons
Declared Current Possessors		
China, France, Russia, United Kingdom, United States		India, Russia, United States (all scheduled to destroy stocks under CWC)
Suspected Possessors		
India, Israel, Pakistan	China, Egypt, Iran, Iraq, Israel, North Korea, Russia, South Korea, Syria, Taiwan, Vietnam	China, Cuba, Egypt, Iran, Iraq, Israel, Libya, Myanmar, North Korea, Pakistan, Syria, Taiwan, Yemen, former Yugoslavia
Suspected of Attempting Acquisition		
Iran, Iraq, Libya, North Korea	Libya	
Abandoned or Reversed Programs		
Algeria, Argentina, Australia, Belarus, Brazil, Canada, Egypt, Germany, Italy, Iraq, Kazakstan, Romania, South Africa, South Korea, Sweden, Switzerland, Taiwan, Ukraine	Canada, France, Japan, South Africa, United Kingdom, United States	Germany, Italy, Japan, United Kingdom

SOURCES: U.S. Congress, Office of Technology Assessment, *Proliferation of Weapons of Mass Destruction: Assessing the Risks* (Washington, D.C.: U.S. Government Printing Office [U.S. GPO], August 1993), pp. 80–82; Department of Defense, *Proliferation: Threat and Response 1997* (Washington, D.C.: U.S. Department of Defense, November 1997), available at <www.defenselink.mil/pubs>; and Gordon M. Burck and Charles C. Flowerree, *International Handbook on Chemical Weapons Proliferation* (New York: Greenwood Press, 1991), pp. 164–165.

Russia, China, Great Britain, France, and the United States are the five declared nuclear weapon states.[84] Each state has a large, secure military nuclear arsenal with sophisticated delivery systems, such as ballistic missiles, cruise missiles, and strike aircraft. Three "threshold states" — India, Israel, and Pakistan — possess significant but unacknowledged nuclear weapon capabilities.[85] Finally, a handful of states — Iran, Iraq, North Korea, Libya, and possibly Egypt, Syria, and Algeria — are believed to be interested in acquiring, or are actively seeking to acquire, nuclear weapons. The delays in their acquisition of nuclear weapons are generally attributed to opposition in the international community to their plans, their own ambivalence about the project, and their limited technical resources and their lack of access to sufficient quantities of fissile material.

No less interesting than the states that have sought to acquire nuclear weapons are the ones that have not, or that have renounced previously established nuclear weapons programs. Australia, Sweden, South Korea, Taiwan, Germany, Italy, and Switzerland all gave serious consideration to acquiring nuclear weapons but decided against it and joined the Nuclear Non-Proliferation Treaty (NPT) of 1968 as non–nuclear weapon states.[86]

---

84. In 1996, the United States possessed approximately 7,150 deployed nuclear weapons, Russia had roughly 12,000, France had 450, Britain had approximately 260, and the best estimates on Chinese nuclear holdings suggest that it possesses approximately 400 deployed nuclear weapons. See *Bulletin of the Atomic Scientists*, Vol. 52, No. 5 (September/October 1996), p. 63; *Bulletin of the Atomic Scientists*, Vol. 52, No. 6 (November/December 1996), pp. 64–67; and *Bulletin of the Atomic Scientists*, Vol. 53, No. 1 (January/February 1997), p. 70. The United States and Russia also have stockpiles of thousands of additional weapons that have been withdrawn from active deployment.

85. Israel is estimated to possess fewer than 100 nuclear weapons. Leonard S. Spector, Mark S. McDonough, and Evan S. Medeiros, *Tracking Nuclear Proliferation, 1995* (Washington, D.C.: Carnegie Endowment for International Peace, 1995), p. 135. Estimates of the size of India's nuclear arsenal range from 25 weapons to more than 80. Ibid. pp. 89–91; and *Strategic Assessment 1997* (Washington, D.C.: Institute for National Strategic Studies, National Defense University, 1997), p. 128. Pakistan's arsenal is estimated to contain only a handful of weapons; *Strategic Assessment 1997*, p. 128.

86. See Paul M. Cole, *Nuclear Bombast: Nuclear Weapon Decision-making in Sweden 1945–1972*, Occasional Paper No. 26 (Washington, D.C.: Henry L. Stimson Center, April 1996). Switzerland went so far as to stockpile several hundred tons of uranium ore for possible manufacture of nuclear weapons if the international

Brazil and Argentina had fledgling nuclear programs but abandoned them, agreed in 1991 to reciprocal inspections of each other's nuclear facilities, and in 1994 accepted international inspections. Argentina also acceded to the NPT in 1995.[87] South Africa built and tested nuclear weapons, but dismantled its small arsenal starting in 1990, and in 1991 acceded to the NPT.[88] Belarus, Kazakstan, and Ukraine each formally renounced nuclear weapons after they seceded from the former Soviet Union; each state returned to Russia the Soviet nuclear weapons stored on its territory within a few years of independence.[89] North Korea appears to have frozen its nuclear weapons program at least temporarily because of international pressure in 1993–95.[90] Finally, Iraq developed a full-scale, clandestine nuclear weapons program that was dismantled under UN supervision after the 1990–91 Persian Gulf War.[91]

The roster of states believed to possess biological weapons is considerably less certain than the list of those possessing nuclear and chemical weapons. Prior to World War II, France, Japan, and the United Kingdom all

---

security environment worsened dramatically. This stockpile was eliminated only in 1989. See Robert Uhlig, "Swiss Kept Nuclear Arms Secret for 43 Years," *The Daily Telegraph*, May 23, 1996. On South Korea, see Mitchell Reiss, *Without the Bomb: The Politics of Nuclear Nonproliferation* (New York: Columbia University Press, 1988), pp. 78–108; and Joseph Yager, "Northeast Asia," in Joseph Yager, ed., *Nonproliferation and U.S. Foreign Policy* (Washington, D.C.: Brookings, 1980), pp. 47–65.

87. Spector, McDonough, and Medeiros, *Tracking Nuclear Proliferation*, pp. 147, 153.

88. Ibid., p. 161.

89. See William C. Potter, *The Politics of Nuclear Renunciation: The Cases of Belarus, Kazakhstan, and Ukraine*, Occasional Paper No. 22 (Washington, D.C.: Henry L. Stimson Center, April 1995).

90. North Korea may possess sufficient separated plutonium for one or even two bombs, but it has suspended plutonium production. It is unknown whether North Korea possesses the technology to make deliverable weapons out of its available materials. Spector, McDonough, and Medeiros, *Tracking Nuclear Proliferation*, pp. 103–106; Michael J. Mazarr, "Going Just a Little Nuclear: Nonproliferation Lessons from North Korea," *International Security*, Vol. 20, No. 2 (Fall 1995), pp. 92–122; and Michael J. Mazarr, *North Korea and the Bomb: A Case Study in Nonproliferation* (New York: St. Martin's, 1995).

91. See Shahram Chubin, *Eliminating Weapons of Mass Destruction: The Persian Gulf Case*, Occasional Paper No. 33 (Washington, D.C.: Henry L. Stimson Center, March 1997).

had biological warfare programs. Canada and the United States began biological weapons programs in 1941 that continued after the war's conclusion.[92] The United States renounced its biological program (but continued research into defensive measures) in 1969 and destroyed its last stocks of biological agents in 1975.[93]

The Biological Weapons Convention of 1972 (BWC), which had been ratified by 140 states as of May 1997,[94] outlaws the possession and use of biological weapons, but some member states have developed biological warfare capabilities in secret. The Soviet Union officially renounced biological weapons when it became a signatory to the Biological Weapons Convention; however, it continued to work on biological agents at least until 1992, and elements of the program may still exist (see Box 3, Soviet Biological Weapons Program, p. 68). Iran, Libya, Syria, Israel, North Korea, China, and Taiwan are all suspected of producing biological weapons in operational quantities.[95] Iraq had an extensive biological weapons program, including biological weapons mounted on missiles, that was discovered only after the 1990–91 Gulf War (see Box 10, Iraqi NBC Programs, p. 255). Iraq may still have several missiles armed with biological warheads, as well as agent seed stocks, weaponized agent, and biological weapons production

---

92. Stockholm International Peace Research Institute (SIPRI), *The Problem of Chemical and Biological Warfare*, Vol. I: *The Rise of CB Weapons* (New York: Humanities Press, 1971), pp. 111–119.

93. On the American renunciation, see SIPRI, *The Problem of Chemical and Biological Warfare*, Vol. II: *CB Weapons Today* (New York: Humanities Press, 1973), pp. 185–186. On the destruction of the U.S. offensive biological warfare stockpile, see *Arms Control Reporter*, January 1997, p. 701.A.5.

94. Arms Control and Disarmament Agency (ACDA), Fact Sheet, May 3, 1997, reproduced on the ACDA web site at <www.acda.gov/treaties/bwcsig.htm>. For additional up-to-date information on the BWC (and CWC), see the Internet site of the Harvard-Sussex Program on CBW Armament and Arms Limitation, <fas-www.harvard.edu/~hsp>.

95. See Office of the Secretary of Defense (OSD), *Proliferation: Threat and Response* (Washington, D.C.: U.S. GPO, April 1996); and Office of Technology Assessment (OTA), *Proliferation of Weapons of Mass Destruction: Assessing the Risks* (Washington D.C.: U.S. GPO, August 1993), p. 65.

Box 3
The Soviet Biological Weapons Program and the Sverdlovsk Accident

In April and May 1979, the Soviet city of Sverdlovsk — now Yekaterinberg, Russia — suffered an outbreak of human pulmonary anthrax.[1] Information about the outbreak was tightly controlled by the Soviet government, and leaked out only gradually. In March 1980, the U.S. government privately asked the Soviets to explain the outbreak, and publicly implied that the event marked a violation of the 1972 Biological Weapons Convention. The Soviet Union denied the accusations both publicly and privately.[2]

The debate over the Sverdlovsk outbreak continued for more than a decade. The U.S. government concluded that the outbreak involved primarily pulmonary anthrax and was due to an accidental release from a biological weapons laboratory long known to U.S. intelligence. Soviet authorities claimed that the outbreak was primarily intestinal anthrax, with a few cutaneous cases, but refused to allow an investigation by non-Soviet experts. Soviet physicians involved in the medical response to the outbreak met with specialists from both inside and outside the U.S. government on several occasions in the mid-1980s, and presented a sophisticated and internally consistent account of the outbreak as resulting from contaminated black-market meat.[3]

The same explanation was presented to the 1986 Biological Weapons Convention Review Conference.[4] Some non-government experts concluded that the Soviet story was credible. However, the U.S. government continued to maintain that the Russian story was false, on the basis of intelligence reports about the facility in question, reports that the human victims had suffered not gastric but pulmonary anthrax, associated with an aerosol release, and on the basis of other intelligence information.[5] Lack of access to pathological evidence and lack of independent on-site investigation left the question unsettled during the 1980s, however.

In 1990, under the liberalizing Gorbachev regime, articles started to appear in the Russian press questioning the official story. These reported that the victims had died of pulmonary anthrax, that extensive efforts to decontaminate the city had taken place after the outbreak, that medical records related to the outbreak had been confiscated by the KGB, and that the government's own investigation had shown that the outbreak was due to a release from the military facility.[6] On his visit to the United States in January 1992, Russian President Boris Yeltsin, who had been the top Communist Party official in the Sverdlovsk region during the outbreak, admitted that there had been "a lag in implementing" the Biological Weapons

Box 3, Soviet BW Program, *cont.*

Convention.[7] When pressed on whether Russia was still making biological weapons, Yeltsin would only say, "in the next few months we're going to take steps to discontinue this kind of activity in accordance with international agreements."[8] In May 1992, the Russian press quoted Yeltsin as saying that "the KGB admitted that our military developments were the cause" of the Sverdlovsk outbreak.

In 1992–93, U.S. and Russian scientists carried out a detailed study in Sverdlovsk, including examination of remaining medical records, interviews, mapping, and review of meteorological records. This study confirmed that the outbreak was of pulmonary anthrax, and was caused by an accidental release of aerosolized anthrax bacteria from a military biological weapons facility in Sverdlovsk.[9] At least 68 civilians downwind of the release died, and at least 15 farm animals as far as 50 kilometers downwind of the release point were infected with anthrax and had to be slaughtered.[10] An undisclosed number of military casualties also occurred.[11]

Accidental release of anthrax could be explained by a number of activities not prohibited by the Biological Weapons Convention (BWC). Nevertheless, the Sverdlovsk outbreak was only a small indicator of a much larger offensive biological warfare program, a program that continued under the Russian government until at least 1992 in violation of the BWC. Extensive Soviet and Russian disclosures, as well as information released by the U.S. government, show that the program involved multiple research and production facilities and several test sites, and that it employed genetic engineering techniques, among others, in its search for militarily useful agents.[12] The continuation of the program under the Russian government led to intense political pressure from the U.S. and British governments, including legislation linking U.S. financial assistance for Russian disarmament to Russian compliance, but there are still some indications that elements of the program persist.[13]

According to a high-level defector who was formerly second-in-command of a branch of the program, the Soviet BW program is said to have included smallpox as an agent.[14] Smallpox is the only disease mankind has succeeded in eradicating, by means of an intensive international program of vaccination and outbreak monitoring. It is also a highly infectious and deadly disease, and renewed outbreaks of smallpox in unvaccinated populations could easily result in devastating and widespread epidemics reaching far beyond the target population. These facts make Soviet work with the agent particularly unethical, because of the risk that smallpox could have been released in a biological warfare accident, not to mention the possibility of intentional use of smallpox weapons.

Box 3, Soviet BW Program, *cont.*

That this program continued and thrived in the Soviet Union, and later Russia, for nearly two decades after the entry into force of the Biological Weapons Convention shows that both the Soviet regime and the Yeltsin government have been willing to disregard arms control treaty commitments. It is reassuring that U.S. intelligence correctly identified many of the facilities involved in the violations, and correctly interpreted the Sverdlovsk outbreak. But U.S. accusations of toxin weapons use in Southeast Asia in the Yellow Rain controversy, which now appear almost certain to have been mistaken,[15] and the long-term difficulty of proving Soviet cheating, illustrate the difficulty of gathering, assessing, and using information about even very large biological weapons programs.

NOTES

1. For a detailed account of the outbreak itself, see Matthew Meselson, Jeanne Guillemin, Martin Hugh-Jones, et al., "The Sverdlovsk Anthrax Outbreak of 1979," *Science*, Vol. 266, No. 5188 (November 18, 1994), pp. 1202–1208. An account of the debate as of the end of 1987 can be found in Elisa D. Harris, "Sverdlovsk and Yellow Rain: Two Cases of Soviet Noncompliance?" *International Security*, Vol. 11, No. 4 (Spring 1987), pp. 41–95. A very useful summary of the revelations in the Russian press in the early 1990s can be found in Milton Leitenberg, "Anthrax in Sverdlovsk: New Pieces to the Puzzle," *Arms Control Today* (April 1992), pp. 11–12. For an overview of Soviet biological warfare activities, see Milton Leitenberg, "The Biological Weapons Program of the Former Soviet Union," *Biologicals*, Vol. 21, No. 3 (September 1993), pp. 187–191.

2. Harris, "Sverdlovsk and Yellow Rain, " pp. 45–46.

3. Meselson et al., "The Sverdlovsk Anthrax Outbreak of 1979," pp. 1202–1203.

4. Leitenberg, "Anthrax in Sverdlovsk," p. 11.

5. Harris, "Sverdlovsk and Yellow Rain," pp. 46–49.

6. Leitenberg, "Anthrax in Sverdlovsk," pp. 11–12.

7. Ibid., p. 10.

8. Ibid., p. 10.

9. This study and its results are described in Meselson et al., "The Sverdlovsk Anthrax Outbreak of 1979," pp. 1202–1208.

10. Ibid., pp. 1203–1204, 1206.

11. Leitenberg, "Anthrax in Sverdlovsk," p. 12.

12. Leitenberg, "The Biological Weapons Program of the Former Soviet Union," pp. 187–191.

13. Leitenberg, "The Biological Weapons Program of the Former Soviet Union," p. 189. For a recent look at this problem, see Raymond A. Zilinskas, "The Other Biological-Weapons Worry," *New York Times*, November 28, 1997, p. A39.

Box 3, Soviet BW Program, *cont.*

14. See Tim Weiner, "Soviet Defector Warns of Biological Weapons," *New York Times*, February 24, 1998, p. A1; and Richard Preston, "The Bioweaponeers," *The New Yorker*, March 9, 1998, pp. 52–65.

15. For example, an article on the history of biological weapons published by scientists from the U.S. Army Medical Research Institute for Infectious Diseases characterizes the Yellow Rain allegations as "widely regarded as erroneous." See George W. Christopher, Theodore J. Cieslak, Julie A. Pavlin, et al., "Biological Warfare: A Historical Perspective," *Journal of the American Medical Association*, Vol. 278, No. 5 (August 6, 1997), p. 415. This and other more extensive sources on the Yellow Rain controversy are cited in note 121 on p. 80.

---

capability, despite extensive efforts by the United Nations to dismantle the program.[96] Other countries that have renounced biological warfare and claim to have destroyed their biological weapons stockpiles include France, which dismantled its arsenal in 1972, Canada, and the United Kingdom.

Many states possess or are believed to possess some form of chemical weapons capability. As of December 1997, 106 states had ratified the Chemical Weapons Convention of 1993 (CWC).[97] By joining the CWC, these states have forsaken the use and possession of chemical weapons and promised to destroy existing chemical weapons stockpiles by April 2007. Among the chemical weapons arsenals scheduled for destruction are those of Russia, India, and the United States.

Other states with chemical weapons capability include Iraq, which is believed to retain agent stocks and substantial amounts of production equipment, despite the destruction of much of its pre–Gulf War capacity by United Nations teams; and Iran, which developed chemical weapons in response to Iraq's chemical attacks during the 1980–88 war, and probably

---

96. See "The History: 7 Years of Evasion, Tons of Illicit Arms," *New York Times*, November 11, 1997, p. A10; Testimony of Ambassador Rolf Ekeus, Executive Chairman of UNSCOM, Senate Hearings 104-422, *Global Proliferation of Weapons of Mass Destruction*, Part II, Hearings before the Permanent Subcommittee on Investigations of the Committee on Governmental Affairs, U.S. Senate, 104th Cong., 2nd Sess. (Washington, D.C.: U.S. GPO, 1996), pp. 90–104; and Report by the Executive Chairman of the Special Commission, U.N. Security Council Document S/1997/301, April 11, 1997, pp. 12–13.

97. See <fas-www.harvard.edu/~hsp/cwcsig.html>. Sixty-one more states had signed but not ratified.

used them.[98] Both Israel and Syria are suspected of having chemical weapons capability, including indigenous production capability. Egypt has had a chemical weapons capability since the 1960s.[99] Libya reportedly began, and then halted, construction of a large underground chemical munitions plant to replace a previous plant that had attracted international attention but may have been destroyed by fire.[100] Another state widely suspected of possessing chemical weapons is North Korea, which may have indigenous production capability.[101] Some reports suggest that Taiwan has a chemical weapons stockpile, although these claims remain unconfirmed. Although China certainly has the technical capability for chemical warfare, it is not believed to possess a significant arsenal.[102] There are also reports that Myanmar (Burma) may possess limited chemical weapons capability.[103]

One difficulty in assessing the chemical warfare capability of a nation is the similarity that a defensive chemical warfare program bears to an offensive chemical warfare program: developing a sophisticated chemical warfare defense system requires detailed knowledge of various offensive agents likely to be used in an attack. The fact that most modern states with mature chemical industries have the capacity to produce a wide variety of chemical agents further complicates efforts to determine chemical weapons possession. The Chemical Weapons Convention seeks to address some of these issues by monitoring the production and use of chemicals that could

---

98. Gordon M. Burck and Charles C. Flowerree, *International Handbook on Chemical Weapons Proliferation* (New York: Greenwood Press, 1991), pp. 237–266.

99. Ibid., pp. 222–231.

100. See OSD, *Proliferation: Threat and Response*, pp. 26–27; Robert Walter, "The Libyan Threat to the Mediterranean," *Jane's Intelligence Review*, Vol. 8, No. 5 (May 1, 1996), p. 225; Porcher Taylor, "Spy Satellites Give U.S. Advantage, Political Headaches," *Army Times*, September 23, 1996, p. 29; and Robert Walter, "Libyan CW Raises the Issue of Pre-emption," *Jane's Intelligence Review*, Vol. 8, No. 11 (November 1, 1996), p. 522.

101. For details of the North Korean chemical weapons program, see Joseph S. Bermudez, Jr., "Inside North Korea's CW Infrastructure," *Jane's Intelligence Review*, Vol. 8, No. 8 (August 1996), pp. 378–382.

102. Burck and Flowerree, *International Handbook on Chemical Weapons Proliferation*, pp. 416–424.

103. Ibid., pp. 428–429.

be used in the manufacture of weapons, and by controlling the export of some such chemicals to states not parties to the treaty.

THREATS OF NBC USE. There is a long record of states having threatened to use nuclear weapons to deter or, less frequently, to coerce their opponents.[104] During the Cold War, U.S.-Soviet deterrence was essentially a dynamic of constant, mutual, and implicit nuclear threat, one that until the Cuban Missile Crisis was frequently reinforced by explicit warnings and heated rhetoric.[105] The United States threatened China with nuclear attack throughout the 1950s, and the Soviet Union did the same in 1969. The Soviet Union threatened Britain and France during the Suez crisis of 1956.[106] The United States made veiled threats to use nuclear weapons against North Korea during the Eisenhower administration, against North Vietnam during the Johnson and Nixon administrations, and against Iraq during the Bush administration.[107] British and especially French military doctrine have

---

104. See Richard Betts, *Nuclear Blackmail and Nuclear Balance* (Washington, D.C.: Brookings, 1987); Gordon H. Chang, "To the Nuclear Brink: Eisenhower, Dulles, and the Quemoy-Matsu Crisis," *International Security*, Vol. 12, No. 4 (Spring 1988), pp. 96–123; Roger Dingman, "Atomic Diplomacy during the Korean War," *International Security*, Vol. 13, No. 3 (Winter 1988/89), pp. 50–91; Rosemary J. Foot, "Nuclear Coercion and the Ending of the Korean Conflict," *International Security*, Vol. 13, No. 3 (Winter 1988/89), pp. 92–112; Scott D. Sagan, "SIOP-62: The Nuclear War Plan Briefing to President Kennedy," *International Security*, Vol. 12, No. 1 (Summer 1987), pp. 22–51; and Marc Trachtenberg, "The Influence of Nuclear Weapons in the Cuban Missile Crisis," *International Security*, Vol. 10, No. 1 (Summer 1985), pp. 137–163.

105. See Joseph S. Nye, Jr., "Nuclear Learning and U.S.-Soviet Security Regimes," *International Organization*, Vol. 41, No. 3 (Summer 1987), pp. 386, 389–390.

106. Betts, *Nuclear Blackmail and Nuclear Balance*, pp. 62–65.

107. Shortly before the beginning of Operation Desert Storm in the 1990–91 Gulf War, U.S. Secretary of State James Baker delivered to Iraqi Foreign Minister Tariq Aziz a letter from President George Bush addressed to Iraqi President Saddam Hussein. The letter stated that "The United States will not tolerate the use of chemical or biological weapons or the destruction of Kuwait's oil fields and installations. Further, you will be held directly responsible for terrorist actions against any member of the coalition. The American people would demand the strongest possible response. You and your country will pay a terrible price if you order unconscionable acts of this sort." "Statement by Press Secretary Fitzwater on President Bush's Letter to President Saddam Hussein of Iraq," January 12, 1991, in *Public Papers of George Bush*, Book 1: *January 1 to June 30, 1991*. Privately, Bush had

historically recognized nuclear retaliation as an optional response to conventional military aggression, as did NATO doctrine during the Cold War. All three of the threshold states — India, Israel, and Pakistan — have signaled their willingness to use nuclear weapons if attacked by their regional military adversaries: Pakistan did so explicitly in its 1990 border dispute with India.[108] Of the nuclear powers, only China maintains a "no-first-use" declaratory policy.

Since the end of World War II, no state has explicitly threatened to use biological weapons, a fact likely explained by the advent of nuclear weapons and the opprobrium attached to the use of biological weapons.[109] A few blustery threats have been made involving chemical weapons — such as Saddam Hussein's threat against Israel prior to the 1990–91 Gulf War, or North Korea's against the South — but these are the exception.

USE OF NBC WEAPONS IN ATTACKS. Since the end of World War I, NBC weapons have been used in attacks in only a handful of instances. Nuclear weapons have been used in anger only twice, in the 1945 American attacks on Hiroshima and Nagasaki, Japan, resulting in 130,000 and 60,000–70,000 fatalities, respectively.[110]

Depending on how loosely one defines "biological weapon," and how far back one looks, the history of biological weapons use may extend as far

---

ruled out nuclear weapons use against Iraq. James A. Baker III with Thomas M. DeFrank, *The Politics of Diplomacy* (New York: G.P. Putnam's Sons, 1995), p. 359.

108. Disagreement remains over how explicit the signal sent by Pakistan to India was. Some reports claim that Pakistani F-16s were armed with nuclear weapons and sat on runway alert during the crisis, although other observers and participants deny this. See Devin T. Hagerty, "Nuclear Deterrence in South Asia: The 1990 Indo-Pakistani Crisis," *International Security*, Vol. 20, No. 3 (Winter 1995/96), pp. 91–101; and Seymour Hersh, "On the Nuclear Edge," *New Yorker*, March 29, 1993, pp. 56–73.

109. For a related discussion of various principles surrounding the non-use of weapons of mass destruction, see Richard M. Price, *The Chemical Weapons Taboo* (Ithaca, N.Y.: Cornell University Press, 1997); and Richard Price and Nina Tannenwald, "Norms and Deterrence: The Nuclear and Chemical Weapons Taboos," in Peter J. Katzenstein, ed., *The Culture of National Security: Norms and Identity in World Politics* (New York: Columbia University Press, 1996), pp. 114–152.

110. See The Committee for the Compilation of Materials on Damage Caused by the Atomic Bombs in Hiroshima and Nagasaki, *Hiroshima and Nagasaki: The Physical, Medical and Social Effects of the Atomic Bombings*, Eisei Ishikawa and David L. Swain, trans. (originally published as *Hiroshima Nagasaki no genbaku saigai*) (Tokyo: Iwanami Shoten, 1981).

back as the twelfth century, when the Mongols are said to have catapulted plague-infected corpses over city walls.[111] In more recent times, Japan experimented with and used a variety of biological warfare agents during World War II, especially in Manchuria (see Box 4, Japan's Unit 731, p. 76). There are no confirmed reports that any state has used modern biological weapons — that is, infectious or toxic agents disseminated as respirable aerosols — as a means of attack.

Chemical weapons have been used by many states in war.[112] They were used extensively by all sides in the trench warfare of World War I, beginning with the German chlorine gas attack near Ypres on April 22, 1915.[113] It is estimated that 125,000 tons of gas were employed during the war, and estimates of casualties due to gas range from 530,000 to 1,300,000.[114] The Spanish are believed to have used mustard gas in Morocco in 1925.[115] Even after the signing of the Geneva Protocol of 1925 forbidding the use of chemical weapons, these weapons continued to be used in the interwar period, by Italy in Ethiopia and by Japan in China. There were allegations of British use of chemical weapons in the Middle East in the

---

111. A useful overview of historical cases and allegations of use of biological weapons appears in Christopher, Cieslak, Pavlin, et al., "Biological Warfare," pp. 412–417. For a longer discussion of cases and suspicious incidents through 1970, see SIPRI, *The Rise of CB Weapons*, pp. 214–230.

112. For general histories, see Robert Harris and Jeremy Paxman, *A Higher Form of Killing: The Secret Story of Chemical and Biological Warfare* (New York: Hill and Wang, 1982); Augustin M. Prentiss, *Chemicals in War: A Treatise on Chemical Warfare* (New York: McGraw-Hill, 1937); Edward M. Spiers, *Chemical Warfare* (Urbana: University of Illinois Press, 1986); Edward M. Spiers, *Chemical Weaponry: A Continuing Challenge* (New York: St. Martin's, 1989); and SIPRI, *The Rise of CB Weapons*.

113. See SIPRI, *The Rise of CB Weapons*, pp. 125–141; Ludwig F. Haber, *The Poisonous Cloud: Chemical Warfare in the First World War* (Oxford: Clarendon Press, 1986); and Donald Richter, *Chemical Soldiers: British Gas Warfare in World War I* (Lawrence: University Press of Kansas, 1992).

114. Jeffrey Legro, *Cooperation under Fire: Anglo-German Restraint during World War II* (Ithaca, N.Y.: Cornell University Press, 1995), p. 145.

115. SIPRI, *The Rise of CB Weapons*, p. 142.

Box 4
Unit 731: Japanese Biological Weapons, 1932–45

In 1932, the Japanese Army created Unit 731, a biological weapons research center in Beiyinhe, Manchuria, under the command of Major Ishii Shiro.[1] For the next thirteen years, the unit conducted an offensive biological weapons research and development program, which included medical experiments on Chinese and Russian civilians, and on American, British, Chinese, Korean, and Russian prisoners of war.

The first Japanese experiments with biological weapons were crude. Unit 731 studied diseases including anthrax, glanders, and plague by infecting prisoners. The victims were studied as the diseases progressed. When they survived, prisoners were used for further studies until they became too weak to be of use, and then they were killed. Pathologists conducted autopsies on the victims, and sometimes dissected living victims to study the intermediate stages of a disease. Later, Unit 731 used human subjects to research typhoid, paratyphoid A and B, typhus, smallpox, tularemia, infectious jaundice, gas gangrene, tetanus, cholera, dysentery, scarlet fever, undulant fever, tick encephalitis, whooping cough, diphtheria, pneumonia, venereal diseases, tuberculosis, salmonella, and frostbite.

The Beiyinhe facility was abandoned in late 1937, and Unit 731 was transferred to a larger facility at Ping Fan, near Harbin, and experiments continued. Large-scale production of some biological warfare agents was also carried out at Ping Fan, and at other Japanese military facilities in occupied China.

In 1949, one former member estimated that the Ping Fan unit could, when operating at full capacity, produce 300 kilograms of plague bacteria monthly. Other biological warfare facilities could produce "500–600 kilograms of anthrax germs, or 800–900 kilograms of typhoid, paratyphoid or dysentery germs, or as much as 1000 kilograms of cholera germs."[2]

The Japanese developed a variety of crude biological weapons delivery systems and used them against Chinese and Soviet civilian and military targets. Porcelain bombs were used to deliver plague-infected fleas, and fleas were also scattered from low-flying planes. Most of Japan's biological weapons attacks, however, were conducted by saboteurs, including Ishii himself. In July 1942, he led a biological weapons expedition to Nanking, China, where he prepared and distributed chocolates filled with anthrax spores to youngsters. On another occasion, 3,000 Chinese prisoners of war were given a "holiday treat" of dumplings injected with typhoid or paratyphoid; they were then released, causing a wider outbreak.[3]

There are some reports that Unit 731 also attempted to attack U.S. military forces and civilians with biological weapons. A team of saboteurs reportedly sailed for Saipan Island in June 1944, intending to deny U.S. forces

Box 4, Japan's Unit 731, *cont.*

access to the airstrip by scattering plague-infected fleas. An American submarine torpedoed their ship before it could reach its target.[4] Japanese researchers also developed plans (some fanciful) to use balloon bombs to carry disease across the continental United States, to use aircraft carried by submarines to drop plague-infected fleas on West Coast cities (an operation planned for September 1945), and to use all manner of biological weapons to repel an American invasion of Japan.[5]

Neither Ishii nor his men were tried for war crimes; they avoided prosecution in exchange for providing the United States with data derived from their experiments.[6]

NOTES

1. This account is drawn from Sheldon H. Harris, *Factories of Death: Japanese Secret Biological Warfare, 1932–45, and the American Cover-up* (New York: Routledge, 1994); and Peter Williams and David Wallace, *Unit 731: The Japanese Army's Secret of Secrets* (London: Hodder & Stoughton, 1989).

2. Harris, *Factories of Death*, p. 55.

3. Ibid., p. 77.

4. Williams and Wallace, *Unit 731*, p. 81.

5. Thomas B. Allen and Norman Polmar, *Code-Name Downfall: The Secret Plan to Invade Japan and Why Truman Dropped the Bomb* (New York: Simon & Schuster, 1995), p. 257.

6. See Harris, *Factories of Death*, pp. 173–223; and George W. Christopher, Theodore J. Cieslak, Julie A. Pavlin, et al., "Biological Warfare: A Historical Perspective," *JAMA*, Vol. 278, No. 5 (August 6, 1997), p. 414.

interwar period as well.[116] Chemical weapons use was much less frequent in World War II, although a few incidents were reported.[117] The United Kingdom considered using chemical weapons to repel a German invasion of the British Isles and to retaliate against German V-1 and V-2 attacks on

116. Ibid.

117. See Frederic J. Brown, *Chemical Warfare: A Study in Restraints* (Princeton, N.J.: Princeton University Press, 1968); John Ellis van Courtland Moon, "Chemical Weapons and Deterrence: The World War II Experience," *International Security*, Vol. 8, No. 4 (Spring 1984), pp. 3–35; and John Ellis van Courtland Moon, "United States Chemical Warfare Policy in World War II: A Captive of Coalition Policy?" *The Journal of Military History*, Vol. 60, No. 3 (July 1996), pp. 495–511.

British cities,[118] and explored the option of biological weapons use against German livestock and possibly civilians. Germany considered using chemical weapons on the Eastern front in 1942, after the disaster of Stalingrad, and at the end of the war, after the firebombing of Dresden. U.S. military planners considered their use in the planned invasion of Japan.[119]

Chemical weapons have also been used since World War II, most extensively in the 1980–88 Iran-Iraq War (see Box 8, Iran-Iraq War, p. 226). Other modern incidents involving chemical weapons include their suspected use during the Yemeni civil war, Libya's use of Iranian-made chemical weapons against Chadian troops in 1987,[120] and suspected use or inadvertent release of chemical weapons during the 1990–91 Gulf War.

COVERT NBC ATTACKS. No clear evidence exists that any state has attempted to deliver nuclear, biological, or chemical weapons by covert means since Japan's biological weapons attacks during World War II, other than in a few assassination attempts. In 1981, the United States alleged that the Soviet Union and its Asian allies had used toxin weapons against the Hmong tribesmen in Laos and against civilians and Khmer Rouge forces in Kampuchea (Cambodia) during the 1970s. Known as the "Yellow Rain" controversy, these allegations were not based on careful scientific analysis, and have been discredited.[121] South Africa is alleged to have used anthrax

---

118. See Moon, "Chemical Weapons and Deterrence," pp. 9–21.

119. See Legro, *Cooperation under Fire*, pp. 163, 173, 189, 192–193; and John Ellis van Courtland Moon, "Project SPHINX: The Question of the Use of Gas in the Planned Invasion of Japan," *The Journal of Strategic Studies*, Vol. 12, No. 3 (September 1989), pp. 303–323.

120. OSD, *Proliferation: Threat and Response*, p. 25.

121. Good summaries of the debate on Yellow Rain can be found in Julian Robinson, Jeanne Guillemin, and Matthew Meselson, "Yellow Rain in Southeast Asia: The Story Collapses," in Susan Wright, ed., *Preventing a Biological Arms Race* (Cambridge, Mass.: MIT Press, 1990), pp. 220–238; Julian Perry Robinson, Jeanne Guillemin, and Matthew S. Meselson, "Yellow Rain: The Story Collapses," *Foreign Policy*, No. 68 (Fall 1987), pp. 100–117; Peter Barss, "Epidemiological Field Investigation as Applied to Allegations of Chemical, Biological, or Toxin Warfare," *Politics and the Life Sciences*, Vol. 11, No. 1 (February 1992), pp. 13–16; and Elisa D. Harris, "Sverdlovsk and Yellow Rain: Two Cases of Soviet Noncompliance?" *International Security*, Vol. 11, No. 4 (Spring 1987), pp. 41–95. A short historical overview of biological weapons use published by scientists from the U.S. Army Medical Research Institute for Infectious Diseases (USAMRIID) characterizes the Yellow Rain allegations as "widely regarded as erroneous." See Christopher,

in the 1978–80 Rhodesian civil war, and possibly to have released an exceptionally virulent strain of malaria in Angola in the 1980s, but these reports are unconfirmed.[122] During the 1950s and 1960s, the United States conducted a number of secret field tests in its own cities using live but non-pathogenic organisms to simulate biological warfare agents (see Box 5, U.S. BW Program), but these do not qualify as biological weapons attacks (although there have been some claims of ill effects in the exposed population). There were unsubstantiated allegations of U.S. biological weapons use in the Korean War.[123] In May 1997, Fidel Castro accused the United States of conducting covert biological attacks in 1996 against Cuban crops — particularly sugar — to undermine the Cuban economy; this was only the latest in a series of Cuban accusations of U.S. biological weapons use that began in 1964.[124] Aside from these questionable allegations, biological weapons use by states since World War II appears to be confined

---

Cieslak, Pavlin, et al., "Biological Warfare: A Historical Perspective," p. 415. However, some U.S. officials and former officials contend that still-classified information would prove the Yellow Rain charges true.

122. See James Adams, "The Dangerous New World of Chemical and Biological Weapons," in Roberts, Terrorism with Chemical and Biological Weapons, p. 24; and Office of Technology Assessment (OTA), Technologies Underlying Weapons of Mass Destruction (Washington, D.C.: U.S. GPO, 1993), p. 110.

123. For a brief discussion of allegations against the United States, see SIPRI, The Rise of CB Weapons, pp. 224–225. The allegations were made by the North Korean, Soviet, and Chinese governments, which refused to allow independent experts to investigate.

124. Cuba's 1964 allegations are discussed in ibid., pp. 226–227. The recent allegation centers around a grayish smoke emitted by a U.S. State Department aircraft that flew over Cuba in transit to Colombia in October 21, 1996. Cuba claims that the aircraft released insects responsible for several crop infestations. The U.S. government claims that the aircraft, flying a regular route over Cuba with Cuban government approval, used a smoke generator to alert a nearby plane of its presence. See Anthony Goodman, "Cuba Accuses U.S. of Biological Aggression," Reuters North American Wire, May 5, 1997. Although the Cuban claim appears specious, it is being investigated by representatives of several Biological Weapons Convention member states. "Cuban Accusations of U.S. Insect Raid on Island to Be Studied," New York Times, August 28, 1997, p. A7.

Box 5
The American Biological Weapons Program and Open-Air Tests

The American biological weapons program originated during World War II, when a large-scale research, development, and production program was established in response to concerns that Germany was developing a similar program.[1] At the conclusion of the war, the biological weapons program was continued, in part out of fear of a Soviet biological weapons program and in part to develop defensive measures to protect both troops and civilian populations.[2]

In the 1950s and 1960s, a series of tests were conducted on U.S. cities using non-pathogenic bacteria and other materials, in order to investigate both biological weapons delivery systems and U.S. vulnerability to large-scale covert attacks. The tests were conducted in secret by the U.S. Army to avoid a public outcry. Revelations in the mid-1970s about the tests, and allegations that one agent used had caused at least one death, led to Senate hearings and strong public criticism of the program.[3]

At least 239 open-air tests were conducted between 1949 and 1968 throughout the United States, in environments from the New York City subway system, to National Airport in Washington, D.C., to the entire city of San Francisco.[4] Tests involving large-scale dissemination of simulated agents by aircraft were also conducted. Monitoring stations more than 1,200 miles away from dispersal points detected traces of the simulants.[5] In the New York City tests, personnel threw light bulbs filled with the simulated agent onto the subway train tracks and into the ventilation system. The study concluded that disseminating the agent through the subway system would expose a large portion of the working population of downtown Manhattan.[6]

In 1969, President Richard Nixon declared an end to all offensive biological weapons research and development.[7] Before the American program was dismantled, approximately 40,000 liters of anti-personnel biological warfare agents were in storage, along with 5,000 kilograms of anti-plant agents and 45,000 toxin-coated bullets and flechettes, small darts intended to carry the agent into the bloodstream.[8] All were destroyed after the decision to eliminate the offensive biological weapons stockpile. U.S. research into biological warfare continues today, albeit on a smaller scale and for defensive purposes only.

NOTES
1. For two histories of the early American biological weapons programs, see Leonard Cole, *Clouds of Secrecy: The Army's Germ Warfare Tests over Populated*

Box 5, U.S. BW Program, *cont.*

Areas (Totowa, N.J.: Rowman & Littlefield, 1988), particularly chapters 1 and 2; and Barton Bernstein, "Origins of the Biological Warfare Program," in Susan Wright, ed., *Preventing a Biological Arms Race* (Cambridge, Mass.: MIT Press, 1990), pp. 9–25.

2. Cole, *Clouds of Secrecy*, pp. 16–17.

3. The bacteria and fluorescent tracers used for these purposes were believed to be non-pathogenic. Some of the bacteria turned out to pose some risk of infection for people with weakened immune systems, however. Furthermore, some of the tracers could be toxic in large concentrations, though this risk would primarily affect personnel operating the dispersal equipment. For a strongly critical view of the testing program, see Cole, *Clouds of Secrecy*, pp. 44–58, 75–84; and Leonard Cole, *The Eleventh Plague* (New York: W.H. Freeman & Company, 1997), pp. 61–66, 71–72. For an explanation of why the case for human fatalities from the testing program remains inconclusive, see George W. Christopher, Theodore J. Cieslak, Julie A. Pavlin, et al., "Biological Warfare: A Historical Perspective," *JAMA*, Vol. 278, No. 5 (August 6, 1997), p. 414.

4. Cole, *Clouds of Secrecy*, pp. 65–69, 152–153.

5. Cole, *The Eleventh Plague*, pp. 19–24.

6. Cole, *Clouds of Secrecy*, pp. 65–69.

7. See Susan Wright, "Evolution of Biological Warfare Policy, 1945–1990," in Wright, *Preventing a Biological Arms Race*, pp. 38–39; and Stockholm International Peace Research Institute (SIPRI), *The Problem of Chemical and Biological Warfare*, Vol. II: *CB Weapons Today* (New York: Humanities Press, 1973), p. 264, n. 3.

8. See SIPRI, *CB Weapons Today*, p. 234.

---

to a handful of state-directed assassinations employing biological agents and toxins.[125]

---

125. On a number of occasions in the twentieth century, states have used biological toxins or chemical poisons to assassinate political opponents. On Israel's spectacular failure to assassinate Khaled Meshal, a Hamas leader, in Jordan, in September 1997, see Alan Cowell, "The Daring Attack that Blew Up in Israel's Face," *New York Times*, October 15, 1997, p. A1. On the KGB-assisted Bulgarian assassination of Bulgarian defector Georgi Markov in London in 1978, see Associated Press, "Soviets Linked to 1978 Death of Bulgarian," *Chicago Tribune*, April 5, 1991, p. 24; Glenn Frankel, "Bulgaria to Probe Poison-Pellet Murder of Exile Who Criticized Zhivkov," *Washington Post*, January 11, 1990, p. A25; and Bernard D. Nossiter, "Exotic Instrument of Exile's Murder; Scotland Yard Says Bulgarian Was Murdered," *Washington Post*, September 30, 1978, p. A1. On Soviet plans in the 1950s to assassinate Tito, the ruler of Yugoslavia, see Natasha Alova, "Soviets Plotted to

SPONSORSHIP OF NBC TERRORISM. No documented case can be found of a state sponsor of terrorism deliberately assisting a terrorist organization in acquiring or using nuclear, biological, or chemical weapons.[126] During the 1990–91 Gulf War, Iraq is rumored to have considered using terrorists as agents to deliver chemical and possibly biological weapons against Western cities, but nothing came of these plans.[127]

PROLIFERATION MOTIVES AND CONSTRAINTS

A vast literature details the causes of, and constraints on, the proliferation of weapons of mass destruction, especially nuclear weapons, and it need not be duplicated here.[128] For the purposes of understanding the present

---

Assassinate Tito with Poisoned Jewel Box," Associated Press, June 12, 1993. For extensive discussion of CIA assassination plots against Fidel Castro of Cuba and Patrice Lumumba of the newly independent Congo, see U.S. Senate, Select Committee to Study Governmental Operations with Respect to Intelligence Operations, *Alleged Assassination Plots Involving Foreign Leaders: An Interim Report* (New York: Norton, 1976). There are some indications that the white minority government of South Africa poisoned opposition leaders on a number of occasions. See Lynne Duke, "Drug Bust Exposes South African Arms Probes; Apartheid-Era Officer's Arrest Puts Focus on Questions about Chemical Weapons," *Washington Post*, February 1, 1997, p. A15; and James Adams, "Gadaffi Lures South Africa's Top Germ Warfare Scientists," *Sunday Times* (London), February 26, 1995. On the poisoning of Frank Chikane, former president of the South African Council of Churches, see Gina Kolata, "Poisoning of African Church Leader Charged," *New York Times*, June 9, 1989, p. A8.

126. In 1996, the U.S. State Department's list of state sponsors of terrorism included Cuba, Iran, Iraq, Libya, North Korea, Sudan, and Syria. U.S. Department of State, *Patterns of Global Terrorism 1996*; see <www.state.gov/www/global/terrorism>.

127. According to Jonathan B. Tucker, "during the Gulf War, U.S. intelligence reportedly foiled a number of Iraqi-sponsored terrorist attacks against American targets, some of which may have involved chemical/biological weapons." Tucker, "Chemical/Biological Terrorism," p. 170. A similar claim is also made in William E. Burrows and Robert Windrem, *Critical Mass: The Dangerous Race for Superweapons in a Fragmenting World* (New York: Simon & Schuster, 1994), p. 49. For a source citing unnamed government officials, see Michael Wines, "After the War: Terror; International Teamwork May Have Foiled Terror," *New York Times*, March 4, 1991, p. A11. We are grateful to Jonathan Tucker for bringing this source to our attention.

128. On the causes of nuclear proliferation, see Scott D. Sagan, "Why Do States Build Nuclear Weapons? Three Models in Search of a Bomb," *International Security*, Vol. 21, No. 3 (Winter 1996/97), pp. 54–86; Benjamin Frankel, "The Brooding

and future threat of covert NBC attacks by hostile states, two key questions are of interest: (1) what drives some states to acquire nuclear, biological, or chemical weapons capabilities? and (2) why do other states, even in comparable circumstances, decide against NBC acquisition? The answers can help identify the states that are the most likely sources of covert NBC threat now and in the future.

SECURITY CONCERNS ARE THE PRIMARY MOTIVE FOR NBC ACQUISITION. In most cases, states are driven to acquire NBC weapons principally by their own security concerns, be they defensive or offensive, real or imagined. The details of any particular state's NBC acquisition and deployment programs will vary with its unique geopolitical circumstances, technological development, bureaucratic politics, and strategic choices, but the quest for security lies at the heart of most decisions to acquire NBC weaponry. Thus, Japan sought biological weapons because some of its scientists and military officers believed that these weapons could become decisive weapons of war; Great Britain developed an offensive biological weapons program as an ultimate deterrent against Nazi invasion; the United States rushed to develop nuclear weapons before an adversary could acquire them first, and to end World War II;[129] the Soviet Union developed nuclear weapons to avoid strategic inferiority to the United States;[130] France developed nuclear

---

Shadow: Systemic Incentives and Nuclear Weapons Proliferation," in Zachary S. Davis and Benjamin Frankel, eds., *The Proliferation Puzzle*, special issue of *Security Studies*, Vol. 2, Nos. 3/4 (Spring/Summer 1993), pp. 100–124; and Richard K. Betts, "Paranoids, Pygmies, Pariahs, and Non-Proliferation Revisited," in Davis and Frankel, *The Proliferation Puzzle*, pp. 100–124. For a study of the consequences of nuclear proliferation, see Scott D. Sagan and Kenneth N. Waltz, *The Spread of Nuclear Weapons: A Debate* (New York: Norton, 1995); David J. Karl, "Proliferation Pessimism and Emerging Nuclear Powers," *International Security*, Vol. 21, No. 3 (Winter 1996/97), pp. 87–119; and Scott D. Sagan, "The Perils of Proliferation: Organization Theory, Deterrence Theory, and the Spread of Nuclear Weapons," *International Security*, Vol. 18, No. 4 (Spring 1994), pp. 66–107.

129. On first hearing the proposal that the United States should research the possibility of the bomb, Roosevelt is reported to have said, "What you're after is to see that the Nazis don't blow us up." See Richard Rhodes, *The Making of the Atomic Bomb* (New York: Simon and Schuster, 1986), pp. 313–314.

130. The Soviet Union, alerted by intelligence reports of serious U.S. and British work on fission weapons, and of at least some German interest, decided in May 1942 to launch its own bomb program. The effort was greatly accelerated at the end of the war, both because of the perceived need to end the U.S. nuclear monopoly,

weapons in part to allay its doubts about the reliability of U.S. extended deterrence of the Soviet Union;[131] Pakistan reacted to its earlier defeats by India and to India's nuclear acquisitions;[132] Israel acquired nuclear weapons to deter attack by its neighbors;[133] and Iran has sought weapons of mass destruction to protect itself against Iraq and to deter unilateral American or Israeli action.[134]

A variety of other forces can also play a significant role in proliferation decisions. Domestic forces, including leaders' search for domestic political legitimacy, the efforts of technological and military entrepreneurs to promote nuclear weapons, and the degree of influence or control of militaries in government decision-making, have played a key role in some states, most notably India, but also in Argentina and Brazil.[135] International influences other than military security also matter. At times, perceptions of weapons — particularly nuclear weapons — as tokens of international power and prestige have influenced states' decisions. This motive is particularly evident in the second wave of nuclear weapon states — most notably

---

and because the program's heavy demands on scientific and industrial resources were easier to meet. See Richard Rhodes, *Dark Sun: The Making of the Hydrogen Bomb* (New York: Simon and Schuster, 1995), pp. 61, 175–178, 180–182.

131. See Wilfrid L. Kohl, *French Nuclear Diplomacy* (Princeton, N.J.: Princeton University Press, 1971), pp. 35–41; and Wolf Mendl, *Deterrence and Persuasion: French Nuclear Armament in the Context of National Policy, 1945–1969* (London: Faber & Faber, 1970), pp. 69–109.

132. Spector, McDonough, and Medeiros, *Tracking Nuclear Proliferation*, pp. 97–99.

133. See Shai Feldman, *Nuclear Weapons and Arms Control in the Middle East*, CSIA Studies in International Security (Cambridge, Mass.: MIT Press, 1997), pp. 95–120. See also Peter Pry, *Israel's Nuclear Arsenal* (Boulder, Colo.: Westview, 1984); Yair Evron, *Israel's Nuclear Dilemma* (Ithaca, N.Y.: Cornell University Press, 1994); and Seymour M. Hersh, *The Samson Option: Israel's Nuclear Arsenal and American Foreign Policy* (New York: Random House, 1991).

134. See Chubin, *Eliminating Weapons of Mass Destruction*; and Ahmed Hashim, *The Crisis of the Iranian State: Domestic, Foreign and Security Policies in Post-Khomeini Iran*, International Institute for Strategic Studies, Adelphi Paper No. 296 (Oxford: Oxford University Press, 1995).

135. See Sagan, "Why Do States Build Nuclear Weapons?" pp. 63–69; and Mitchell Reiss, *Bridled Ambition* (Washington, D.C.: Woodrow Wilson Center Press, 1995), pp. 45–88.

France[136] — and in some Third World countries' quests for rudimentary chemical weapons and ballistic missile capabilities. Since the late 1960s, however, and especially since the signing of the Nuclear Non-Proliferation Treaty in 1968, weapons of mass destruction have grown less and less legitimate in the eyes of the international community, and NBC acquisition is now more likely to damage a state's prestige than to enhance it, a consideration that has influenced some states' decisions.[137] Simultaneously, the international consequences of violating entrenched nonproliferation norms have grown more serious as more states have shown a willingness to apply political and economic levers to prevent or reverse proliferation. Contrary to the fears of earlier analysts,[138] states such as Brazil, Indonesia, and Nigeria no longer contemplate nuclear weapons acquisition as a means to solidify their roles as dominant regional powers or the leaders of the nonaligned movement. Prestige considerations now appear to exert a modest influence on proliferation decisions.

TECHNICAL BARRIERS DELAY AND COMPLICATE NBC ACQUISITION. An array of technical obstacles must be overcome as an aspiring proliferator designs, develops, fabricates, and deploys specific types of weapons of mass destruction. The effort can be costly and arduous, especially if the state in question lacks a developed, industrialized economy, or if the weapons are intended for use in large-scale military operations.[139] Two technical barriers are particularly significant: access to fissile material for nuclear weapons, and the weaponization of pathogenic microorganisms or toxins for biological weapons. The vast quantity of chemical agents required for effective, large-scale military use is less a technical than an economic and logistical barrier, but it does impede proliferation in some cases.

---

136. See Sagan, "Why Do States Build Nuclear Weapons?" pp. 73–80; and Lawrence Scheinman, *Atomic Energy Policy in France Under the Fourth Republic* (Princeton, N.J.: Princeton University Press, 1965).

137. See Sagan, "Why Do States Build Nuclear Weapons?" pp. 80–82; Steven E. Miller, "The Case against a Ukrainian Nuclear Deterrent," *Foreign Affairs*, Vol. 72, No. 3 (Summer 1993), pp. 67–80; Reiss, *Bridled Ambitions*, pp. 89–182; and Potter, *Politics of Nuclear Renunciation*.

138. Betts, "Paranoids, Pygmies, Pariahs," p. 164.

139. NBC weapons intended for limited usage by terrorists can be considerably simpler. See Chapter 2 for a full discussion, especially Box 6, Terrorist vs. Military Weapons, p. 100.

Access to sufficient quantities of fissile material is an absolute prerequisite for nuclear weapons acquisition. Unless fissile material is directly purchased or stolen (a rising concern since the collapse of the Soviet Union), it must be produced indigenously. For a state to produce fissile material itself, it must possess either a uranium-enrichment facility to produce highly enriched uranium, or a nuclear reactor and reprocessing plant to produce plutonium. All methods of fissile material production are expensive and technically complex.[140] Iraq, for example, is estimated to have spent more than $10 billion over a decade in an ultimately futile attempt to produce enough fissile material for even one nuclear weapon.[141] U.S. intelligence has concluded that, similarly, "Iran will not be able to produce sufficient plutonium to create a weapon until well into the next century, unless it receives significant foreign assistance."[142] North Korea's reprocessing of spent reactor fuel was detected by International Atomic Energy (IAEA) inspectors, triggering a major international effort to compel North Korea to halt its production of plutonium.[143] Producing fissile material is much more challenging than building a simple nuclear weapon once enough of the material is on hand.[144] Consequently, international export controls are in place to try to prevent nuclear aspirants from acquiring key fissile-material production technologies.[145]

---

140. Niels Bohr, one of the greatest physicists of the twentieth century and the man who explained the differences between the fissile and non-fissile isotopes of uranium, did not believe that isotopic separation was technically feasible until he saw the U.S. uranium-enrichment plant at Oak Ridge, Tennessee. Rhodes, *The Making of the Atomic Bomb*, p. 294.

141. See David Albright and Mark Hibbs, "Iraq's Bomb: Blueprints and Artifacts," *Bulletin of the Atomic Scientists*, Vol. 48, No. 1 (January/February 1992), pp. 30–40; and David A. Kay, "Denial and Deception Practices of WMD Proliferators: Iraq and Beyond," *Washington Quarterly*, Vol. 18, No. 1 (Winter 1994), p. 85.

142. Quoted in Tony Capaccio, "CIA: Iran Holding Limited Stocks of Biological Weapons," *Defense Week*, August 5, 1996, p. 1.

143. See Mazarr, "Going Just a Little Nuclear," pp. 94–96; and Mazarr, *North Korea and the Bomb*, pp. 94–99.

144. This issue is discussed in greater detail in Chapter 2.

145. In addition to IAEA safeguards required of all non–nuclear weapon state signatories to the Nuclear Non-Proliferation Treaty, the Zangger Committee and the Nuclear Suppliers Group (NSG) regulate the sale, transfer, and use of all materials and equipment that could potentially be used in a nuclear weapons program. Both

The effective weaponization of biological agents is a significant technical hurdle to biological weapons acquisition. As Chapter 2 explains, growing biological agents is often quite simple, but turning these agents into potent military instruments — which requires both a reasonable shelf life for storage and transport, and efficient dispersal in a stable, respirable aerosol — is substantially more difficult.[146] Iraq, despite years of effort and multimillion-dollar investments, does not appear to have been able to produce high-performance biological agent preparations, relying instead on relatively inefficient liquid slurries.[147] Likewise, "technical shortcomings, combined with limitations in Libya's overall ability to put agents into deliverable munitions, will preclude [its] production of militarily effective biological warfare systems for the foreseeable future," according to the U.S. Department of Defense.[148]

While these and other technical hurdles pose real obstacles to would-be proliferators, some nonproliferation analysts and policymakers tend to exaggerate the importance of technical impediments to the acquisition of NBC weapons. Over the long term, no technical barrier should be regarded as insurmountable by a determined state with moderate industrial capacity. Instead, these obstacles should be thought of as the principal explanation for the time lag between a state's decision to acquire a particular NBC capability and its actual deployment of the weapons system. These lags are often quite long: decades, in the case of many developing countries. But, except for a few states presenting marginal proliferation risks that are either truly impoverished or ambivalent about the merits of NBC acquisition, technical obstacles do not explain why most states have decided against acquiring weapons of mass destruction. Many advanced industrialized nations, including Germany, Japan, Taiwan, South Korea, and Sweden,

---

the materials themselves (such as plutonium and highly enriched uranium) and the "triggers" and other technologies associated with nuclear weapons, are subject to scrutiny by members of the two nonproliferation regimes, which include most of the industrialized states.

146. OTA, *Technologies Underlying Weapons of Mass Destruction*, pp. 94–99.

147. Some evidence, however, suggests Iraq may also have produced dried anthrax spores, which are much easier to aerosolize. Raymond A. Zilinskas, "Iraq's Biological Weapons: The Past As Future?" *JAMA*, Vol. 278, No. 5 (August 6, 1997), p. 421.

148. OSD, *Proliferation: Threat and Response*, p. 27.

have decided not to acquire NBC weapons, despite possessing the technological capacity to develop and fabricate such weapons indigenously.

INTERNATIONAL EFFORTS HAVE DISSUADED MANY STATES FROM ACQUIRING NBC WEAPONS. The international community, led by the United States and, for a time, by the Soviet Union, has established a wide variety of formal and informal regimes designed to discourage, delegitimize, detect, prevent, and sometimes even reverse NBC proliferation. Although there are no certain techniques for dissuading states from seeking NBC weapons capabilities — and the uncertainties are even greater in the case of non-state actors — much of the international community's nonproliferation effort over the past decades has consisted of diplomatic and political steps intended to make NBC weapons acquisition less attractive than it would otherwise be, and economic steps intended to make acquisition slower, more visible, and more costly.

Perhaps the most effective means of dissuading states from acquiring NBC weapons is for outside powers, such as the United States, to provide for their security.[149] This can be done in different ways, ranging from promoting arms control (i.e., coordinated, reciprocal threat reduction), to launching international peacemaking and peacekeeping missions, to offering security guarantees or assistance of various kinds, to exerting pressure on the states or groups that are the potential proliferator's perceived threat.[150] These activities have become almost routine elements in the foreign policy of most major states, a result of both their widely dispersed national interests and their general sense of responsibility for maintaining peace. The nonproliferation benefits of such policies are often barely noticed byproducts.

External security guarantees, however, are costly and risky, and thus rarely extended to other states, while international confidence-building and peacemaking efforts are not always successful. Any state, even one with purely defensive aims and powerful friends or allies, could reasonably reach the conclusion that the added military capabilities of nuclear,

---

149. Challenging this conventional wisdom is Sagan, "Why Do States Build Nuclear Weapons?" pp. 54–86.

150. It is usually not feasible to provide security directly to the states that present the "hardest" proliferation cases — such as Iraq, Iran, Libya, and North Korea — since their behavior in other areas makes them politically unsupportable.

biological, or chemical weapons are required for its survival.[151] As sovereign entities with great resources at their disposal and an inherent right to self-defense, states can acquire any sort of weapon they wish, unless they have forfeited this option through a military defeat, a treaty, or the acceptance of international common law. Thus, another effective means of dissuading other states from seeking to acquire NBC weapons is to establish global norms and generalized prohibitions against acquisition, possession, and use of weapons of mass destruction. To a large extent, the international community has succeeded in establishing such norms, which are embodied in various international agreements and treaties.[152] While often lacking effective enforcement mechanisms, these treaties establish a standard for judging a state's behavior, which in turn helps convey the message that NBC acquisition, possession, or use is condemned by the international community and carries long-term consequences. The existence of clear norms of behavior should also make it easier to build international coalitions against violators of the norms.

Toothless treaties and sometimes discriminatory norms will not dissuade a ruthless or highly insecure regime committed to acquiring weapons of mass destruction, so coercive measures may also be necessary. These can include general declaratory threats against states that acquire or use NBC weapons, as well as more focused instruments directed at particular states, including political pressure, diplomatic isolation, economic sanctions, military threats, selective air strikes, or war. To a large extent, however, the deterrent effect of these coercive options depends on the potential proliferator's assessment of the likelihood of detection of its clandestine NBC weapons program by outside powers.

States with NBC weapons must contend with a wide variety of long-term costs associated with their proliferation decisions: provoking destabilizing fear and hostility in their neighbors and in the larger international community; incurring international economic sanctions;

---

151. See Shai Feldman, *Israeli Nuclear Deterrence: A Strategy for the 1980s* (New York: Columbia University Press, 1982), pp. 7–52.

152. Among the most important of these normative agreements are the 1925 Geneva Protocol, which bans the use of chemical weapons in warfare; the 1968 Nuclear Nonproliferation Treaty (NPT), which permits only five states to possess nuclear weapons; the 1972 Biological Weapons Convention (BWC), which bans offensive biological weapons programs; and the 1993 Chemical Weapons Convention (CWC), which bans chemical weapons possession and requires the destruction of existing chemical weapons stockpiles.

enduring treatment as international pariahs; triggering regional arms races or alliance formation; and even suffering preventive military attack by other threatened states. The long-term costs of NBC weapons acquisition explain, in part, the Israeli, Indian, and Pakistani preference for opaque (secret) proliferation. These costs are a major reason why many states have decided not to initiate NBC weapons programs, or have renounced NBC weapons programs already in existence.

WHY NBC ATTACKS HAVE BEEN SO RARE

As noted earlier, NBC weapons have been used in war only a handful of times in the eight decades since World War I. No state is known to have delivered modern NBC weapons by covert means, and there is no evidence that any state sponsor of terrorism has ever assisted a terrorist group in acquiring or using weapons of mass destruction. Conventional weapons, however, have been used in vast numbers, with great frequency, and to horrible effect in the organized violence of states. Why has NBC warfare not been more frequent or extensive?

RISKS OF RETALIATION DETER STATES FROM NBC USE. The most compelling reason why most states have decided against using NBC weapons against their adversaries is the risk of near-term military retaliation, such as a response in kind or an escalation in some other arena of the conflict. Chemical weapons were used by all sides in the trench warfare of World War I, but the dominant lesson drawn from this experience was that even though each side was capable of inflicting massive losses on the other, any gains from this carnage were only temporary and tactical. Massive human losses in the trenches of France and Belgium had a profound impact on the home front but did not translate into significant strategic achievements.[153] Since this war, almost all confirmed instances of a state using weapons of mass destruction have been against adversaries with minimal capacity to retaliate in kind or to escalate, as Table 3 shows.

With the advent of nuclear weapons and their rapid accumulation by the United States and the Soviet Union, the potential consequences of a retaliatory second strike grew enormously, further dampening any incentive a state might have to initiate a nuclear, biological, or chemical exchange. U.S.-Soviet nuclear deterrence in the Cold War also discouraged

---

153. See SIPRI, *The Rise of CB Weapons*, pp. 125–141.

Table 3. Instances of NBC Use by States in the Twentieth Century.

Nuclear Weapons	Chemical Weapons
• United States against Japan, 1945	• World War I, unrestrained use in Europe
	• Russian Civil War, 1919–21
	• Spain against Morocco, 1925
	• Britain in the Middle East, 1920s (?)
	• Italy in Ethiopia, mid-1930s
Biological Weapons	• Japan in Manchuria, late 1930s
• Japan against China and the Soviet Union, 1937–45	• Egypt against Yemen, 1967–68
	• Iran-Iraq War, 1983–88
	• South Africa, 1980s (?)
	• Libya against Chad, 1987
	• Iraq against Kurds, 1988

SOURCES: Stockholm International Peace Research Institute (SIPRI), *The Problem of Chemical and Biological Warfare*, Vol. I: *The Rise of CB Weapons* (New York: Humanities Press, 1971), pp. 125–293; Gordon M. Burck and Charles C. Flowerree, *International Handbook on Chemical Weapons Proliferation* (New York: Greenwood Press, 1991).

use of biological and chemical weapons in regional wars, because even limited NBC aggression could potentially escalate into a global nuclear conflict.[154] The most extensive use of any weapon of mass destruction since World War I was the heavy chemical weapons use in the 1980–88 Iran-Iraq War (see Box 8, Iran-Iraq War, p. 226), a conflict somewhat insulated from superpower involvement by the independence of Saddam Hussein's Iraq and the Ayatollah Khomeini's Iran.

In the post–Cold War environment, deterrence remains the most significant check on NBC weapons use, although an increasing number of

---

154. This probably also explains the lack of attention to the issue of chemical and biological weapons. In the Cold War, the primary security threat was perceived to come from nuclear rather than chemical or biological weapons.

analysts have begun to question its efficacy.[155] Despite reductions in the U.S. defense budget, the United States has retained enormously capable conventional military forces and significant strategic and tactical nuclear forces, which would weigh heavily on the mind of any rational leader contemplating the use of NBC weapons against the United States or its friends and allies.[156] Even barring direct U.S. involvement, there is no guarantee that regional powers that initiate nuclear, biological, or chemical warfare would be able to terminate the war successfully — where "success" is defined as meeting original strategic objectives.[157]

The international community has a major stake in maintaining the norm against NBC use, so victims of NBC attacks — and the states acting on their behalf — are likely to benefit from some increased moral authority. Even if there is no immediate military retaliation, any state that initiates NBC use runs the risk of provoking an international response, possibly including economic sanctions and long-term political isolation. For all these reasons, the great destructive power of weapons of mass destruction does not easily translate into useful coercive power. Weapons of mass destruction can rationally be turned toward only relatively few strategic objectives, deterrence being the most important among them. This fact, more than any other, explains the rarity of NBC weapons use since World War I.

COVERT ATTACKS HAVE LIMITED MILITARY UTILITY. A few instances of NBC use by states have occurred since the 1920s, but except for Japan's biological warfare activities in China in the 1930s and 1940s, none have involved covert means of delivery. Indeed, if one looks at the deployment pattern of NBC weapons across many states and over time, it is clear that most have considered traditional military delivery systems — especially artillery,

---

155. See, for example, Keith B. Payne, "Deterring the Use of Weapons of Mass Destruction: Lessons from History," *Comparative Strategy*, Vol. 14, No. 4 (October–December 1995), pp. 349–351.

156. Paradoxically, an understanding of the power of NBC deterrence might also heighten the incentive to proliferate among some states, especially if they perceive themselves to be significantly weaker in conventional military power than their likely adversaries. But if deterrence of a more powerful adversary is the baseline motive for proliferation, then the state is likely to want a true military arsenal of NBC weapons, not a limited number of weapons suitable mainly for covert, surprise delivery against soft targets.

157. Brad Roberts discusses the issue of NBC war termination in "Rethinking How Wars Must End: NBC War Termination in the Post–Cold War Era," unpublished manuscript.

ballistic missiles and military aircraft — the weapons of choice.[158] Thus, a second question relevant to this study is why almost none of the states that have used NBC weapons has employed covert means of delivery, and have why almost all have relied instead on overt means such as aircraft and artillery.

The most compelling explanation of the historical rarity of covert NBC attacks by states is that the military utility of most conceivable covert NBC attacks is limited. Covert delivery presents an effective means of killing large numbers of civilians in cities, but this is a second-order objective for even the most bloodthirsty aggressors. Inherent limitations of covert delivery operations generally would restrict attacks to a limited number in any case, making them a weapon of terror but not one that would assure even tactical military victory. The foremost security concern of states in most wars is the organized armed forces of their adversaries. To counter an adversary's armed forces with NBC weapons, traditional military delivery systems are generally superior to covert means of delivery, because they can be fired repeatedly in salvos with accuracy, promptness, and reliability. For this reason, states that want NBC weapons capabilities generally want not a few weapons for limited clandestine operations, but an arsenal of weapons linked with prompt, reliable, survivable, and accurate delivery systems in the hands of trained military units.

The fundamental reason why states prefer militarily usable NBC arsenals is that conflicts involving NBC weapons are very high-stakes games; in the canonical worst case — all-out nuclear war — the very existence of the state could be jeopardized. Because the stakes are so high, states that decide to base their national security strategy on NBC weapons should also be willing to make the additional investments needed to buy or build modern military means of delivery, such as ballistic missiles, cruise missiles, and strike aircraft. While it could be useful in some circumstances, covert delivery cannot meet all of a state's military needs, whether for deterrence or for offensive use. Prompt, reliable, survivable means of delivery, such as ballistic missiles, strengthen deterrence by ensuring delivery against even the most vigilant adversary, as well as offering the attacker reliable options for escalation.

Thus, states that decide to acquire NBC weapons in the first place are unlikely to be satisfied with only the limited military potential of covert delivery options. This does not mean that covert NBC attacks would have

---

158. It is also worth noting that the historical record contains no instance of NBC weapons delivery by ballistic missile.

no role in their strategic plans. Indeed, selective covert NBC use could have profound effects in an unfolding conflict, particularly against a more powerful adversary (as we describe in Chapter 4). Moreover, a state in possession of NBC weapons but lacking a sufficient number to constitute a military arsenal, or lacking effective means of military delivery, might resort to covert means of delivery for lack of a better alternative. To date, however, no such attacks have occurred. A covert means of delivery would reduce the likelihood that the attacker could be promptly identified and counterattacked. This would weaken deterrence of NBC use, though the possibility of identification means that the risk to the attacking state would still be immense.

STATES LACK CONFIDENCE IN THE TERRORISTS THEY SPONSOR. As noted earlier, there appears to be no case in which a state sponsor of terrorism has assisted a non-state actor to acquire an NBC weapons capability. All of the explanations given above for the rarity of covert NBC attacks apply also to this circumstance, but there are two additional reasons for the absence of any known cases of state-sponsored NBC terrorism.

First of all, state sponsorship of even conventional terrorism is itself quite rare. The U.S. Department of State currently lists only seven state sponsors of terrorism: Cuba, Iran, Iraq, Libya, North Korea, Sudan, and Syria. Each of these states has suffered in various ways from complicity with international terrorist movements, an issue that frequently succeeds in uniting the international community. State sponsorship was somewhat more common during the Cold War, when terrorism was often associated with Communist-inspired revolutionary movements,[159] but in the post–Cold War world, it has been stripped of whatever moral legitimacy it may once have had. Because of the great risks associated with state sponsorship of terrorism, it is likely to remain a strategy pursued only by the most hardened, choleric nations, and even then only when it "serves the prime objectives of the respective leadership."[160]

Second, any nation's leaders would have to be truly desperate to hand over NBC weapons to a terrorist group with even the slightest degree of

---

159. See Walter Laqueur, "Postmodern Terrorism," *Foreign Affairs*, Vol. 75, No. 5 (September/October 1996), pp. 24–25.

160. Uwe Nerlich, "The Political and Strategic Analysis of Nuclear Non-state Actors and Sponsoring States: What to Look For?" Stiftung Wissenschaft und Politik, AP 2908 (June 1995), p. 45.

autonomy.[161] As discussed in the previous section, the use of an independent group to deliver the weapon would heighten a state's already extreme risks in carrying out a covert NBC attack. Imperfect state control, possible conflict between differing political agendas, and even the risk that the group would turn the weapons against the sponsor itself make states unlikely to follow such a path. Furthermore, states are likely to fear that they would be punished for any NBC attack carried out by a group they sponsored, whether or not they had supplied the weapons. This fear alone is reason enough for state sponsors of terrorism to oppose any sponsored group's efforts to acquire NBC weapons.

NORMS AGAINST NBC USE MAY INFLUENCE STATES. Finally, it is possible that the existence of norms in the international community against using NBC weapons has contributed to the relative rarity of NBC weapons use. There is a special stigma attached to nuclear, biological, and chemical weapons use that does not seem to apply to other weapons, even when they are used to kill large numbers of people. And there is no shortage of declarations and formal international commitments calling for weapons of mass destruction never to be used.

It is impossible, of course, to separate the extent to which these pious statements and commitments are the product of a sense of morality rather than a rational, self-interested calculus. When Mikhail Gorbachev and Ronald Reagan declared that "a nuclear war cannot be won and must never be fought,"[162] were they motivated principally by moral belief or by self-interest? The question is not an academic one, for it goes directly to the issue of what would happen if it became rational for a state to employ NBC weapons. Would norms, beliefs, or psychological barriers stop state leaders from using such weapons? Such constraints may influence some leaders, and for that reason we argue in Chapter 5 that some attention to strengthening norms is worthwhile. Norms alone, however, are not an adequate guarantee of any nation's national security.

---

161. A related argument appears in Laqueur, *The Age of Terrorism*, p. 317. Making the opposite case is Adams, "The Dangerous New World of Chemical and Biological Weapons," p. 41. Nerlich also argues that state-sponsored nuclear terrorism is the "most plausible case." Uwe Nerlich, "Nuclear Non-state Actors: Lessons from the RAF-GDR Connection?" paper prepared for Sandia National Laboratories, August 1993, p. 8.

162. From "Text of the Joint U.S.-Soviet Statement," as published in the *New York Times*, November 22, 1985, p. 15.

Conclusion

Many states have built weapons of mass destruction, but few have used them in the modern era. A few non-state actors have dabbled with nuclear, biological, or chemical weapons, but only Aum Shinrikyo has crossed the motivational and technical thresholds that have prevented all others from posing a serious terrorist threat of mass destruction. If this situation persists into the future, modern societies have little to fear from the prospects of covert NBC aggression, their acute vulnerability notwithstanding.

As we discuss in Chapter 2, however, society's vulnerability to clandestine attack is high, and some of the technical barriers to NBC acquisition and delivery are eroding. The existence of a vulnerability, and even the increasing availability of the relevant weapons, does not mean that the threat will inevitably become acute. As we argue in Chapters 3 and 4, however, there is growing evidence that motivational restraints against nuclear, biological, and chemical weapons use by both states and non-state actors are eroding. An array of factors, ranging from an apparent change in the nature of terrorism, to U.S. invulnerability to most forms of conventional attack, appear to be shifting the decision calculus of potential NBC attackers, creating an environment in which weapons of mass destruction are more likely to be used than in the past. These trends, balanced by any countervailing efforts the United States and its allies take against them, will largely determine whether the threat grows significantly worse.

Chapter 2

NBC Acquisition and Covert Delivery

Technical Possibilities and Technical Constraints

The threat of covert attack with nuclear, biological, or chemical weapons is exaggerated as often as it is underestimated. Polarized threat assessments result in part from incomplete or incorrect understandings of the difficulty of covert NBC weapons acquisition and use. The purpose of this chapter is to provide a clear and accurate technical assessment of the vulnerability of open societies to covert NBC attacks by states and non-state actors. The question of why a particular state or non-state actor might decide to carry out such an attack is taken up in Chapters 3 and 4. This chapter looks only at the range of technical possibilities for potential attackers with different levels of capability.

Vulnerability is a function of an adversary's access to a particular weapon type, its ability to use the weapon in an offensive mode, the target's ability to defend itself against this attack, and the consequences of a successful attack. Accordingly, this chapter addresses three basic questions.[1] First, how accessible are nuclear, biological, and chemical weapons? Second, how feasible is covert weapons delivery against targets in an open society? And third, what is the range of possible physical effects of successful covert NBC attacks?

The difficulty of obtaining and using nuclear, biological, and chemical weapons varies widely, both between and within the weapon types. Many factors are relevant: the size, sophistication, and type of the weapon being sought; the availability of the technical information needed to design the weapon; the accessibility of essential precursor materials and equipment;

---

1. As noted in the Preface, we deliberately try not to provide a guide to weapons acquisition in this chapter. Therefore, we restrict our discussion to general information widely available from many sources, and leave out most specific technical information that would ease the task of a would-be NBC attacker. Because the technical barriers to chemical weapons acquisition are particularly low, we leave most technical details out of the section on chemical weapons acquisition. We also deliberately refrain from extensive discussion of delivery methods and employment concepts likely to increase the damage or the political utility of covert NBC attacks. In general, however, relevant information on these subjects can be assembled by a focused, competent researcher with access to a good library.

the difficulty of weapon design and construction; the extent to which the peculiarities of the weapon complicate the organization of a clandestine acquisition effort; and the existence of externally observable signatures that increase the likelihood of discovery. Moreover, the ability to surmount the technical and organizational barriers to NBC weapons acquisition varies enormously among states and non-state actors. Taking all of these factors into account, however, it is clear that weapons of mass destruction suitable for covert use are within the reach of a wide range of states and many non-state actors.[2]

Chemical weapons suitable for mass-casualty attacks can be acquired by virtually any state and by non-state actors with moderate technical skills. Certain very deadly chemical warfare agents can quite literally be manufactured in a kitchen or basement in quantities sufficient for mass-casualty attacks. Production procedures for some agents are simple, are accurately described in publicly available sources, and require only common laboratory glassware, good ventilation, and commercially available precursor chemicals. Greater expertise and some specialized equipment are required to fabricate the most toxic chemical warfare agents, but the acquisition of quantities sufficient for mass-casualty attacks would still be within the reach of some technically capable non-state actors. The Japanese cult Aum Shinrikyo produced tens of kilograms of the nerve gas sarin, demonstrating the technical feasibility of chemical weapons acquisition by capable non-state actors. The actual use of a highly toxic chemical agent as a weapon of mass destruction is not difficult in principle.[3]

Many states and moderately sophisticated non-state actors could construct improvised but effective biological weapons. Quite detailed information on the relevant science and technology is available from open sources. Culturing the required microorganisms, or growing and purifying toxins, is inexpensive and could be accomplished by individuals with college-level training in biology and a basic knowledge of laboratory technique. Acquiring the seed stocks for pathogenic microorganisms is also

---

2.   The argument of this chapter rests on the differences between high-performance military weapons and weapons for covert use, which may be less sophisticated, but still capable of causing mass casualties. See Box 6, Terrorist vs. Military Weapons, p. 100.

3.   It is worth noting that Aum Shinrikyo failed at this aspect of the problem in the Tokyo attack, delivering the sarin ineffectively and causing only a fraction of the potential fatalities (see Box 1, Aum Shinrikyo, p. 19). However, the failings of a particular terrorist group cannot be taken as a guarantee of public safety.

not particularly difficult, but the easiest acquisition option — placing an order with a biological supply service — has been largely closed off within the United States by new regulations. The most significant technical challenge in fabricating a biological weapon is effectively disseminating bulk biological agent as a respirable aerosol. The most efficient aerosolization systems, which could produce extremely high casualties over wide areas, would require considerable technological sophistication, and remain beyond the reach of most states and most conceivable non-state actors. However, less efficient aerosolization techniques are available, and could be mastered by many states and some technically skilled non-state actors. The effects of biological attacks could vary greatly, but a single biological weapon could kill or incapacitate as many as tens of thousands of people even with an inefficient delivery system, especially if directed against large indoor targets.

Nuclear weapons are within the reach of tens of states, with the most significant constraint being the ability to produce plutonium or highly enriched uranium (HEU). If this obstacle were avoided through the theft or purchase of fissile material, almost any state with a reasonable technical and industrial infrastructure could fabricate a crude nuclear weapon, with a yield in the range of 10 kilotons (the equivalent of 10,000 tons of high explosive). This is roughly the magnitude of the explosion that destroyed Hiroshima. Some exceptionally capable non-state actors could also design and build a nuclear weapon, particularly if they had access to a substantial quantity of HEU metal, which allows an inefficient but simple weapon design to be used. Such groups might also be able to build a weapon with plutonium or with HEU oxide.[4] Non-state actors would find it hard to predict the yield of their device. They would also be more likely to have design and execution problems leading to a "fizzle" yield anywhere between zero and 1 or 2 kilotons. The collapse of the Soviet Union, which has exposed large stockpiles of fissile material to an unprecedented risk of theft and diversion, has heightened the risk of risk of nuclear weapons acquisition by non-state actors and states without an indigenous fissile material production capability.

---

4.   A very wide range of states and non-state actors could also construct radiological weapons from common radioactive materials and waste products, but these would be far less destructive than nuclear weapons, and would generally be less deadly than chemical or biological weapons of comparable accessibility. See Introduction, p. 15.

Box 6
Terrorist Weapons are
Easier to Build than Military Weapons

Much conventional wisdom on the difficulty of acquiring weapons of mass destruction is based on the lessons learned from the weapons programs of the United States and, to a lesser extent, the programs of other states. These lessons are important, but it is also important to emphasize that acquiring a small number of usable improvised weapons of any type is considerably easier than building and maintaining a militarily usable arsenal of weapons.

Weapons for military use are needed in large numbers, must be deliverable by normal military means, must be effective against properly equipped military forces on the battlefield, must be rugged and reliable, and must have adequate shelf life and predictable effects. These requirements increase the cost and difficulty of acquiring weapons of mass destruction for military use. In contrast, weapons of mass destruction intended for covert use can be produced inefficiently and in small quantities. They can be delivered by non-military means, such as by boat or truck, making possible the use of weapons, including improvised nuclear weapons, that are too large and unwieldy to be delivered in combat. Similarly, backpack-sized chemical or biological weapons, too small, improvised, and fragile to have an impact on a battlefield or against soldiers equipped for chemical and biological defense, could nonetheless be devastating against some civilian targets. Shelf life and reliability must be adequate for the intended use, but just-in-time agent production would be suitable for many kinds of attacks, largely eliminating shelf-life constraints. Finally, while covert attackers would want predictable weapons effects, they would generally require less precision than a military commander needs on the battlefield. These factors significantly change the basis on which the accessibility of weapons should be judged. A vulnerability assessment needs to consider the potential for attack with any of the weapons available, not just with high-performance weapons.

Weapons of all three types could be delivered by covert means against a variety of civilian targets, and against some military or political targets, with good chances of success and limited risk of detection and attribution. The basic reason for this uncomfortable fact is that NBC weapons can be easily delivered in ways that are virtually indistinguishable from the normal background of civilian traffic and commerce, making detection likely only after the weapon has been detonated or the harmful agent released. The information required to deliver an NBC weapon successfully is significantly less complicated and easier to obtain, at least for most targets, than the information needed to build the weapon in the first place. Some talent for planning and conducting dangerous covert operations would be required to ensure that the attack is effective and that the perpetrators are able to escape undetected; these skills are distinct from the technical ability to build a weapon. Barring specific intelligence warning or a major error on the part of the perpetrators, it is unlikely that the authorities would be able to detect and defeat a covert NBC attack before it is too late.

The effects of a successful covert attack with a nuclear, biological, or chemical weapon would vary widely depending on the weapon, the target, and the effectiveness of the delivery means. However, if used against a concentrated, unprotected population, even a single chemical weapon would likely kill hundreds or thousands of people, significantly more than any previous terrorist attack. Such an attack would cause significant economic damage, might contaminate the target for an extended time, and would almost certainly cause popular anxiety and panic disproportionate to the physical effects of the weapon. At the high end of the scale, a single well-placed biological or nuclear weapon could cause tens of thousands, even hundreds of thousands, of casualties, as could a campaign of lesser attacks. The resulting casualties and contamination would damage the economy and could destabilize society.

The next three sections of this chapter assess the difficulty of state and non-state actor acquisition of weapons of mass destruction by evaluating the technical requirements for building chemical, biological, and nuclear weapons suitable for covert use. The fourth section discusses the requirements for effective weapons delivery against specific target types. The concluding section outlines the likely effects of nuclear, biological, and chemical weapons attacks, and the nature of post-attack response options.

Chemical Weapons: Most States and Many Non-state Actors

Of the three weapon types under consideration here, chemical weapons are the easiest to acquire. Virtually all states could muster the technical expertise and resources necessary to acquire a minimal chemical weapons capability, as could a wide range of non-state actors, including many with far fewer resources than Aum Shinrikyo.[5] At a minimum, a clandestine effort aimed at producing a simple but effective chemical weapon would require at least one smart, technically educated person, preferably with practical experience in chemistry or chemical engineering. It would also require at least one technician able to build simple devices for agent dissemination, a simple laboratory facility with appropriate equipment, and a small machine shop. The required equipment and supplies could be bought for no more than tens of thousands of dollars, perhaps even less. The time required would be somewhere between several weeks and a year, depending on the group's size, knowledge, finances, and skills, and on the sophistication and size of the weapon sought.

To aid an understanding of the technical barriers to the acquisition of a basic chemical weapons capability, we emphasize five points. First, many of the precursor materials that are essential to the synthesis of simple but effective chemical warfare agents — including some used in the trenches of World War I — also have legitimate commercial uses and are commercially available. Second, producing significant quantities of some basic but effective chemical agents from the appropriate precursor materials requires only a moderate knowledge of chemistry, easily acquired equipment, and a few hours or days of work. Third, once a sufficient quantity of chemical warfare agent is on hand, producing an effective weapon of mass destruction is not difficult and could be done in a few days. Fourth, although several aspects of a chemical weapons program have distinctive characteristics that might be observed by watchful law enforcement agencies, these signatures can be concealed if the acquisition effort is designed and conducted with care. Finally, while the effectiveness of outdoor chemical weapons attacks would be limited by the scale of the production facility and the size and number of the weapons used, even a bare-bones effort could

---

5. The Office of Technology Assessment concluded that more than 100 countries could produce "simple chemical weapons such as phosgene, hydrogen cyanide, and sulfur mustard," while a smaller number could produce nerve agents. U.S. Congress, Office of Technology Assessment (OTA), *Technologies Underlying Weapons of Mass Destruction* (Washington, D.C.: U.S. Government Printing Office [U.S. GPO], December 1993), p. 16. These estimates appear to apply to large-scale production for military purposes. Militarily significant use of chemical weapons generally requires many tons of agent, imposing manufacturing and logistics burdens that many countries cannot easily meet. The less demanding laboratory-scale production that would be needed to supply weapons for covert or terrorist attacks is within reach for many more states.

produce a reliable weapon that could kill thousands of people if used in a crowded, enclosed space.

PRECURSOR MATERIALS ARE LARGELY DUAL-USE AND COMMERCIALLY AVAILABLE

Chemical warfare agents are produced by reacting other chemicals, known as precursors, in appropriate ratios and according to prescribed procedures. Most agents can be produced by several production routes, requiring different combinations of precursor materials. Many of these synthesis procedures are described in the open literature. Furthermore, many of the precursor materials required to produce chemical warfare agents have legitimate industrial uses, and are widely available from commercial sources. Even some of those subject to domestic or international controls may be obtained with only modest difficulty and risk.

In the United States and many other countries, a wide variety of chemicals are used in research and industry. Some chemical weapons precursors, like many other chemicals, can be ordered in small quantities for domestic delivery without arousing undue suspicion, if adequate thought is given to cover stories that explain the need for any of the more specialized chemicals.[6] Most chemical suppliers, and particularly large mail-order suppliers, take considerable care to ensure that their customers are legitimate researchers or commercial enterprises, and often require documentation, such as business licenses, to prove it.[7] In an extreme case, it might prove necessary to set up a front company to obtain the chemicals. This would create a paper trail that might benefit post-attack investigation, and require additional knowledge and skills. But even this obstacle can be avoided by finding a less careful supplier, or by choosing an agent and production pathway that uses more common precursors. Chemical weapons precursors are subject to export controls, and large domestic orders from an unknown customer would probably arouse concern that the chemicals might be intended for illegal export. Quantities in the tens of kilograms are unlikely to arouse such suspicions, however.

---

6. This statement is based on authors' discussions with an industrial chemical supplier serving local industry in a major U.S. city. All of the major domestic chemical suppliers carry at least a few important precursor chemicals, both in bulk for industrial use, and in small quantities for laboratory use.

7. This statement is based on authors' discussions with two chemical suppliers, one local and one national.

Even with the entry into force of the Chemical Weapons Convention (CWC), which requires international declarations of production and use of precursor chemicals, controls and reporting requirements on small-quantity domestic sales are almost nonexistent. The CWC requires reporting of all facilities that use, on an annual basis, more than 1 metric ton of a defined set of high-risk precursors in moderately widespread commercial use, and 30 metric tons of a defined set of dual-use chemicals that are used commercially in large quantities.[8] The U.S. implementing legislation for the CWC will make chemical suppliers liable to prosecution for selling precursors to anyone they know intends to use them for chemical weapons. This is likely to increase suppliers' awareness of the risks, but legitimate-seeming customers will still be able to buy the chemicals they need.[9]

Although international commerce in chemical weapons precursors is regulated somewhat more systematically, and the system will become

---

8. Reporting thresholds are 100 g for military chemical warfare agents with no commercial use (twelve chemicals or chemical families are specified). Three particularly dangerous chemicals in commercial use have specific thresholds: benzilate, 1 kg; Amiton and PFIB, 100 kg. Amy E. Smithson, ed., *The Chemical Weapons Convention Handbook*, Stimson Center Handbook No. 2, rev. ed. (Washington, D.C.: Henry L. Stimson Center, September 1995), p. 24.

9. On May 23, 1997, the CWC implementing legislation passed the Senate. 143 Congressional Record S. 5080. In November 1997, the bill passed the House, attached to an unrelated measure sanctioning Russia for missile sales which will require negotiations with the Senate and which may make the legislation difficult for the president to sign into law. Jonathan B. Tucker, "Congress has Undermined Chemical Weapons Ban," *Monterey County Herald*, March 15, 1998, p. A11. For up-to-date information on the status of this and other legislation, see the on-line legislative information service of the Library of Congress, at <thomas.loc.gov>. The legislation does not impose record-keeping or transaction reporting requirements for small-scale precursor purchases. Chemicals useful for the manufacture of illegal drugs, in contrast, are subject to much tighter controls and reporting requirements. "The Chemical Diversion and Trafficking Act of 1988 establishes customer identification, recordkeeping, reporting and notification requirements relating to the distribution, import, and export of certain precursor and essential chemicals and tableting and encapsulating machines utilized in the manufacture of controlled substances [illegal drugs]," Statement of Max Turnipseed, Chemical Manufacturers Association, in Senate Hearings 101-744, *Global Spread of Chemical and Biological Weapons*, Hearings before the Committee on Governmental Affairs, Permanent Subcommittee on Investigations, U.S. Senate (Washington, D.C.: U.S. GPO, 1990), p. 429.

tighter during the first few years of the CWC, export controls may not prevent small-scale weapons acquisition for covert use.[10] Under an arrangement known as the "Australia Group," the international community's main chemical suppliers have worked since 1985 to strengthen and harmonize their export controls on the most important precursor chemicals and equipment, particularly to certain states suspected of having chemical weapons programs.[11] Alternate suppliers and illegal exports have made this system imperfect, but it has improved over time, and additional suppliers have joined the group or agreed to follow its guidelines.[12] The entry into force of the CWC will make it harder to evade Australia Group controls, since it requires end-user certificates for member states' shipments of precursor chemicals to non-member states, and prohibits trade in certain precursor chemicals with non-member states after the treaty has been in force for three years.[13]

---

10. For a good short discussion of the international availability of precursor chemicals, see OTA, *Technologies Underlying Weapons of Mass Destruction*, pp. 28–31.

11. For an overview and assessment of Australia Group efforts to limit the spread of chemical weapons, see Julian P. Perry Robinson, "The Australia Group: A Description and Assessment," in Hans Günter Brauch et al., eds., *Controlling the Development and Spread of Military Technology: Lessons from the Past and Challenges for the 1990s* (Amsterdam: VU University Press, 1992), pp. 157–176. An overview of the U.S. export control system and guide to business compliance can be found in *Exporter's Encyclopedia, 1996/97* (Bethlehem, Pa.: Dun & Bradstreet Information Services), pp. 3.47–3.84. A more detailed discussion of the institutional arrangements can be found in Cecil Hunt, Deputy Chief Counsel for Export Administration, U.S. Department of Commerce, "Export Controls," in *Going International: Fundamentals of International Business Transactions* (Philadelphia: American Law Institute, 1996), pp. 431–462.

12. National and international export control efforts impeded but did not prevent very large exports of chemical weapons precursors to Iraq in the last years of its war with Iran. Gordon M. Burck and Charles C. Flowerree, *International Handbook on Chemical Weapons Proliferation* (New York: Greenwood Press, 1991) pp. 48–49, 553–560.

13. Amy E. Smithson, *Separating Fact from Fiction: The Australia Group and the Chemical Weapons Convention* (Washington, D.C.: The Henry L. Stimson Center, March 1997), p. 25. This provision will not make Australia Group controls more effective against states such as Iran that have joined the CWC but are still believed to have chemical weapons programs.

International control efforts are more likely to impede acquisition by non-state actors in developing countries than to impede states' efforts to build chemical weapons on a small scale. States will generally have greater resources, and can either synthesize appropriate precursors on a laboratory scale or attempt to evade international controls. Export controls can sometimes be evaded via false end-user certificates or customs declarations, and are directed mainly at impeding large-scale military chemical weapons programs, not preventing or detecting small-scale chemical weapons programs aimed at covert use. Exports of chemical weapon precursors to states that are not suspected of posing chemical weapons proliferation risks are not subject to tight controls, which means that a non-state actor operating in such a state, especially one in an Australia Group country, might be able to purchase precursor materials from suppliers in another Australia Group country with little difficulty. In most such cases, however, seeking a domestic supplier would lower the risk of detection by an intelligence agency.

REQUIREMENTS OF AGENT PRODUCTION ARE MODERATE
The published literature on chemical warfare, combined with the technical literature in chemistry and chemical engineering, provides a wealth of information on chemical warfare agents. Data on agent toxicities and effects, on precursor chemicals and their sources, and on different production processes are available in many technical libraries. Given the right precursors, and chemistry knowledge at the college level or sometimes less, a single individual could produce certain chemical warfare agents easily, in processes requiring very little specialized equipment or expertise. Test runs of production processes might take only hours to complete for production of simple agents from ideal precursors, or could take weeks or months in more complicated cases. Production runs on the scale of a few kilograms each could be carried out in hours or days with direct precursors, but might take weeks or months starting from indirect precursors.

Equipment and safety requirements would vary substantially, depending on the agents in question, the synthesis path chosen, and the quantity and purity of product required. In general, nerve agents would be more demanding than older, less toxic agents to synthesize safely, in part because of their high toxicity and in part because most of them require difficult synthesis steps.[14] Some of the less common precursors involved would also be more difficult to order without arousing suppliers' suspicion. Some reactions, such as those involving gaseous, corrosive, or highly toxic reagents or elevated ·temperatures, would require more specialized equipment and more expertise. High agent purity would be difficult to achieve by some production processes without special equipment.[15] Equipment needs can, however, be limited by choosing agents and production paths that avoid high-energy, high-pressure, and high-temperature reactions. Some simple but still highly toxic chemical agents can be synthesized in kilogram quantities in laboratory glassware. The required equipment for small-scale production of more difficult agents by more difficult routes can be obtained from laboratory equipment supply companies in any industrialized country. Equipment for small-scale synthesis also falls below the size thresholds for export control established by the Australia Group's guidelines.[16]

WEAPONIZATION IS NOT DIFFICULT

Chemical weapons do not require sophisticated dispersal methods. Unlike biological agents, chemical agents do not die or become inactivated through poor dissemination.[17] Chemical warfare agents can enter the body through the skin, lungs, or mucous membranes, although death by skin exposure usually requires a higher dose.[18] They can be effective, therefore, as large liquid droplets on the victims' skin or clothing, as aerosols (fine droplets or

---

14.   On the relative difficulty of synthesizing various chemical agents, see OTA, *Technologies Underlying Weapons of Mass Destruction*, pp. 21–27; and Burck and Flowerree, *International Handbook on Chemical Weapons Proliferation*, pp. 587–592.

15.   Impure agents have reduced toxicity and can have limited shelf-life, but can still be used in effective attacks. The sarin used in the Tokyo subway attack, for example, was of low quality.

16.   See Annex 2, "Australia Group Control List of Dual-Use Chemical Manufacturing Facilities and Equipment and Related Technology," in Smithson, *Separating Fact from Fiction*, pp. 36–43.

17.   Certain agents are, however, flammable, and can be destroyed by fire if dispersed by explosive means.

18.   For data on the lethal dosage of chemical agents, see Burck and Flowerree, *International Handbook on Chemical Weapons Proliferation*, pp. 580–581; and Stockholm International Peace Research Institute (SIPRI), *The Problem of Chemical and Biological Warfare*, Vol. II: *CB Weapons Today* (New York: Humanities Press, 1973), pp. 42–43.

dust suspended in the air), and as vapor (individual molecules that become mixed with the air as the agent evaporates). Agents that are effective in all these forms are easy to disseminate effectively using improvised sprayers or bursting charges, as there is no need to create high–quality respirable aerosols.[19] If adequate quantities of agent are used, even a spray of widely varying droplet size will quickly produce lethal levels of agent vapor, while the droplets themselves will settle onto the victims, both poisoning them directly and contaminating them.

Building an improvised chemical agent delivery device would take at least a day of work even using standard parts and materials (such as pre-made timers, seals, valves, batteries, spray nozzles, gas cylinders, and detonators), and such parts would provide important forensic evidence if left at the attack site. More time, but not necessarily more than a week, would be needed if the device were made from relatively untraceable raw materials. The most important requirement in constructing such a device is making sure that delivery personnel will not be killed by leaks, which requires the agent to be stored in a well-sealed, uncontaminated container prior to dissemination. Leak-proof storage has to be combined with a dispersal device, making the overall munition somewhat more complicated to build than, for example, a mail bomb. Machine shop facilities and simple electrical and electronics equipment would be needed for constructing delivery devices. A skilled electrical and mechanical technician could build adequate sprayers or explosive bursters.

The safety problems associated with synthesizing, weaponizing, and delivering some lethal chemical agents can be minimized by producing binary weapons. Binary devices store two less toxic precursor chemicals and

---

19. "Most hazardous industrial chemicals and military-unique chemicals can be effectively disseminated using explosive ordnance or commercial sprayers." Testimony of James A. Genovese, *Global Proliferation of Weapons of Mass Destruction*, Part I, Hearings before the Permanent Subcommittee on Investigations of the Committee on Governmental Affairs, U.S. Senate, 104th Cong., 1st Sess. (Washington, D.C.: U.S. GPO, 1996), p. 125. The various simple dispersal systems used during World War I illustrate this. See Stockholm International Peace Research Institute (SIPRI), *The Problem of Chemical and Biological Warfare*, Vol. I: *The Rise of CB Weapons* (New York: Humanities Press, 1971), pp. 28–38. Some analysts, however, argue that delivery devices are a significant problem. "Devising and testing an effective CW agent delivery system, such as a bomb or spray device, poses another major technical hurdle — one that caused Aum Shinrikyo particular difficulties." Jonathan B. Tucker, "Chemical/Biological Terrorism: Coping with a New Threat," *Politics and the Life Sciences*, Vol. 15, No. 2 (September 1996), p. 172.

combine them at the last possible moment, causing them to react to form a lethal chemical warfare agent, which is then disseminated.[20] For covert use, a binary delivery device could easily use a small, battery-powered pump to mix the two components before dissemination. Aum Shinrikyo attempted to use an improvised binary device to produce cyanide gas in an attack following the police raids on its compound, but the device was discovered before it produced lethal concentrations of gas (see Box 1, Aum Shinrikyo, p. 19). Given the proper precursor materials, producing a simple binary device would be only slightly more difficult than producing a standard chemical dispersal device, and in some cases would offer significant safety benefits.

VISIBLE ACQUISITION SIGNATURES CAN BE AVOIDED

The process of acquiring chemical weapons has several distinctive signatures or indicators that may arouse suspicion if observed by law enforcement or intelligence agencies. The most significant of these indicators would be: the purchase of certain well-known precursor chemicals; explosions, fires, or detectable environmental emissions from a secret chemical laboratory; and suspicious illnesses or deaths. Even without visible external signatures, accidental detection by health and safety regulators could also occur. A careful proliferator has a variety of options for minimizing risk in each of these areas, though sometimes at the price of increasing the cost, complexity, or difficulty of the project as a whole.

Precursor purchases would entail some risk of supplier suspicion, but this hazard can be minimized with a little thought and effort. Some chemical weapons precursors are subject to export controls. Others that are highly toxic or reactive are subject to shipping restrictions and other health and environmental regulations. Furthermore, because many chemicals pose risks of injury due to misuse or accidents, industrial suppliers are often cautious in supplying chemicals to unknown customers. Exporters are generally aware of the potential weapons applications of dual-use chemicals, as are some domestic suppliers, and many chemical suppliers would notify law enforcement agencies if they became suspicious of a particular order. Nevertheless, precursors for certain agents have broad enough uses that small purchases would go unnoticed. Purchase of other precursors might require a commercial cover story, and perhaps a front

---

20. OTA, *Technologies Underlying Weapons of Mass Destruction*, p. 34. OTA further reports that Iraq developed improvised binary warheads that required a soldier to add the second chemical component just before firing.

company. No record-keeping or reporting requirements have been put in place to detect unusual domestic trade in chemical weapons precursors, although chemical dealers are required by law to report bulk purchases of certain chemicals used in the manufacture of illegal drugs.[21] A trained chemist or chemical engineer would have an excellent chance of buying precursors without provoking suspicion, and an intelligent person without extensive chemistry training, proceeding carefully, would have a good chance.

A chemical weapons production facility would face risks from fire and explosions, but certain simple agent production processes would raise no special risks, and the hazards of other agents can be minimized with the right equipment and practices. A simple production facility would also produce exhaust fumes that might, depending on the chemicals in use and the amounts released, have strong offensive odors or even cause sickness or death to people or animals nearby. Such effects would not present a problem for a state, but a facility run by a non-state group would be likely to draw official attention, unless the facility had no neighbors.[22] If these issues were considered in the planning stage, however, a proliferator could avoid them by careful choice of precursors and production paths, or by choosing an isolated location. A non-state group would also face a risk of detection if agent releases in the laboratory led to illnesses or deaths among members of the group. Especially if members sought outside medical care after an accident, agent effects might make medical and public health personnel suspicious. Again, agents and production pathways can be chosen to minimize this risk, and dual-use equipment is easily available to allow more demanding processes to be conducted safely, at least on a small scale. In a properly equipped laboratory, normal safety measures, including

---

21. Regulations issued by the Drug Enforcement Administration, under the authority of the Chemical Diversion and Trafficking Act of 1988 and related laws, require chemical dealers to maintain records on certain chemicals, and to report suspicious purchasers and purchases in excess of certain quantities, which vary depending on the chemicals. Title 21, *Code of Federal Regulations*, parts 1300–1316, especially parts 1309–1310. Some of the controlled chemicals, such as acetone, sulfuric acid, and hydrochloric acid, are used for a very wide range of legitimate purposes. Similar reporting requirements might be appropriate for some chemical weapons precursors.

22. It is worth noting, however, that Aum Shinrikyo's production plant drew exactly this kind of attention in 1994 with a release of an unknown chemical. Police came to investigate, but did not enter the cult's buildings.

fume hoods and measures to avoid ignition of flammable chemicals, would suffice to protect personnel up to the final process step, even in nerve agent production. When supertoxic agents are finally produced, working in negative-pressure glove boxes and wearing protective clothing and gas masks would be prudent, especially with nerve agents. Adequate equipment of this sort could be improvised easily.

Detection through normal regulatory activity would also be possible, but not likely. A wide range of academic, business, and industrial facilities are subject to regulations that provide local, state, and federal health, safety, and environmental agencies the right to enter and inspect them. Such inspections are not thorough enough to ensure the detection of chemical weapons production facilities, but they would place such facilities at risk of exposure. Government inspections also usually depend on a facility being properly licensed and registered, and a covert facility might escape attention for years, especially if sited carefully. The risk of detection by law enforcement or other government agencies would rise sharply with the size of a production effort, both because the larger amounts of equipment and precursors needed would be more likely to raise supplier suspicions, and because the larger facility would be more visible and more prone to attract normal regulatory attention. Nevertheless, a facility capable of producing agents on the scale of hundreds of kilograms per year need not be larger than a house, nor look unusual from the outside.

The entry into force of the Chemical Weapons Convention (CWC) brings into existence an international verification system that includes provisions for challenge inspections.[23] That system is designed to detect militarily significant chemical agent production, however, not tens of kilograms. While challenge inspections might uncover suspected small-scale production sites if intelligence identifies them, the CWC regime will not on its own detect such sites, and cannot be expected to detect diversion from legitimate uses of the small quantities of precursors that would be needed for weapons for covert attacks. Moreover, the CWC does not provide for inspections in states not party to the treaty.

---

23. Smithson, *The Chemical Weapons Convention Handbook*, pp. 31–34.

Biological Weapons: Many States and a Few Non-state Actors

Many states and a few non-state actors could build effective biological weapons.[24] The project is beyond the level of any of the "terrorist cookbooks" mentioned in the press, but a biological weapons project faces no fundamental barriers that would be insurmountable by a small team of individuals with good skills in experimental microbiology and engineering, provided they are capable of carrying out a multi-stage research and development project. The minimum desirable group would have one competent microbiologist (undergraduate-level training or higher), one experimental physicist or mechanical engineer able to work with aerosol technology, and sufficient funds — less than a few hundred thousand dollars would be needed — for research, testing, production, and weaponization.[25] The facilities required would fit in a large apartment.

Producing a biological weapon involves three essential technical steps. The first is to acquire a seed stock of a pathogenic or toxin-producing organism. The second is to produce the microorganism or toxin in bulk. The third is to develop a system capable of dispersing the chosen agent in infectious or toxic concentrations as a respirable aerosol, without deactivat-

---

24. OTA, *Technologies Underlying Weapons of Mass Destruction*, p. 85, quotes an estimate that "more than 100 countries have the capability ... to develop at least improvised biological weapons based on standard microbial and toxin agents," citing "Testimony of Thomas Welch, Deputy Assistant Secretary of Defense (Chemical Matters), reported in *Defense Week*, May 9, 1988." An international panel of scientific experts convened by the United Nations concluded in 1969 that "any developing country could, in fact, acquire ... a limited capability in [biological warfare]." United Nations Report No. E 69. I. 24, 1969, *Chemical and Bacteriological (Biological) Weapons and the Effects of Their Possible Use* (New York: Ballantine, 1970), p. 142.

25. This cost estimate is based on discussions with biotechnology industry consultants and biological defense specialists, and is meant to be conservative, allowing enough resources to support a project that could take more than a year to bear fruit. Some cost estimates are much lower. Kathleen Bailey, a national security analyst and a former assistant director of the U.S. Arms Control and Disarmament Agency, has argued publicly that the correct figure is in the tens of thousands of dollars. Leonard Cole, *The Eleventh Plague* (New York: W.H. Freeman, 1997), citing interviews with Bailey, states that she "is 'absolutely convinced' that a major biological arsenal could be built in a room 15-by-15 feet, with $10,000 worth of equipment."

ing it in the process. The main obstacle to biological weapons acquisition on a small scale is carrying to completion the multi-stage effort required to succeed at all three tasks, combining a deadly biological agent with an effective dissemination device. Within this general constraint, the equipment and expertise needed to build biological weapons would vary greatly depending on the desired characteristics of the weapon.[26] Certain approaches to biological warfare, such as creating entirely new pathogens through genetic engineering, lie at or beyond the limits of current biological knowledge. Other effective approaches, however, use well-known and easily acquired agents, and require only common, dual-use production equipment and simple delivery systems.

We make six key points about the technical aspects of biological weapons acquisition. First, the pathogenic biological agents most suitable for weapons applications are identified in widely published sources, and the technical information on how to produce them in bulk is available in the scientific literature. Second, the seed stocks for many biological warfare agents can be obtained from a range of sources. Third, the equipment and supplies needed to produce biological warfare agent in bulk have legitimate commercial applications and can be procured with little difficulty. Fourth, preparing an agent for effective aerosol dissemination, and manufacturing an appropriate sprayer system, poses a significant technical hurdle to biological weapons acquisition, but it is one that can be overcome if the proliferator is willing to adopt a less efficient dissemination technique based on liquid slurries, rather than the more efficient dry powders. Fifth, clandestine biological weapons acquisition has few externally observable indicators to arouse the suspicions of law enforcement agencies, although some procurement options would create a trail for post-attack investigators to follow. Sixth, even with an inefficient agent dissemination system, a single biological weapon could produce thousands or tens of thousands of casualties in a densely populated target; a more efficient dissemination technique, or attacks involving larger amounts of agent, could cause hundreds of thousands of casualties.

---

26. For example, some characteristics desirable in military biological weapons are difficult to achieve even with well-known agents, as explained in Box 6, Terrorist vs. Military Weapons, p. 100. OTA, *Technologies Underlying Weapons of Mass Destruction*, pp. 82–97.

INFORMATION ON SELECTION AND PRODUCTION OF AGENTS IS READILY
AVAILABLE

Agent selection depends on a number of variables, four of which — the kind
of organism affected, the effects on the victims, the requirements of agent
cultivation, and the requirements of agent delivery — determine the main
outlines of a biological weapons effort. An attacker can choose an agent to
affect humans, animals, or plants, though attacks on humans are the
primary concern of the present study.[27] Agents can be chosen to sicken,
incapacitate, or kill; to spread from person to person or to affect only those
initially exposed; and to be susceptible or resistant to medical treatment.[28]
Biological warfare agents also vary in how difficult they are to cultivate and
to disseminate.

The literature on biological weapons contains extensive discussions of
the advantages and disadvantages of the various pathogens and toxins that
have been considered as biological warfare agents. This literature includes
assessments of the difficulty of cultivating specific agents, the problems and
methods of aerosolization, the expected agent lethality in humans, and the
history of past research and development by states. Thus it provides
enough guidance on agent selection that any state or group with research
skills and access to a good library could select a biological warfare agent
without any laboratory work at all. Production methods are widely
published in the scientific literature, and are not difficult to master for some
bacteria and toxins that are among the most effective biological warfare
agents. Library research would yield a sound book-knowledge of agent
production, guiding later laboratory work in the right direction.

---

27. The choice is essentially between weapons aimed at military forces or civilians
and those aimed at economic targets such as cattle or cereal crops. This study
focuses on the risk of attacks causing substantial human casualties. Covert attacks
aimed purely at causing economic damage, while potentially important, are less
likely to shape the strategic environment or sharply limit U.S. foreign policy
options.

28. For discussions of the effects of various representative biological warfare
agents, see SIPRI, *The Problem of Chemical and Biological Warfare*, Vol. II: *CB Weapons
Today*, pp. 59–71; and David R. Franz et al., "Clinical Recognition and Management
of Patients Exposed to Biological Warfare Agents," *Journal of the American Medical
Association (JAMA)*, Vol. 278, No. 5 (August 6, 1997), pp. 399–411.

AGENT SEED STOCKS ARE ACCESSIBLE

Technically and operationally competent attackers could acquire an appropriate seed stock for agent production with little risk of detection, although doing so might require some time and effort. The seed stocks needed to produce biological warfare agents can be obtained from commercial suppliers, stolen, or extracted from natural sources. The scientific and medical communities have a legitimate need for active samples of many different types of biological agents, including those with weapons applications, and this need is met by a variety of biological supply services. In the United States, the principal supplier of biological agent seed stocks is the American Type Culture Collection (ATCC), a private organization in Rockville, Maryland, that maintains a vast library of microbial cultures for scientific use.[29] At least until recently, it has been extremely easy for states and individuals to obtain seed stocks from the ATCC. During the 1980s, for example, orders from Iraq for candidate biological warfare agents were filled by the ATCC, with U.S. government acquiescence.[30] In 1995, Larry Wayne Harris, a white supremacist in Ohio, ordered and obtained plague bacteria from the ATCC by mail (see Box 2, Larry Wayne Harris Case, p. 40).

U.S. export controls have since been tightened, and the Australia Group agreed in 1990 to impose export restrictions on pathogens and toxins.[31] On the domestic front, the Harris case helped prompt new regulations restricting the transfer of certain organisms and toxins, requiring all users of relevant pathogens and toxins in the United States to register with the Department of Health and Human Services, requiring recipients of cultures to give their registration number with each order, and requiring record-

29.   Descriptive information on the ATCC, as well as its online catalogue, can be found at the ATCC website, <www.atcc.org>. The website also points out that permits are required for domestic and international orders of certain pathogens.

30.   See "Senator Says U.S. Let Iraq Get Lethal Viruses," *New York Times*, February 10, 1994, p. A9; and "New Look Urged on Gulf Syndrome," *New York Times*, December 10, 1996, p. A1. The first story and its title are slightly inaccurate, referring to anthrax incorrectly as a virus (it is bacteria).

31.   The Australia Group reached agreement on lists of controlled items during 1992. Smithson, *Separating Fact from Fiction*, p. 16. The Australia Group control list of agents and dual-use equipment appears at ibid., pp. 44–51.

keeping for all transfers.[32] These reforms have made the process of obtaining agent seed cultures from U.S. suppliers less easy than it has been in the past, and have heightened supplier sensitivity to this important indicator of a clandestine biological weapons program. Seed cultures can, however, still be obtained commercially if a plausible front company can be established, or from suppliers in other countries. For example, the former Soviet republics, several of which have large scientific research communities, have very lax controls over weapons-related exports, including biological exports.[33] Nevertheless, because of growing international sensitivity to biological threats, cross-border requests for pathogenic strains might risk supplier suspicion.

If purchasing biological seed stocks from a commercial supplier is too difficult or too risky, the appropriate agents can also be stolen from legitimate users. Some laboratories and firms maintain seed cultures, sometimes including organisms with weapons applications. The U.S. government does not regulate how individual laboratories and companies must secure and account for the biological warfare agents in their possession, in contrast to its strict control of nuclear weapons materials.[34] The security of these widely dispersed seed cultures is highly variable. A laboratory employee at a facility that works with pathogens could probably steal a seed culture. Only a minute sample is required to produce vast

---

32. See "CDC Urges Rule to Track Killer Germs: Terrorism Fears Spark Shipping Crackdown," *Atlanta Journal and Constitution*, June 19, 1996, p. A5. For an overview of the new regulations, and of legislation aimed at preventing biological terrorism, see James R. Ferguson, "Biological Weapons and U.S. Law," *JAMA*, Vol. 278, No. 5 (August 6, 1997), pp. 359–360. For the regulations themselves, see "Additional requirements for facilities transferring or receiving select agents: Final rule," *Federal Register*, Vol. 61, No. 207 (October 24, 1996), p. 55190.

33. For an overview of developments in the export control systems of the Soviet successor states, see Gary Bertsch, ed., *Restraining the Spread of the Soviet Arsenal: NIS Nonproliferation Export Controls* (Athens, Ga.: Center for International Trade and Security, University of Georgia, 1996); and Rustam Safaraliev, "Russia's Export Controls, Current Status and Future Tasks," *The Monitor*, Vol. 3, No. 1 (Winter 1997), pp. 1, 7–9.

34. The new CDC regulations, Code of Federal Regulations, Vol. 42, Part 72, do require laboratory safety and containment measures proportionate to the public health danger of an accidental release. These are distinct from security measures against theft, and the CDC explicitly declined to provide more than very general guidance on laboratory security measures.

quantities of agent, making it possible that the theft would never be noticed. While an inside job could be easy, it might be hard for an outside group to find out what company or laboratory to target, making this route less likely for groups without insiders.

Finally, many bacterial agents are endemic to large parts of the world, among them those that cause anthrax, tularemia, and brucellosis, and the bacterium that produces botulinum toxin. If a natural reservoir can be located, the organism can be cultured from nature. This process could be slow, and would be particularly difficult for groups at the lower end of the range of technical capability, but would minimize the externally observable indicators of this stage of a clandestine program. Finding an outbreak of the disease could provide a shortcut, since a tissue sample from a sick or dead animal would provide an abundant culture of a virulent strain.[35] Different natural strains of a given organism can also vary widely in their ability to withstand the stresses of dissemination and in their virulence. The need to experiment with the agent, and perhaps to seek alternate strains, would add costs and delays to a biological weapons program that used seed cultures derived from nature. Ricin, the toxin that is involved in most known non-state biological weapons incidents, comes from the seeds of the castor bean plant, a common garden shrub.[36] The seeds are available not only in nature, but by mail order from garden catalogues.

PRODUCTION EQUIPMENT AND SUPPLIES HAVE COMMON, LEGITIMATE USES
Equipment and supplies for culturing bacteria and for extracting toxins are common, with a wide range of legitimate applications in biotechnology, the food industry, and medicine. Modern biotechnology has made available high-performance culture equipment capable of efficiently producing large amounts of biological products under controlled conditions.[37] Small-scale

---

35. In 1997, for example, there was an outbreak of anthrax among cattle in Tatura, Australia. See "Lethal Spores Wake Down Under," *Financial Times*, March 15–16, 1997, p. 4.

36. Most known cases of activities involving ricin are food-borne poisoning attempts or other small-scale efforts aimed at poisoning individuals. Since they are not large-scale attacks, they do not qualify as biological weapons events by the standards of the present study. The easy availability of the seeds probably explains the frequency of these occurrences, but they are no more serious for the purposes of this study than poisonings involving cyanide.

37. See Tucker, "Chemical/Biological Terrorism," p. 174.

production of bacteria could also be conducted with more primitive types of equipment,[38] including, for example, microbrewery fermenters, although with more difficulty and less efficiency. Culture medium is also widely available, and can be improvised from common food products by a competent microbiologist, also at some cost in efficiency. Equipment for measuring key process parameters such as temperature, acidity, and oxygen content is widely available.

Producing bacterial pathogens or toxins would require competence in microbiology laboratory technique, a good understanding of the published information on the bacterium under cultivation, and persistence and experimentation to overcome process problems. Extracting or concentrating bacterial toxins would require further knowledge, but would not be as difficult as growing the bacteria in the first place, provided only improvised agent preparations were desired. Producing ricin, a plant toxin, is not difficult: it requires farming the castor bean plant, harvesting and crushing the seeds, and extracting the toxin with solvents. Producing viral agents, while possible for some states and particularly capable non-state actors, is substantially more difficult than producing bacterial agents and toxins, and is thus unlikely to be attempted in a program intended only to produce an improvised weapon of mass destruction.[39]

Personnel producing certain very deadly agents, including anthrax and some toxins, would face minimal health risks, provided they were careful to observe good laboratory technique and some simple protective practices.[40] The containment and personnel protection measures now required in the United States for work with highly infectious pathogens are

---

38. Testimony of Edward M. Eitzen, U.S. Army Medical Research Institute of Infectious Diseases, in *Global Proliferation of Weapons of Mass Destruction*, Part I, p. 118; and authors' discussions with biotechnology industry consultants with experience in vaccine production.

39. OTA, *Technologies Underlying Weapons of Mass Destruction*, p. 88.

40. "A developing country seeking to develop biological weapons would probably use much less elaborate containment measures. During World War II, for example, the Japanese Army's Unit 731 produced vast quantities of highly infectious agents, yet the workers were protected only by wearing rubberized suits, masks, surgical gloves, and rubber boots, and by receiving vaccinations against the agents they were working with." OTA, *Technologies Underlying Weapons of Mass Destruction*, p. 92. Many of the agents in question were far more infectious than anthrax.

sophisticated and somewhat expensive.[41] But certain biological warfare agents, such as anthrax, are not particularly infectious except by the aerosol route, and working with them does not require unusual equipment.[42] Toxins, provided they are not ingested, injected, or inhaled, remain harmless.[43] Gloves, filter masks, hoods, good ventilation, sound laboratory technique, and regular decontamination, perhaps supplemented with antibiotic prophylaxis or vaccination, would be adequate. Risks would rise sharply if agents were aerosolized and tested, or if agents were dried and milled into powders.

DELIVERY DEVICES CAN BE DEVELOPED WITH SOME DIFFICULTY
A variety of effective biological weapons delivery options exist, including some simple but effective means within the reach of non-state actors. The efficiency and capacity of the dispersal device will largely determine a weapon's area of effect, and thus its effectiveness against a given target. Efficient, large-scale dissemination may elude less technically sophisticated

---

41. For descriptions of the equipment and practices recommended in the United States for handling dangerous microorganisms, see Centers for Disease Control and National Institutes of Health, *Biosafety in Microbiological and Biomedical Laboratories*, 3rd. ed. (Washington, D.C.: U.S. GPO, 1993); also available on the World Wide Web at <www.cdc.gov/od/ohs/biosfty/bmbl/bmbl-1.htm>.

42. The CDC's recommendations on anthrax state: "Biosafety Level 3 practices, containment equipment and facilities are recommended for work involving production volumes or concentrations of cultures, and for activities which have a high potential for aerosol production. In these facilities immunization is recommended for all persons working with the agent, all persons working in the same laboratory room where the cultures are handled, and persons working with infected animals." See <www.cdc.gov/od/ohs/biosfty/bmbl/sect7c.htm#Bac>. Level 3 practices include the use of biosafety cabinets (air-handling devices analogous to chemistry laboratory fume hoods), practices designed to minimize contamination and aerosol production, and vaccination of personnel. These standards are intended to eliminate laboratory infections, and while a proliferator could meet most of them with affordable equipment, moderate shortfalls would produce only limited risks. Immunization with the FDA-approved vaccine would presumably be desirable, and the vaccine is available through CDC, but requesting it would draw attention to the fact that the personnel were working with anthrax.

43. The major exceptions are certain trichothecene mycotoxins, which can be absorbed through the skin. OTA, *Technologies Underlying Weapons of Mass Destruction*, p. 81.

proliferators, but even at low efficiency levels, attacks against indoor targets could be quite deadly.

The key to effective large-scale use of biological weapons is aerosol delivery.[44] A variety of other methods of dissemination are possible, including via food or water, direct injection, animal or insect vectors, and human-to-human contagion. All but the last of these delivery techniques are difficult to use for mass-destruction attacks, since they generally affect only small numbers of victims, require extremely large quantities of agent to overcome dilution effects, or are impaired by normal hygiene measures.[45] Contaminating a city's water supply is a frequently discussed scenario, but large dilution factors, the normal breakdown of agents in water, and the effects of chlorination make such attacks more demanding than they might appear, and constrain their size.[46] A handful of contagious agents could conceivably be released to cause epidemics, but the spread of a contagious disease depends on a number of variables beyond the control of an attacker, making that sort of attack both unreliable and uncontrollable.[47] Most military biological warfare programs have avoided highly contagious

---

44. "If bacteriological (biological) warfare ever occurred, the aerosol technique would thus be the one most likely to be used, simply because the respiratory tract is normally susceptible to infection by many microorganisms, because of the wide target area which could be covered in a single attack and because ordinary hygienic measures are ineffective in preventing the airborne route of attack." United Nations, *Chemical and Bacteriological (Biological) Weapons and the Effects of Their Possible Use*, p. 34.

45. There have been a few cases of food-borne pathogen attacks that affected tens or hundreds of people. The largest known was carried out by members of a cult based in Oregon, who contaminated salad bars in several restaurants with *Salmonella* bacteria, apparently in a dry run for a planned effort to win an election by making local voters too ill on election day to vote. See Thomas A. Török, Robert V. Tauxe, Robert P. Wise, et al., "A Large Community Outbreak of Salmonellosis Caused by Intentional Contamination of Restaurant Salad Bars," *JAMA*, Vol. 278, No. 5 (August 6, 1997), pp. 389–395.

46. See the discussion in World Health Organization, *Health Aspects of Chemical and Biological Weapons* (Geneva: World Health Organization, 1970), pp. 113–120.

47. It remains true that "biological weapons using agents that are highly contagious ... may pose a global threat greater than that posed by large-scale nuclear war." Karl Lowe, Graham Pearson, and Victor Utgoff, *Potential Values of a Simple BW Protective Mask* (Washington, D.C.: Institute for Defense Analyses, September 1995), p. 3.

pathogens, partly for these reasons, and partly to avoid the risk of an epidemic that might spread to friendly troops or populations.[48]

Aerosol delivery makes it possible to overcome many of these problems. An aerosol is a cloud of droplets or particles suspended in the air: smoke and fog are familiar examples. Effective aerosol dissemination of a biological agent requires spraying or otherwise producing agent particles of 1 to 5 micron size, easy to inhale deep into the lungs and small enough to remain suspended in the air.[49] This allows efficient, wide-area dissemination of infectious or toxic concentrations of agent particles, necessary for small biological weapons to be highly destructive. Lethal doses of toxins and infectious doses of pathogens are in some cases substantially lower when the agent is inhaled rather than ingested.[50] The aerosol transmission route, because it creates lung infections of organisms that normally enter the body by other routes, sometimes produces extremely severe symptoms even with pathogens that are not usually fatal in humans.

States and technically sophisticated non-state actors could develop or acquire aerosolization devices suitable for covert biological attacks. A simple aerosol generator could be built from scratch by an engineer familiar with the extensive published literature on aerosols. Buying an industrial or agricultural sprayer is an alternative, though most off-the-shelf aerosol generators would not generate effective biological aerosols, and most that do have very low output rates. Agricultural aerosol generators, for example, generate large particles intended to settle out of the air and onto crops. While they might be used with anti-crop agents or to cause panic, they would produce little respirable agent and cause little risk to people, unless

---

48. OTA, *Technologies Underlying Weapons of Mass Destruction*, p. 77. Notable exceptions are Japan's biological weapons program in World War II (see Box 4, Japan's Unit 731, p. 76), and the Soviet biological weapons program, which reportedly developed smallpox weapons (see Box 3, Soviet BW Program, p. 68).

49. OTA, *Technologies Underlying Weapons of Mass Destruction*, p. 96; David R. Franz, "Physical and Medical Countermeasures to Biological Weapons," in Kathleen C. Bailey, ed., *Director's Series on Proliferation*, No. 4 (Livermore, Calif.: Lawrence Livermore National Laboratory, 1994), pp. 55–65; or see the extensive literature on aerobiology, e.g., Bruce O. Stuart, "Deposition of Inhaled Aerosols," *Archives of Internal Medicine*, Vol. 131 (January, 1973), pp. 60–73. A micron is a millionth of a meter, or about 40 millionths of an inch.

50. Tularemia is one example. SIPRI, *The Problem of Chemical and Biological Warfare*, Vol. II: *CB Weapons Today*, p. 65. Ricin, saxitoxin, and T-2 mycotoxin are others. Jonathan B. Tucker, "Chemical/Biological Terrorism," pp. 55, 59.

specially modified or used with carefully tuned agent preparations. Medical aerosol generators specially designed to create respirable aerosols generally have very small outputs, appropriate for use in single-patient inhalation treatment, and would have little utility as weapons. To be sure of high output rates and adequate efficiency, a would-be attacker would have to build or modify a device and test its output. Commercially available aerosol measurement equipment makes this problem considerably easier, however.

Highly advanced techniques are probably beyond the reach of most non-state actors, but are not necessary for effective attacks.[51] Dry agent powders are among the advanced technologies most useful for biological warfare. High-quality powder preparations can be aerosolized with very high efficiency with simple equipment, and can improve agent stability, but they require sophisticated techniques to prepare. Technologies such as microencapsulation, in which small particles of a pathogen or toxin are covered with a chemical coating to protect them from exposure to the environment, make aerosol delivery possible for a wider range of agents. Careful engineering of liquid agents and specialized sprayers makes efficient aerosolization of liquid agent slurries possible as well. Large-scale biological aerosol attacks are much more likely to be effective with high-performance technologies such as these, which can efficiently produce large, stable clouds of respirable aerosol.

Outdoor aerosol delivery of biological weapons is acutely sensitive to weather conditions, the quality of the dispersal system, and the characteris-

---

51. "It would be technically difficult for a terrorist group to produce a dry biological agent in the right particle size for inhalation.... It is possible, however, that some groups have this level of expertise or could obtain support from a country which has an offensive BW program." Senate testimony of Edward M. Eitzen, *Global Proliferation of Weapons of Mass Destruction*, Part I, p. 118. See also discussions in World Health Organization, *Health Aspects of Chemical and Biological Weapons*, pp. 93–94; United Nations, *Chemical and Bacteriological (Biological) Weapons and the Effects of Their Possible Use*, pp. 115–117; and OTA, *Technologies Underlying Weapons of Mass Destruction*, pp. 93–97. The difficulty of building militarily useful biological weapons capable of disseminating the large quantities of agent required for large outdoor attacks — i.e., achieving a lethal or infectious dose of agent over an area measured in square kilometers — can be seen from the limited capabilities of Iraq's biological weapons. Iraq sought biological weapons over a period of at least six years, but inspections by UN teams in the years since the Gulf War suggest that the program yielded only limited capabilities for effective use. See Raymond A. Zilinskas, "Iraq's Biological Weapons: The Past as Future?" *JAMA*, Vol. 278, No. 5 (August 6, 1997), pp. 418–424.

tics of the agent used. The characteristics of the particular bacterial strain, its growth conditions, the age of the culture, and the methods of preparing and preserving the agent before dissemination can strongly affect its ability to survive spraying and cause disease. Mechanical stresses and exposure to air, humidity, and ultraviolet light rapidly kill many microorganisms, making aerosol dissemination of all but a few hardy species technologically challenging.[52] Atmospheric mixing can quickly dilute an aerosol to concentrations so low as to be harmless. Variation in any or all of these factors can easily degrade the effectiveness of an attack by factors of thousands to millions, making the difference between an unnoticed failure and a sudden plague that wipes out most of a city.[53] Indoor delivery of biological weapons would be less affected by the vagaries of weather, and the dilution rates in buildings are more predictable and generally lower than outdoor rates. Furthermore, the exposure time of people in a building is likely to be longer than exposure to a passing cloud. As a result, weapons with low respirable-aerosol output may nevertheless be effective against indoor targets.

BIOLOGICAL WEAPONS PROGRAMS LACK STRONG EXTERNALLY OBSERVABLE INDICATORS

The attempted acquisition of simple biological weapons by a competent non-state actor is unlikely to be detected by law enforcement agencies in advance of an attack. A terrorist effort focused on bacterial agents that are easy to produce and disseminate, acquiring seed stocks from natural sources, and using only common, dual-use equipment and supplies, should attract no outside attention, whether from suppliers or curious neighbors. A basement laboratory and machine shop could handle the work needed to learn and test production processes, as well as the fabrication and testing (using only simulated agents) of aerosol generators. Weapons development would take time, probably at least months for a small program, even with very competent scientists. Once the processes had been mastered, however, agent production and weapon filling for bacterial weapons would take only

---

52. See OTA, *Technologies Underlying Weapons of Mass Destruction*, pp. 93–94 and 95–97; SIPRI, *The Problem of Chemical and Biological Warfare*, Vol. II: *CB Weapons Today* (New York: Humanities Press, 1973), pp. 64–65 and 67–68.

53. See Box 1, Aum Shinrikyo, p. 19, for a description of Aum Shinrikyo's biological weapons dissemination failures, which apparently included three attacks in Tokyo, each of which failed to produce casualties.

days for moderate quantities of an immediate-use agent in crude liquid form.

Biological weapons fabrication, carried out on the small scale needed for covert attacks, has few distinctive indicators likely to be detectable from outside the facility. Fermentation odors are one, though these could be covered by distance or by pretexts such as beer brewing. Waste water or solid wastes from the facility would carry biochemical signatures that could identify the agents being produced, but only if someone had reason to sample and analyze them. Any agent aerosols accidentally generated in the production facility might be detected outside, but only if infections resulted, if air samples were taken when the release occurred, or if soil samples could detect agent that had settled out of the air. Electricity consumption would be moderate. Water consumption during production and clean-up might be higher than normal for a household or business, but no more than it might be for other reasons, such as refilling a swimming pool or running a photographic darkroom.

Plant toxin production would look rather different, but would be equally hard to detect. The main candidate plant toxin, ricin, is an extract of castor beans. Castor beans are farmed in many countries, and are commonly grown as ornamental shrubs, but producing enough ricin for a biological aerosol weapon would require too many plants to fit in a suburban yard. Given room to farm the plant, however, or with beans bought or stolen in large quantities, extracting the toxin would require limited space and equipment, and would be unlikely to attract attention.

The infection or poisoning of people or animals by accidental aerosol releases could reveal the presence of a weapons effort. If aerosol testing of the actual agent was avoided, however, the risk of outside infection would be very low for many agents.[54] The risk of accidental infection of production workers is difficult to assess, and would depend heavily on the agent in use, the competence of the personnel, and the equipment available. At least for anthrax, however, a combination of relatively simple measures, including containment, sterilization, protective equipment, and antibiotic prophylaxis, would reduce the risk to a sufficiently low level that a small weapons program conducted by competent personnel would probably experience no accidental infections. Many people who might be interested in mass

---

54. It is worth noting that accidental releases from aerosol testing are possible even from more sophisticated facilities, as in the case of the accidental release of *Bacillus anthracis* aerosol at Sverdlovsk in the Soviet Union. See Box 3, Soviet BW Program, p. 68.

destruction weapons are not trained in laboratory techniques, however. For these reasons, health authorities should treat the diagnosis of anyone with a disease associated with biological warfare as possible evidence of a biological weapons program, either as a part of the program or as a victim of an early test or accident, and public health systems should add biological warfare illnesses to their list of diseases that physicians are required to report.[55]

Only weapon testing would require producing agent aerosols in advance of an attack. Because of the risk of exposing the personnel involved, such testing would be extremely dangerous. Indoor testing can be carried out using closed test chambers, but the facilities would have to be relatively elaborate and equipped to filter and sterilize air, and there would be a heightened risk of accidental agent release and worker infections. An unsophisticated proliferator could probably carry out effective open-air tests in an isolated area, where the agent cloud would have space to dissipate before reaching unintended victims. Human and animal epidemiological monitoring would increase the chances of detecting such a test.[56] Weapon testing might be avoided altogether by testing the dispersal device with a non-pathogenic simulated agent to ensure that it would produce a respirable aerosol. A non-state actor willing to treat its first attack as a weapon test, at the risk of affecting far fewer or far more victims than planned, might simply use a rugged agent and a proven sprayer design, and bypass even simulant testing. However, an attacker wishing to kill large numbers of people reliably — a state targeting U.S. troops marshaling for transport overseas, for example — might reasonably believe there would be only one opportunity, making prior weapons testing indispensable.

Law enforcement awareness of possible indicators of biological weapons acquisition would increase the likelihood of early detection of a program, especially if the people involved were already under suspicion and observation. These indicators include purchasing growth media or aerosolization equipment, collecting soil or animal tissue samples in areas of endemic disease or disease outbreaks, and acquiring brewing equipment, microscopes, glassware and laboratory supplies, sterilizing agents, and filter masks. Heightened awareness in industry and academia of unusual

55. See National Science and Technology Council, *Global Microbial Threats in the 1990s* (Washington, D.C.: The White House, 1996), p. 2.

56. See Chapter 5 for further discussion of the potential value of epidemiological surveillance in detecting biological weapons acquisition and attacks.

requests for equipment, microbial cultures, or information related to biological warfare organisms will also improve the chances of early detection, but only if suspicions are reported to law enforcement agencies, and only if those agencies know how to use the information.

Nuclear Weapons: With Fissile Material, Many States and a Few Non-state Actors

Nuclear weapons require fissile material: highly enriched uranium or plutonium.[57] Once an adequate supply of fissile material is at hand, the technical difficulty of assembling a nuclear weapon varies greatly with the weapon design and the type and purity of fissile material available: it ranges from the extremely sophisticated to the merely difficult. Only highly enriched uranium (HEU) allows a simple gun-type weapon design to be used. Most states and some exceptionally capable non-state actors could build an immensely destructive gun-type nuclear weapon in as little as several months,[58] at a cost of a few hundred thousand dollars, if they could acquire an adequate quantity of highly enriched uranium. If plutonium were the only available fissile material, or the builders wanted to use available HEU as efficiently as possible, an implosion design would be required.[59] An implosion weapon is harder to build, but is no more

---

57. See Box 7, Fission Weapon Design, p. 160, for a summary of the principles of fission explosives.

58. This time estimate is for a covert weapon project as a whole, not the time required to construct the weapon itself. The time to assemble a weapon could be reduced to as little as a few days, and perhaps lower in some cases, but only if detailed preparations had been made in advance, if all parts of the process had been tested thoroughly, and if no unexpected problems were encountered. See J. Carson Mark, Theodore Taylor, Eugene Eyster, et al., "Can Terrorists Build Nuclear Weapons?" in Paul Leventhal and Yonah Alexander, eds., *Preventing Nuclear Terrorism* (Lexington, Mass.: Lexington Books, 1987), pp. 59–60.

59. A 1977 OTA study argues that given an adequate supply of fissile material and "a fraction of a million dollars," a small group of people "could possibly design and build a crude nuclear explosive device" on the basis of published information. Such a group "would probably not be able to develop an accurate prediction of the yield of their device." Nevertheless, low-technology devices made from weapons-grade materials can achieve yields in the range of 10 to 20 kilotons. OTA, *Nuclear Proliferation and Safeguards*, pp. 140–142. For an argument that non-state actors could build nuclear weapons from HEU or plutonium metal, or even uranium or

destructive. First-generation weapons of either type would almost certainly be large and difficult to transport, but could be delivered by boat or truck. The likely yields of these first-generation weapons would be on the order of 10 kilotons, but errors in design or construction could reduce or eliminate the yield.[60] Crude implosion weapons made from HEU and plutonium oxides are also conceivable, but yields would be hard to predict in advance.[61] Fewer states could produce their own HEU or plutonium, a process that requires expensive, specialized facilities. Fissile material production is also subject to international monitoring, and is likely to be detected. It is extremely unlikely that any non-state actor will be able to produce fissile material on its own in the near future.

We make five key points about the technical possibility of clandestine nuclear weapons acquisition. First, all of the scientific information necessary to design a simple nuclear weapon is publicly available. Second, the increased possibility of stealing fissile material, or acquiring it from smugglers, has lowered the most significant technical barrier to nuclear weapons acquisition. Third, with a sufficient quantity of pure HEU in metallic form, nuclear weapons design and construction requires only limited resources, equipment, and expertise, and could be accomplished by many states and a few exceptionally capable non-state actors. Fourth, although building nuclear weapons with plutonium and non-metallic or impure HEU would present greater technical challenges, it could be accomplished by many states, and would be possible for some non-state actors. Finally, although an active effort to obtain fissile material exposes

---

plutonium oxides, see Mark, Taylor, Eyster, et al., "Can Terrorists Build Nuclear Weapons?" pp. 55–65. See also Mason Willrich and Theodore B. Taylor, *Nuclear Theft: Risks and Safeguards* (Cambridge, Mass.: Ballinger, 1974), or the excerpt from it reproduced as "Nuclear Theft: Risks and Safeguards," in Augustus R. Norton and Martin H. Greenberg, eds., *Studies in Nuclear Terrorism* (Boston: G.K. Hall, 1977), pp. 59–84, arguing that weapons with yields of at least 100 tons (.1 kT) can conceivably be built in as little as a few weeks by a few people or even a single person, even with plutonium or HEU oxide. Taylor later retreated slightly from elements of this assessment in "Can Terrorists Build Nuclear Weapons?"

60. Mark, Taylor, Eyster, et al., "Can Terrorists Build Nuclear Weapons?" p. 61. A very low-technology weapon, or one that was not well designed and well built, would face a higher risk of producing only a nuclear "fizzle" (see Box 7, Fission Weapon Design, p. 160), either by failing to achieve high criticality, or by fissioning prematurely.

61. Mark, Taylor, Eyster, et al., "Can Terrorists Build Nuclear Weapons?" p. 61.

nuclear aspirants to considerable risk of detection by law enforcement and intelligence agencies, the clandestine fabrication of a nuclear weapon has few distinctive, easily observable indicators. We discuss these five points next.

NUCLEAR WEAPONS DESIGNS CAN BE DEVELOPED FROM PUBLISHED DATA

A handful of skilled personnel could successfully design a simple nuclear weapon using publicly available information. Nuclear weapons designs are not, however, available on the Internet. What one finds on the Internet are rough sketches illustrating basic design concepts.[62] These concepts have been publicly available for years, but considerably more is required to build a nuclear weapon.[63] The designers of an improvised nuclear weapon would need to determine the criticality characteristics of the fissile material they intended to use in the weapon, which govern how much material would need to be assembled how fast to produce a nuclear explosion. The designers would also need to know the performance characteristics of the explosives, propellants, and firing circuitry used to assemble the fissile material. Raw data on the behavior of nuclear weapons materials is available in numerous published sources. Indeed, the scientific data required to understand and model nuclear reactions is now available at a level of detail far beyond that available to the Manhattan Project scientists in 1945. The physics of nuclear interactions is well described in the literature, but the calculations would need to be performed by someone with some advanced training.[64] The criticality calculations could be carried

---

62. Two examples are "Todd's Atomic Homepage," at <neutrino.nuc.berkeley.edu/neutronics/todd/nuc.bomb.html>; and "Nuclear Weapons Frequently Asked Questions," at <www.milnet.com/milnet/nukeweap/nfaq0.htm>.

63. "Schematic drawings of fission explosive devices of the earliest types showing in a qualitative way the principles used in achieving the first fission explosions are widely available. However, the detailed design drawings and specifications that are essential before it is possible to plan the fabrication of actual parts are not available. The preparation of these drawings requires a large number of man-hours and the direct participation of individuals thoroughly informed in several quite distinct areas." Mark, Taylor, Eyster, et al., "Can Terrorists Build Nuclear Weapons?" p. 58.

64. For example, extensive information on criticality calculations for reactor design is given in Yigal Ronen, ed., CRC Handbook of Nuclear Reactor Calculations (Boca Raton, Fla.: CRC Press, 1986), 3 volumes. The same principles and data can be applied to weapons design. Writing an accurate computer simulation program would require considerable effort. A full simulation of a bomb's nuclear reactions

out by a talented person with as little as a good undergraduate education in physics or nuclear engineering. Today's powerful personal computers would further simplify the nuclear modeling problem. Designing the triggering and assembly mechanisms would require good mechanical and possibly electrical engineering skills. In sum, developing a viable nuclear weapons design is a serious technical problem, but one that can be solved by a state or non-state actor that possesses, or can recruit or hire, a handful of intelligent scientists and engineers.[65]

INSECURE FISSILE MATERIAL LOWERS THE MOST IMPORTANT BARRIER
Fissile material needs to be carefully guarded, in recognition of the acute proliferation risk it presents. This is especially true of materials such as metallic HEU and plutonium, which require no chemical processing to be used in weapons.[66] Unfortunately, security measures against theft of weapons material, and even of test devices, have not always been adequate, even in the United States.[67] Nevertheless, weapons-usable material has

---

and explosion dynamics would be out of reach for most non-state actors, making weapon yield hard to predict. Non-state actors could develop adequate criticality-modeling programs, however, leaving out the explosion dynamics and thus sacrificing any hope of accurate yield prediction. As with reactor design, uncertainties in key nuclear constants would make subcritical nuclear experiments desirable. These could be used to confirm the results of the simulation, and to prevent accidental criticality when assembling the first weapon.

65. Aum Shinrikyo provides an interesting example of the problems encountered by a group that recruited several well-educated but apparently not highly competent scientists. See Box 1, Aum Shinrikyo, p. 19.

66. Other materials could serve as sources of fissile material for weapons, but using them poses additional problems. Spent fuel from nuclear power reactors, for example, contains plutonium. Extracting and purifying the plutonium to use in a bomb, however, requires dissolving the fuel in acid and chemically extracting the plutonium, a complex process that is made even harder and more dangerous by the high radiation levels involved.

67. See *Nuclear Weapons Facilities: Adequacy of Safeguards and Security at Department of Energy Nuclear Weapons Production Facilities*, Hearings before the House Committee on Energy and Commerce, H. Hrg. 99-143, 99th Cong., 2nd Sess. (Washington, D.C.: U.S. GPO, 1986); John McPhee, *The Curve of Binding Energy* (New York: Farrar, Strauss, Giroux, 1974); and Willrich and Taylor, *Nuclear Theft*. Congress acted again in November 1997 to address concerns about nuclear security at DOE facilities. See Peter Eisler, "Unit to Probe Nuke Safety Is Approved: Action

generally been difficult to steal. This obstacle, combined with the cost and difficulty of producing weapons material, has been an effective barrier to nuclear weapons acquisition for all but the most advanced or determined states.[68] However, this old constraint on improvised nuclear weapons acquisition has been seriously eroded by the collapse of the Soviet Union.[69]

The Soviet system for controlling fissile materials has been severely degraded by the deep social, political, and economic transformations underway in the former Soviet Union, a fact of enormous significance to the global problem of preventing nuclear proliferation. The Soviet Union produced vast quantities of fissile material for its nuclear weapons, reactor, and research programs. It is estimated, for instance, that the Russian inventory stood at over one million kilograms of HEU in 1994.[70] This is enough for some twenty thousand nuclear weapons, even using an

---

Follows Revelation of Lapses at Arms Facilities," *USA Today*, November 7, 1997, p. 5A.

68. For an overview of fissile material production processes, see David Albright, Frans Berkhout, and William Walker, *Plutonium and Highly Enriched Uranium 1996: World Inventories, Capabilities, and Policies* (New York: Oxford University Press, 1997), pp. 12–25; or Leonard S. Spector, *Nuclear Ambitions: The Spread of Nuclear Weapons, 1989–1990* (Boulder, Colo.: Westview, 1990), pp. 417–420.

69. This argument is developed at length in Graham T. Allison, Owen R. Coté, Jr., Richard A. Falkenrath, and Steven E. Miller, *Avoiding Nuclear Anarchy: Containing the Threat of Loose Russian Nuclear Weapons and Fissile Material*, CSIA Studies in International Security (Cambridge, Mass.: MIT Press, 1996). The theft and sale of operational nuclear weapons from Russian stockpiles could provide an even quicker, more certain, and less detectable route to nuclear status, provided the buyer is able to overcome any security devices built into the weapon to prevent its detonation. For a journalistic account of U.S. efforts to improve the security of Russian nuclear weapons, see Andrew Cockburn and Leslie Cockburn, *One Point Safe* (New York: Anchor, 1997). At times there has also been cause for concern over the security of nuclear weapons and weapons-usable materials at U.S. facilities at home and abroad. See Thomas D. Davies, "What Nuclear Means and Targets Might Terrorists Find Attractive?" in Leventhal and Alexander, eds., *Preventing Nuclear Terrorism*, pp. 54–67.

70. Albright, Berkhout, and Walker, *Plutonium and Highly Enriched Uranium 1996*, pp. 399–400.

inefficient, gun-type design.[71] Much of the fissile material in the former Soviet Union can be directly used in nuclear weapons without chemical processing.[72] Large quantities of such fissile material are being removed from nuclear weapons, and are accumulating in poorly secured, makeshift facilities.[73] Because Russia and the other former Soviet republics can no longer be relied upon to secure their fissile material stockpiles from theft and illicit diversion, the possibility of a state or non-state actor making a small number of improvised nuclear weapons from illicitly acquired fissile material has increased. This possibility of "nuclear leakage" increases the number of states with near-term nuclear potential from about a dozen to several dozen, and the number of non-state actors that could conceivably acquire nuclear weapons from zero to a few.

NUCLEAR WEAPONS FABRICATION WITH HEU IS DIFFICULT BUT FEASIBLE

While there are some technical difficulties associated with fabricating even the simplest nuclear bomb, none is so severe as to be insurmountable by a determined state or a highly capable non-state actor. HEU permits the use of the simplest nuclear weapon design, which uses an assembly mechanism based on a gun. In essence, a gun-type nuclear weapon uses a small artillery piece to fire a "bullet" of HEU into a stationary mass of HEU, forming a supercritical assembly. It requires an HEU projectile and catcher assembly, carefully designed to remain assembled after a high-velocity collision; a machined tamper to surround the HEU assembly; the barrel of a small artillery piece and a propellant charge to fire the "bullet" into the assembly; fusing and firing circuitry; and in some cases a neutron generator to trigger the explosion. A gun-type weapon requires about 100 pounds of HEU, with

---

71.   About 55 kg (121 pounds) of HEU was used in each of South Africa's weapons. David Albright, *South Africa's Secret Nuclear Weapons* (Washington, D.C.: Institute for Science and International Security, May 1994), p. 12. Rhodes, *The Making of the Atomic Bomb*, p. 601, gives an estimate of about 42 kg (92.6 pounds) HEU for the Hiroshima bomb.

72.   There is considerable uncertainty about the precise composition of fissile material stockpiles in the former Soviet Union, but it is known that hundreds of tons of weapons-usable material were produced there. See Albright, Berkhout, and Walker, *Plutonium and Highly Enriched Uranium 1996*, pp. 50–59, 113–116.

73.   Russian weapons disassembly is not subject to verification, and there is some uncertainty about the rate. Secretary of Defense William J. Perry gave a figure of 2000 warheads per year in "A Legacy of Readiness: An Interview with Secretary of Defense William J. Perry," *Sea Power*, October 1995, p. 11.

no option of using plutonium. Non-nuclear testing of gun-type weapons is so reliable that the gun-type weapon dropped on Hiroshima was not tested first.

Many states, and some sophisticated non-state groups, could build a functioning gun-type weapon if supplied with a sufficient quantity of HEU in metallic form.[74] Many states, and perhaps fewer non-state actors, could also overcome the additional barrier of converting highly-enriched uranium oxide into metal form. Aside from acquiring HEU metal and developing a workable design, fabricating the gun barrel would be the largest obstacle to making a gun-type weapon. In many countries, however, an appropriately strong, smooth tube could be purchased from an industrial supplier without much risk of arousing suspicion. The design requirements for the gun mechanism also need not be demanding. A high-performance gun-type weapon, small and light enough for air delivery, might use a 1.5-meter gun barrel, and would thus require a high-performance design and specialized propellants to achieve the necessary projectile velocity in the short distance available.[75] A truck-delivered weapon, in contrast, might use an improvised gun with a longer barrel and a lower propellant pressure to achieve the same projectile velocity; the gun and the tamper could also be made thicker and heavier, simplifying some of the engineering problems. "Little Boy," the gun-type bomb that the United States dropped on Hiroshima in August 1945, was 10.5 feet in length, including the external ballistic casing, demonstrating that even a first-generation design can employ a relatively short gun barrel.[76] For comparison, the cargo compartment of the longest truck that can be rented from Ryder, a large truck-rental firm, by a person without a truck-driver's license is 24 feet long.

---

74. This claim is consistent with published analyses written by a number of well-qualified nuclear weapons experts, including former weapons designers. See, for example, Mark, Taylor, Eyster, et al., "Can Terrorists Build Nuclear Weapons?" pp. 55–65; and OTA, *Nuclear Proliferation and Safeguards*, pp. 140–142. Steve Fetter estimates that "about thirty countries have the sort of industrial infrastructure and scientific talent that could support the successful construction and operation of nuclear facilities and nuclear weapons on a crash basis." See Steve Fetter, *Verifying Nuclear Disarmament* (Washington, D.C.: Henry L. Stimson Center, October 1996), p. 38. Many more could carry out the much easier task of weaponizing material acquired from external sources.

75. South Africa's weapon, for example, was about 1.8 meters long. Albright, *South Africa's Secret Nuclear Weapons*, p. 12.

76. Rhodes, *The Making of the Atomic Bomb*, p. 701.

Machining the HEU metal would present some unusual problems, because of the metal's hardness and high chemical reactivity, but these could be overcome through techniques learned from library research and practice on natural uranium. A skilled machinist would be needed to fabricate the uranium parts, but standard machine tools and common machine-shop measuring equipment would be adequate to ensure the necessary precision for a gun-type weapon. Non-fissile mock-ups of the final weapon, preferably using natural uranium in place of the fissile components, would also have to be tested to be certain that the weapon would properly assemble the fissile material. The resulting weapon would be large, unsafe, and very inefficient in its use of fissile material, but it could produce an explosive yield on the order of 10 kilotons.

FISSILE MATERIAL IMPURITIES COMPLICATE WEAPONS FABRICATION

HEU in the form of oxide, or with substantial impurities that would affect the nuclear reaction, could not be fabricated directly into weapons components, and would add a number of challenging new chemical and metallurgical steps to the weapons fabrication process, requiring significant additional equipment and specialized expertise.[77] If, for example, the nuclear material were obtained in oxide form, it would have to be chemically reduced to metal and then recast into ingots before it could be used in a gun-type bomb.[78] HEU (or plutonium) mixed with other elements or contained within spent reactor fuel would have to be chemically separated (reprocessed), then reduced to metal and recast. These tasks would require additional equipment and facilities, including foundry equipment and specialized supplies. Removing non-radioactive impurities, or those that pose a low radiation hazard, would require additional time, expertise, and equipment, although they would pose limited barriers.[79] Reprocessing

---

77. HEU and plutonium oxide could be used in a crude implosion device, but the odds of weapons failure or low yield are higher. See Mark, Taylor, Eyster, et al., "Can Terrorists Build Nuclear Weapons?" pp. 55–65.

78. Although HEU oxide can theoretically be used in gun-type weapons, the masses involved make such designs impractical. Ibid., pp. 55–65.

79. For example, extracting plutonium from glass logs (one proposed form for disposing of surplus military plutonium) would require additional effort, but would not pose a major new barrier. The National Academy of Sciences Committee on International Security and Arms Control concluded that "most potential proliferators with the technical expertise, personnel, and organization required to produce an operable nuclear weapon from separated plutonium — a substantial

highly radioactive spent fuel would require much more sophistication, appropriate remote handling equipment, and pumps and tanks for handling, mixing, and separating large volumes of radioactive and corrosive process solutions. These requirements would pose further significant hurdles to any weapons program, reducing a non-state group's chances of success, and imposing significant delays on less industrialized states.[80] Only a very well funded non-state actor with access to very good scientific and engineering talent would have a good chance of overcoming all of the additional problems associated with extracting plutonium from spent fuel.[81]

FABRICATION OF PLUTONIUM WEAPONS IS A SIGNIFICANT CHALLENGE

All common isotopic blends of plutonium can produce nuclear explosions, including the plutonium created in civilian nuclear reactors.[82] But the simple gun-type design cannot be used to make a plutonium bomb; instead, a significantly more complex implosion design is required. Although it uses less fissile material than a gun-type weapon to produce a similar explosive yield, an implosion bomb poses greater design, fabrication, and testing

---

technical task in itself — would also be able to extract plutonium chemically from a glass log not spiked with radioactivity." See *Management and Disposition of Excess Weapons Plutonium* (Washington, D.C.: National Academy Press, 1994), pp. 189.

80. A good overview of the nature and special requirements of the processes involved can be found in Manson Benedict, Thomas Pigford, and Hans Levi, *Nuclear Chemical Engineering* (New York: McGraw-Hill, 1981), a well-regarded reference in the field.

81. The feasibility of reprocessing by non-state actors has been debated for years. A good overview and guide to other sources is "The Spent Fuel Standard: How Accessible Is Plutonium in Spent Fuel?" in U.S. Department of Energy Report DOE/NN-0007, *Nonproliferation and Arms Control Assessment of Weapons-Usable Fissile Material Storage and Excess Plutonium Disposition Alternatives* (Washington, D.C.: DOE Office of Arms Control and Nonproliferation, January 1997), pp. 52–55.

82. A 1997 Department of Energy publication discusses the utility of various grades of plutonium, and concludes that all types of the element, with the exception of nearly pure Pu-238, can be used to build nuclear weapons. It further states: "At the lowest level of sophistication, a potential proliferating state or subnational group using designs and technologies no more sophisticated than those used in first-generation nuclear weapons could build a nuclear weapon from reactor-grade plutonium that would have an assured, reliable yield of one or a few kilotons (and a probable yield significantly higher than that)." Ibid., pp. 37–39.

challenges than a gun bomb (see Box 7, Fission Weapon Design, p. 160). It would require a wider variety of advanced technical skills, a wider range of specialized equipment, and considerable opportunity for high-explosive testing to ensure success in the first nuclear detonation.[83] These requirements would delay states attempting to build a plutonium bomb, and would put such weapons out of reach for some non-state groups that might be capable of building a gun-type bomb.

The first implosion weapon was designed during the Manhattan Project to overcome the high neutron emission rate that makes plutonium impossible to use in a gun-type weapon. An implosion weapon uses high explosives to compress a sphere of fissile material from a subcritical configuration (a hollow sphere, for example, or a solid but subcritical sphere of normal density) into a supercritical configuration (a solid sphere, often of increased density achieved by the force of the high-explosive compression). Even the simplest implosion weapons require carefully machined spherical assemblies of fissile material and tamper materials, surrounded by high-explosive lenses;[84] high-performance detonation

---

83. Provided sufficient tests are carried out to ensure the implosion system works as intended, nuclear testing is not necessary to ensure that an implosion weapon will work the first time it is used. See OTA, *Technologies Underlying Weapons of Mass Destruction*, p. 152. The United States did carry out a full nuclear test of the "Fat Man" implosion design that was used in the weapon dropped on Nagasaki three weeks later. That test, meant to prove the combination of two entirely new technologies — explosive lenses and nuclear fission — was successful. Nevertheless, almost all nuclear-armed states have conducted tests, in part to provide extra confidence and in part to develop smaller, lighter designs. Israel and Pakistan are believed not to have tested, but both states probably benefited from foreign design advice and perhaps test data. See Spector, *Nuclear Ambitions*, pp. 93, 152, 156–157. There is also some evidence to suggest that Israel may have played a role in a South African test in 1979. See Frank Barnaby, *The Invisible Bomb: The Nuclear Arms Race in the Middle East* (London: I.B. Tauris, 1989), pp. 14–21. Whether such a test ever occurred remains an unresolved question, however. See David Albright and Corey Gay, "A Flash from the Past," *Bulletin of the Atomic Scientists*, Vol. 53, No. 6 (November/December 1997), available at <www.bullatomsci.org/issues/1997/nd97/nd97albright.html>.

84. Explosive lenses are assemblies of two or more different explosives, constructed so that the differing speed of propagation of the detonation wave in each explosive shapes the wave front into a desired shape. In a nuclear implosion weapon, the full assembly of lenses, when triggered simultaneously, together form a perfectly synchronized spherical implosion. Rhodes, *The Making of the Atomic*

systems capable of detonating all of the explosive lenses simultaneously; a neutron generator timed to start the chain reaction near the moment of maximum compression; and fusing and firing circuitry able to synchronize the implosion and the neutron initiation.[85] Casting, forming, and machining high explosives for an implosion weapon would require specialized equipment and safety precautions, preferably including the use of an isolated facility, to minimize the consequences of unwanted explosions. Furthermore, testing and diagnosis of the behavior of the explosive lens system — a crucial part of the design and prototyping process — would best be done with specialized equipment such as high-speed cameras and flash x-ray equipment, although simpler equipment can also be used.

All processes involving plutonium would carry substantial safety risks due to the high toxicity of the metal and its extreme chemical reactivity.[86] This would require a variety of safety measures, possibly including handling plutonium in glove boxes, wearing protective clothing and filter masks, conducting some machining operations in an inert atmosphere, handling and storing machining wastes carefully, and ventilating work areas thoroughly.

FISSILE MATERIAL ACQUISITION IS THE MOST SIGNIFICANT INDICATOR OF A CLANDESTINE NUCLEAR PROGRAM

The most significant indicator of a clandestine nuclear weapons effort is an attempt to purchase or steal fissile material. States and non-state actors that seek to acquire fissile material by illicit means run substantial risks of being detected by watchful governments. Fissile material is present at a large but finite number of facilities, which are watched by national intelligence, law enforcement, and national security agencies, and in some cases by international inspectors. Law enforcement agencies have conducted sting operations in the nuclear black market, and have caught a number of

---

Bomb, pp. 575–576.

85. It may be possible to relax some of these requirements and still produce a working weapon, but figuring out with confidence which corners can safely be cut, and to what degree, could require more expertise than designing and building a weapon to tight specifications.

86. Willrich and Taylor, "Nuclear Theft," pp. 59–84.

freelance nuclear smugglers, a few with weapons-usable materials.[87] Although employees of the post-Soviet nuclear complex have endured a horrific socio-economic decline, many still have the integrity to resist and report suspicious overtures. The system for keeping tabs on worldwide stockpiles of fissile material is far from perfect, but all clandestine attempts to acquire nuclear weapons must seek to obtain fissile material, or weapons themselves, illegally. This indicator offers the most important opportunity for obtaining advance warning of incipient covert nuclear threats.

It is, however, important to recognize that illicit trafficking in nuclear weapons materials may in some cases eliminate what has been the most important signature of secret national nuclear weapons programs: fissile material production facilities. The production of weapons-usable nuclear materials generally requires large facilities and substantial expenditures. The facilities themselves, and the process of obtaining materials, equipment, and expertise for their construction and operation, create a variety of indicators that frequently lead to their detection. By removing the need to make fissile material, nuclear smuggling could sharply reduce the personnel, equipment, and facilities a proliferator would need for a weapons program, making covert nuclear weapons programs harder for international intelligence agencies to detect and reducing the time required for a bomb project.

For non-state actors, testing of the gun or the high-explosive systems are the only other indicators of a clandestine nuclear weapons program that are likely to attract attention. Machining a long gun barrel or a large tamper assembly might arouse the suspicion of an observer who had thought about the physical components of a nuclear weapon, but such individuals are rare. Most interested observers would probably think many of the individual purchases and activities required to build an improvised nuclear weapon peculiar, but without seeing the full effort or knowing what to look for, most would also think them innocuous.

---

87. For a listing of actual and alleged cases of nuclear diversion and smuggling, see *Nuclear Successor States of the Former Soviet Union: Nuclear Weapon and Sensitive Export Status Report*, No. 4 (Washington, D.C.: Carnegie Endowment for International Peace, and Monterey, Calif.: Monterey Institute of International Studies, May 1996), pp. 75–96, and earlier issues in the same series.

Open Societies Are Highly Vulnerable to Covert NBC Attack

Vulnerability is a function not only of an attacker's access to a particular weapon type, but also of its ability to use the weapon, and of the target state's ability to defend itself. The more effective the delivery method, and the less effective the defense, the greater the vulnerability. With military technologies, the relative effectiveness of offensive and defensive systems is a subject of constant study within and outside of government. Much less attention has generally been given to the vulnerability of population centers to covert NBC attack.[88] This is in part because there has never been a covert NBC attack against the United States, but it is also because the results of any serious analysis of this kind are so obvious and so discouraging.

Free and open societies such as the United States are acutely vulnerable to covert NBC attack. The attacker is presented with a vast array of possible mass-casualty targets, as well as many different options for effective covert delivery. The defenders, who include the whole of the target state's law enforcement, national security, intelligence, medical, and emergency response agencies, face a situation of pervasive vulnerability. They cannot protect all possible targets, and cannot passively prevent weapon transportation or delivery. Moreover, the defenders' ability to protect itself is likely to be limited by the absence of timely, specific intelligence on covert NBC threats. It is also limited by political and legal constraints on domestic surveillance and security measures, constraints fundamental to the nature and values of the United States and many other liberal democracies.

OFFENSE: MULTIPLE TARGETS AND DELIVERY OPTIONS
In a covert NBC threat scenario, the attacker's task is straightforward: deliver a weapon into or near an appropriate target and set it off. The attacker is able to undertake advance planning and to select the time, place, and scope of the strike. The attacker also needs to exploit only a single vulnerability. Should one target become difficult, a multitude of other targets are available.

---

88. The U.S. Army carried out extensive analyses of U.S. vulnerability to biological attack, and extensive field testing with simulated biological agents in U.S. cities, between 1949 and 1968. George W. Christopher, Theodore J. Cieslak, Julie A. Pavlin, et al., "Biological Warfare: A Historical Perspective," *JAMA*, Vol. 278, No. 5 (August 6, 1997), p. 414. See also Box 5, U.S. BW Program, p. 80. This testing, however, apparently did not lead to significant preparations for defense against or response to the consequences of covert biological attacks on cities.

For weapons suitable for area attacks, including nuclear weapons and large biological weapons, delivery is a simple matter of transporting the weapon to the target area. For smaller chemical and biological weapons, maximum effectiveness may require placing the weapon in a target building. After weapon emplacement or detonation, most attackers would attempt to escape the scene of the attack, and perhaps to remove or destroy evidence that might make post-attack attribution easier, since the victim is certain to seek retribution. These requirements add complexity to the attacker's task and require talents that are quite distinct from those necessary to produce an NBC weapon in the first place. However, a variety of individuals with paramilitary, terrorist, or criminal backgrounds would possess such skills, and others with cool heads and calm nerves could develop them.

Improvised NBC weapons can easily be made indistinguishable from the vast and complex background of civilian commerce and traffic within a target state's borders, a fact that works for the attacker. The wide variety of transportation options available, from privately owned vehicles to commercial cargo services, allows hidden NBC weapons to be moved from point to point with no questions asked, and with little risk of detection. Illustrating the scale of the problem, 1.5 million vehicles enter Manhattan's central business district daily, and over 7 million trucks a year cross the George Washington Bridge into Manhattan, an average of over 19,000 a day.[89] Approximately 167,000 people ride the subway during the typical morning commute in Washington, D.C.[90] The volumes of traffic are staggering, and without specific intelligence warning of an attack, it is impossible to find and stop a single vehicle or a few people.

The need to cross national borders would increase the chances of detection somewhat, since all persons and cargoes entering a country are subject to potential search and impoundment. However, there is an enormous volume of daily border traffic at most nations' official points of entry and exit — the United States has over 300 — and in most countries the border police and customs officials lack the resources, time, and political

---

89. Authors' telephone interview with a New York City government official, who cited figures compiled by the New York Metropolitan Transportation Council. Manhattan's central business district is defined as the area south of 60th Street.

90. Authors' telephone interview with a staff member at the Washington, D.C., Metro planning office, who cited internal statistics.

mandate to search all persons and cargoes crossing the border.[91] According to the Customs Service, almost 10 million shipping containers entered the United States during 1994, and trade continues to grow.[92] The failure of U.S. interdiction efforts to put drug smugglers out of business is a good measure of the difficulty of reliable border control.[93] If the risks of detection at the border appear too high, an attacker can manage them in a number of different ways. For example, an attacker could smuggle a weapon or its components into any of a large number of uncontrolled harbors by boat. This method would add costs, impose delays, and require knowing how to operate an ocean-going boat, but the chance of being caught would be small.[94] Alternatively, a foreign group could fabricate a weapon within the

---

91. In the absence of specific intelligence warning, weapons and weapons components are also unlikely to be discovered in physical searches. The Customs Service has put in place systems to focus its limited resources on cargoes most likely to contain contraband, but even so it can only inspect 22 percent of the 3.3 million shipping containers deemed "high risk" for narcotics. The difficulty of reliably determining risk is illustrated by the fact that the 3.3 million shipping containers designated "high risk" represent 35 percent of the containers shipped. Percentages are for FY 1994. U.S. Customs Service, *New Directions: The Year In Review 1994* (Washington, D.C.: U.S. Customs Service, no date), p. 7. Even if shipping containers are opened, nuclear weapons or weapons components might be hard to recognize. Especially in a gun-type design, the parts could be made to look like odd but not suspect castings and machine parts. The fissile material and the gun propellant, however, if detected, would cause suspicion. Chemical and biological weapons, and especially containers of chemical and biological warfare agents, could also be quite small and unlikely to attract attention.

92. Ibid., p. 7.

93. In another recent example, a Florida businessman was arrested for smuggling 180 tons of freon refrigerant into the United States from Russia. The arrest would be evidence of good border security if the man hadn't already smuggled 4,000 tons of the chemical into the United States in the previous three years. "CFC Smuggling, Production Cool Optimism: Continued Demand, Defiance of Ban May Delay Mending of Earth's Ozone 'Hole' for Decades," *Washington Post*, September 16, 1997, p. A3.

94. Persons making landfall at U.S. ports and airports without Customs control are required to notify the Customs Service by phone of their arrival, and to await inspection. See U.S. Customs Service Publication No. 513, *Guide for Private Flyers: 1995 Edition* (Washington D.C.: U.S. GPO, December 1994), pp. 7–22; and No. 544, *Pleasure Boats: Reporting Requirements* (no publication data), pp. 3–4. Except for boats and planes arriving in regions with substantial drug smuggling, however, only

target state. For many foreign groups, such an effort would risk attracting exposure, especially if their lack of technical expertise were likely to arouse the suspicion of necessary suppliers. Nonetheless, a group able to live and work in the United States, and technically confident in its chosen project, might find the added risk of detection outweighed by the advantages of widely available equipment and supplies and easy access to targets.

IMPROVISED NUCLEAR WEAPONS. Improvised nuclear weapons are likely to range from one to several tons in weight,[95] and from one to a few meters in length. Very large improvised weapons could be transported by freight truck or boat. Smaller, more sophisticated nuclear weapons stolen from a nuclear weapon state could be light enough to transport in a van or light truck. Several people or a small hoist would be needed to load even a small weapon into a vehicle, but only a driver would be needed for delivery.

Nuclear weapons, or fissile material and other weapons components, can be smuggled into the United States. The large size and weight of a weapon limits the transportation options and makes detection by Customs more likely. Nuclear materials also emit radiation, which in principle can be detected at a distance. Radiation detectors at border crossings can thus increase the chances of detecting weapons smuggling, provided the material is not shielded to reduce the signature.[96] A weapon or its components could be concealed in other cargo, however, and might easily go unnoticed. Alternatively, an attacker could ship a fully assembled nuclear weapon via a major port, with a time-delay, global-positioning, or tamper-sensitive detonating system. Making the port of entry the target, or simply

---

limited resources are devoted to detecting unannounced arrivals.

95. Mark, Taylor, Eyster, et al., "Can Terrorists Build Nuclear Weapons?" p. 60.

96. Weapons-usable fissile material emits radiation — plutonium more so than HEU — including alpha particles, gamma rays, and neutrons, which can in principle be detected by passive radiation detectors. In practice, however, the existence of natural background radiation, the low emission rates from weapons materials, and the small amount of material needed for a weapon combine to make these signatures difficult to detect except at short range, even if a radiation detector is on hand. See Steve Fetter et al., "Detecting Nuclear Warheads," *Science and Global Security*, Vol. 1, Nos. 3–4 (1990), pp. 225–302. The U.S. Customs Service is putting radiation detection equipment in place at ports of entry, a measure that will improve the chances of detecting nuclear material and nuclear weapons. Coverage is likely to be limited, however, and shielding can defeat even the best radiation detectors, albeit at the cost of making the smuggled item larger and heavier.

accepting it as a secondary target, would remove concern about border inspection.

Within the target country, a nuclear weapon could be shipped by commercial transport services, whole or in pieces. Weapons delivered in this way could either be fused to detonate on their own — for example, at a particular time or when their container is opened — or received by agents at or near the target for final assembly, delivery, or detonation. Unaccompanied delivery by commercial transport would entail only minimal risk, and would allow the attacker plenty of time to disappear. Sending personnel to receive the weapon would probably entail delay and greater risk of detection, failure, and identification. Shipment by commercial transport would require the attacker to give up tight control over the weapon, but unless the transport company became suspicious, detection would be unlikely.

Cities, ports, and military bases all are vulnerable to nuclear weapons. Final delivery of a nuclear weapon against most targets would carry little risk. Most targets could be destroyed from at least several city blocks away, making a truck-bomb attack on any target in an urban area, or against a city itself, easy to carry out. Some military targets protected by large security perimeters might be difficult to reach, if entering vehicles are subjected to search. The fallout left behind by a nuclear blast would provide information on the design of the bomb, but would incinerate most of the forensic evidence other types of truck bomb leave behind.

IMPROVISED BIOLOGICAL AND CHEMICAL WEAPONS. Biological and chemical weapons can be transported within or smuggled into a target country more easily than nuclear weapons. The high potency of many pathogens and toxin agents means that only small quantities are needed for significant attacks. A kilogram of a concentrated biological agent — enough, in the case of anthrax bacteria, to kill tens of thousands of people — could be mailed or hand-carried across a border with little risk of detection. However, attackers relying on weapons involving liquid bacterial cultures or impure chemical agents may need to transport the agent from production to attack site quickly, in some cases within as little as a few days, because of shelf-life constraints. This would limit the means of transportation available for agent smuggling, requiring foreign attackers to use air transport to reach the United States, for example. Use of air transport would create a record of the entry of people or cargo near the time of the attack, making it easier for a post-attack investigation to find the lead, and might increase the odds of detection at the border.

In general, however, biological and chemical agents have very limited signatures before release, making detection and interdiction difficult.[97] Unless they leak and cause noticeable effects, chemical weapons are unlikely to attract attention. Biological weapons based on microorganisms and most toxins might not be detected even if they leak, since these agents might easily fail to cause casualties if unaerosolized, and even if anyone were affected, the onset of symptoms might be delayed for days. Concealed in cargo, these weapons would have about the same chance of getting through Customs as any other smuggled item. While chemical and biological agent dispersal would generally involve sprayers or explosives of some type, these might be small enough to conceal in baggage or in the trunk of a car for border crossings. Even large weapons would be unlikely to be detected in domestic transportation. They simply would not attract much attention in the back of a pickup truck on the highway.

To be fully effective, biological and chemical weapons require more careful final delivery than nuclear weapons. Weather, atmospheric dilution, and population density can strongly affect the performance of chemical and biological weapons, which complicates the attacker's ability to conduct outdoor area attacks. These problems can be partially avoided by attacking indoor targets. Indoor attacks may require placing the weapon in very close proximity to its intended victims, thus raising the odds of pre-attack detection and post-attack identification.[98] Attacks of this kind could in principle be carried out with concealed bombs or sprayers delivered by mail or courier, but the effects of such an imprecise delivery system would be highly variable. To achieve the full mass-casualty potential of simple

---

97. A variety of physical signatures of chemical and biological agents can be detected before release, including, for example: acoustic resonance spectra, which can be measured with special transducers in contact with the container; neutron activation signatures from sulfur or phosphorous in chemical agents, which could be detected with large, fixed scanners; and nuclear magnetic resonance signatures. Detecting any of these signatures requires special equipment, much of it expensive, and application to large cargo flows would be costly. A wide variety of other chemical, biochemical, and biological methods can be used to characterize samples once they are taken out of the container, but such sampling and testing cannot easily be applied to more than a small percentage of containers entering the United States.

98. In the case of biological weapons, it may be possible for the attacker to recover the dispersal devices after the attack but before the physical symptoms of the attack are noticed.

chemical and biological weapons, some knowledge of the air flow and other structural characteristics of the target is necessary, and a human operative would likely be required to introduce the dispersal device into the building and perhaps into the ventilation system. One exception to this would be biological weapons that can disseminate very large quantities of agent as stable, respirable aerosols, which could be used in open-air attacks affecting large areas. Some protection against such area attacks could be provided by appropriate filtering in the ventilation systems of important buildings, and on tall buildings simply by locating air intakes high above ground.

DEFENSE: PERVASIVE VULNERABILITIES AND LIMITED OPTIONS FOR PROTECTION

The task of the defender in a covert NBC attack scenario is not at all straightforward: to anticipate specific threats before they emerge, defend all possible targets against an attack that could come at any time from any direction, and minimize the damage that could result from a successful attack. As an operational challenge, the defender's task is orders of magnitude more difficult than the attacker's.

The key to defeating a specific covert NBC attack is to know about it in detail in advance. If specific, detailed warning of an attack is available, most states will be able to mobilize an effective operational response that overwhelms the attacker's limited personnel and resources. Covert attackers rely on remaining undetected, not on their ability to fight a stronger opponent. Unfortunately, the defender is unlikely to have any idea that an attack is coming, much less know its origin, target, timing, and other relevant operational specifics. The level of commerce and movement in a modern nation is simply too high for a government to be fully aware of what is going on within its jurisdiction; even totalitarian societies suffer from various forms of criminality, terrorism, and smuggling. In an open society like the United States, people are free to move about without notifying anyone in advance, and to do more or less as they please in their homes and businesses, with constitutionally protected rights against arbitrary search and arrest. Strong legal constraints on the state's ability to know what is happening within its borders are integral to limited democratic governance; to change this would be to abandon the basic values of liberal society.

It is possible that the defender will have some general warning or information on a possible covert NBC threat. However, even in this case, the options for detecting and defeating the attack are extremely limited. Both site security and wide-area searches present profound operational problems. Most buildings and public spaces can be entered without difficulty. Air intake ducts and ventilation systems are almost never guarded or even monitored. Even facilities with tight security usually only control the entry of people at the immediate perimeter of the building, and packages are searched only after they enter the structure, if at all. Although building security can be improved on short notice by closing points of entry and exit, increasing guard presence, and enhancing search procedures, these measures are costly, and are impractical for some types of targets. In the case of nuclear weapons, technology may offer assistance in the form of remote sensing equipment,[99] but in general the only reliable way to detect a concealed weapon is to recognize it or its component parts in a close physical search. Over a wide area in a short period of time, it is not possible to search all potential vehicles, containers, and buildings for hidden NBC weapons.

Thus, in the absence of specific intelligence, a serious effort to locate and defeat a particular covert NBC attack would require a state to clamp down vigorously on all forms of civilian commerce, traffic, and civil liberties. Lesser measures, such as a higher state of alert by law enforcement and border-control agencies, could increase the chances of detecting a covert NBC attack somewhat, but are unlikely to be especially effective in a real emergency. Even if oppressive defensive measures could be ordered by an elected official and effectively implemented by government agencies, they offer no guarantee of success. NBC weapons are simply too easy to disguise, and a developed economy offers too many places in which they can be hidden, for an open society ever to have a complete defense against covert NBC attack.

The defender also faces a problem of not knowing when its preparations are inadequate. A covert NBC attack is an extremely uncommon event, and is without precedent in the United States. This absence of attacks can be mistaken for the absence of vulnerability, since both have identical manifestations. Without real incidents, the defender's weaknesses are indistinct to most observers, and are easily ignored by inattentive or complacent leaders. This fundamental political reality limits the ability of the United States to respond effectively to a shifting threat environment.

As hopeless as the situation may sound when looked at in terms of vulnerability, most potential attackers lack the resources, knowledge, skill, and luck required to exploit fully the openings that exist. Even marginal improvements in certain capabilities may significantly increase the chances

---

99. Fetter et al., "Detecting Nuclear Warheads," pp. 225–302. Detection is further discussed in Chapter 5.

of detecting and stopping attacks before they happen. Although perfection in customs interdiction of NBC weapons is infeasible, certain improvements can raise attackers' risk of detection and improve the chances of successful defense. Better equipment, appropriate training, and further improvements in border monitoring each have a part to play. Raising the barriers an attacker would have to cross can put covert NBC attacks out of reach of some attackers, and can increase the chances of detecting and stopping the others. When overseas attackers are not stopped at the border, or when an attack originates in the United States, pre-attack detection will rest on domestic policing and on security measures at target sites. Police work and security measures will have at best a limited ability to detect attack planning and preparations, but if the proper personnel are prepared to recognize signs of NBC activity when they see them, luck (perhaps aided by other criminal activity on the part of the would-be attacker) may provide opportunities to uncover attacks in the planning stage.[100]

If a nation like the United States has any advantage in defending itself against specific covert NBC threats, it is that American society is not generally supportive of violent conspiracies. Terrorists and foreign agents in the United States are unlikely to find many sympathizers in the general population. Instead, they will find an essentially content citizenry that can be quite watchful and xenophobic, and that is tightly netted together by an efficient and pervasive media. Americans are prone to report suspicious or threatening activities to local law enforcement officials, especially outside of the nation's largest cities, and the government's efforts are augmented somewhat by investments that businesses have made in security services and equipment. This aspect of American society is a source of modest optimism, and suggests that if the government receives advance warning of an impending covert NBC attack, it is as likely to come from the fortuitous observation and action of a citizen as from the purposeful efforts of a state agency.

Finally, it is important to bear in mind that an attacker would face increasing difficulty and risk of detection with each successive attack and each corresponding escalation of the target's defensive measures. Carrying out tens of attacks would expose the perpetrators to a high risk of detection and retaliation, a risk few would be willing to face, and would also demand

---

100. The Japanese police repeatedly missed opportunities to stop Aum Shinrikyo's escalating series of attacks and other broad patterns of illegal behavior. Missing this kind of extensive and overt evidence of terrorist activity is a mistake that the United States should seek not to emulate. See Box 1, Aum Shinrikyo, p. 19.

extraordinary resources and logistical capabilities. However, as the next section makes clear, even one or two nuclear attacks or large biological attacks would cause considerable damage and loss of life, and even a single chemical attack could easily be the most damaging terrorist event in the history of the United States. Such attacks would also cause political and psychological damage far outside the area of their physical effects. But they would not threaten destruction on the scale of nuclear war, a danger long feared but now almost forgotten.

The Effects of a Covert NBC Attack Could Be Severe

A society's vulnerability to a specific form of attack depends on the consequences that would follow a successful attack. In the Introduction, we outlined the immediate physical effects of nuclear, biological, and chemical weapons attacks, and noted that such attacks could have additional second-order effects on the psychology, social structure, economy, and political system of a society. In this section, we describe the physical effects of NBC attacks in greater detail, showing how even a limited number of covert attacks involving improvised NBC weapons could cause severe damage and loss of life.

CHEMICAL ATTACK EFFECTS

Covert chemical attacks are likely to affect hundreds or thousands of victims. Effects of this magnitude are within the potential reach of small non-state groups capable of making tens of kilograms of agent, provided they use well-designed weapons in well-planned and well-executed attacks on crowded indoor targets. Larger numbers of casualties are conceivable for attackers able to produce and deliver hundreds of kilograms of agent.

Chemical agent effects vary widely, but most agents act in a matter of minutes. Nerve gases inhibit the action of acetylcholinesterase, a crucial enzyme in the nervous system, causing symptoms such as tightness in the chest and difficulty breathing, runny nose, dizziness, dim vision, vomiting, twitching, and respiratory paralysis, which leads to death by asphyxiation. Victims exposed to heavy inhaled doses die in under a minute; those receiving lower doses, and those exposed through the skin, die more slowly.[101] Some older agents, such as cyanide, also kill quickly by inhalation. Mustard gas at low concentrations may cause only mild initial irritation of

---

101. SIPRI, *The Problem of Chemical and Biological Warfare*, Vol. II: *CB Weapons Today*, pp. 58–59.

the eyes and mucous membranes, even while doing fatal damage, leaving victims to die in hours or days. For some agents, decontamination is the only way to reduce damage, but the effects of many chemical agents are treatable with antidotes. However, many of these antidotes have significant adverse side effects, and can be difficult to administer.

In any chemical attack scenario, different victims will receive widely varying doses. Although some victims may die quickly, a prompt and effective emergency response could save a substantial fraction of the lives at risk, and sharply reduce the number and severity of permanent injuries. Victims would have to be removed from contaminated areas, treated with antidotes, decontaminated at the scene, and taken to hospitals for evaluation and supportive care. U.S. cities presently have very limited capabilities for such an effective response, however. Furthermore, even with quick action it would be difficult to prevent large numbers of deaths in a well-executed chemical attack.

Attacks on crowded indoor targets are likely to be the most destructive. Such attacks would require carrying munitions into the target building and emplacing them before the attack, or introducing agent into ventilation intakes, operations that would increase the planning and operational requirements of an attack, and the risk of detection. It would be necessary to use a few kilograms of even the most highly toxic agents in attacks on targets where thousands of people might be exposed. For example, if one kilogram (about 2.2 pounds) of VX, the most toxic of the standard nerve agents, were vaporized and evenly dispersed in a large assembly hall 100 meters square and 10 meters high, everyone in the room would receive the median fatal dose in about 3 minutes.[102] Unless immediately removed from the room and injected with atropine, half would die. VX is a relatively non-volatile agent, and 1 kilogram is all that can be vaporized in a room that size at normal temperatures. Ten kilograms of sarin, which vaporizes more easily, would give a median fatal dose in one minute. In practice, sudden and even dispersal of an agent across a large space would be difficult or impossible, however, and an attacker's calculations would be considerably

---

102. Authors' calculation. The estimates we present here are oversimplified and thus worst-case. We believe they provide a reasonable picture of the numbers of deaths likely in covert chemical attacks, without providing much information on how to calculate the quantity of agent needed for an effective attack. The respiratory toxicity of VX is expressed as an LCt50 of 36 mg-min per cubic meter. An LCt50 is the concentration that will prove lethal to half the people who breathe it for one minute.

complicated by uneven dispersal of agent and by ventilation. With sarin or VX, two of the most toxic chemical agents, larger targets could require hundreds of kilograms or even tons of agent, released at multiple points.[103] Even attacks on crowded places can, if poorly handled, be ineffective, as demonstrated by the Aum Shinrikyo sarin attack in the Tokyo subway (see Box 1, Aum Shinrikyo, p. 19). Representative figures for fatalities in various attack scenarios are given in Table 4.

An outdoor attack intended to affect any significant area requires far larger quantities of agent, due largely to the dilution and removal of the agent by wind.[104] The Office of Technology Assessment cites an estimate of 60 to 200 deaths from a single-point attack with 300 kilograms of sarin in a normal urban area (population density of three thousand to ten thousand people per square kilometer), with a moderate wind.[105] A relatively simple outdoor attack, involving no more planning and execution than a large truck-bomb attack, is thus likely to kill people in numbers comparable to the number of dead in the bombing of the Oklahoma City Federal Building, but would require a quantity of agent that is unlikely to be produced in a basement laboratory. Another estimate provides representative results of calculations based on U.S. Army data. The minimum amount of sarin required to achieve 50 percent casualties among unprotected people in open terrain is 80 kilograms per square kilometer, under ideal weather conditions. Cold, windy weather can raise the required quantity to 3400 kilograms per square kilometer. These figures assume release by many small, ground-level devices scattered over the target area, a requirement

---

103. Killing the occupants of a large building would also require an understanding of ventilation rates and other factors governing exposure levels in the target building, and the difficulty of producing and delivering excess agent would make it difficult to solve these problems through overkill.

104. Overestimates of the potential severity of chemical attacks are common. "With a basic knowledge of chemistry and a small amount of money, such groups [terrorist organizations] can easily produce enough chemical agent to threaten an average-size city." Prepared statement of Elisa D. Harris, in Senate Hearings 101-744, *Global Spread of Chemical and Biological Weapons*, Hearings before the Committee on Governmental Affairs, Permanent Subcommittee on Investigations, United States Senate (Washington, D.C.: U.S. GPO, 1990), p. 276.

105. U.S. Congress, Office of Technology Assessment, *Proliferation of Weapons of Mass Destruction: Assessing the Risks* (Washington, D.C.: U.S. GPO, August 1993), p. 53.

Table 4. Chemical Weapons Attack Effects.

Agent	Mass of agent	Area affected	Population exposed	Estimated fatalities
Open Air Attack[1]				
Point source				
Sarin	300 kg	0.22 sq km	660–2,200	60–200
Line source[2]				
Sarin	1000 kg	0.8 sq. km	2,400–8,000	400–800
Indoor Attack[3]				
Movie theater				
VX	~ 1kg	Building only	1,000	500
Phosgene	Tens of kgs	Building only	1,000	500
Subway car				
VX	Hundreds of grams	Car only	100–200	50–100

SOURCES: U.S. Congress, Office of Technology Assessment (OTA), *Proliferation of Weapons of Mass Destruction: Assessing the Risks* (Washington, D.C.: U.S. GPO, August 1993); Gordon M. Burck and Charles C. Flowerree, *International Handbook on Chemical Weapons Proliferation* (New York: Greenwood Press, 1991), pp. 580–581; and authors' calculations based on toxicity data in Stockholm International Peace Research Institute (SIPRI), *The Problem of Chemical and Biological Weapons*, Vol. II: *CB Weapons Today* (New York: Humanities Press, 1973), pp. 42–43;.

NOTES

1.   Both open-air estimates are from OTA, *Proliferation of Weapons of Mass Destruction*, pp. 53–54. Both assume moderate weather conditions. OTA does not give estimates for the population exposed. The numbers given here are the population of the affected area in the OTA estimates, computed by multiplying the affected area by the population range given by OTA: 3000–10,000 per sq. km.

2.   Assumes moderate weather conditions. "Line source" means that the agent is dispersed at a large number of points along a line, or disseminated from a vehicle or aircraft moving along a line. Line source delivery is logistically more demanding, but is more efficient in creating lethal agent concentrations over large areas.

3.   Authors' calculations. The calculations on which these figures are based are intentionally oversimplified, assuming very efficient dispersal, ignoring ventilation, and assuming that the average victim receives the median lethal dose before escaping. Actual effects could vary substantially depending on the dispersal method and the rate of ventilation.

that a covert attacker might find hard to meet.[106] Both the difficulty of producing large amounts of agent and the increased risk of detection during delivery would make such attacks hard to carry out.

BIOLOGICAL ATTACK EFFECTS

Fatalities from effective biological attacks against densely populated indoor or outdoor targets are likely to range from thousands to hundreds of thousands.[107] These figures assume both an effective weapon disseminating a deadly agent, and the absence of timely, effective medical intervention. The high end of the range also assumes efficient dissemination of large quantities of agent aerosol, over a wide area, under good meteorological conditions. Even a weapon with limited aerosol output, if correctly used against a large indoor target, could be expected to expose a high percentage of the people inside — perhaps as many as tens of thousands — to a potentially lethal infection or intoxication. The actual number of victims would depend on the size and efficiency of the weapon used, on the agent chosen, on whether or not the weapon was well suited for the target chosen, and on the timeliness and effectiveness of medical response efforts.

The lethality of biological agents varies widely, as does the incubation period, and both often depend on the dose inhaled.[108] Symptoms of biological attack will usually begin to appear in a matter of hours or days, depending on dose and individual susceptibility. Fatality rates without medical treatment are close to one hundred percent for some accessible

---

106. SIPRI, *The Problem of Chemical and Biological Warfare*, Vol. II: *CB Weapons Today*, p. 137.

107. Projections of the effects of biological releases are based on laboratory tests of such agents, including inhalation tests on animals and human volunteers, on field tests of weapons on animals, and on field tests of the aerosol dispersal of simulant agents. Outdoor aerosol attacks against humans are unknown, except for the three alleged failed attempts in Tokyo by Aum Shinrikyo (see Box 1, Aum Shinrikyo, p. 19). An accidental release of anthrax from a Soviet military biological warfare laboratory in 1979 provides the only example of effective large-scale outdoor aerosol dissemination of a live biological warfare agent affecting humans (see Box 3, Soviet BW Program, p. 68).

108. For a primer on the medical effects of biological warfare agents, see David R. Franz, Peter B. Jahrling, Arthur M. Friedlander, et al., "Clinical Recognition and Management of Patients Exposed to Biological Warfare Agents," *JAMA*, Vol. 278, No. 5 (August 6, 1997), pp. 399–411.

Table 5. Biological Weapons Attack Effects.

Agent	Amount of agent	Area affected	Population exposed	Estimated fatalities
Indoor attack (arena)				
Anthrax[1]	1–100 liters crude liquid	Inside building	10,000–50,000	8,000–40,000
Brucellosis[2]	1–100 liters crude liquid	Inside building	10,000–50,000	160–800 (8,000–40,000 sick)
Open-air attack (city)[3]				
Line Source[4]				
Tularemia[5]	50 kg dry powder	40 sq. km	500,000	19,000 (250,000 sick)
Anthrax[6]	50 kg dry powder	40 sq. km	500,000	100,000 (250,000 sick)
Anthrax[7]	100 kg dry powder	300 sq. km	1–3 million	1–3 million
Point Source				
Anthrax[8]	30 kg dry powder	10 sq. km	30,000–100,000	30,000–100,000

agents, such as anthrax.[109] Other agents cause severe illnesses, but few deaths: brucellosis, for example, causes a severe, flu-like illness lasting for weeks or months, but kills fewer than 5 percent of untreated victims.[110] Toxin effects also vary widely, from incapacitating to lethal. The effects of an attack would thus depend strongly on the agent used and on the virulence of the specific strain. Table 5 provides representative estimates for attacks using a variety of agents against indoor and outdoor targets.

---

109. Ibid., pp. 401–402.

110. Ibid., p. 402.

Table 5, *cont.*

SOURCES: Estimates of fatalities from representative biological and chemical attacks against population centers are given in World Health Organization (WHO), *Health Aspects of Chemical and Biological Weapons* (Geneva: WHO, 1970), pp. 96, 98–99. The mass of aerosolized toxins needed to produce a median fatal dose over a 100-square-kilometer area is discussed in David R. Franz, *Defense Against Toxin Weapons*, (Frederick, Md.: U.S. Army Medical Research and Materiel Command, ca. 1993), pp. 8–10. Comparative fatality estimates for representative single-weapon NBC attacks on Washington, D.C., are given in Office of Technology Assessment, *Proliferation of Weapons of Mass Destruction: Assessing the Risks* (Washington, D.C.: U.S. GPO, August 1993), pp. 53–54.

NOTES

1. Authors' estimate, based on a crude liquid agent, a range of aerosol efficiencies, and a high inhaled dose. Fatality figures assume that the attack goes unnoticed, and that early medical care is not provided.

2. Authors' estimate, based on low-efficiency dispersal of a concentrated liquid agent slurry, and a high inhaled dose.

3. Note that these estimates are for attacks using high-quality dried agent preparations, efficiently disseminated. Not all states and non-state actors capable of making crude biological weapons could make effective dry agents, a process that requires greater expertise, as well as better equipment and facilities.

4. "Line source" means that the agent is dispersed at a large number of points along a line, or disseminated from a vehicle or aircraft moving along a line. Line source delivery is logistically more demanding, but is more efficient in creating lethal agent concentrations over large areas.

5. WHO, *Health Aspects of Chemical and Biological Weapons*, p. 98. Estimate is for an attack on a city of 5 million people in an industrial country using a high-quality agent preparation, under ideal weather conditions. Population exposed was calculated on the basis of an urban population density model, and averages 12,500 per square kilometer. Fatality estimate assumes that antibiotic therapy reduces fatalities from 25 percent of infected cases to 7.5 percent.

6. Ibid., p. 98. Estimate is for an attack on a city of 5 million people in an industrial country using a high-quality agent preparation, under ideal weather conditions. Population exposed was calculated on the basis of an urban population density model, and averages 12,500 per square kilometer. Fatality estimate assumes antibiotic therapy reduces fatalities by half (to 35–40 percent of those infected, rather than 70–80 percent).

7. OTA, *Proliferation of Weapons of Mass Destruction*, p. 54. Population exposed calculated on the basis of 3,000–10,000 unprotected people per square kilometer. Note that the number exposed is equal to the number of fatalities, presumably reflecting the near-100 percent fatality rate of untreated inhalation anthrax.

8. Ibid., n. 53. Assumes moderate weather conditions.

Following covert attacks with even the most lethal bacterial agents, medical care can, in theory, save many of those exposed.[111] Medical treatment is possible for all of the easily used bacterial agents and many toxins, so in theory an adequate medical response could save most of the people exposed in a large biological attack. Table 6 presents estimates of the impact of medical care in two scenarios. The results show not only that early medical care can save many lives, but also that quick prophylactic treatment of exposed individuals can substantially reduce the total dollar cost for medical care over the course of the disaster.[112] The cost reduction comes about primarily because early treatment keeps many people from needing expensive hospital care.

With its current level of preparedness, however, the United States can presently expect to save only a fraction of the victims, mostly people who sicken more slowly because they are less heavily exposed. A well-executed attack would have a good chance of going unnoticed until the victims started to get sick, and early prophylactic treatment would no longer be possible. Some agents are effectively untreatable once they become symptomatic. In addition, although the onset of sickness would vary from person to person, across the exposed population it could be quite sudden and explosive in character, resulting in thousands or tens of thousands of deaths within the span of a few days, and completely overwhelming medical resources. Even if individual patients were susceptible to treatment, the logistical problems of providing medicines quickly to large numbers of people, and of providing intensive care support to large numbers of acutely ill patients, would be insurmountable. Furthermore, the United States currently lacks adequate stocks of antitoxins, other medicines, and respirators needed to care for large numbers of biological warfare casualties. (These problems are further discussed in Chapter 5.)

---

111. For an analysis of the effects of medical care on fatalities and economic damage in several attack scenarios, see Arnold F. Kaufmann, Martin I. Meltzer, and George P. Schmid, "The Economic Impact of a Bioterrorist Attack: Are Prevention and Postattack Intervention Justifiable?" *Emerging Infectious Diseases*, Vol. 3, No. 2 (April–June 1997), pp. 1–12.

112. Prophylactic treatment is treatment designed to prevent a disease from occurring. In the cases under consideration, antibiotics would be given before victims became ill. In the anthrax case, anthrax vaccine would also be given to boost the victims' immune response.

Table 6. Impact of Early Medical Intervention on Biological Attack Consequences.

	Number infected	Deaths	Medical costs[1]
Anthrax			
Immediate prophylaxis	50,000	5,000	$28m to $355m
Treatment starts Day 6	50,000	32,875	$194m to $237m
Tularemia			
Immediate prophylaxis	82,500	1,000	$43m to $155m
Treatment starts Day 6	82,500	6,188	$445m to $543m

SOURCE: Arnold F. Kaufmann, Martin I. Meltzer, and George P. Schmid, "The Economic Impact of a Bioterrorist Attack: Are Prevention and Postattack Intervention Justifiable?" *Emerging Infectious Diseases*, Vol. 3, No. 2, pp. 1–12, <www.cdc.gov/ncidod/EID/vol3no2/kaufman.htm>.

NOTE

1. The model presented by Kaufmann, Meltzer, and Schmid assumes that in the prophylaxis cases, when 100,000 people are exposed, anywhere between five and fifteen times that many will show up for medical treatment. The wide range in cost estimates in the prophylaxis cases reflects this. In the late-treatment cases, only the sick need to be treated, and the range of medical cost estimates reflects differences in the costs of hospital care in different parts of the country. Cost range for anthrax treatment is based on use of two alternate drugs, as well as on whether five or fifteen times the exposed population come for treatment in the immediate prophylaxis case. The study also models the costs due to lost wages and productivity; these estimates run into the billions of dollars.

NUCLEAR ATTACK EFFECTS

A first-generation nuclear weapon might reasonably be expected to have an explosive yield on the order of 10 kilotons.[113] The bombings of Hiroshima and Nagasaki are ample reminders that such an explosion can destroy the core of a city. By comparison, the Oklahoma City bomb was equal to about 2 tons of TNT, about one five-thousandth as powerful as a small nuclear weapon. The number of likely deaths depends on the population density and the kind of buildings in the target area. Even an improvised nuclear weapon with only a 1-kiloton yield would cause very severe damage.

---

113. One kiloton (kT) is a measure of explosive power equivalent to 1,000 tons of TNT.

Nuclear explosions cause immediate injury through blast, thermal radiation, and nuclear radiation.[114] Indirect injury caused by building collapse could also be a significant factor. Most of the damage would occur almost instantly after the weapon was detonated. In a populous area, large numbers of people would be killed immediately, while many others would receive serious injuries. In addition to the direct blast damage to buildings, the heat of the explosion would start fires, which could spread. In the days after the attack, radiation from fallout would cause further injury. The strain on the local medical infrastructure, and on disaster-assistance resources brought in from outside, would be tremendous.

Because of the complexity of weapons effects, and because the damage would depend on how the weapon was used and where, calculating fatality estimates is difficult. Table 7 contains simplified estimates, based on the assumption that everyone out to the radius at which brick apartment buildings collapsed would die in the blast, and that no one outside that radius would die.[115] It shows that even a 1-kiloton explosion would destroy the heart of a city. The blast would distort the frames of reinforced-concrete-frame office buildings within four hundred fifty feet of the detonation point, and would blow down their interior partitions.[116] Solidly built brick apartment houses would be leveled more than a quarter of a mile away, and wood-frame houses even farther away would collapse. In a densely populated city, tens of thousands of people would die immediately, even before fallout took its toll, and the damage to property would be many billions of dollars. Similar blast effects from a 10-kiloton explosion would extend to about twice the distance in each case, and thus would cover four

---

114. See *The Effects of Nuclear Weapons*, 3rd ed. (Washington, D.C.: U.S. Department of Defense and U.S. Department of Energy, 1977). Our discussion draws heavily on this book.

115. This approximation, although rough, is accurate enough to demonstrate that the effects of an attack would be severe. This is a long-standing rule of thumb for rough estimates of total fatalities. See U.S. Congress, Office of Technology Assessment (OTA), *The Effects of Nuclear War* (Washington, D.C.: U.S. GPO, May 1979), p. 19. Actual effects might vary considerably, and secondary effects, such as fires and fallout, might add to casualties.

116. Data taken from tables 5.139a, p. 214, and 5.139b, *The Effects of Nuclear Weapons*, 3rd ed., pp. 215–216. These tables present data for optimum air bursts, which are more destructive than ground bursts. A covert nuclear attack would presumably be a ground burst, so the blast radii shown here have been adjusted downward by a factor of 0.75 in accordance with instructions given in ibid., p. 218.

Table 7. Nuclear Weapons Attack Effects (Prompt Blast Damage Only).

Weapon yield	Radius within which buildings collapse		Population per sq. km[1]	Number of deaths
	Reinforced concrete	*Brick apartment houses*		
1 kiloton (kT) ground burst	150 m	450 m	5,000–15,000	3,200–9,600
12.5 kT ground burst	450 m	1100 m	5,000–15,000	19,000–57,000
Hiroshima (12.5 kT air burst)			10,000 (est.)	68,000–140,000[2]
Nagasaki (22 kT air burst)			3,000 (est.)	38,000–70,000[3]

SOURCES: *The Effects of Nuclear Weapons*, 3rd ed. (Washington, D.C.: U.S. Department of Defense and U.S. Department of Energy, 1977); and Richard Rhodes, *The Making of the Atomic Bomb* (New York: Simon and Schuster, 1986).

NOTES

1. Population density is a crucial factor in determining the number of people killed in a nuclear blast. The figure of 5,000–15,000 per square kilometer used in our estimates is representative for core areas of dense U.S. cities, but does not encompass the top end of the range found in the United States. Manhattan, for example, has a density of well over 30,000 per square kilometer during a working day. See *The Effects of Nuclear Weapons*, 3rd ed., p. 544.

2. The number of people killed at Hiroshima has been difficult to determine precisely, largely because the 1945 population density of the city is not accurately known. The lower end of the range of fatalities corresponds to the population density estimate given here; both are based on data from Table 12.09, *The Effects of Nuclear Weapons*, 3rd ed., p. 544. The higher end of the range of fatality estimates is from Rhodes, *The Making of the Atomic Bomb*, p. 734. Our estimate for fatalities from a ground burst of the same size as the Hiroshima air burst is substantially lower, even at the high end of the population density estimate, because a ground burst produces less damage than an air burst at optimum altitude.

3. The number killed at Nagasaki is uncertain. The low end of the range of fatality estimates corresponds to the population density estimate given here, based on data from Table 12.09, *The Effects of Nuclear Weapons*, 3rd ed., p. 544. The high end is from Rhodes, *The Making of the Atomic Bomb*, p. 740.

times the area.[117] Disaster response efforts could save some lives, but most of the damage would occur in the first seconds after the attack, and could be neither prevented nor reversed.

Conclusion

We have argued that nuclear, biological, and chemical weapons are potentially available to states and non-state actors; that such weapons, whether they originate at home or abroad, can be delivered against targets in the United States with limited likelihood of detection; and that the effects of such weapons would be severe if used in attacks on densely populated areas. The United States is thus acutely vulnerable to covert NBC attack.

The threat spectrum, however, is wide. Chemical weapons are potentially available to a broad range of groups and states, but cause the least damage. Biological weapons are within the reach of many states and a few non-state actors, and could cause death on a scale comparable to nuclear weapons. Nuclear weapons are potentially available to many states and a few non-state actors, if weapons-usable fissile material is available. First-generation nuclear weapons could cause large numbers of deaths and large-scale physical destruction. Weapons of all three classes are deliverable against a wide range of targets, and defense is difficult. The stakes are high for the United States, and could be very high if biological or nuclear weapons are involved.

This analysis has implications for policies aimed at reducing vulnerability. First, while reliable denial is hard to achieve, targeted measures to control precursor access could delay or impede weapons acquisition. Stronger efforts to ensure the security of fissile material stocks offer the best hope of preventing access to nuclear weapons, because of the difficulty of producing such material. Precursor materials, equipment, and expertise for chemical or biological weapons are too widespread to control completely, but controls and supplier awareness measures for key precursors can impede proliferators. Such measures have already been put in place domestically for biological seed stocks, but could be tightened in other countries. Second, even if denial efforts are imperfect, intelligence and warning efforts can be improved by watching transactions in key materials and equipment more closely. Improved supplier awareness and improved awareness among law enforcement personnel can greatly increase the

---

117. Blast effects scale with the cube root of the yield, so the area destroyed is less than linearly proportional to the yield.

chances of detecting a weapons acquisition effort before it succeeds, and of catching the perpetrators after an attack. Finally, because effective emergency response can save many of the victims of chemical and biological attacks, there is good reason to develop the necessary capabilities. Chapter 5 provides specific policy recommendations derived from these general observations.

Box 7
Fission Weapons Physics and Design Concepts

To fuel the reactions that power them, nuclear weapons require fissile material: material whose nuclei are capable of being split by high-energy neutrons, releasing energy and more neutrons.[1] Nuclear weapons explode by rapidly splitting the nuclei of many atoms of fissile material, releasing far more energy than is available in normal chemical explosives. They accomplish this by creating a rapidly growing chain reaction, in which the fissioning — splitting — of one nucleus releases high-energy neutrons, some of which go on to split another nucleus and release more neutrons, and so on. A nuclear chain reaction can only sustain itself in an assembly of fissile material large and dense enough to keep many of the neutrons from escaping. An assembly in which, on average, each fission makes one other nucleus split, sustaining the reaction at a steady rate, is called "critical." A smaller or less dense assembly is called subcritical because it allows more neutrons to escape, and the reaction dies down. A supercritical assembly contains enough of the neutrons that each fission triggers on average more than one in the next generation, causing the reaction to grow exponentially. An assembly that is only slightly supercritical will produce a slow-growing reaction, and will heat up and melt, rather than exploding. All nuclear weapons rapidly assemble a highly supercritical mass of fissile material. When the weapon is detonated, the nuclear reaction grows so fast that large amounts of energy are released before the weapon destroys itself.

Weapons-usable Materials

Uranium-235 is the only fissile material that occurs naturally in large quantities.[2] It is present as only 0.7 percent of natural uranium, however, and concentrating — "enriching" — it to the level of purity required to make a bomb is a complicated and expensive undertaking.[3] The mass of uranium required to build a bomb varies strongly with its uranium-235 content. Enrichments below about 10 percent cannot cause a fission explosion, even in theory. Uranium enriched to more than 20 percent is referred to as highly enriched uranium (HEU). Material of 20 percent enrichment could conceivably be used in a workable explosive device, but such a device would have to be very large, and in practice much higher enrichments are desirable. "Weapons-grade" uranium is enriched to over 90 percent U-235. Other frequently mentioned weapons-usable isotopes are uranium-233, which can be made by bombarding thorium with neutrons in a nuclear reactor, and most of the isotopes of plutonium, which can be made from uranium-238 by the same method. The mass of plutonium required for a bomb varies with

Box 7, Fission Weapon Design, *cont.*

isotopic composition, but most isotopic mixes could be used in a practical explosive device.[4] "Weapons-grade" plutonium is nearly pure plutonium-239. "Reactor-grade" plutonium, which contains a higher proportion of plutonium isotopes 240 and above, poses an increased radiation hazard, and emits heat and neutrons at rates that impose some additional engineering challenges, but can still be used in weapons.[5] Uranium-233 has rarely been produced in bulk.

Basic Design Concepts

Two basic methods are used to assemble fissile material in a weapon into a highly critical configuration: gun assembly and implosion. In a gun-type weapon, a subcritical projectile of HEU is fired down a gun barrel and collides with a subcritical HEU assembly waiting at the end. The two together combine to form a supercritical assembly, which explodes. In an implosion weapon, high explosives are used to compress a subcritical assembly of HEU or plutonium, usually a hollow or solid sphere, into a sphere of greatly increased density. The high densities achieved in implosion decrease the required critical mass and increase the efficiency of the nuclear chain reaction, sharply reducing the amount of fissile material needed for a given explosive yield. Because fissile material is difficult and expensive to make, most states that have made nuclear weapons have chosen implosion designs for most of their weapons, to conserve their scare fissile materials and to maximize the number of weapons they could produce. South Africa is an exception to this generalization.[6]

In either design, the process of creating a highly supercritical assembly starts with the weapon in a subcritical configuration, and passes through criticality and low levels of supercriticality on its way to full assembly. A gun-type weapon carries out this process relatively slowly, relying on the low probability that a low energy "fizzle," resulting from a stray neutron starting the nuclear reaction when the weapon is only slightly supercritical, will destroy the weapon before it has a chance to explode properly. Plutonium releases a steady stream of neutrons from the spontaneous decay of its nuclei. The resulting stray neutrons are almost certain, if plutonium is used in a gun-type bomb, to initiate the chain reaction early, causing a "fizzle" that will destroy the weapon without producing a large nuclear yield. Thus, building a weapon out of plutonium requires the use of a high-explosive implosion system to compress the plutonium quickly into a highly supercritical configuration. When this is done quickly enough, the chance of a stray neutron being present at the wrong time becomes small.

Box 7, Fission Weapon Design, *cont.*

It is widely agreed among nuclear weapons experts that reliable first-generation nuclear explosive devices of either the gun-type or implosion design can be built without full-scale nuclear testing. Extensive testing of the gun or implosion mechanisms with non-fissile materials would be needed to ensure that assembly would occur correctly, but actual nuclear detonations are not needed. In fact, in the first use of a nuclear weapon in war, a gun-type bomb dubbed "Little Boy" was dropped on Hiroshima on August 6, 1945. The design was judged simple and reliable enough that the United States did not subject it to a full nuclear test before using it in combat. That design was based on measurements of essential physical data, such as fission cross-sections, that would be considered crude by today's standards. The United States and most other states with nuclear arsenals have tested their implosion weapons, but such tests are more important for reducing the size and improving the efficiency of more advanced weapons than for assuring the detonation of a first-generation design.

The requirements for building improvised nuclear weapons have been a subject of public debate for at least two decades, as has the ease or difficulty with which non-state actors such as terrorist groups could build such weapons. Credible sources, including former weapons designers, have argued that small non-state groups could make simple nuclear explosive devices out of improvised materials, such as uranium or plutonium oxides.[7] Arguments against the possibility of non-state groups building nuclear weapons tend to focus on the challenges of implosion designs or the problems of making weapons small and deliverable, problems that a group building a basic gun-type weapon need not solve.[8]

Some discussions of clandestine weapons programs also conclude that the challenges of gun-type and implosion nuclear weapons acquisition are roughly equivalent. These arguments often rest on the claim that the gun design is more difficult than it appears, because of the required characteristics of the gun itself.[9] However, a gun design can be considerably simpler both to design and to construct, provided the length and weight of the gun are not constrained by the traditional requirement that the weapon be deliverable by air. A longer, larger-diameter gun makes it easier to achieve the required projectile velocity without a high-performance design.[10] A gun-bomb project would also be less challenging in other respects than an implosion project, particularly for a non-state group. To begin with, use of a gun-type design eliminates the need to design and test explosive lenses and to synchronize them in an effective implosion system. Thus, the physics

Box 7, Fission Weapon Design, *cont.*

is simpler, because implosion need not be modeled, and the nuclear processes need only be modeled at normal densities. Acquiring the other materials, parts, and test equipment needed for a basic gun-type weapon project would also be easier and less expensive than for an implosion project. Not only is the gun design conceptually simpler and easier to fabricate, it avoids the requirement for large quantities of high-quality explosives. The purchase of explosives is controlled in many states, imposing a barrier that non-state actors may find hard to circumvent without risk of detection. While it would be challenging to design a mechanism capable of reliably forming a supercritical assembly when the projectile hits the catcher at 600 miles an hour, testing the mechanics of a gun design is easier than testing an implosion mechanism.

Finally, a gun-type design apparently makes it possible to eliminate the neutron initiator, albeit with some sacrifice in yield. South Africa is the only state known to have done this.[11] Presumably, the designers relied on neutron emissions from the HEU itself (which do occur in weapons-grade uranium, but at a low rate) or from natural background radiation to trigger a chain reaction. Because a gun-type weapon does not involve a terribly violent assembly system, and because it does not create an ultra-compressed and therefore short-lived critical assembly, a weapon can apparently be designed so that assembly happens quickly, but not so violently as to blow the critical assembly apart before a stray neutron can start the chain reaction. How difficult this is to achieve depends on the skills of those building the weapon. South Africa, which has a large arms industry that makes high-quality artillery and other weapons, had access to experienced engineers, a luxury that might not be available to a non-state group. But the builders of an improvised weapon could simplify the problem somewhat by overdesigning certain weapons components, albeit at some cost in greater weight. The weight increase would be intolerable in a military weapon meant for air or missile delivery, but would matter much less in a truck bomb. Mock-up assemblies would also have to be built and test-fired to ensure that the assembly behaved as expected under the intense forces generated by the high-velocity impact.

NOTES

1. This discussion draws on a number of previously published summaries of nuclear weapons physics and design concepts. See Thomas B. Cochran, William M. Arkin, and Milton M. Hoenig, *Nuclear Weapons Databook,* Vol. I: *U.S. Nuclear Forces and Capabilities* (Cambridge, Mass.: Ballinger, 1984), pp. 22–26; U.S. Congress, Office of Technology Assessment (OTA), *Nuclear Proliferation and Safeguards* (New York: Praeger, 1977), pp. 139–144; OTA, *Technologies Underlying*

Box 7, Fission Weapon Design, *cont.*

Weapons of Mass Destruction (Washington, D.C.: U.S. GPO, December 1993), pp. 173–175; Leonard S. Spector, *Nuclear Ambitions: The Spread of Nuclear Weapons, 1989–1990* (Boulder, Colo.: Westview, 1990), pp. 417–422; and Robert Serber, *The Los Alamos Primer* (Berkeley: University of California Press, 1992). Considerable information on the development of the first atomic bombs and on the underlying science and technology can also be found in Richard Rhodes, *The Making of the Atomic Bomb* (New York: Simon and Schuster, 1986); and in Lillian Hoddeson, Paul W. Henriksen, and Roger A. Meade, *Critical Assembly: A Technical History of Los Alamos During the Oppenheimer Years, 1943–1945* (New York: Cambridge University Press, 1993).

2. Uranium-235 is one of several isotopes of uranium. A chemical element, such as uranium, is identified by the number of electrons orbiting its nucleus, which determines its behavior in chemical reactions. A given element can be further categorized by its various isotopes, which have slightly different masses, contain different numbers of neutrons in their nuclei, and have different characteristics in nuclear reactions such as fission and radioactive decay.

3. Because different isotopes of an element are nearly identical chemically, normal chemical separation processes are almost useless for separating them. As a result, uranium enrichment is extremely difficult and expensive. A thorough technical overview is given in Manson Benedict, Thomas Pigford, and Hans Levi, *Nuclear Chemical Engineering* (New York: McGraw-Hill, 1981), pp. 812–931. A brief overview can be found in OTA, *Technologies Underlying Weapons of Mass Destruction*, pp. 176-180.

4. See U.S. Department of Energy, Office of Arms Control and Nonproliferation, *Nonproliferation and Arms Control Assessment of Weapons-Usable Fissile Material Storage and Excess Plutonium Disposition Alternatives* (Washington, D.C.: U.S. Department of Energy, January 1997), pp. 37–39.

5. Reactor grade plutonium is plutonium produced in power reactor fuel. Economical operation of power reactors requires long fuel-residence times in the core, causing much of the plutonium-239 produced to be converted to plutonium-240 by neutron bombardment. The ratio of plutonium-240 to plutonium-239 is about 1 to 3 under normal conditions. Plutonium-240 emits neutrons and heat that make materials containing large amounts of it harder to use in weapons. "Weapons-grade" plutonium, in contrast, would have no more than 7 percent plutonium-240. National Academy of Sciences, *Management and Disposition of Excess Weapons Plutonium: Reactor Related Options* (Washington, D.C.: National Academy Press, 1995), p. 45.

6. See David Albright, *South Africa's Secret Nuclear Weapons* (Washington, D.C.: Institute for Science and International Security, May 1994).

Box 7, Fission Weapon Design, *cont.*

7. See OTA, *Nuclear Proliferation and Safeguards*, pp. 140–143; Mason Willrich and Theodore B. Taylor, *Nuclear Theft: Risks and Safeguards* (Cambridge, Mass.: Ballinger, 1974); or the excerpt from it reproduced as "Nuclear Theft: Risks and Safeguards," in Augustus R. Norton and Martin H. Greenberg, eds., *Studies in Nuclear Terrorism* (Boston: G.K. Hall, 1977), pp. 59–84; and J. Carson Mark, Theodore Taylor, Eugene Eyster, et al., "Can Terrorists Build Nuclear Weapons?" in Paul Leventhal and Yonah Alexander, eds., *Preventing Nuclear Terrorism* (Lexington, Mass.: Lexington Books, 1987), pp. 55–65. The latter article revises elements of Taylor's earlier views, but supports his central contention that nuclear weapons could be built by small groups of people with the right skills.

8. See, for example, Karl-Heinz Kamp, "An Overrated Nightmare," *Bulletin of the Atomic Scientists*, Vol. 52, No. 4 (July/August 1996), pp. 32–33.

9. "The difficulties of the gun assembly are often not appreciated: a large mass of high density must be accelerated to a high speed in a short distance, putting quite unusual requirements on the gun design." OTA, *Nuclear Proliferation and Safeguards*, p. 142.

10. In other words, "The problem of fabricating a nuclear device is even simpler if the purpose is only to demonstrate nuclear capability and no premium is placed on such military requirements as low weight and deliverability." Ted Greenwood, George W. Rathjens, and Jack Ruina, *Nuclear Power and Weapons Proliferation*, Adelphi Paper No. 130 (London: International Institute for Strategic Studies, 1976), p. 6.

11. David Albright, a physicist who has investigated South Africa's nuclear weapons program, reports that its six gun-type bombs apparently did not use a neutron trigger of any sort to initiate the intended nuclear explosion. See David Albright, *South Africa's Secret Nuclear Weapons*, p. 12.

Chapter 3

The Threat of Nuclear, Biological, or Chemical Attack by Non-State Actors

How serious is the threat of covert nuclear, biological, or chemical attack by a terrorist group or other hostile non-state actor? Countless non-state actors with hostile intent have arisen in the past decades, but only one — Aum Shinrikyo — has combined the technological capability needed to mount a terrorist act involving a real weapon of mass destruction with the intent of doing so. This is a remarkable fact, especially against the backdrop of the most murderous century in human history.[1]

In Chapter 1, we explained why this particular form of violence has been so rare. Many of the factors that have discouraged NBC terrorism in the past will continue to do so. But a threat assessment based solely on extrapolation from the past would be misleading. Changes in the nature of non-state violence, in the ease of acquiring NBC weapons, and in the role of the United States in the world suggest that the probability of significant non-state NBC attacks is greater than zero now, and is growing larger.

There is a growing body of expert and official opinion, especially in the United States, that the threat of non-state violence involving weapons of mass destruction is becoming one of the most serious security challenges of the modern era. Senator Sam Nunn, after the Tokyo incident, came to the belief that "this attack signals the world has entered a new era."[2] A year before becoming secretary of defense, Senator William Cohen noted that "it does not require much imagination to envision that those who hire terrorists to blow up jumbo jets might enlist them to poison our populations."[3] In an

---

1. It is estimated that 110 million people have been killed in major armed conflicts in the twentieth century, compared to 19 million in the nineteenth and 7 million in the eighteenth.

2. "Opening Statement of Senator Nunn," in U.S. Congress, *Global Proliferation of Weapons of Mass Destruction*, Part I, Hearings before the Permanent Subcommittee on Investigations, Committee on Governmental Affairs, U.S. Senate, 104th Cong., 1st Sess. (Washington, D.C.: U.S. Government Printing Office [U.S. GPO], October 31 and November 1, 1995), p. 5.

3. "Opening Statement of Senator Cohen," in U.S. Congress, *Global Proliferation of Weapons of Mass Destruction*, Part I, p. 8.

initiative that was spearheaded by Senators Sam Nunn, Richard Lugar, and Pete Domenici in 1996, Congress overwhelmingly passed legislation designed to improve domestic preparedness for NBC terrorism (see Box 11, Nunn-Lugar-Domenici, p. 262). Director of Central Intelligence John Deutch stated in May 1996 that the "proliferation of nuclear, biological, and chemical weapons and their potential use by states or terrorists is the most urgent challenge facing the national security, and therefore the intelligence community, in the post–Cold War world."[4] Walter Laqueur, a terrorism expert once skeptical of the risk of NBC terrorism, wrote in 1996 that "proliferation of weapons of mass destruction does not mean that most terrorist groups are likely to use them in the foreseeable future, but some almost certainly will, in spite of all the reasons militating against it."[5] According to FBI Director Louis Freeh, "the acquisition, proliferation, threatened or actual use of weapons of mass destruction by a terrorist group or individuals constitutes one of the gravest threats to the United States. The government's policy recognizes that there is no higher priority than preventing the acquisition of this capability or removing this capability from terrorist groups potentially opposed to the United States."[6]

We believe that the growing concern about the possibility of NBC terrorism is justified. In Chapter 1, we argued that there is a range of reasons why few non-state actors have emerged with both the technical capacity and the motivation to acquire and use nuclear, biological, and chemical weapons. The ability to acquire and use NBC weapons is quite distinct from interest in causing mass casualties, which in turn is distinct from wanting to use weapons of mass destruction to do so (a relationship depicted in Figure 1). A specific threat of NBC terrorism arises when a

---

4.   John M. Deutch, Speech to Harvard–Los Alamos Conference on Nuclear, Biological, and Chemical Weapons Proliferation and Terrorism, Washington, D.C., May 23, 1996, <www.odci.gov/cia/public_affairs/speeches/archives/1996/dci_speech_052396.html>.

5.   Walter Laqueur, "Postmodern Terrorism," *Foreign Affairs*, Vol. 75, No. 5 (September/October 1996), p. 34. Laqueur had earlier written: "For a variety of reasons [NBC weapons] are not rational weapons for non-state actors.... While the use of these weapons can never be ruled out, the probability remains low." Walter Laqueur, *The Age of Terrorism* (Boston: Little, Brown, 1987), p. 319.

6.   Louis J. Freeh, "Counterterrorism," Statement before the Senate Appropriations Committee, U.S. Senate, May 13, 1997, available at <www.fbi.gov/congress/counter/terror.htm>.

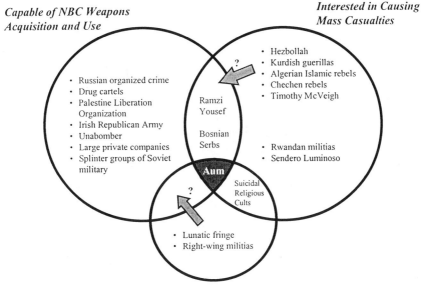

*Capable of NBC Weapons
Acquisition and Use*

*Interested in Causing
Mass Casualties*

- Russian organized crime
- Drug cartels
- Palestine Liberation Organization
- Irish Republican Army
- Unabomber
- Large private companies
- Splinter groups of Soviet military

Ramzi Yousef

Bosnian Serbs

?

- Hezbollah
- Kurdish guerillas
- Algerian Islamic rebels
- Chechen rebels
- Timothy McVeigh

- Rwandan militias
- Sendero Luminoso

Aum

?

Suicidal Religious Cults

- Lunatic fringe
- Right-wing militias

Interested in Using NBC

Figure 1. Non-state Actors, Mass Casualties, and NBC Weapons.

group emerges that falls into all three categories: capable of NBC weapons acquisition and use; interested in causing mass casualties; and interested in using NBC weapons to this end. We argue that the threat of NBC terrorism is growing more serious with time because large-scale societal trends are gradually expanding the number of groups simultaneously capable of acquiring weapons of mass destruction and interested in inflicting mass casualties. The purpose of this chapter is to identify these large-scale trends and to clarify their relationship to the long-term threat of NBC terrorism.

First, the range of non-state actors capable of acquiring and using NBC weapons is clearly increasing. This trend results from broad phenomena, particularly the expansion of the social knowledge base and the increasing ease of access to information, as well as from specific NBC-related developments, such as the erosion of the Soviet nuclear custodial system.

Second, there is a growing body of evidence that non-state actors are becoming more interested in causing human casualties on a massive scale. This is a relatively new development, and is poorly understood. The classic conceptual model of a terrorist organization — that of an established group with limited political aims, a strategy of controlled violence for achieving them, and an interest in self-preservation — appears to be breaking down. New groups are emerging with hazier objectives, shorter life spans, and a more direct interest in violence for its own sake, often for reasons rooted in religious fundamentalism or political radicalism. The ascendance of Western culture and U.S. power in the post–Cold War international system is making the United States and its allies increasingly attractive as targets of terrorism. In short, the nature of terrorism is changing in a way that suggests there will be an expanding range of groups that are both capable of using weapons of mass destruction and interested in inflicting human casualties at levels well beyond the terrorist norms of the previous decades. We explore this point in the second section below.

But will such groups actually employ nuclear, biological, or chemical weapons? There is scant evidence of an increase in the number of groups interested in having anything to do with weapons of mass destruction in the first place, a fact that makes this question hard to answer. Virtually all known groups continue to find that the tried-and-true arsenal of conventional weapons provides the tools they need. Aside from the Aum Shinrikyo case, only a handful of individuals and groups — most of them on the lunatic fringe — have been caught in possession of, or attempting to acquire, materials or equipment that could be used in a chemical or biological weapon. These few cases are not a strong indicator of a rising level of interest in NBC weapons among hostile non-state actors, making it difficult to do more than speculate as to whether Aum Shinrikyo was an anomaly or the first of many NBC-armed non-state actors. We consider this issue further in the third section below.

In sum, we argue that the threat of NBC terrorism is growing because an increasing number of non-state actors are simultaneously NBC-capable and interested in causing mass casualties. At best, these two trends suggest that conventional non-state violence is likely to become more deadly. At worst, they suggest that violent non-state actors are moving into position for more frequent and more effective forays into the largely uncharted territory of NBC terrorism. It is possible that none of these capable, bloodthirsty groups will choose to resort to NBC weapons, but considering the consequences that would result from such a decision, it would be imprudent for the United States to continue to assume that the threat of NBC terrorism will lie dormant indefinitely.

Non-state Actors are Growing More Capable of Acquiring and Using NBC Weapons

Building or stealing a weapon of mass destruction is a difficult, complex, risky, often expensive task, but the basic technical requirements for building

NBC weapons are established and are not becoming any more difficult. Indeed, as argued in Chapter 2, the acquisition of several types of improvised NBC weapons is actually growing easier, as the materials, equipment, and expertise necessary for a successful acquisition effort — some not very hard to get in the first place — become more readily and widely available to non-state actors. The technical barriers to NBC acquisition are at best fixed, and are probably declining.

The latent ability of non-state actors to master the challenges associated with NBC attack is rising in all modern societies. This gradual increase in potential NBC capabilities is in part a byproduct of economic, educational, and technological progress. Furthermore, in most modern societies, particularly those that have entered the information age, the ability of the state to monitor and counter illegal or threatening activities is being outpaced by the increasing efficiency, complexity, technological sophistication, and geographic span of the activities, legal or illegal, of non-state actors. Taken together with the factors discussed in Chapter 2, these trends imply that the number of non-state actors with the latent capacity to build or use weapons of mass destruction is increasing.

THE IMPACT OF ECONOMIC, EDUCATIONAL, AND TECHNOLOGICAL PROGRESS
The technological and scientific challenges associated with covert NBC acquisition and use are significant, but they are also not getting any harder. The amount of HEU needed to produce a nuclear explosion is the same today as it was in 1945; the particle size necessary to create a stable, respirable aerosol of anthrax spores is the same today as it has always been; and the chemical structure of sarin remains unchanged from 1939, when the substance was discovered by a German chemist trying to produce a better pesticide. Meanwhile, non-state actors are growing more capable, primarily as a consequence of the economic, educational, and technological progress of their societies. As a result, the number and range of non-state actors with NBC potential is expanding. Since the fundamental cause is social progress, this expansion of latent non-state actor NBC potential is inexorable, and is not reversible or even manageable by governments.

How and why is the underlying capacity of non-state actors to master the technical challenges of NBC acquisition and use increasing? The first reason is that the basic science behind these weapons is being learned by more people, better than ever before. In the United States alone, the number

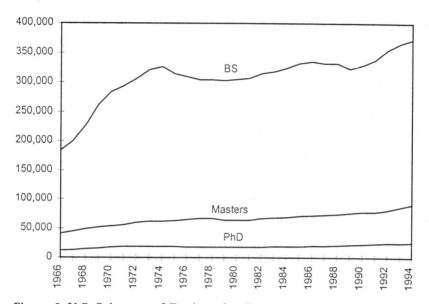

Figure 2. U.S. Science and Engineering Degrees, 1966–94.
SOURCE: National Science Foundation, Science and Engineering Degrees: 1966–94, NSF 96-321 (Arlington, Va.: National Science Foundation, 1996), Table 1, p. 35.

of people receiving bachelor's, master's, and doctoral degrees in science and engineering fields each year more than doubled between 1966 and 1994 (see Figure 2). Over the same time period, the number of B.S. degrees awarded in biology increased by 122 percent, and the number of Ph.Ds grew by 144 percent; more than 60,000 advanced degrees were granted in biology each year by 1994 (see Figure 3). Some of these increases result from cyclical fluctuations in the college-age population, but it is also the case that the number of science and engineering bachelor's degrees awarded for every thousand 22-year-olds in the U.S. population has increased steadily over the last 30 years, from 65 in 1966 to 103 in 1994.[7] These statistics suggest that the underlying scientific and technical competence of the U.S. population is rising with time. Education data on other countries suggest similar trends.

---

7.   National Science Foundation, *Science and Engineering Degrees: 1966–94*, NSF 96-321 (Arlington, Va.: National Science Foundation, 1996), Table 56, p. 90. Master's degrees per capita have increased much more slowly, and Ph.Ds per capita have increased hardly at all, holding steady at about 5–7 per 1,000 30-year-olds.

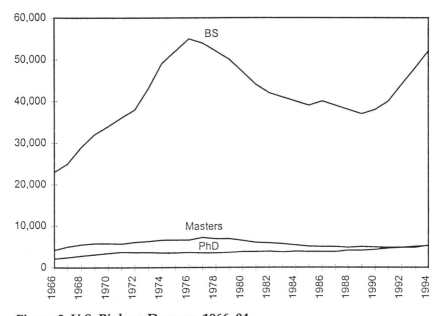

Figure 3. U.S. Biology Degrees, 1966–94.
SOURCE: National Science Foundation, Science and Engineering Degrees: 1966–94,
NSF 96-321 (Arlington, Va.: National Science Foundation, 1996), Table 49, p. 83.

An even more important gauge of the ability of non-state actors to build
and use weapons of mass destruction is the increasing level of knowledge
available even in high school science courses, not to mention undergraduate
or graduate-level courses, as well as the sophistication of the laboratory and
analytical tools, from computers to laboratory-scale fermentation equipment, that are now routinely available. The new physics that the Manhattan
Project scientists — many of the world's most brilliant — had to discover to
make nuclear weapons possible is now standard textbook fare for young
physicists and engineers. No undergraduate of the 1930s could reasonably
have expected to perform the criticality calculations necessary to determine
how much of a particular type of fissile material would need to be
assembled to produce a nuclear explosion; in 1998, however, some
undergraduates can, not least because they have access to high-quality data
on the relevant nuclear reactions, and to quite capable computers. In other
words, increasing numbers of people are receiving increasingly sophisticated scientific and technical educations, and are simultaneously gaining
access to increasingly sophisticated information and tools.

Nowhere is this phenomenon more pronounced than in biology. In the past forty years, since Watson and Crick identified the structure of DNA in 1954, major scientific advances have greatly expanded the understanding of biological processes, and in particular have created new abilities to manipulate genetic material and produce specific biological substances, such as human hormones, in bulk. In the mid-1970s, a new "biotechnology" industry emerged that sought to exploit the commercial potential of the rapid advances in the biological sciences. Biotechnology has emerged as a key area of American comparative advantage in the global economy, but the more profound impact of biotechnology is the growing ability of human beings to control the biological and genetic processes of virtually all living things.[8]

The biotechnology revolution will have two basic effects on the long-term risks posed by biological weapons. First, the advance of the biological sciences is creating a situation in which a sophisticated offensive program can more easily produce advanced biological weapons with heightened resistance to prophylaxis or treatment, increased virulence, controllable incubation periods and agent longevity, and conceivably even a selectivity that targets groups of people according to their genetic makeup.[9] If such

---

8. A useful overview of the science behind biotechnology, and its commercial applications, is Office of Science and Technology Policy, National Critical Technologies Report, March 1995, Chapter 5, <www.whitehouse.gov/WH/EOP/OSTP/CTIformatted/chap5/5living.html#head1>; John H. Gibbons, "Biotechnology: Opportunity and Challenge," speech to the National Biotechnology Summit, Omni Shoreham Hotel, Washington, D.C., January 24, 1994, <www.whitehouse.gov/WH/EOP/OSTP/other/sp940124.html>; and Susan Aldridge, *The Thread of Life: The Story of Genes and Genetic Engineering* (Cambridge: Cambridge University Press, 1996).

9. See Erhard Geissler, "Implications of Genetic Engineering for Chemical and Biological Warfare," in Stockholm International Peace Research Institute (SIPRI), *World Armaments and Disarmament: SIPRI Yearbook 1984* (London: Taylor & Francis, 1984), pp. 421–451; U.S. Congress, Office of Technology Assessment (OTA), *Technologies Underlying Weapons of Mass Destruction* (Washington, D.C.: U.S. GPO, December 1993), pp. 113–117; Leonard A. Cole, *Clouds of Secrecy: The Army's Germ Warfare Tests over Populated Areas* (Totowa, N.J.: Rowman & Littlefield, 1988), pp. 121–135; and Charles Piller and Keith R. Yamamoto, *Gene Wars: Military Control over the New Genetic Technologies* (New York: Beech Tree Books, 1988), pp. 93–126. States may also find that biotechnology makes it easier to produce effective vaccines to protect their own troops and people from their weapons. Jonathan B. Tucker, "Gene Wars," *Foreign Policy*, No. 57 (Winter 1984–85), pp. 58–79. For a brief discussion of

sophisticated weapons are developed, they are most likely to be found in the secret arsenals of relatively advanced states, since developing weapons of this kind will be considerably more difficult than producing naturally occurring biological warfare agents.

Naturally occurring biological agents, however, retain their potential as weapons of mass destruction. The second impact of the biotechnology revolution is to increase the number of people with the knowledge to use such agents, and to make the agents easier to produce and employ as weapons. The biotechnology industry's growth is causing a steady increase in the number of people who understand how simple biological processes (such as growing bacteria) can be used in a practical way, and who are capable of manipulating these processes for their own ends. According to the Biotechnology Industry Organization, in 1996, 118,000 people were employed by 1,287 U.S. firms focused specifically on biotechnology, up from virtually zero in the early 1980s.[10] As the biotechnology sector becomes entrenched in the global economy, the number of people with the skills necessary to undertake a basic biological weapons program will inevitably grow.[11] Just as important, the industry's growth has made available a wide range of tools and supplies — such as efficient fermenters for producing large amounts of bacteria in small facilities, and increasingly sophisticated tools for measuring aerosols — that would make a proliferator's biological weapons procurement effort easier.

Finally, even apart from rising education levels and growing familiarity with relevant technologies, the latent NBC potential of non-state actors is growing because the ability to acquire information of all kinds, quickly and

---

the possibilities of genetically tailoring biological agents to attack particular ethnic groups, see Malcolm Dando, "'Discriminating' Bio-Weapons Could Target Ethnic Groups," *Jane's International Defense Review*, March 1977, pp. 77–78. Note, however, that designing organisms for specific purposes is still a difficult and uncertain process. Standard biological warfare agents remain the primary risk. See U.S. Department of Defense, *Advances in Biotechnology and Genetic Engineering: Implications for the Development of New Biological Warfare Agents* (Washington, D.C.: U.S. Department of Defense, June 1996), <www.acq.osd.mil/cp/biotech96.htm>.

10. See <www.bio.org>.

11. According to the 1992 Census of Manufacturers, there were 750 establishments engaged in pharmaceutical preparations and 268 engaged in producing biological products. Terence Taylor and L. Celeste Johnson, *The Biotechnology Industry of the United States: A Census of Facilities* (Stanford, Calif.: Center for International Security and Arms Control, July 1995), p. 5.

with ease, is increasing. The Internet contains a vast amount of information relevant to the planning and execution of complex violent acts, ranging from information on specific targets to detailed accounts of previous terrorist incidents and tactics, and even basic design information for nuclear, biological, and chemical weapons. Much of this information has been present in libraries for years, but access to it has never been easier. Today's violent non-state actors are able to start substantially higher on the terrorist learning curve, compared to their predecessors of even a decade ago, if they can conduct even a modest computerized search for information.

NON-STATE EFFICIENCY AND FLEXIBILITY IS OUTPACING THAT OF THE STATE
National governments will seek to suppress non-state efforts to acquire weapons of mass destruction on their territory. The difficulty of clandestine NBC acquisition, therefore, depends in part on the interested non-state actor's effectiveness at eluding the surveillance and enforcement efforts of state agencies. The relationship between any particular non-state actor and its pursuers is likely to be idiosyncratic, but as a general matter it appears that the efficiency of non-state operations is outpacing the efficiency of state operations, at least in the United States, and probably everywhere in the developed world.[12] Non-state actors are improving their ability to hide faster than states are improving their ability to seek.

A complex, illegal activity like clandestine NBC weapons acquisition has several different constituent parts, any of which may be vulnerable to law enforcement surveillance. A team of like-minded, appropriately skilled individuals must be assembled; places must be found for them to work; they must be able to communicate with one another, possibly over great distances; financing must be secured; information, materials, and equipment must be gathered, possibly from abroad; and a dangerous weapon must be assembled and delivered without misstep. This is a challenging set of tasks, and would entail risks of detection in any state able to provide for its internal security. The rapid development of communications and transportation systems makes several of these tasks easier, however, at the same time as the explosion of legitimate use of such systems makes criminal usage harder to spot. Today, the Internet and other networked systems allow far-flung groups to communicate with ease, and like-minded individuals to locate one another at an anonymous distance. Some kinds of

---

12. A similar argument is made in Jessica T. Matthews, "Power Shift," *Foreign Affairs*, Vol. 76, No. 1 (January/February 1997), pp. 50–66.

information are much easier to gather electronically than from paper sources. Supplies and weapons are increasingly easy to transport quickly and reliably.

Fundamentally, this phenomenon results from advances in the private sector's ability to communicate.[13] Whereas non-state actors once had access to little more than analog phone lines and the mail, today they can communicate by fax, cellular or satellite telephone, teleconference, alphanumeric pagers, e-mail, computer modem, and computer bulletin boards. They can quickly transport at least certain kinds of weapons and supplies via Federal Express, United Parcel Service, DHL, and numerous other highly efficient shipping services. Telecommunications traffic has increased vastly in both volume and variety over the last decades, easily outpacing the state's ability keep track of it all.[14] The communications systems available to non-state actors also now have the potential to be more secure than ever. Strong encryption systems were once "the exclusive domain of governments,"[15] but today virtually unbreakable encryption software is now readily available on the global software market, and easily downloaded off the Internet.[16] The benefits to legitimate users are considerable, but the implications of this trend for the ability of law enforcement agencies to cope with increasingly sophisticated non-state actors are profound. According to FBI Director Louis Freeh:

Law enforcement is in unanimous agreement that the widespread use of robust unbreakable encryption ultimately will devastate our ability to fight crime and prevent terrorism. Unbreakable encryption will allow drug lords, spies, terrorists and even violent gangs to communicate about their crimes and their

---

13.   A related argument is made in John Arquilla and David Ronfeldt, *The Advent of Netwar* (Santa Monica, Calif.: RAND, 1996), pp. 15–16, 81–82.

14.   Likewise, with respect to physical traffic, "huge increases in the volume of goods and people crossing borders and competitive pressures to speed the flow of trade by easing inspections and reducing paperwork make it easier to hide contraband." Matthews, "Power Shift," p. 58.

15.   Richard C. Barth and Clint N. Smith, "International Regulation of Encryption: Technology Will Drive Policy," in Brian Kahin and Charles Nesson, eds., *Borders in Cyberspace: Information Policy and the Global Information Infrastructure* (Cambridge, Mass.: MIT Press, 1997), p. 263.

16.   For an overview of the relevant issues, see National Research Council, *Cryptography's Role in Securing the Information Society* (Washington, D.C.: National Research Council, 1996).

conspiracies with impunity. We will lose one of the few remaining vulnerabilities for the worst criminals and terrorists upon which law enforcement depends to successfully investigate and prevent the worst crimes.[17]

Government efforts to control the availability of unbreakable encryption software have failed, and the nature of the technology makes them unlikely to succeed in the future.[18]

Before the information age, this situation was markedly different: state agencies had clear technological dominance over their non-state challengers, in areas ranging from sophisticated eavesdropping equipment to advanced surveillance cameras. Law enforcement and intelligence gathering continue to benefit from improving technology, but generally cannot increase their effectiveness at detecting hidden illegal activities at the same rate because of the constraints of law, manpower, financial resources, and technology. As one study has put it, "power is migrating to actors who are skilled at developing networks, and at operating in a world of networks.... Non-state adversaries — from warriors to criminals, especially those that are transnational — are currently ahead of government actors at using, and being able to use, this mode of organization and related doctrines and strategies."[19] In this competition between a centralized process, in which the state seeks the needle of criminal activity in the haystack of an increasingly complex society, and decentralized criminal processes where effectiveness is limited only by human competence, resources, and ever-advancing technology, the state is clearly at a disadvantage.[20]

---

17.   Louis J. Freeh, "The Impact of Encryption on Public Safety," Statement before the Permanent Select Committee on Intelligence, U.S. House of Representatives, September 9, 1997, available at <www.fbi.gov/congress>.

18.   For a useful description of the technical issues associated with government control over encryption technology, see Hal Abelson, Ross Anderson, Steven M. Bellovin, et al., *The Risks of Key Recovery, Key Escrow, and Trusted Third Party Encryption: A Report by an Ad Hoc Group of Cryptographers and Computer Scientists*, May 1997, <www.crypto.com/key_study>.

19.   Arquilla and Ronfeldt, *The Advent of Netwar*, p. 43.

20.   As Eugene Skolnikoff has put it, "it is therefore a reasonable, though qualitative, conclusion that the introduction of information technologies (and other technologies that play a synergistic role) tend, on balance, to have consequences that are biased in the direction of increased limitations on the centralization of political power and toward greater openness within a society." Skolnikoff, *The*

Organized Non-state Violence is Becoming Increasingly Lethal

Non-state actors interested in inflicting mass casualties are not as rare as they once were, and the general aversion to large-scale organized killing appears to be diminishing. In combination with the growing capabilities of non-state actors discussed above, this trend toward more lethal non-state violence suggests that larger numbers of violent groups may acquire the motivational and operational prerequisites of NBC terrorism.

What evidence supports this claim of rising lethality? On the whole, the behavior of violent non-state actors is very poorly understood, making general claims about their conduct suspect. Such groups are highly idiosyncratic and often ephemeral, and the community of experts who study them has so far failed even to agree on a common typology for categorizing them.[21] Good data are, however, gathered on acts of international terrorism, and these data bear out the conclusion that this particular form of non-state violence is becoming less frequent but more lethal. According to the U.S. State Department, "while the incidence of international terrorism has dropped sharply in the last decade, the overall threat of terrorism remains very serious. The death toll from acts of international terrorism rose from 163 in 1995 to 311 in 1996, as the trend continued toward more ruthless attacks on mass civilian targets and the use of more powerful bombs."[22] Based on the most detailed database of terrorism incidents in the public domain — the RAND–St. Andrews Chronology of International Terrorist Incidents — Bruce Hoffman similarly concluded that

---

Elusive Transformation: Science, Technology and the Evolution of International Politics (Princeton, N.J.: Princeton University Press, 1993), p. 101.

21. For a survey of the different typologies and definitions that have appeared in the terrorism literature, see Wayman C. Mullins, *A Sourcebook on Domestic and International Terrorism: An Analysis of Issues, Organizations, Tactics and Responses*, 2d ed. (Springfield, Ill.: Charles C. Thomas, 1997), pp. 16–40.

22. U.S. Department of State, *Patterns of Global Terrorism 1996* (Washington, D.C.: U.S. Department of State, April 1997), p. 1, available at <www.state.gov/www/global/terrorism>. The overall drop in the incidence of terrorism noted by the State Department results from the post–Cold War decline in left-wing, ideologically motivated terrorism (e.g., the Red Army Faction in Germany, the Italian Red Brigades, Japan's United Red Army), and a marked drop in state-sponsored international terrorism.

"while terrorists were becoming less active, they were also becoming more lethal. For example, at least one person was killed in 29 percent of terrorist incidents in 1995: the highest percentage of fatalities to incidents recorded in the Chronology since 1968."[23] Although data of this kind must be treated with some caution, the general conclusion of decreasing prevalence and increasing lethality is very widely held among terrorism experts.[24]

International terrorism is, however, only a subset of the broader phenomenon of organized non-state violence. Unfortunately, the data available on other types of violent non-state actors is even less systematic and conclusive. Many countries, including the United States, suffer from terrorism of a purely domestic character, but information on these incidents is not gathered or released in all countries, and there exists no global compilation. Limited anecdotal evidence (e.g., the 1995 Oklahoma City bombing, the series of bombings of women's health clinics) suggests that the lethality of domestic terrorism is also rising. The 1995 FBI report on terrorism noted that "large-scale attacks designed to inflict mass casualties appear to be a new terrorist method in the United States."[25] Another form of non-state violence of concern, ethnic conflict and guerrilla warfare, has been more deadly than terrorism — international or domestic — by several orders of magnitude. The years since the end of the Cold War have seen an explosion of exceptionally deadly internal conflicts, in Algeria, Bosnia, Somalia, Rwanda, Sudan, Tajikistan, and Afghanistan. Such conflicts also

---

23. Bruce Hoffman, "Terrorism and WMD: Some Preliminary Hypotheses," *Nonproliferation Review*, Vol. 4, No. 3 (Spring–Summer 1997), p. 47. See also Bruce Hoffman, "Terrorist Targeting," *Terrorism and Political Violence*, Vol. 5, No. 2 (Summer 1993), pp. 14–19.

24. There are two key problems in attempting to use the available data to make firm conclusions on terrorist trends. The first is that the casualty figures for any individual year tend to be dominated by any extremely lethal single event that occurs, such as the destruction of an airliner or major building. Thus, an increase in the average lethality of terrorist attacks in a single year may have everything to do with the idiosyncratic lethality of a single attack, and nothing to do with the intentions of the terrorists involved in all other incidents that year. The second problem is that the overall incidence of international terrorist incidents is strongly correlated to wars, major regional crises, and other divisive world events. Thus, apparent trends in terrorist incidents might not indicate any change in underlying "terrorist motivations," but could simply reflect fluctuations in inter-state tension.

25. U.S. Department of Justice, Federal Bureau of Investigation, *Terrorism in the United States 1995* (Washington, D.C.: FBI, 1996), <www.fbi.gov>.

appear to be becoming more lethal than they were in the past, but there are insufficient data to know with certainty whether today's hostile actors really want to kill more people than their predecessors did, or whether instead the impression of increasingly lethal internal conflicts results primarily from other factors or an exaggerated emphasis on current headlines.[26]

The questions of greatest interest for present purposes are really two, and neither can be conclusively answered by statistical analysis alone. First, is the number of groups interested in killing large numbers of people growing? And second, is the level of killing that violent non-state actors believe necessary to achieve their objectives rising? Despite the limitations of the available data, we believe that the answer to both questions is "yes."

In Chapter 1, we argued that there were four principal reasons why non-state actors, and particularly terrorist organizations, have chosen to kill fewer people than they are capable of killing: first, mass-casualty attacks tend to undermine political support for the organizations that commit them and the causes that motivate them; second, mass casualties raise the risks of unfettered reprisal by affected governments; third, increasing casualties does not clearly reduce the difficulty of terrorist coercion; and fourth, decisions to increase the level of violence tend to increase internal dissension, thus jeopardizing group preservation. While these considerations will continue to discourage much mass-casualty violence in the future, changes in the character of non-state violence in the 1990s, particularly in the types of non-state actors committing violent acts, appear to be weakening the past disincentives to mass-casualty attacks.

Five trends, often tightly interrelated, point toward increasingly lethal non-state violence. First, violence and terrorism motivated by religion are becoming more common and more lethal. Second, local opposition to U.S. influence and military presence appears to be intensifying in the moderate, pro-American sheikdoms of the Persian Gulf region, resulting in increasingly frequent and damaging anti-American terrorist attacks. Third, right-wing terrorism appears to be growing both more prevalent and more lethal. In the United States, this was seen most clearly in the 1995 bombing of the Federal Building in Oklahoma City. Fourth, "amateur" terrorists appear to be growing more common, suggesting that terrorism is becoming more spontaneous and that the groups responsible for these acts of violence are

---

26. In 1995, major internal conflicts were underway in 35 regions. For a summary, see Michael E. Brown, "Introduction," in Michael E. Brown, ed., *The International Dimensions of Internal Conflict*, CSIA Studies in International Security (Cambridge, Mass.: MIT Press, 1996), pp. 3–8.

less concerned with group preservation than were the terrorist organizations of the 1970s and 1980s. Finally, racism and ethnic hatred continue to motivate extreme acts of violence in guerrilla wars throughout the world, leading to ever-mounting casualties in a series of conflicts that have erupted in the wake of the Cold War. If these trends continue into the future, the number of violent non-state actors, and the severity of their attacks, will continue to grow. We discuss these five trends next.

RELIGIOUS VIOLENCE IS BECOMING MORE PREVALENT AND MORE LETHAL

Non-state violence appears to be becoming more lethal because it is increasingly motivated by extreme and absolutist religious doctrines, a phenomenon that has manifested itself in several different ways.[27] Religious terrorism has undergone something of a renaissance in the last two decades, as the number of known terrorist groups motivated primarily by religious causes has grown markedly. In 1968, none of the eleven identified international terrorist groups was religiously motivated; in 1980, two of 64 were believed to be; in 1992, eleven of approximately fifty.[28] Although the data are poor, the number of domestic terrorist groups motivated by religion also appears to be rising, particularly in the Middle East, especially in Algeria, Egypt, Turkey, and Israel. This rise in religious terrorism is often attributed to the Iranian Revolution of 1979, which not only radicalized some Islamic fundamentalists, but also created an active state sponsor of religiously motivated terrorism abroad. However, although Islamic

---

27. For good discussions of the character and prevalence of religious terrorism, see Bruce Hoffman, *'Holy Terror': The Implications of Terrorism Motivated by a Religious Imperative*, P-7834 (Santa Monica, Calif.: RAND, 1993); Bruce Hoffman, "The Contrasting Ethical Foundations of Terrorism in the 1980s," *Terrorism and Political Violence*, Vol. 1, No. 3 (July 1989), pp. 361–377; Mark Juergensmeyer, ed., *Violence and the Sacred in the Modern World* (London: Frank Cass, 1992); and Mark Juergensmeyer, *The New Cold War? Religious Nationalism Confronts the Secular State* (Berkeley: University of California Press, 1993). An excellent study of the relationship between terror and religion is David C. Rapoport, "Fear and Trembling: Terrorism in Three Religious Traditions," *American Political Science Review*, Vol. 78, No. 3 (September 1984), pp. 658–77.

28. Data from the RAND–St. Andrews University Chronology of International Terrorist Incidents, Centre for the Study of Terrorism, St. Andrews University, St. Andrews, Scotland.

(especially Shi'ite) terrorist attacks have been bloodier than most,[29] nearly all religions contain violent content, and many have had a connection to terrorism.[30] In recent years, violent religious fanatics have come from Jewish, Christian, Hindu, and Buddhist denominations as well as Islamic ones.[31]

Many of the reasons why secular, politically motivated non-state actors have tended to refrain from causing mass casualties apply with limited

---

29.   The various Shi'ite Islamic groups, for instance, have committed only 8 percent of all international terrorist incidents since 1982, but they are responsible for 30 percent of the total number of deaths. Data from the RAND–St. Andrews Chronology of International Terrorism, reported in Hoffman, *Holy Terror*, p. 5.

30.   The symbols, rituals, myths, and sacred texts of all major religions contain elements of violence, either suffered or inflicted. A religious identity may entail an expectation, understanding, and appreciation of violence and, among the most fervent believers, a willingness to endure and inflict it. See Mark Juergensmeyer, "The Logic of Religious Violence," in David Rapoport, ed., *Inside Terrorist Organizations* (New York: Columbia University Press, 1988), pp. 172–192.

31.   The main Jewish terrorist organization active today is Kach, founded by the Israeli-American rabbi Meir Kahane, and its offshoot Kahane Chai. Baruch Goldstein, who attacked praying Muslims with a machine gun at the al-Ibrahimi mosque in the West Bank town of Hebron in February 1994, was affiliated with Kach. For general background, see R. Cohen-Almagor, "The Kahanist Phenomenon," in R. Cohen-Almagor, ed., *The Boundaries of Liberty and Tolerance* (Gainesville: University of Florida Press, 1994), pp. 154–173; Marda Dunsky, "Incubator of Violence: Let's Stop Pretending that Israeli Extremists are Crazy," *Washington Post*, January 12, 1997, p. C1; and Ehud Sprinzak, *The Ascendance of Israel's Radical Right* (New York: Oxford University Press, 1991). In another incident, Jewish extremists attempted to blow up Islam's third holiest shine, the Dome of the Rock in Jerusalem, in 1984, reportedly with the hope of triggering a nuclear war that would destroy their Arab enemies. See Hoffman, "Terrorism and WMD," p. 48. Christian fundamentalists were responsible for some of the domestic terrorism in the United States in the 1990s, such as the bombings of abortion clinics perpetrated by right-to-life extremists. In December 1992, Hindu militants attacked and destroyed the Babri mosque in Ayodhya, India, triggering waves of sectarian riots. See Šumit Ganguly, "Conflict and Crisis in South and Southwest Asia," in Brown, *International Dimensions of Internal Conflict*, pp. 146–147. Aum Shinrikyo was nominally a Buddhist cult. See Murray Sayle, "Nerve Gas and the Four Noble Truths," *The New Yorker*, April 1, 1996, pp. 56–71.

force or not at all to terrorists motivated by religious beliefs.[32] Most violent non-state actors of the past have been politically motivated, and have sought either to extract specific concessions from a state, or to foment or block social and political change. These purposes are not often served by causing mass casualties. Killing large numbers of people does not make the terrorists' problem of coercing political concessions out of a state significantly easier, and indeed might even make it worse, since escalating death counts tend to undermine popular support, encourage more vigorous countermeasures, and exacerbate the group's internal dissension. Mass killing also is also at best an imperfect instrument for guiding social change.

Religious violence follows a different logic. For religious terrorists, violence can become a sacramental act, dictated and legitimized by theology. The religious movements most prone to extreme violence are those that attract intensely committed followers and that conceive a Manichean struggle between themselves and secular authority. With this attitude, only absolute victory and absolute defeat are possible: compromise would mean acquiescence in the dominance of the ungodly, and is thus tantamount to defeat. The targets of violence are often dehumanized as infidels, oppressors, or both.[33] The primary purpose of violent acts is not to coerce particular concessions, but to fulfill a spiritual requirement.[34] The relationship between the objectives of a religious movement and acts such as blowing up the Dome of the Rock in Jerusalem, massacring Algerian villagers, bombing the Paris subway, attacking American military bases abroad, bringing down the World Trade Center, pumping cyanide into a synagogue, bombing an abortion clinic, or accelerating the apocalypse by releasing nerve gas in the Tokyo subway may be obscure to outsiders, but

---

32. This argument has been developed in greatest detail by Bruce Hoffman. See Hoffman, *Holy Terror*, pp. 11–14; Hoffman, "Contrasting Ethical Foundations," pp. 368–375; Hoffman, "Terrorist Targeting," pp. 22–24; and Hoffman, "Terrorism and WMD," pp. 48–50.

33. One reason why religious terrorists might refrain from using indiscriminate weapons, or weapons whose operation and effects are poorly understood (e.g., NBC weapons), is that while they feel morally justified in killing members of the "outgroup," they may be quite reluctant to risk accidentally killing their fellow believers, which may be sinful.

34. This thesis is developed and applied to Sikh religious violence in Juergensmeyer, "The Logic of Religious Violence," pp. 185–190.

the linkages can become mortally compelling in the belief systems of religious fanatics.[35]

Loss of popular support is of little concern to the religious terrorist, since the act is done for God, or God's clerical proxy, not public opinion.[36] Group cohesion is threatened less by practical matters, such as disagreements over the tactically and morally appropriate level of violence, than by the possibility of appearing unfaithful to the belief system that binds the group together. Harsh countermeasures by secular authorities are expected, but the deterrent effects of this prospect are relatively modest for religious terrorists: in their own minds, zealots are already locked in a life-and-death struggle with their opponents, and heightened oppression serves mainly to reinforce the teachings of fanatical spiritual leaders. When the ideology of religious violence takes hold, individuals can be inspired to great sacrifice with the promise of martyrdom and rewards in the afterlife, as in the 1996–97 campaign of suicide bombings carried out in Israel by Hamas. For all these reasons, the inhibitions on mass-casualty violence are markedly lower in religiously inspired terrorism than in secular, political terrorism. As a result, as religiously inspired terrorism becomes more prevalent, non-state violence in general will become more lethal.

Several cautions should be borne in mind in thinking about religious violence and terrorism. While the correlation between religious inspiration and highly lethal incidents is unmistakable, and violent fanaticism in many different settings appears to have the common elements just described, generalizations across dissimilar cultures and belief systems about the motives of religious terrorists are hazardous. Most major religions are basically peaceful most of the time, and only a tiny minority of their

---

35. "Every set of millenarian beliefs is, in effect, an intellectual system with an inner logic, albeit a logic not always evident to the casual observer. Because such beliefs often diverge markedly from those that prevail in the larger society, they are commonly stigmatized as 'irrational' or 'insane.' Yet they have an internal consistency for believers ... to organize experience and make apparent sense out of ... events." Michael Barkun, "Millenarian Groups and Law Enforcement Agencies: The Lessons of Waco," *Terrorism and Political Violence*, Vol. 6, No. 1 (Spring 1994), p. 92.

36. See Hoffman, "Terrorism and WMD," pp. 48–49; Hoffman, "Contrasting Ethical Foundations," pp. 361–377; and Brian Jenkins, "Understanding the Link between Motives and Methods," in Brad Roberts, ed., *Terrorism with Chemical and Biological Weapons: Calibrating Risks and Responses* (Alexandria, Va.: Chemical and Biological Arms Control Institute, 1997), p. 48.

adherents ever become violent or form terrorist organizations.[37] Some other variable must intervene to provoke the violent expression of religious fervor. Part of the explanation may lie in individual psychology, since some — perhaps many — of the individuals who choose to participate in violent religious organizations are attracted by the opportunity to fulfill their own compulsions, whether pathological or political.[38] The appearance of a charismatic demagogic leader such as Shoko Asahara, the guru of Aum Shinrikyo, may matter greatly where religious teachings and mind-control techniques are used to manipulate gullible followers into implementing the leader's agenda. Yet the emergence of religious terrorism requires more than a collection of suitably motivated individuals and a spiritual leader; it also requires an organization, operational leaders, financing, and a concept of action. How and why all these factors come together is idiosyncratic, but rarely is religious violence completely apolitical. Religious terrorism is most likely to emerge when a spiritual cause coincides with, and is reinforced by, major political developments that affect whole communities. Triggering events can include the active sponsorship of a state, such as Iran; political and social grievances in countries with closed political systems, as in the

---

37. Nevertheless, many religions have motivated large-scale violence at one time or another. Protestants and Catholics fought wars in Europe over theological differences that seem minor to modern Europeans; Catholicism underpinned the Crusades; Islam in its youth motivated the conquest of lands stretching from India to Morocco, north across much of eastern Europe, and into Spain; divine guidance motivated or justified the Jewish conquest of the "promised land" thousands of years ago, and is part of the motivation for the continued occupation of the West Bank. The Shi'ite and Sikh religions, while they have not produced wars of a similar scale, have produced some particularly violence-prone offshoots in recent decades. On the Shi'ites, see Amir Taheri, *Holy Terror: The Inside Story of Islamic Terrorism* (London: Sphere Books, 1987). On the Sikhs, see Paul Wallace, "Political Violence and Terrorism in India: The Crisis of Identity," in Martha Crenshaw, ed., *Terrorism in Context* (University Park: Pennsylvania State University Press, 1995), pp. 357–381; Juergensmeyer, "The Logic of Religious Violence"; and Bernard Imhasly, "A Decade of Terrorism in the Punjab," *Swiss Review of World Affairs*, Vol. 40, No. 12 (March 1991), pp. 23–25.

38. See Jerrold M. Post, "Terrorists' Psycho-Logic: Terrorist Behavior as a Product of Psychological Forces," in Walter Reich, ed., *Origins of Terrorism: Psychologies, Ideologies, Theologies, States of Mind* (New York: Cambridge University Press, 1990), pp. 25–40; and Leonard Weinberg and William Lee Eubank, "Cultural Differences in the Behavior of Terrorists," *Terrorism and Political Violence*, Vol. 6, No. 1 (Spring 1994), pp. 1–28.

Shah's Iran or in some of the sheikdoms of the Arabian Peninsula; a history of ethnic or religious persecution, such as the Holocaust; or nationalism resulting from a people's lack of a homeland, as in the Palestinian case.

Although most of the underlying causes of religious terrorism are particular to specific groups, at least one factor has the potential to cut across many different cultures: the coming of the millennium. Many experts have identified a relationship between major events in the calendar and the incidence of religious fanaticism, often associated with prophesies of Armageddon.[39] Most of this millennial activity is peaceful, or merely self-destructive,[40] but groups may emerge "who feel impelled either to hasten the redemption associated with the millennium through acts of violence or, in the event that the year 2000 passes and redemption does not occur, to attempt to implement Armageddon by the apocalyptic use of weapons of mass destruction."[41] According to *The Economist*, "those who dismiss the coming of 2000 as a non-event do so at their peril. History shows that the crossing of 1,000-year watersheds can provoke strange passions in the human soul."[42]

---

39. See David C. Rapoport, "Some General Observations on Religion and Violence," in Juergensmeyer, *Violence and the Sacred in the Modern World*, p. 131; Ernest R. Sandeen, *The Roots of Fundamentalism: British and American Millenarianism, 1880–1930* (Chicago: University of Chicago Press, 1970); Gustav Niebuhr, "On the Furthest Fringes of Millennialism, *New York Times*, March 28, 1997; and Jane Gross, "In the Hunt for Answers, Only Questions Arise," *New York Times*, March 28, 1997, p. A21.

40. There have been several incidents of mass suicide involving millennial groups in the 1990s. In April 1993, eighty members of the Branch Davidian cult died when their armed compound ("Rancho Apocalypse") in Waco, Texas, burned down as federal law enforcement agencies attempted forcible entry. Seventy-four members of the "Order of the Solar Temple" cult committed suicide in two separate incidents in Switzerland (1994) and Quebec (1997). Thirty-nine members of the "Heaven's Gate" cult committed suicide in San Diego, California, in March 1997, prompted by their guru and the arrival of the Hale-Bopp comet. See Todd S. Purdum, "Tapes Left by Cult Suggest Comet was the Sign to Die," *New York Times*, March 28, 1997; and Barry Bearak, "Eyes on Glory: Pied Pipers of Heaven's Gate," *New York Times*, April 28, 1997.

41. Hoffman, *Holy Terror*, p. 14.

42. "The Millennial Itch," *The Economist*, January 4, 1997, p. 83. *The Economist* further noted, "Besides, Christ may return."

INTENSIFYING EFFORTS AGAINST U.S. PRESENCE AND INFLUENCE IN THE
PERSIAN GULF

Religious and political motives for terrorism clearly reinforce one another
in the Middle East, especially the Persian Gulf, and they do so in a manner
that suggests that this is the region where the risk of mass casualty
terrorism against U.S. targets is growing most rapidly. This risk has become
visible as a result of two major bombings in Saudi Arabia: the first at the
offices of the U.S. program manager for security assistance with the Saudi
Arabia National Guard (OPM-SANG) in Riyadh on November 13, 1995,
killing seven and wounding 40; and the second at the Khobar Towers
housing complex for U.S. Air Force personnel in Dhahran on June 25, 1996,
killing 19 Americans and injuring more than 500.[43] Exactly who was
responsible for the two bombings remains somewhat mysterious, but the
rationale behind the attack is fairly clear. Certain strands of Islam,
particularly some elements of radical Shi'ism, are profoundly hostile to
what some Islamists perceive as the dominance of Muslim lands by foreign
powers, especially the United States. Radicalized by a long colonial history,
the Arab-Israeli conflict, and the 1990–91 Gulf War, significant numbers of
Muslims see the U.S. regional presence and influence as fundamentally
incompatible with Islamic faith, primarily because America abets secular
governance and transmits a Western culture that some Muslims consider
depraved. In the Gulf region, this religious hostility is magnified by the
realpolitik of Iran and Iraq, whose aspirations toward regional hegemony are
blocked by the forward U.S. presence, and by the anti-Americanism of
many ordinary Arabs and Muslims, some of whom hold the United States
responsible for their own poverty and political powerlessness. Because of
this combination of religious, geopolitical, and social factors, the risk of
mass-casualty terrorist attacks against U.S. interests in the Persian Gulf
appears to be rising, and this possibility jeopardizes the precarious political
foundations on which the American presence in the region rests.

---

43. On the Khobar bombing, see U.S. Department of State, Bureau of Diplomatic
Security, *Significant Incidents of Political Violence against Americans 1996* (Washington,
D.C.: U.S. Department of State, July 1997), p. 29; U.S. Congress, *Bomb Attack in Saudi
Arabia*, Hearings before the Committee on Armed Services, U.S. Senate, 104th Cong.,
2nd Sess. (Washington, D.C.: U.S. GPO, 1997); and U.S. Congress, *Terrorist Attack
against United States Military Forces in Dhahran, Saudi Arabia*, Hearings before the
Committee on National Security, U.S. House of Representatives, 104th Cong., 2nd
Sess. (Washington, D.C.: U.S. GPO, 1997).

None of the U.S. allies in the Gulf is wholly comfortable with the presence of American military forces. U.S. troops are now stationed in six moderate Gulf sheikdoms: Bahrain, Kuwait, Oman, Qatar, Saudi Arabia, and the United Arab Emirates.[44] Several of these states, most importantly Saudi Arabia, had refused to permit the permanent stationing of American military forces on their territories prior to the 1990–91 war with Iraq. Foreign soldiers, especially Americans, offer many uncomfortable reminders: of local regimes installed by colonial powers; of overly generous oil concessions; of Zionism and the mistreatment of Arabs; of American unilateralism; of national weakness; of the incompatibility between Islamism and Western culture; of democracy. The American military presence heightens the internal threats faced by these undemocratic, Sunni fundamentalist, rentier regimes, and is tolerated only because Iraq's invasion of Kuwait revealed an even more serious external threat.

The OPM-SANG and Khobar attacks appear to have been aimed directly at the political substructure of the American military presence in the Gulf, and there is reason to fear that anti-American terrorist groups and states will continue to exploit this unique vulnerability of the world's only superpower. Although the American national security elite recognizes the importance of a forward presence in protecting vital U.S. interests in the Gulf, a mounting American death toll might change popular opinion on this matter, as it did in Lebanon in 1983 and Somalia in 1993. Moreover, this possibility would worsen if the host nation, concerned with its own internal political circumstances, were to appear callous, ungrateful, or duplicitous in its handling of an anti-American terrorist incident. Successful anti-American terrorism could make it politically impossible to sustain the foundation of U.S. policy in the region — a forward military presence.

The OPM-SANG and Khobar bombings provide the most compelling evidence of an intensifying effort against U.S. influence and military presence in the Persian Gulf. It remains possible, though unproven, that the two incidents are part of an organized campaign, but the coincidence is worrisome even if there is no conspiracy. Some evidence points to Iranian sponsorship of the Khobar bombing, but it is also possible that the bombers took action without any state's encouragement. They may have had help from Usama Bin Ladin, a dissident Saudi millionaire and terrorist financier now based in Taliban-controlled Afghanistan, who "has announced his intention to stage terrorist and guerrilla attacks against U.S. personnel in

---

44. U.S. Central Command Posture Statement, <www.centcom.mil/97posture.htm>, p. 8.

Saudi Arabia in order to force the United States to leave the region," and has been linked to numerous international terrorist incidents.[45] The Saudi government has failed to cooperate fully with the U.S. investigation of the incidents, and U.S. officials have refused to accept the Saudi explanations of the attacks at face value. In April 1996, four Sunni Saudi nationals confessed responsibility for the OPM-SANG attack after prolonged Saudi interrogation, but were beheaded before they could be questioned by U.S. investigators. In November 1996, the Saudi government reportedly provided Washington with evidence that the Khobar bombing was unconnected to the OPM-SANG bombing and was instead carried out by Shi'ite Saudi extremists trained in Lebanon and supported by Iran.[46] Thus, while the U.S. government has strong suspicions that Iran was behind the Khobar attack, the Federal Bureau of Investigation has not yet been able to confirm independently the information provided by the Saudis or to ascertain what role, if any, Iran played. Transnational Shi'ite terrorists have long been active in the Gulf region, but there is evidence that they are increasing their presence and operations in the moderate sheikdoms. With the Khobar attack it is now clear that they are willing to target U.S. forces

---

45. See *Saudi Arabia Travel Advisory, Public Announcement*, U.S. Department of State, February 25, 1997; and *Patterns of Global Terrorism 1996* (Washington, D.C.: U.S. State Department, April 1997), pp. 3, 20–21, 25. Bin Ladin has repeatedly announced his intention to stage attacks against American forces in the Persian Gulf. In a May 1997 interview with CNN, for example, Bin Ladin stated that "we have focused [our] declaration of *jihad* [holy war] on striking at the U.S. soldiers inside Arabia, the country of the two holy places, Mecca and Medina. In our religion, it is not permissible for any non-Muslims to stay in Arabia. Therefore, even though American civilians are not targeted in our plan, they must leave. We do not guarantee their safety." Stephen Frazier, Peter Arnett, and Joelle Attinger, "IMPACT Interviews Islamic Radical," *CNN Impact*, May 11, 1997, Federal Document Clearinghouse, Inc., transcript no. 97051100V55.

46. U.S. officials are concerned not only that the Saudi government may be attempting to distract attention from a purely domestic insurgent problem, but also that the Saudi government, which is Sunni, may unfairly be trying to blame Shi'ite Iran for the attack, and thus provoke U.S. military reprisal or international economic sanctions. R. Jeffrey Smith, "Saudis Offer Data to U.S. Linking Extremists, Bomb," *Washington Post*, December 11, 1996.

directly.[47] Since Iran is a long-standing sponsor of Shi'ite terrorism, especially the Lebanese Hezbollah, suspicion of an Iranian connection is warranted.

Both attacks on U.S. forces in Saudi Arabia involved enormous bombs. The OPM-SANG car bomb contained an estimated 200–250 pounds of explosive, while Khobar was hit with an estimated 5,000 pounds of TNT in a tanker truck. Both attacks were directed against large numbers of American personnel in high-rise buildings. Both were clearly intended to cause massive, indiscriminate casualties. Hundreds were injured in the two explosions, but fatalities were held at a relatively low level because the targeted structures withstood the blasts without collapsing. However, if terrorist attacks against the U.S. military presence in the Gulf continue, it is likely that the perpetrators will continue to employ highly lethal techniques. The usual inhibitions against mass-casualty attacks would apply with little force in this case. The immediate objective of the terrorists appears to be to compel the removal of U.S. forces from the region, and they have reason to believe that higher casualties increase the probability of success.[48] The potential loss of popular support is probably not an issue, since the Khobar and OPM-SANG bombers were appealing mainly to a constituency that is already strongly anti-American: Islamic fundamentalists. And the fear that escalating fatalities will provoke heightened countermeasures is probably no more than a moderate concern to the religiously inspired terrorists. Despite its almost medieval brutality, the Saudi criminal justice system is not believed to be particularly effective at penetrating transnational Islamic terrorist organizations. Moreover, the Saudi king, as the "Custodian of the Two Holy Mosques," must take care not to oppress the Saudi religious community too severely. The United States can retaliate militarily only against the state sponsors of terrorist attacks, and can only do so when they can be conclusively identified. In conjunction with the general effects of rising religious violence, the specific characteristics of the U.S. presence in

---

47. In addition to the Saudi allegations about an Iranian-Lebanese connection to the Khobar bombing, the government of Bahrain announced in June 1996 the discovery of a Bahraini Hezbollah cell that was recruited, trained, and supported by Iran and had been assisted by a Hezbollah cell based in Kuwait. *Patterns of Global Terrorism 1996*, Middle East overview, <www.state.gov/www/global/terrorism/1996report/middle.html>.

48. The nineteen fatalities of the Khobar bombing caused the U.S. Air Force to relocate its base from urban Dhahran to the Prince Sultan Air Base at Al Kharj, deep in the desert.

the Persian Gulf diminish many of the usual incentives against mass-casualty terrorism, making the region a particularly dangerous one for U.S. forces, citizens, and interests.

Three final points must be made about the possibility of mass-casualty terrorism in the Gulf. The first is that while Iran is typically identified as the most likely state sponsor of this activity, Iraqi sponsorship of anti-American terrorism is also a serious possibility. While the secular Iraqi regime lacks the religious motives of Iran and its fanatical Shi'ite followers, Baghdad's geopolitical interest in forcing an American withdrawal from the region is at least as compelling as Tehran's. Saddam Hussein is also likely to have an even stronger desire for revenge against the United States than the Iranian ayatollahs, given the defeat Iraq suffered at American hands in 1991, the unrelenting embargo and sanctions regime, the U.S.-enforced no-fly zones in northern and southern Iraq, U.S. support for the Kurds, and Washington's attempts to remove Saddam from power. Aside from allegations that Iraq sponsored the 1993 bombing of the World Trade Center,[49] the only known incident of Iraqi-sponsored terrorism against American targets since the 1990–91 Gulf War was the failed April 1993 assassination attempt against former President George Bush, which prompted the United States to retaliate with cruise missile strikes against Iraqi intelligence headquarters in Baghdad.[50] Yet Saddam is a well known risk-taker with few options. The

---

49. Although no Iraqi connection to the World Trade Center Bombing of February 26, 1993, has been publicly suggested by American law enforcement or intelligence authorities, analyst Laurie Mylroie argues that various pieces of evidence suggest that Ramzi Yousef, the mastermind behind the bombing, was an Iraqi agent. Mylroie argues that Iraqi intelligence probably learned of the small group of fundamentalists plotting bombings in New York when one of the conspirators made extensive calls to an uncle in Iraq with Palestinian-terrorist ties. Iraq, she suggests, sent Yousef to use this group both to carry out attacks and to obscure any Iraqi connection. Her argument that Yousef is an Iraqi agent focuses on Yousef's uncertain identity and his ties to Iraq. One link is the fact that he traveled to the United States under an Iraqi passport. Another is that he fled under a temporary Pakistani passport which he obtained by using the identity of a Pakistani national, a permanent resident of Kuwait, who had disappeared during the Iraqi occupation, and whose identity files in Kuwait had been tampered with, presumably by the Iraqis. See Laurie Mylroie, "The World Trade Center Bomb: Who is Ramzi Yousef? And Why it Matters," *The National Interest*, No. 42 (Winter 1995/96), pp. 3–15.

50. On June 26, 1993, the United States fired 23 Tomahawk missiles at Iraq's intelligence headquarters; 20 are believed to have hit their target.

possibility of Iraqi-sponsored terrorism in the Gulf region should thus not be discounted.

Second, states that sponsor terrorist attacks against U.S. forces or citizens run enormous risks, since the United States has a strong record of taking unilateral military action in response to specific, proven incidents of direct state sponsorship.[51] Both Iran and Iraq have much to lose from further antagonizing the United States and the international community, but the attraction of a high-lethality terrorist campaign against the institutions of U.S. power in the Gulf is precisely that it offers at least the possibility of anonymity. The United States has found it difficult to determine who was responsible for the OPM-SANG and Khobar bombings, and the answers may never be known. State sponsorship, moreover, can take many forms, ranging from day-to-day operational control to routine logistic support; the reality of the relationship will rarely be apparent to an outside observer. The United States has not yet reached the point where it will retaliate against state sponsors of terrorism without strong confirmation of a direct connection between the sponsoring state and a terrorist act.[52]

Finally, it is worth noting that since the Khobar bombing, the U.S. military has initiated a major set of policy and operational reforms aimed at reducing the vulnerability of forward-deployed U.S. forces to terrorist attacks. The outline of these reforms was laid out in a detailed report prepared by General Wayne Downing, who shortly after his retirement from the Army led an investigation into the Khobar Towers incident at the request of Secretary of Defense William Perry.[53] All large military deployments expose U.S. personnel to some level of vulnerability, but most of Downing's recommended enhancements in U.S. force protection are now in place, leaving U.S. forces in the Gulf significantly less vulnerable to a conventional terrorist attack. In the past, some terrorist groups have

---

51. On April 16, 1986, for instance, U.S. aircraft attacked military and intelligence facilities in Libya in retaliation for Libya's sponsorship of the terrorist bombing of a Berlin discotheque.

52. However, some terrorism experts have argued that the United States should be prepared to retaliate against state sponsors of terrorism even when it cannot be proven that the state sponsor specifically ordered the attack. See L. Paul Bremer III, "Terrorist Patrons Must Pay a Price," *Wall Street Journal*, August 5, 1996, p. 18.

53. See Department of Defense, Office of the Assistant Secretary of Defense (Public Affairs), "Background Briefing on Force Protection Measures," News Briefing, June 20, 1997; available at <www.defenselink.mil>.

responded to reduced target vulnerabilities by changing tactics,[54] but it remains to be seen if and how the anti-American terrorists in the Gulf will do so. General Downing is not alone, however, in suggesting that reducing the vulnerability of U.S. forces to conventional forms of terrorism — i.e., large chemical explosives — may simultaneously increase the incentive to employ weapons of mass destruction.[55]

INCREASING RIGHT-WING VIOLENCE WITHIN STATES

The problem of right-wing violence, while by no means new, appears to have grown worse since the mid-1980s. Internationally, an escalation in right-wing violence and fringe political agitation has been seen in England, Germany, France, Israel, Russia, and several other states of the former Soviet Union, manifested most often in racially motivated attacks on foreign residents.[56] Right-wing extremism and violence have also risen significantly in the United States. The deadliest terrorist attack ever committed on U.S. soil — the April 19, 1995, bombing of the Alfred P. Murrah Federal Building

---

54. The clearest example of terrorist adaptation following security countermeasures is in aircraft hijacking, which surged after the 1967 Six-Day War, but declined precipitously with the introduction of more effective and comprehensive airport security measures in the early 1970s. See Peter St. John, *Air Piracy, Airport Security, and International Terrorism: Winning the War against Hijackers* (New York: Quorum Books, 1991).

55. The post-Khobar reviews of the security of U.S. forces in Saudi Arabia reportedly included "scrutinizing the bug-spraying routine — a measure intended to guard against the prospect that forces hostile to the United States might spread lethal chemical weapons." Douglas Jehl, "How U.S. Missteps and Delay Opened Door to Saudi Blast," *New York Times,* July 7, 1996, p. 6.

56. See Stan Taylor, "The Radical Right in Britain," in Peter H. Merkl and Leonard Weinberg, eds., *Encounters with the Contemporary Radical Right* (Boulder, Colo.: Westview, 1993), pp. 165–184; Ekkart Zimmermann and Thomas Saalfeld, "The Three Waves of West German Right-Wing Extremism," in Merkl and Weinberg, *Encounters with the Contemporary Radical Right,* pp. 50–74; William Safran, "The National Front in France: From Lunatic Fringe to Limited Respectability," in Merkl and Weinberg, *Encounters with the Contemporary Radical Right,* pp. 19–49; Ehud Sprinzak, "The Israeli Radical Right: History, Culture, and Politics," in Merkl and Weinberg, *Encounters with the Contemporary Radical Right,* pp. 132–161; Vladislav Krasnov, "Pamiat: Russian Right-Wing Radicalism," in Merkl and Weinberg, *Encounters with the Contemporary Radical Right,* pp. 111–131; and Paul Wilkinson, "Violence and Terror and the Extreme Right," *Terrorism and Political Violence,* Vol. 7, No. 4 (Winter 1995), pp. 82–93.

in Oklahoma City — resulted from extreme right-wing anti-government sentiment. Whether this trend will continue remains unknown, but the precedent for massively destructive domestic terrorism has been set.

Right-wing violence is fundamentally chauvinistic. Opponents are seen not just as politically or ideologically mistaken but as inferior, sub-human, and properly subordinate, usually for reasons of race, religion, or sexual orientation.[57] The individuals associated with extreme right-wing groups hold a broad range of idiosyncratic beliefs, but only a minority choose to resort to violence. Beyond the common element of hate, the violent fringe of the radical right is characterized by a great variety of group types and ideologies. The United States in particular has a great diversity of right-wing groups.[58] Some are basically racist and provincial in character, such as the Ku Klux Klan, now just a shadow of its former self. Others are militant white supremacist groups, such as the Christian Identity movement, Aryan Nations, and The Order (now defunct), many of which have a strong religious or mystical quality and elaborate doctrines based on their opposition to the conspiracies of a "Zionist Occupation Government (ZOG)." There are survivalists and millenarians living in fortified rural compounds, like the Branch Davidians in Waco, Texas. There are Neo-Nazis, skinheads, and Holocaust revisionists. There is a vigorous tax protester movement, the breeding ground of many more right-wing extremists, alongside numerous other anti-government activist groups. There are fanatical anti-abortionists, who because of their religious beliefs terrorize and attack women's health clinics. And there is a popular and growing militia, or "patriot," movement,

---

57. See Wilkinson, "Violence and Terror and the Extreme Right," p. 83; and Ehud Sprinzak, "Right Wing Terrorism in a Comparative Perspective: The Case of Split Delegitimization," *Terrorism and Political Violence*, Vol. 7, No. 1 (Spring 1995), pp. 17–43.

58. See John George and Laird Wilcox, *Nazis, Communists, Klansmen, and Others on the Fringe: Political Extremism in America* (Buffalo, N.Y.: Prometheus Books, 1992); Mullins, *A Sourcebook on Domestic and International Terrorism*, pp. 185–229; James Coates, *Armed and Dangerous: The Rise of the Survivalist Right* (New York: Hill and Wang, 1987); James A. Aho, *This Thing of Darkness: A Sociology of the Enemy* (Seattle: University of Washington Press, 1994); and the very useful web page of the Southern Poverty Law Center, a watchdog of domestic right-wing extremists, at <www.splcenter.org/klanwatch/kw-2.html>.

which provides its members with paramilitary training and equipment, often as preparation for the collapse of civic society.[59]

The groups of the far right are by no means uniformly dangerous or effective. To begin with, only some are inclined to violence. A handful have well developed organizations, considerable resources, and an active membership, but others are little more than a single extremist with a photocopier and a mailing list. In both organization and ideology, the radical right is exceptionally fluid and eclectic: groups form and disband frequently, and individuals move from group to group often and with ease. Indeed, ideology is not the prime concern of many of the individuals who become involved in these organizations; rather, many appear to be drawn by a need to feel powerful, superior, and accepted, where in reality they are weak, socially marginal, and looked down upon. As a social phenomenon, the radical right is of concern not just because of its ability to sprout violent, capable organizations, but because the chauvinism it represents has a ready audience of considerable size. The prevalence of right-wing extremists is in some ways a barometer of society's latent hatred and bigotry, and the views such groups espouse in turn feed those forces, providing a constant, ready justification for violence.

Most of the groups and individuals that should be regarded as "extreme right wing" do not engage in acts of physical violence. Many of them appear satisfied with reading and disseminating conspiratorial or hate literature (increasingly through the Internet); acquiring paramilitary training and weapons; attending gun shows, rallies, and conventions; withdrawing to isolated compounds; or intimidating and insulting individual Jews, blacks, homosexuals, and others when the opportunities arise. Of those who do resort to violence, street fights and other random acts of violence against unfortunate persons are more common than the premeditated use of lethal force. Violent right-wing extremists do commit individual murders, assassinations, and small bombings and arson, but these incidents usually produce only limited casualties and often result in the prompt arrest of the perpetrators.[60] The individual targets of organized

---

59. For an overview of several different terrorist typologies, see Mullins, *A Sourcebook on Domestic and International Terrorism*, pp. 16–27.

60. U.S. law enforcement agencies have been able to penetrate most of the established violent right-wing organizations in the United States with relative ease, in part because these groups have a constant need to take on new members, in part because they have a tendency to boast of their aggressive acts though right-wing media, and in part because they are often little more than amateur criminals of

right-wing groups are most often government employees, especially tax agents and federal law enforcement officials. Prominent members of minority groups have also sometimes been targeted for assassination by groups with a particular grudge. A handful of these incidents have gained national notoriety, but in general these attacks cannot be regarded as part of a coherent plan.[61]

Most attacks by right-wing groups, whether successful or only attempted, are not systematic, do not seek to cause mass casualties, and do not appear to be part of a sensible political strategy. Even most bombings and other indiscriminate attacks attributed to right-wing groups have been neither especially lethal, nor particularly coordinated. Only in one case, the attacks against abortion clinics, has the violence taken the form of a campaign. In the last twenty years, there have been over 220 attempted and successful bombings and arsons of abortion clinics in the United States, though together these incidents have produced only a handful of casualties.[62] A variety of other attacks, attempts, or conspiracies have occurred, but with much less destructive effect. In the summer of 1993, for instance, two members of the "Fourth Reich Skinheads" were arrested in Los Angeles and charged with planning a series of bombings against Jewish targets.[63] In November 1993, the leader, or perhaps the sole member, of the "Aryan Liberation Front" was charged with bombing a synagogue in Sacramento, California, the local office of the NAACP, and the home of an Asian-American politician.[64] In October 1995, an unknown right-wing group derailed an Amtrak train in Arizona, causing one fatality and a

---

modest intelligence.

61. In 1984, for example, the Denver talk radio host Alan Berg was murdered by "The Order," a short-lived but violent white supremacist group. This incident attracted considerable public concern, and resulted in several books and a Hollywood film.

62. See data on anti-clinic violence at <www.cais.com/agm/main/violence.htm>.

63. Bruce Hoffman, "Responding to Terrorism across the Technological Spectrum," *Terrorism and Political Violence*, Vol. 6, No. 3 (Autumn 1994), pp. 375–376.

64. Ibid., pp. 375–376; and Ramon Coronado, "Accused Firebomber in Court," *Sacramento Bee*, January 13, 1994, p. A1.

dozen serious injuries.[65] A right-wing individual or group is suspected of having set off the pipe bomb that exploded during the Atlanta Olympics in August 1996.[66] Given this pattern of unconnected, low-lethality attacks, right-wing organizations in the United States appear to share the aversion to mass casualties that was described in Chapter 1.

The signal exception to this general pattern was the Oklahoma City bombing, which killed 168 and injured hundreds more. Timothy McVeigh and his accomplice Terry Nichols were both members of the right-wing fringe.[67] While the precise logic behind the bombing remains obscure, it is clear that at least McVeigh drew inspiration from *The Turner Diaries*, a 1978 novel that has emerged as one of the canonical texts of the American far right.[68] Written under the pseudonym "Andrew Macdonald" by William Pierce, the well-educated leader of a neo-Nazi group, *The Turner Diaries* provides what many see as a vision of, and blueprint for, right-wing terrorism of ever increasing lethality.[69] *The Turner Diaries* taps into many of the ideological strands of the radical right that may make mass-casualty tactics more likely in the future. The protagonist is a hate-filled, disillusioned racist who considers himself a patriot for trying to free the United States from the control of an illegitimate government that he believes is the puppet of an international Jewish conspiracy. It is by no means certain that a domestic right-wing group will ever again seek to kill as many people as

---

65. According to the FBI, at the site of the crash "investigators also found four typed letters. These letters mentioned the Bureau of Alcohol, Tobacco, and Firearms, the FBI, 'Ruby Ridge,' and 'Waco.' They were signed 'Sons of the Gestapo.'" FBI, *Terrorism in the United States, 1995*, available at <www.fbi.gov/publish/terror/terrorin.htm>.

66. Letters to Atlanta newspapers have claimed responsibility for three later bombings, of abortion clinics and a gay nightclub, in the name of "The Army of God." Physical evidence has linked the three bombings with the 1996 bombing at the Atlanta Olympics. Rick Bragg, "Group Tied to 2 Bombings Says It Set Off Clinic Blast," *New York Times*, February 3, 1998, p. A10.

67. For a detailed study of Terry Nichols' right-wing leanings, see "The Second Man: Terry Nichols and the Oklahoma City Bombing," *Klanwatch*, Special Report by the Klanwatch/Militia Task Force Projects of the Southern Poverty Law Center, 1997.

68. Andrew Macdonald (pseud. for William Pierce), *The Turner Diaries*, 2nd ed. (New York: Barricade Books, 1996).

69. Mullins, *A Sourcebook on Domestic and International Terrorism*, p. 209.

Timothy McVeigh did, since his example is not obviously sympathetic or encouraging. But since the tactics of the past have clearly been ineffective — whether the end is bringing down the U.S. government, "cleansing" the nation of ethnic minorities, or whatever else — more people on the far right might come to see monumental attacks and massive human casualties as the only way of breaking the superior power of the government.

THE RISE OF "AMATEUR" TERRORISM

The prototypical terrorist group is an organization with a well-defined command and control system, whose members have specialized training in terrorist or paramilitary techniques and are engaged in clandestine conspiracies as a full-time avocation. Reality has never been quite so tidy. It now appears that more and more non-state violence is committed by *ad hoc* collections of like-minded individuals who come together for specific purposes, sometimes to commit a single attack. Bruce Hoffman has termed this phenomenon the rise of "amateur" terrorism, a phase which refers more to the spontaneity of the group's formation than to the skill level of its members.[70] The attacks on the World Trade Center and Oklahoma City were both carried out by groups Hoffman would describe as "amateurs," in the sense that they did not belong to established, professional terrorist organizations. It appears likely that most of the small bombings in the United States, like the pipe bomb explosion at Centennial Park during the Atlanta Olympics, are also not the work of organized groups.[71]

The factors behind this growth in "amateur" terrorism are not entirely clear, but it probably has something to do with the changes described earlier that reduce the would-be terrorist's need for a large institutional base. One consequence of the explosion of new communications technologies, including the Internet, has been to make it much easier for geographically scattered but ideologically similar individuals to make contact and sustain communications. As a result, whether the underlying interest group

---

70. Bruce Hoffman, "Terrorism and WMD," p. 50.

71. The Olympic bombing is believed to be part of a series of small bombings in Atlanta and Birmingham, carried out by the "Army of God." However, these appear to be the work of a single person or a small group. "People claiming to be connected to the Army of God have been taking responsibility for bombings in the United States for more than a decade. Law enforcement experts question whether any such group exists as a formal organization, rather than as a collection of far-flung individuals acting independently under the same banner." See Bragg, "Group Tied to 2 Bombings Says It Set Off Clinic Blast."

comprises a thousand sufferers of a rare illness organizing to lobby for research, or a hundred people who believe that the U.S. government is conspiring to enslave its citizens and that the United Nations may invade at any time, groups are able to coalesce and organize much more easily. This new ability frees people at the most violence-prone fringes of political and religious discourse from some of the constraints they have previously faced. Where once an anti-government zealot might have stayed involved in a more moderate political movement, constrained from violence by his inability to act alone and restrained by the influence of his peers, such a person can now more easily find fellow travelers as radical as himself, making it easier to form violent groups. The rise of radical ideologies, whether political, racial, or religious, also provides a pool of people from which members can be drawn.

According to the FBI, "loosely affiliated extremists ... represent the most difficult international terrorist challenge to the law enforcement and intelligence communities."[72] Furthermore, while amateur terrorists probably have a somewhat lower capacity to carry out mass-casualty attacks, the motivational restraints on their ability to do so are also likely to be considerably lower. Thus, if amateur terrorism continues to spread, casualties from major terrorist attacks will probably continue to rise. Established terrorist groups, like any other political organization, are concerned fundamentally with their own survival, a fact that contributes to their basic conservatism in the use of destructive force.[73] This characteristic is most evident in the terrorist groups that have continued to fight long after their cause has vanished or become irrelevant, as appears to be the case with the Basque ETA, German Red Army Faction, and Japanese Red Army. Amateur terrorist groups are quite different, since they have no political organization to worry about, and form only to commit a limited number of violent acts. Amateur groups, especially those pursuing a goal they believe is ordained by God, or motivated by a political ideology that is more a justification for violence than a political blueprint, may not feel the force of this constraint.

---

72. FBI, *Terrorism in the United States 1995*, p. 13.

73. Crenshaw, "An Organizational Approach to the Analysis of Political Terrorism."

LARGE-SCALE ETHNIC AND RELIGIOUS CONFLICT

The most extreme acts of non-state violence have occurred in large-scale internal conflicts, usually along ethnic or religious lines. The numbers of deaths are staggering: 30,000–60,000 killed in Algeria since 1992; 100,000 in Burundi in 1993; 100,000–500,000 in Angola since 1992; 150,000 in Liberia since 1989; 200,000 in Bosnia since 1992; 400,000 dead in Somalia since 1990; 800,000 killed in Rwanda in a few months of 1994; a million dead in the Cambodian genocide of 1975–79; more than a million dead in the wars in Afghanistan since 1978; more than a million dead from the Sudanese civil war that began in 1983.[74] The numbers of people displaced and injured in these conflicts are even higher. The problem of internal and ethnic conflict is not new, but it appears to have entered into a particularly bad spell in the last decades of the twentieth century.

Although large-scale ethnic conflict is often carried out by non-state actors, it obeys a logic very different from that of terrorist violence.[75] The combatants in an internal conflict generally do not have limited political objectives. Rather, their aim is at a minimum to survive, and at a maximum to secure total control over a contested piece of territory. Both aims can lead to exceptionally vicious tactics. Once the factions in an internal conflict begin a life-and-death struggle, their mutual fears of one another can escalate to the point where all sides come to believe that they can only be secure if the contested piece of territory is "cleansed" of opposing ethnic, political, or religious groups, whether by coerced expulsion, genocide, or

---

74. These data are taken from Michael E. Brown, "Introduction," in Brown, *The International Dimensions of Internal Conflict*, pp. 4–7.

75. For a discussion of the causes and nature of ethnic conflict see Brown, *The International Dimensions of Internal Conflict*, pp. 1–31; Ted Robert Gurr and Barbara Harff, *Ethnic Conflict and World Politics* (Boulder, Colo.: Westview, 1994); Donald L. Horowitz, *Ethnic Groups in Conflict* (Berkeley: University of California Press, 1985); and Stephen Van Evera, "Hypotheses on Nationalism and War," *International Security*, Vol. 18, No. 4 (Spring 1994), pp. 5–39. For analyses of Bosnia and the Balkans, see V.P. Gagnon, Jr., "Ethnic Nationalism and International Conflict: The Case of Serbia," *International Security*, Vol. 19, No. 3 (Winter 1994/95), pp. 130–166; and Susan Woodward, *Balkan Tragedy: Chaos and Dissolution after the Cold War* (Washington, D.C.: Brookings, 1995). For discussions of the genocide in Rwanda, see Alain Destexhe, *Rwanda and Genocide in the Twentieth Century* (New York: New York University Press, 1995); and Gerard Prunier, *The Rwanda Crisis: History of Genocide* (New York: Columbia University Press, 1995). See also Rene Lemarchand, *Burundi: Ethnic Conflict and Genocide* (New York: New York University Press, 1995).

both. Ruthless leaders of opposing factions, or of neighboring states, manipulate the fears and prejudices of their followers for their own selfish purposes, thus worsening the bloodshed. The aversion to mass casualties evident in most other forms of non-state violence does not apply to the dedicated guerrilla group or the mob inflamed by racial hatred and fear.

Highly lethal conflicts of this kind will continue to erupt around the world, leaving tens of thousands dead. Whether such conflicts will grow more or less prevalent remains to be seen, but it is clear that this is the most deadly form of non-state violence. To date, no non-state faction in an internal conflict has chosen to employ any weapon except conventional ones, although there was some risk of this in the case of the Bosnian Serbs.[76] Knives and guns are perfectly adequate for killing the most common victim of internal wars: defenseless civilians.

Why Interest in NBC Weapons Might Increase

The technical ability to acquire and deliver a nuclear, biological, or chemical weapon is a necessary condition for a non-state actor to pose a threat of NBC terrorism. An interest in causing mass casualties is a second necessary condition. Even together, however, these two conditions are not sufficient: it does not follow that all highly capable non-state actors that want to cause mass casualties will attempt to do so with weapons of mass destruction. To date, the requisite proficiency, interest in mass casualties, and interest in weapons of mass destruction has combined only in Aum Shinrikyo (see Figure 1, p. 169). Even an ingenious killer like Ramzi Yousef, the World Trade Center bomber, chose to rely on tried-and-true conventional

---

76. The fact that both the Serb-dominated Yugoslavian army and the predominantly Muslim Bosnian army possessed chemical weapons is a cause for concern, although it appears that neither used them in the conduct of the war. The Bosnian government acknowledged in 1992 that it had chemical weapons and, before the cease-fire was reached in 1995, had threatened to use them as defensive measures against the Serbs. The Serbs have chemical weapons too, notably sarin and mustard gas, but they apparently have not used them. It appears that most of the chemical weapons in Yugoslavia were moved to Serbia from a storage place outside of Sarajevo early in 1992 after the dissolution of the country. Philip Shenon, "Rights Group Suspects Yugoslav Army May Have Chemical Arms," New York Times, March 28, 1997, p. A5.

explosives in his attempt to kill thousands of people.[77] Mass destruction can be wrought without weapons of mass destruction, and many non-state actors have managed to kill very large numbers of people without employing exotic technologies. Moreover, acquiring and using NBC weapons, while feasible for capable non-state actors, presents risks and challenges beyond those associated with conventional weapons, such as greater technological difficulty, more severe health hazards, unpredictable effects, and (as we explain in Chapter 2) increased risks of detection.[78] Weapons of mass destruction, therefore, are unlikely to be attractive to an attacker that seeks the simplest, least costly, least risky, and most reliable means of attack available.

Thus, while there is good reason to believe that non-state violence and terrorism involving conventional weapons is growing increasingly lethal, it is far from certain that the groups that perpetrate these acts will turn to weapons of mass destruction. Indeed, to date there is relatively little evidence of a rising interest in NBC weapons among capable non-state actors interested in mass casualties. Aside from Aum Shinrikyo, only a few indications of interest in weapons of mass destruction have been uncovered in groups that present a plausible threat of mounting an attack with a nuclear, biological, or chemical weapon. Numerous groups and individuals have been caught in possession of, or even having used, chemical poisons and biological toxins (mainly ricin), but the individuals involved in most of

---

77.   The Yousef case is particularly interesting in that he clearly wanted to cause mass casualties, was technically competent, is reported to have made previous chemical weapons threats (against the Philippines), and is reported to have possessed chemical weapons "cookbooks." Prepared Statement of John F. Sopko and Alan Edelman, in U.S. Congress, *Global Proliferation of Weapons of Mass Destruction*, Part III, Hearings before the Permanent Subcommittee on Investigations, Committee on Governmental Affairs, U.S. Senate, 104th Cong., 1st Sess. (Washington, D.C.: U.S. GPO, March 27, 1996), p. 23. Despite these indicators of possible interest in chemical weapons, however, he still decided to use only conventional explosives. According to the Secret Service agent who interviewed Yousef as he was being extradited from Pakistan, Yousef claimed to have considered a "poison gas attack," but decided it would be "too expensive to implement." Benjamin Weiser, "As Trade Center Smoldered, Suspect Watched, Jury Hears," *New York Times*, October 23, 1997, p. A31.

78.   Walter Laqueur, for example, has suggested that "while terrorism seems to be tending toward more indiscriminate killing and mayhem, terrorists may draw the line at weapons of superviolence likely to harm both foes and large numbers of relatives and friends — say, Kurds in Turkey, Tamils in Sri Lanka, or Arabs in Israel." Laqueur, "Postmodern Terrorism," p. 31.

these cases appear to have been neither interested in nor capable of building and using the dissemination system required to create mass casualties. Technical information on chemical and sometimes biological weapons has been found in the possession of a few hostile non-state actors, and others have been found in possession of quantities of chemicals, toxins, or bacterial cultures, demonstrating that they were at least aware of the possibility of NBC weapons acquisition and use.[79] However, without other indications of an NBC acquisition effort, available evidence does not demonstrate that most groups had any intention of putting the information to use. Minor cases of possession or use of chemical poisons, toxins, and biological agents have occurred for decades without leading to NBC attacks by non-state actors.

National security threats often, however, consist of high-consequence events that have a low probability of occurring or are completely unprecedented. The fact that no state has ever fired an NBC-armed ballistic missile in anger does not prevent the U.S. security establishment from treating this possibility with utmost seriousness, spending tens of billions of dollars in an ongoing effort to create defenses against ballistic missile attack. Similarly, even without clear evidence of a trend toward greater interest in NBC weapons, the threat cannot be dismissed out of hand. One must also consider why a non-state actor capable of NBC acquisition and use, and interested in inflicting mass casualties, might decide to employ a weapon of mass destruction rather than a less complicated conventional weapon. Five basic, often complementary, reasons are plausible: (1) an interest in producing casualty levels so high that they could not easily be caused by a single conventional attack (more than 1,000 dead, for example); (2) a desire to create, and possibly to manipulate, terror of unprecedented scale and intensity; (3) an aspiration to mimic the functions and trappings of a state, and thus to enhance the legitimacy of a non-state actor's assertion of sovereignty; (4) an innate curiosity or fascination with exotic weapons; and (5) a wish to equal the precedent set by Aum Shinrikyo or some other previous NBC incident, including those perpetrated by states. These reasons are discussed below.

VERY HIGH CASUALTIES

The clearest reason why a capable non-state actor might decide to use an NBC weapon rather than something less exotic is a desire to have a single attack produce very high casualties: perhaps a thousand or more dead.

---

79. These cases are discussed in Chapter 1.

This, after all, is the reason why states have developed and used weapons of mass destruction. Conventional explosives, even those used against highly vulnerable targets such as jumbo jets and crowded buildings, rarely kill more than a few hundred people in a single attack (see Table 3, p. 91). Ramzi Yousef allegedly attempted to destroy the World Trade Center's structural support columns, which could have caused the tower to collapse and kill tens of thousands of people.[80] Any similar attempt poses significant technical difficulties, and may even be more difficult than building and using an improvised chemical or biological weapon. It is entirely possible that a few hundred deaths will be regarded as insufficient by an individual or a group that has crossed the motivational barrier to causing mass casualties. If multiple conventional attacks are rejected as insufficiently dramatic, or too taxing for a small terrorist cell, this desire to inflict very high casualties could motivate an interest in acquiring and using weapons of mass destruction. The desire for dramatic results was clearly part of what inspired Aum Shinrikyo to release nerve gas in the Tokyo subway.

Of course, the fact that a non-state actor might decide to use weapons of mass destruction to kill more people than could easily or reliably be killed by a single conventional attack does not explain why the group would want to kill that many people in the first place. The possible reasons were discussed in the previous section: religious conviction; a thirst for revenge; opposition to U.S. power or regional presence; an abhorrence of Western culture; ethnic or racial enmity; a belief in the apocalypse; internal secessionism or the desire to undermine an established political order; and homicidal psychosis. There is no way to predict how any particular group motivated to violence by these or other reasons would decide on the number of people it needs to kill to fulfill its purpose, or on how far it would be willing to push its technical capabilities and internal cohesion to achieve some higher level of lethality. Most highly violent groups in the past have been content with attacks that individually caused only a few dozen casualties; the low hundreds are the upper end of the range.

A hostile group or individual that wishes to exceed this threshold is likely to have some combination of exceptionally intense motivation and psychological disturbance, possibly including extreme alienation from society, psychosis, or megalomania (e.g., a desire to go down in history as

---

80. Evidence of Yousef's intent to cause thousands of casualties by collapsing the World Trade Center comes from an interview he gave to U.S. law enforcement personnel as he was in custody being extradited by plane from Pakistan. See Weiser, "As Trade Center Smoldered," pp. A1, A31.

the most effective mass murderer of all time). As argued in Chapter 1, the more psychologically disturbed an individual is, the less likely he or she is to be able to master the organizational and technical challenges associated with building a team of people who can acquire and use an NBC weapon. Aum Shinrikyo appears to have been a very rare case in which the group overcame these challenges despite its leader's disorders.

EXTREME TERRORISM, REVOLUTION, AND "THE NEXT LENIN"

A non-state actor may also choose to take up NBC weapons as a means of creating terror of unprecedented scale and intensity. Terrorists have long understood the deaths they cause as instrumental, with the real targets being the attitude of the public and the policies of the government. It is possible, however, that the public is growing increasingly inured to bombings and other low-lethality attacks, or that a hostile non-state actor will come to believe that this is so. A single conventional bomb, the most destructive tool of traditional terrorism, can reliably kill at most a few hundred people, but cannot kill a few thousand, much less tens of thousands. Even if a terrorist organization has no particular interest in killing large numbers of people, it may still believe that it must create sufficiently widespread and intense fear to achieve its objectives.[81] "Kill one, frighten 10,000," the Chinese philosopher Sun Tzu is said to have written in the 4th century BC. Terrorists of the modern era may perceive a less advantageous ratio of exchange.

Because of their incredible killing power and malevolent mystique, weapons of mass destruction have an unrivaled capacity to terrorize a society. The very unfamiliarity of weapons of mass destruction, and their macabre images — gruesome airborne diseases, convulsions and poison gas, men in protective suits, radioactive fallout, etc. — would further magnify the psychological impact of a covert NBC attack. Mass panic could result if a terrorist group were to use or credibly threaten to use an NBC weapon against a population, especially if an orchestrated campaign of unstoppable NBC attacks appeared possible. A government would have few options if faced with a situation like this, which could quickly escalate to an existential challenge to the political order of the state. This strategy has not been pursued by the terrorist groups of the past. A hostile non-state actor that is outside of this logic may, however, yet emerge.

The non-state actor most likely to adopt a strategy of "extreme" or "grand" terrorism is one that does not have limited political objectives and

---

81. This idea is suggested in Hoffman, "Terrorism and WMD," p. 49.

that is not concerned with winning domestic or international sympathy.[82] The fact that some religious terrorism already appears to fit this pattern is part of the explanation for the rising lethality of non-state violence evident in the 1990s. A group motivated by secular causes might also adopt a strategy of extreme terrorism. For example, a group that wished to undermine the institutions of a state might well expect an established government to refuse to negotiate a change in its core constitutive principles — a political objective, but hardly a "limited" one — if subjected to a campaign of incremental, low-lethality terrorism. Such a group might, therefore, opt for a strategy of profound social destabilization, bringing intolerable pressure to bear against the targeted government and forcing its disintegration. This is, in effect, the strategy of the kind of revolutionary who seeks to seize power by force from a collapsing state, and is thus little concerned with his own popularity. Fred Iklé has termed such an individual the "next Lenin": a brilliant, merciless leader willing to run great risks for great gains, facing a state that lacks the competence and the ruthlessness required to sustain itself.[83] History contains only a few leaders as capable and committed as Lenin, and precisely how such a person could use mass-destruction terrorism to seize power in the modern era is difficult to predict. But if such a person were to emerge, would he or she eschew weapons of mass destruction?

MIMICRY OF STATE BEHAVIOR

A third reason why a non-state actor might opt to acquire or use weapons of mass destruction rather than conventional weaponry is to strengthen a contested claim to sovereignty by taking on some of the trappings of a state. Weapons of mass destruction have been perhaps the ultimate symbol of state power, and may be sought by a secessionist movement as a symbol to rally around, giving courage to wavering members of the group and providing a counterweight to the superior forces of opposed states. Weapons of mass destruction may come to be seen as useful for creating an

---

82. The term "grand terrorism" was coined by former Assistant Secretary of Defense Ashton B. Carter, and is one of the focal points of his Preventive Defense Project with William J. Perry. See Ashton B. Carter, "Grand Terrorism: A New Threat to National Security," speech before the Air Force National Security Conference on Countering the Proliferation and Use of Weapons of Mass Destruction, National Defense University, July 29, 1997.

83. Fred Iklé, "The Next Lenin," *The National Interest*, No. 47 (Spring 1997), pp. 9–19.

aura of legitimacy around the unrecognized government of a non-existent nation-state. The destructive and deterrent power of NBC weapons adds to their symbolic value.

Several different types of secessionist movements could find this motive for taking up NBC weapons appealing. An ethnic group that lacks a state of its own is the most obvious example, and the incentives for NBC acquisition may be especially strong if the state or states opposed to the group's self-determination are themselves NBC-armed. The Chechens have dabbled with radiological weapons and made numerous threats involving weapons of mass destruction,[84] which is no surprise given that their opponent, Russia, is the most heavily NBC-armed nation on the planet. It is perhaps surprising that the Chechen war has not had a stronger NBC component, though the Chechens may fear provoking Russia. Similarly, the separatist movements in Kurdistan and Tajikistan present potential NBC risks, with both groups reportedly interested in chemical weapons and guilty of mass poisoning attacks.[85] When NBC weapons or materials are unsecured or unaccounted for in the vicinity of the group — as is clearly the case in the former Soviet Union — these risks should be regarded as acute.

Another set of non-state actors that might be motivated to acquire NBC weapons in mimicry of state behavior is the right-wing militia movement in the United States.[86] According to the FBI, "extremists in the United States ... continued a chilling trend by demonstrating interest in — and experimentation with — unconventional weapons."[87] These groups are variously inspired by religion, racism, parochial American patriotism, conspiracy theories, Nazi idolatry, and an unusually intense resentment of having to pay taxes. Some are committed survivalists, who prepare for nuclear or

---

84. See Mark Hibbs, "Chechen Separatists Take Credit for Moscow Cesium-137 Threat," *Nuclear Fuel*, Vol. 20, No. 25 (December 4, 1995), p. 5.

85. Alexander Chelyshev, "Terrorists Poison the Water Supply in Turkish Army Cantonment," TASS, March 29, 1992; Ron Purver, *Chemical and Biological Terrorism: The Threat according to the Open Literature*, Canadian Security Intelligence Service (unclassified), June 1995, pp. 86–87; and "Poisoned Champagne Kills 10 in Tajikistan," Reuters North American Wire, January 2, 1995, cited in Purver, *Chemical and Biological Terrorism*, p. 89.

86. See "Crossing the Threshold: The Increasing Threat of Biochemical Terrorism has Security Experts on High Alert," *Klanwatch Intelligence Report*, No. 85 (Winter 1997), pp. 7–9.

87. FBI, *Terrorism in the United States 1995*, p. 14.

Biblical Armageddon, have a strong fascination with weapons, and undergo organized paramilitary training. Some groups wish to establish an alternative, minimalist government in the place of the current political system, which they perceive as illegitimate and immoral. Unable to achieve this objective on a national scale, some of these groups retreat to armed compounds, where they reject the jurisdiction of the U.S. government, pay no taxes, and occasionally proclaim their independence as "free states."[88] Since the late 1980s, a series of standoffs between groups of this kind and federal law enforcement agencies, often ending in violence, has only reinforced the militias' paranoid sense of being under siege.[89] It is possible that an interest in acquiring weapons of mass destruction will emerge out of this mix, as the groups seek to affirm their own legitimacy to themselves, stand up to the superior power of the federal government, and satisfy their urge to play with exotic weapons. Indeed, a handful of criminal cases in the 1990s have involved individuals associated with right-wing organizations caught in possession of biological and chemical agents, particularly ricin. Given the past behavior of groups like this, the most likely manifestation of this risk is that a group will acquire some type of weapon of mass destruction for essentially defensive or deterrent reasons, in which case any use of the weapon would probably result from a violent confrontation with the authorities. A less likely but more dangerous possibility is that the group might seek to use NBC weapons to advance its own idiosyncratic cause, whether by attacking a government institution, as Timothy McVeigh did, or by attacking a particular ethnic or religious group.[90]

---

88. According to FBI Director Louis Freeh, militia groups "generally view themselves as 'sovereign' citizens who are exempt from the laws and regulations of the United States government." Louis J. Freeh, "Counterterrorism," Statement before the Senate Appropriations Committee, U.S. Senate, May 13, 1997, available at <www.fbi.gov/congress/counter/terror.htm>.

89. One of the most important of these standoffs was the FBI siege at Randy Weaver's cabin in Ruby Ridge, Idaho, in May 1992, which resulted in the deaths of Weaver's wife, his teenage son, and a U.S. Marshal. "Ruby Ridge" has since become a rallying call for the extreme right. See Mullins, *A Sourcebook on Domestic and International Terrorism*, pp. 219–221; Aho, *This Thing of Darkness*, pp. 50–67; and Jeffrey Kaplan, "Right Wing Violence in North America," *Terrorism and Political Violence*, Vol. 7, No. 1 (Spring 1995), pp. 87–88.

90. In an incident that nearly fits this pattern, the German police are reported to have thwarted a neo-Nazi attempt to pump cyanide gas into a synagogue in 1992. See Robert H. Kupperman and David M. Smith, "Coping with Biological Terrorism,"

A major difference between states and non-state actors is that states tend to provide for their own security through military deterrence, while violent non-state actors tend to survive through secrecy. For this reason, it is not at all clear that deterrence would be a rational motivation for a non-state actor's acquisition of NBC weapons. A group with some territorial control, and facing an adversary with little heart for reasserting control over the territory, might have some small chance of successfully deterring a state adversary with NBC weapons, but even so, the risks would be great. NBC threats, and certainly attacks, would have a substantial chance of bringing the full wrath of the state down on the group. It may have made sense for the Chechen rebels to frighten the people of Moscow with radioactive material, but a series of chemical attacks, or a threat based on a stolen nuclear weapon, would probably have focused more of Russia's military resources on suppressing the rebels, at even greater risk to the Chechen people. The key risk, therefore, is that a non-state actor will seek to acquire NBC weapons for irrational reasons, having failed to think through the strategic implications of this decision. In a case like this, any weapons use is most likely to result from a violent confrontation with the state that provokes the non-state actor or causes it to panic.

CURIOSITY AND FASCINATION

Innate curiosity, fascination, or the need to demonstrate their competence and worth to society is a fourth possible reason why individuals or groups might attempt to acquire and even use weapons of mass destruction. Carrying these impulses to such extremes is clearly irrational, and this tendency is not evident in established terrorist organizations, which have historically been highly risk-averse and conservative in their tactics.[91] There is some evidence of such behavior among fringe groups and alienated individuals, however, and these factors might influence individuals or groups for whom the control of exotic weapons, including military ones, is a source of self-esteem and group cohesion. The individuals most likely to respond to influences of this kind probably come from America's large stratum of disaffected, rural young white men, immersed in gun shows, weapons magazines, Army surplus, survivalist manuals, assassination

---

in Brad Roberts, ed., *Biological Weapons: Weapons of the Future?* (Washington, D.C.: Center for Strategic and International Studies, 1993), p. 37; and Purver, *Chemical and Biological Terrorism*, p. 80.

91. See Hoffman, "Terrorist Targeting."

handbooks, conspiracy theories, and military fantasies.[92] People like this compose the right-wing militia groups of the American interior, and it is possible that a militia will come to think of improvised weapons of mass destruction in the same way it thinks of military-issue assault rifles, combat fatigues, and body armor.

Alternatively, a highly intelligent, hubristic individual might be drawn to weapons of mass destruction as a way of proving his or her own superiority, possibly as Theodore Kaczynski (the "Unabomber") was drawn to sophisticated letter bombs. Others might see NBC weapons acquisition as an interesting technological problem, and might want to surmount the associated challenges just for the sake of doing so.[93] It would, however, be a rare individual of this type who would also be motivated to kill on a massive scale, and be willing to disregard his or her own instincts for self-preservation.

COPYCAT EFFECTS AND PRECEDENT

A non-state actor's decision to acquire or use weapons of mass destruction might also be a response to some incident in the past. Until the March 1995 Tokyo subway attack, terrorism involving a modern weapon of mass destruction was essentially a non-existent phenomenon. A precedent has now been set, with several potential effects. On the one hand, future groups may be discouraged from using NBC weapons by the fact that Aum Shinrikyo caused only a fraction of the fatalities it could have, and failed to achieve anything except its own demise. On the other hand, the capable, hostile non-state actors of the future may notice the enormous amount of attention the cult has received, particularly from the U.S. national security establishment, and may seek to attract similar publicity through a similar

---

92. See, for example, the case of James Dalton Bell, a chemist arrested in Vancouver, Washington, for a stink-bomb attack on an IRS office. Bell had discussed assassinating government officials in an Internet forum. Police are said to have found a large assortment of chemicals, including ingredients for chemical weapons, when his house was searched at the time of his arrest. David E. Kaplan, "Terrorism's Next Wave," *U.S. News and World Report*, November 17, 1997, pp. 26–31.

93. In the view of one analyst, weapons of mass destruction could come to represent "scientific power" to a terrorist group. See Harvey J. McGeorge, "The Growing Trend Toward Chemical and Biological Weapons Capability," *Defense and Foreign Affairs*, April 1991, p. 5.

attack — or even a fake attack, such as the B'nai B'rith incident.[94] Another fringe religious group might incorporate similar ideas into its own belief system, and follow Aum Shinrikyo's example by seeking to bring about the apocalypse with an NBC attack. A "copycat" phenomenon has been seen among terrorist groups, cults, and criminals before, and it is certainly not impossible that others will copy Aum Shinrikyo.[95]

The risks of copycat attacks is likely to grow even more severe if weapons of mass destruction begin to be used more frequently and more successfully than they were by Aum Shinrikyo.[96] If a successful NBC attack occurs in the United States, for example, it is likely to attract extensive publicity, demonstrate the acute vulnerability of U.S. targets to this form of aggression, and embarrass the government by revealing the very low level of current preparedness and the paucity of specialized response capability. Uncertainty about the immediate and long-term effects of NBC weapons attacks would diminish, and the norm against using weapons of mass destruction would likely be further eroded. In a scenario like this, the risks of NBC terrorism and covert attack would quickly worsen. Limiting copycat attacks is part of the reason why prevention and preparedness efforts in advance of a real incident are so important.

Finally, it is also possible that the use (and possibly even the mere possession) of NBC weapons by states could set an example that encourages non-state actors to seek to obtain or employ weapons of mass destruction. Some have speculated, for example, that Aum Shinrikyo's interest in

---

94. The incident is described on p. 44 in Chapter 1, and in Matthew L. Wald, "Suspicious Package Prompts 8-Hour Vigil at B'nai B'rith," *New York Times*, April 25, 1997, p. A12; and "Jewish Center Package Causes Alert," *Facts on File Digest*, May 29, 1997.

95. Few other groups are likely to have the personnel and financial resources of Aum Shinrikyo, but a more competent group, even if much smaller and less well funded, could be substantially more destructive than Aum Shinrikyo proved to be.

96. According to a 1984 CIA intelligence estimate, "one successful incident involving such [a biological or chemical] agent would significantly lower the threshold of restraint on their application by other terrorists." Reported in Jack Anderson, "Chemical Arms in Terrorism Feared by the CIA," *Washington Post*, August 27, 1984, cited in Jessica Stern, "Will Terrorists Turn to Poison?" *Orbis*, Vol. 37, No. 3 (Summer 1993), p. 402. Similarly, Brian Jenkins argued that "the historical record well documents the tendency of terrorists to mimic the behavior of others. Once a spectacular event has taken place, it is likely that a similar event will follow." Jenkins, "Understanding the Link between Motives and Methods," p. 49.

chemical weapons was stimulated by the 1990–91 Persian Gulf War.[97] The use of NBC weapons by a state would allow non-state actors to observe the effects of these weapons, and might contribute to the weakening of norms against NBC weapons use. It could also motivate a non-state actor to try to retaliate against a state in kind — that is, with whatever weapons the state had used. This motivation might apply, for example, to the Kurdish rebel groups in southeastern Turkey, northern Iraq, and northwestern Iran, which face a very difficult military situation and which have been the victims of Iraqi chemical weapons attacks in the past. Similarly, Israel's failed October 1997 attempt to assassinate Khaled Meshal, a leader of the Hamas terrorist organization, in Amman, Jordan, with an exotic chemical agent could stimulate interest in chemical attacks among non-state Arab radicals, and might also be used to justify such attacks.[98]

Conclusion: The Risks of NBC Terrorism are Growing

Until Aum Shinrikyo, the non-state actors that have been capable of acquiring and using NBC weapons have been uninterested in doing so, and those that may have been interested in employing weapons of mass destruction have been unable to do so. Now, however, both parts of this generalization are becoming questionable.

First of all, the range of non-state actors that possess the technical capacity to obtain and use weapons of mass destruction is increasing. This process, which results both from growing non-state capabilities and from shrinking NBC acquisition hurdles, is adding new motivational diversity to the set of non-state actors with NBC potential. The diffusion of increasingly sophisticated knowledge of the nuclear, biological, and chemical sciences is increasing the number and range of individuals who understand that NBC weapons acquisition is technically feasible and who, if called upon, would be able to contribute materially to a non-state actor's attempt at secretly acquiring or fabricating an improvised weapon of mass destruction. As more groups and individuals become capable of NBC acquisition and

---

97. Jenkins, "Understanding the Link between Motives and Methods," p. 49.

98. The Israeli assassination team is reported to have used the synthetic opiate Fentanyl, a drug regularly used for anesthesia, but which is usually fatal in large doses. For an account of the Amman debacle, see Alan Cowell, "The Daring Attack that Blew Up in Israel's Face," *New York Times*, October 15, 1997, pp. A1, A8.

use, the odds that one or more will actually wish to use these weapons in a massively destructive attack will rise inexorably.

Terrorist groups and most other non-state actors have historically had little interest in killing large numbers of people with their attacks, and for many non-state actors, the reasons for this aversion will remain compelling. Nonetheless, non-state violence appears to be growing more lethal: mass-casualty terrorist events are becoming more frequent, and the percentage of terrorist attacks that result in fatalities is increasing. The best explanation for this trend is that there are increasing numbers of violent non-state actors for whom the logic of limited lethality applies only weakly, such as fanatical religious groups and cults, anti-American Islamic extremists in the Middle East, right-wing chauvinists, and loosely affiliated terrorists who lack the traditional concern with group preservation.

The net effect of these two trends is that the number of NBC-capable non-state actors with an interest in causing mass casualties will continue to grow in the years ahead. However, conventional weapons have been seen as adequate for virtually all non-state violence in the past, so an increase in the use of NBC weapons does not necessarily follow from an increasing interest in mass casualties. The disincentives to NBC weapons acquisition and use will continue to exist, but at the same time the number of groups that might switch to NBC terrorism will continue to grow. This fact, together with an appreciation of the potential consequences of even a single NBC attack against a civilian population, is the basis for our judgment that the risk of a covert NBC attack against the United States is rising, and that at present it is seriously underestimated by U.S. leaders and officials.

At the moment, there is only the most fragmentary evidence that any specific non-state actor has a current, serious interest in weapons of mass destruction. (If such information were found, the law enforcement and national security agencies of the American and many other governments would move with dispatch to extinguish the threat.) It is possible, however, to suggest elements of the likely "profile" of non-state actors with the capacity, motive, and intention to acquire and use NBC weapons:

- religious extremists, particularly those who have goals coinciding with a political terrorist agenda or an apocalyptic theology;

- Shi'ite terrorists operating in the Persian Gulf against U.S. forces and the moderate sheikdoms, with or without state sponsorship;

- groups that wish to mimic the trappings and functions of a state, such as secessionist guerrilla movements and some militia groups;

- "extreme" terrorists and revolutionaries, who are willing to run the great risks associated with massive casualties and NBC weapons use;

- weapons fanatics, possibly from the radical right, and technophiles for whom the acquisition of an exotic weapon has intrinsic value;

- groups that have themselves been the victim of NBC attacks, such as the Kurds; and

- "copycats," who wish to imitate an incident that has already occurred.

Groups in these categories are by no means certain to make the fateful step of using a weapon of mass destruction. However, if another incident of NBC terrorism does occur, those responsible for the attack will likely fall under one or more of the headings above. As an analytical matter, the likelihood of such an attack cannot be predicted. But as a national security matter, the possibility of such an attack must not be discounted.

Chapter 4

The Threat of Nuclear, Biological, or Chemical Attack by States

How serious is the threat of covert nuclear, biological, or chemical attack against the United States by another state? As Chapter 1 explained, use of NBC weapons has been quite rare in the eight decades since World War I, and many of the factors explaining this historical infrequency can be expected to endure into the future. One might therefore conclude that the threat of a covert NBC attack by a hostile state is so small that it is unimportant to U.S. national security strategy. Such a judgment would be dangerously mistaken. The probability of future events can be judged only in part on the basis of the past incidence of such events.[1] In addition to the growing availability of NBC weapons, discussed in Chapter 2, there are three reasons that the United States should take the threat of covert NBC attack by an international adversary more seriously than it does now.

First, the changing international environment is producing stronger motives for NBC weapons use, and weaker constraints against it, than obtained for most states during the Cold War. States have a variety of potential reasons to acquire or use nuclear, biological, or chemical weapons: to compensate for the loss of superpower patronage; to deter a more powerful adversary, such as the United States, or its coalition partners; to win on the battlefield against a more powerful adversary; to "decapitate" an opposing state by killing its senior officials, thus limiting its ability to fight;

---

1. Covert NBC attack against the United States by another state has been compared to the Japanese attack on Pearl Harbor, and for good reason. The U.S. fleet based at Pearl Harbor was vulnerable to a potentially devastating Japanese attack, but U.S. forces nonetheless allowed themselves to be taken by surprise — in part because of an intellectual failure to understand Japan's strategic options. Attacking the world's only superpower (or one of its allies) with weapons of mass destruction would be a very high-risk strategy for any foreign government. It might, however, still be rational, especially if the government in question was resigned to the inevitability of conflict with the United States. As Thomas Schelling has observed, "if Pearl Harbor was a long shot for the Japanese, so was war with the United States; assuming the decision on war, the attack hardly appears reckless." Thomas C. Schelling, "Foreword," in Roberta Wohlstetter, *Pearl Harbor: Warning and Decision* (Stanford, Calif.: Stanford University Press, 1962), p. vii.

to weaken an adversary's economic strength or political will; or to exact revenge. Nuclear, biological, and chemical weapons are likely tools for any state that opts for an "asymmetric strategy," one that seeks to deter or win by threatening a more powerful opponent's weakest points, and thus to avoid having to fight against the adversary's strengths. Regional powers such as Iraq may face, or may perceive, greater U.S. pressure and a greater threat of U.S. military action than they would have a decade ago. Because the end of the Cold War has also reduced U.S. security interests in many regions, such regional powers may also find it easier to deter the United States by means of NBC threats or attacks.

The second reason for the United States to treat the threat of covert NBC attack seriously is that, for many states — especially states in conflict with the United States — covert attack could have important advantages over more conventional military uses of NBC weapons. While covert delivery is inappropriate for many military purposes, it can provide certain advantages in some scenarios, especially against a more powerful opponent. Covert attacks on civilian populations may be more effective than military attacks in causing panic and sapping political will. Covert delivery may allow attackers to escape identification and retaliation, making it possible to attack an enemy and escape retribution. Moreover, for states without military delivery means to strike the desired target, covert delivery may be the only viable option for NBC use. Successful covert delivery also promises to maximize the element of surprise. Surprise can be a crucial factor in determining a weapon's effectiveness, especially in the case of biological weapons and in nuclear attacks aimed at an adversary's political leadership.

Third, the low priority presently attached to countering covert NBC threats is irrational given the prominence of ballistic missile defense in the U.S. defense budget. There is no reason to believe that the threat of covert NBC delivery is significantly less serious than the threat of NBC delivery by ballistic missile. The covert delivery threat is present now, is not confined to a few technologically advanced states with long-range ballistic missiles, and is very hard to detect and defend against. In U.S. federal government expenditures, however, the resources devoted to ballistic missile defense exceed those devoted to countering covert NBC threats by at least an order of magnitude.[2] As a simple matter of resource allocation, it makes little

---

2.   Unlike ballistic missile defense, which has a defined, largely consolidated piece of the defense budget, defense spending to reduce U.S. vulnerability to covert NBC attack is difficult to measure. One could add up the budgets of every federal, state,

sense to virtually ignore the covert NBC threat, while spending upwards of $3 billion per year on missile defense. Defense against covert attack merits higher priority in U.S. national security planning and resource allocation.

This chapter develops these arguments. The first section examines the potential motives for all forms of NBC use, whether covert or with traditional military delivery means, explaining why a hostile state might decide to use NBC weapons against U.S. territory, military forces, or allies. The second section examines the potential motives for employing covert means of delivery as opposed to more traditional military means. The analysis builds on the discussion in Chapter 1, offering reasons to believe that covert NBC attacks may occur, despite the many disincentives. The final section contrasts the threat of ballistic missiles with the threat of covert delivery in order to demonstrate that the threat posed by both NBC delivery techniques — ballistic missiles and covert delivery — should be considered at least roughly comparable. Together, the three sections help to fix the threat of covert NBC weapons delivery against the United States, its territories, military forces, and allies in its proper place: between the extremes of complacency and paranoia. They form the analytical basis for our argument that the covert NBC threat from states is already significant and is growing with time.

Motives for NBC Attack

Weapons of mass destruction have rarely been used by states in war, and no state is known to have sponsored NBC terrorism. The disincentives to using NBC weapons are strong. A state that uses these weapons faces serious risks of direct retaliation by the targeted state, and of long-term political antagonism and economic penalties, and possibly even military action, by the international community. This fact exerts a deterrent effect on individual NBC use decisions, and makes it hard to conceive of scenarios in which the use of an NBC weapon clearly serves the larger strategic interests of a nation. Similarly, state sponsors of international terrorism lack

---

and local agency involved in law enforcement, counterterrorism, border patrol, emergency management, or medical response, but the figure generated would be meaningless. If one looks only at programs focused specifically on countering covert NBC threats, the figures are far lower. The Nunn-Lugar-Domenici amendment to the 1996 Defense Authorization Act provided about $50 million for programs aimed specifically at reducing U.S. vulnerability to covert NBC attack (see Box 11, Nunn-Lugar-Domenici, p. 262).

perfect control over the groups they support and are therefore unwilling to run the enormous risks associated with assisting them to acquire weapons of mass destruction.

Although these considerations will continue to restrain future NBC use, they do not make such use impossible. Indeed, the incentives in favor of using weapons of mass destruction against the United States or U.S. interests in regional contingencies have probably grown since the end of the Cold War. One result of that shift in the structure of the international system is that nationalist movements, previously held in check by the Cold War, especially by Soviet pressure, have awakened from dormancy, fueling a variety of low-intensity conflicts around the globe. The end of the superpower standoff has also largely removed the risk that regional conflicts might escalate into superpower war, giving the United States greater freedom to involve itself in regional conflicts. Ironically, the end of geopolitical competition with the Soviet Union has simultaneously reduced the importance to the United States of many of its interests in the Third World, making asymmetric deterrence of superior U.S. power more feasible. These large-scale structural changes in the international system may be creating an environment that is more conducive to NBC weapons use than at any time since the end of World War I. Regional powers opposed to U.S. influence may seek to compensate for the conventional military dominance of the United States by acquiring, and perhaps using, weapons of mass destruction.

An NBC attack against an American city or some other part of the continental United States has the potential to do the greatest damage to vital U.S. national interests. But this is probably the least likely scenario, due to the risk that such an attack would provoke the full wrath of the United States, up to and including retaliatory nuclear strikes. Only a state that is supremely confident of escaping blame, or that is making a last-ditch effort to force the end of a losing war, could rationally decide to conduct NBC attacks against U.S. territory. (Irrationality, however, is always a possibility; in particular, one must consider the possibility of revenge attacks against the U.S. leadership or citizenry.) Attacks against U.S. military forces stationed abroad are somewhat more likely, whether as the opening salvo of a war or as a gambit to undermine political support for forward deployment of U.S. troops. As in the case of attacking the U.S. homeland, however, a nuclear, biological, or chemical attack on U.S. servicemen would run the risk of triggering war with the United States. Nuclear, biological, or chemical weapons use against a third country, which might limit the risk of war with the United States, may be the most likely of all. Attacks against third countries might be enough to achieve significant strategic objectives, such as the disruption of opposing military coalitions, while not engaging the United States directly. As demonstrations of a capability to carry out NBC attacks, third-country attacks might also serve as an effective deterrent against U.S. regional involvement.

We argue that NBC weapons are most likely to be used to serve one or more of six basic purposes: (1) to deter or intimidate the United States; (2) to disrupt U.S.-led coalitions by deterring or intimidating potential U.S. allies; (3) to prevail on the battlefield; (4) to "decapitate" an opposing state by killing its leaders; (5) to destabilize the society or undermine the economy of an international rival; and (6) to take revenge against a foe.

DETERRING THE UNITED STATES

After the crushing defeat of the Iraqi army by the U.S.-led coalition, former Indian Army Chief of Staff K. Sundarji is reported to have remarked that "one principal lesson of the Gulf War is that, if a state intends to fight the United States, it should avoid doing so until and unless it possesses nuclear weapons."[3] Saddam Hussein is reported to have believed that the Americans had no stomach for casualties, and clearly hoped that the United States would be deterred from war by the prospect of battlefield losses. Although Saddam probably made an incorrect assumption about the American willingness to incur casualties, Iraq's effort to deter the United States failed principally because Iraq was unable (or unwilling) to make a credible threat of massively destructive counterstrikes against U.S. military forces, much less against American cities. Iraq did not possess nuclear weapons or a long-range military delivery capability, and was not believed to possess a mature offensive biological weapons capability, so Saddam was presumed to pose no major threat to the U.S. homeland. Iraq's chemical weapons, like its conventional forces and short-range ballistic missiles, were a threat to U.S. military forces in the Kuwaiti theater, but a militarily manageable one and, in the end, one that was successfully deterred by explicit American threats.[4] However, even with this relatively modest

---

3.   Quoted in Robert G. Joseph and John F. Reichart, "Deterrence and Defense in a Nuclear, Biological, Chemical Environment," Occasional Paper of the Center for Counterproliferation Research, Institute for National Strategic Studies, National Defense University, 1995, p. 4.

4.   Shortly before the beginning of Operation Desert Storm in the 1990–91 Gulf War, U.S. Secretary of State James Baker delivered to Iraqi Foreign Minister Tariq Aziz a letter from President George Bush addressed to Iraqi President Saddam

spectrum of threats, there was still a real debate in the United States about the war's merits, and some senior American officials expressed considerable hesitancy about risking U.S. lives to expel Saddam from Kuwait.[5] President Bush's resolve to fight and win the war seems to have been unwavering, but what would have happened if Iraq had had nuclear weapons, or if the United States or its allies had known of the scope of Iraq's biological weapons program?[6]

Even though it did not happen in the Iraqi case, it is entirely conceivable that a state threatened militarily by a superior conventional power such as the United States will attempt to deter war, or deter specific military actions, through the threat or the use of NBC weapons against U.S. or allied civilian or military targets. In the words of a 1994 Pentagon report on the Defense Counterproliferation Initiative, "in contrast to the Cold War, today, it is the United States that has unmatched conventional military power, and it is potential adversaries who may use weapons of mass destruction to deter U.S. power projection abroad."[7] Similarly, another U.S.

Hussein. The letter stated that "The United States will not tolerate the use of chemical or biological weapons or the destruction of Kuwait's oil fields and installations. Further, you will be held directly responsible for terrorist actions against any member of the coalition. The American people would demand the strongest possible response. You and your country will pay a terrible price if you order unconscionable acts of this sort." "Statement by Press Secretary Fitzwater on President Bush's Letter to President Saddam Hussein of Iraq," January 12, 1991, in *Public Papers of George Bush*, Book 1: *January 1 to June 30, 1991*. Privately, Bush had ruled out the use of nuclear weapons against Iraq. James A. Baker III with Thomas M. DeFrank, *The Politics of Diplomacy* (New York: G.P. Putnam's Sons, 1995), p. 359.

5. Among others, General Colin Powell, then chairman of the Joint Chiefs of Staff, expressed reluctance to commit forces to such a mission. See Michael R. Gordon and Bernard E. Trainor, *The Generals' War: The Inside Story of the Conflict in the Gulf* (New York: Little, Brown, 1995), pp. 129–131.

6. For a good analysis of this scenario, see Barry R. Posen, "U.S. Security Policy in a Nuclear-Armed World (Or: What If Iraq Had Had Nuclear Weapons?)" *Security Studies*, Vol. 6, No. 3 (Spring 1997), pp. 1–31. Posen argues that if Iraq had had nuclear weapons, the United States would still have had to fight to liberate Kuwait, not because of the intrinsic importance of the emirate, but because of the "general strategic consequences of inaction," which he enumerates.

7. Office of the Deputy Secretary of Defense, *Report on Nonproliferation and Counterproliferation Activities and Programs* (Washington, D.C.: Department of Defense, May 1994), p. 2.

government study has argued that "strategic attack with NBC — or the threat of attack — would most likely be designed to cause the loss of political/public support in an effort to deter the United States from acting or to force withdrawal."[8]

Deterrent threats and attacks could involve a wide range of targets, weapon types, and delivery methods. Absent a history of NBC catastrophes, a powerful state like the United States could easily decide to ignore threats, confident of its ability to prevent or absorb damage to its homeland and military forces, and certain of its ability to retaliate with devastating force. A state seeking to deter the United States might have to carry out demonstration attacks. In principle, such attacks could be carried out equally well during wartime or as bolt-from-the-blue attacks in advance of a planned conflict. Even a completely anonymous attack, demonstrating simply that some unknown actor has the capacity to cause large numbers of casualties, might be an effective deterrent. To deter effectively, however, the attacker would have to demonstrate a plausible ability to carry out further attacks during wartime, even after the target state has taken precautionary measures such as heightening internal security and restricting travel and commerce.

Threats or attacks against a more powerful adversary or its troops in the field would carry great risks. They might strengthen the adversary's resolve by revealing the weaker state as more dangerous than originally assumed, and they could prompt immediate retaliation. Exactly how the United States or any other state might react in a situation like this is, of course, difficult to predict; the response would depend on the severity of the threat or act, the target affected, and the degree to which the target state was already entangled in the conflict. For example, a biological attack against the first U.S. troops deployed to the Gulf after Iraq's invasion of Kuwait, sickening but not killing the first few thousand troops, might have swung U.S. public and official opinion against the war. A large attack on a U.S. city, or the loss of 10,000 soldiers in the field just before the start of the war, might have had the opposite effect. Demonstration attacks for deterrent purposes need not be aimed at their real targets, however. Iraq could, for instance, have used biological weapons during its invasion of Kuwait, demonstrating their efficacy without directly attacking the United States or U.S. forces. It could also have attacked an American ally such as Saudi Arabia or Turkey, or even a non-allied country such as Iran or Syria, perhaps in the latter cases hoping that the target country's poor relations

---

8.   Joseph and Reichart, "Deterrence and Defense," p. 14.

with the United States would allow a demonstration without unduly heightening Washington's hostility.[9]

A deterrent strategy based on the threat of NBC attacks directly against the United States would force Washington to weigh its limited interests in most regional contingencies against the more vital interest of protecting the lives of thousands of U.S. civilians at home.[10] If the issue becomes one of endangering thousands of U.S. civilians in order to achieve less-than-vital objectives abroad, how American political leaders will react is certainly open to question. In the run-up to a regional conflict, the vivid image of thousands of dead civilians in a foreign city, much less an American one, might cause elected U.S. leaders to recoil in horror, rather than harden their resolve.

DETERRING U.S. ALLIES AND COALITION BUSTING

If a state lacks either the ability or the will to threaten U.S. military forces or cities directly with NBC attacks, then it may try to deter a key regional ally of the United States from becoming involved in a crisis or war, or to disrupt a coalition that the United States has built.[11] A deterrent strategy of this kind would exploit U.S. dependence on regional allies for power projection. In almost all conceivable regional wars, the United States must rely on nearby allies to provide the military bases and territories from which U.S. forces can prosecute the war. Deterring a few key regional states from assisting the United States could have a profound effect on the

---

9.   This logic suggests that the most likely targets are states that are neither friendly nor allied with the United States or any other powerful state. This is outside the scope of our present analysis, which is concerned with attacks on the United States and its friends and allies. It is worth noting, however, that Iraq's decision to use chemical weapons against Iran in 1983–88 fits this pattern, as does Libya's use of chemical weapons against Chadian troops in 1986, and possibly even Egypt's use of chemical weapons against Yemen in the 1960s. On these incidents, see Gordon M. Burck and Charles C. Flowerree, *International Handbook on Chemical Weapons Proliferation* (New York: Greenwood Press, 1991), pp. 92–184, 223, 269–270.

10.   On this general question, see Lawrence Freedman, "Great Powers, Vital Interests and Nuclear Weapons," *Survival*, Vol. 36, No. 4 (Winter 1994/95), pp. 35–52.

11.   On this general concern, see Kenneth Watman and Dean Wilkening, *U.S. Regional Deterrence Strategies* (Santa Monica, Calif.: RAND, 1995); and Dean Wilkening and Kenneth Watman, *Nuclear Deterrence in a Regional Context* (Santa Monica, Calif.: RAND, 1995).

outcome of the war. One U.S. government-sponsored study noted: "loss of staging areas/bases in neighboring countries, because of coercive threat to (or actual attack on) those countries, could severely curtail U.S. or coalition operations, possibly compromising the overall prosecution of the campaign (e.g., although an attack may be contained, there may not be sufficient logistic support available to conduct a counterattack)."[12]

After the Iraqi invasion of Kuwait, for instance, a credible nuclear threat — perhaps with a demonstration shot — against Saudi cities and oil fields might have convinced the Saudi government that it would be better off reconciling itself to Saddam's hegemony than inviting the U.S. Army onto its soil. Similarly, Japan's willingness to allow its territory to be used as a staging area for U.S. military forces could be critically important to success in another war on the Korean peninsula. But how would a skittish Japanese government react to a suspicious outbreak of tularemia (a lethal disease induced by a biological warfare agent) in one of its cities during preparations for such a war, especially if the epidemic were coupled with a quietly conveyed warning that the capability to conduct many more such attacks was dispersed widely among Japan's large Korean minority?

The risks of such a deterrent strategy would be high, although probably not as high as targeting the United States or U.S. military forces directly. But the state in question might find these risks preferable to the near certainty of military defeat by a U.S.-led coalition.

WAR FIGHTING

Nuclear, biological, or chemical weapons might also be used tactically in an attempt to achieve the upper hand in open warfare. In this case, the attacker would judge that the strategic risks of retaliation associated with initiating NBC use were outweighed by the opportunity to achieve military victory (or at least to avert military defeat) on the battlefield. Chemical weapons were initially developed for use on the battlefield in the early twentieth century, and used during World War I. More recently, Iraq used chemical weapons in its war with Iran in the 1980s to compensate for its numerically inferior ground forces (see Box 8, Iran-Iraq War, p. 226). Nuclear weapons were initially developed solely for strategic purposes (strikes directly against the enemy's homeland, bypassing the battlefield), but

---

12. Joseph and Reichart, "Deterrence and Defense," p. 14. They also note that differences in the levels of preparation for dealing with NBC attacks among the military forces of the various countries in a coalition could become a serious source of tension and acrimony in the management of the coalition.

Box 8
Chemical Weapons Use in
the Iran-Iraq War, 1980–88

Chemical weapons were used extensively in the Iran-Iraq War of 1980–88, first and most extensively by Iraq, but probably also by Iran.[1] Iran made allegations of Iraqi chemical weapons use as early as 1980, but chemical weapons use before the final months of the third year of the war was never independently confirmed. By late 1983, however, as Iran broadened the front and began to carry the war into Iraqi territory, Iraq began to use chemical weapons on a significant scale, and independent observers began to confirm Iran's reports of chemical weapons use.[2] In March of 1984, a UN investigation examined Iranian casualties and other evidence, and concluded that Iraq had used mustard gas and tabun.[3]

Accounts of chemical weapons use during the remainder of the war differ widely, due largely to the lack of independent verification, and to the likelihood that both Iran and Iraq were inclined to lie about chemical weapons use for propaganda purposes.[4] Large numbers of attacks were reported, and while some of the reports may be true, many could not be confirmed and some seem dubious. Nevertheless, outside investigators confirmed that Iraq used chemicals at least a few times in 1985, and in February 1986 during the Iranian offensive against the Fao Peninsula (including attacks on hospitals and other rear-area targets).[5] UN investigators visiting Iran in April of 1987 again confirmed chemical attacks with mustard gas and possibly tabun. They also confirmed for the first time, in a visit to Iraq in late April and early May, that Iraqi forces had been exposed to mustard gas, but it was impossible to determine whether the exposure was due to Iraq's own chemical operations, or to possible Iranian attacks.[6] In March 1988, Iraq and perhaps Iran carried out chemical attacks that killed an estimated 3,000–5,000 civilians in the town of Halabja and the surrounding area.[7] Additional Iraqi chemical weapons attacks against Iranian troops and rear areas later in the year were also confirmed.[8]

Chemical weapons are not believed to have significantly altered the course of the war, but were tactically significant in some battles.[9] They helped Iraq overcome Iran's manpower advantage, particularly when defending against Iranian offensives, and they helped limit Iraqi casualties, a significant political benefit to Saddam Hussein.[10]

Iraq acquired its chemical weapons both by importing the necessary precursor chemicals, and by manufacturing these precursor chemicals in its own chemical facilities, starting with indigenous petroleum, phosphates, and other feedstocks.[11] In both areas, Iraq had substantial foreign assistance from companies in Europe and the United States. Hundreds of tons of various precursor chemicals for nerve agents and mustard gas were shipped to Iraq

Box 8, CW in the Iran-Iraq War, *cont.*

during the 1980s, including over 500 tons of thiodiglycol shipped under false export documents from a single company in Maryland.[12] Karl Kolb GmbH in Germany, among other companies, greatly aided the Iraqi efforts to build an indigenous chemical weapons production capability by providing complete chemical production lines usable for nerve agent production.[13] Little information about Iranian production capabilities is available, and what is available is less detailed, but a variety of reports, as well as clear evidence of imports of large quantities of precursors such as thiodiglycol (from the same Maryland company that was supplying Iraq) indicate that if Iran did not succeed in producing its own chemical weapons during the war, it at least made substantial progress, and could easily have completed the capability after the war.[14]

The present status of the Iranian and Iraqi chemical programs is uncertain. Iraq's production capacity and agent stocks have been greatly reduced by the ongoing efforts of the United Nations inspection teams, but Iraq is believed to retain significant quantities of agent and of key production equipment (see Box 10, Iraqi NBC Programs, p. 255). Far less is publicly known about Iran's program, but the U.S. government maintains that one exists. Iran, however, has recently joined the Chemical Weapons Convention, agreeing to subject itself to that treaty's fairly intrusive verification provisions, which should make it hard to hide a large program. Iran has not yet submitted the declarations required by the treaty, nor has the treaty's verification organization carried out any inspections there.

NOTES

1. A thorough and careful account of Iraq's chemical warfare program and of the use of chemical weapons in the Iran-Iraq War can be found in Gordon M. Burck and Charles C. Flowerree, *International Handbook on Chemical Weapons Proliferation* (New York: Greenwood Press, 1991), pp. 31–152. A narrower discussion of some of the same issues can be found in Anthony H. Cordesman and Abraham R. Wagner, *The Lessons of Modern War*, Vol. II: *The Iran-Iraq War* (Boulder, Colo.: Westview, 1990), pp. 506–518.

2. Burck and Flowerree, *International Handbook on Chemical Weapons Proliferation*, pp. 31, 32, 93–101.

3. Ibid., p. 103.

4. A good discussion of the problems with the available data can be found in ibid., p. 35.

5. Ibid., pp. 105–107.

6. Ibid., p. 109.

notes continue overleaf

Box 8, CW in the Iran-Iraq War, *cont.*

7. Ibid., pp. 110, 239–240.

8. Ibid., pp. 112–114.

9. Ibid., p. 114.

10. Ibid., pp 114–115.

11. For a detailed discussion, see ibid., pp. 35–49.

12. Ibid., p. 49.

13. Ibid., pp. 42–43.

14. Ibid., pp. 237–256.

---

during the Cold War, both the United States and the Soviet Union developed a vast array of relatively low-yield "tactical" nuclear weapons intended for a variety of battlefield contingencies. While biological weapons are usually too slow-acting to be strictly tactical — that is, able to affect the course of a battle — their ability to affect unprotected troops across large areas within a few days makes their use potentially decisive in regional wars.[13]

Battlefield use of nuclear, biological, and chemical weapons in a future regional war remains a serious possibility, especially as an asymmetric tactic of a conventionally outmatched adversary. The U.S. military, under the Defense Counterproliferation Initiative, has begun a concerted effort to prepare U.S. forces for these contingencies.[14] However, the NBC employment concept of a future American adversary is unlikely to be a simple replay of the chemical weapons attacks against massed infantry seen in World War I and the Iran-Iraq War.

---

13. After decades of producing and weaponizing biological agents, the United States terminated its biological weapons program in 1969. The U.S. military agreed to abandon this class of weapons because their tactical utility was limited, nuclear weapons were capable of performing essential strategic tasks more predictably and promptly, and the U.S. government wished to delegitimize these low-cost weapons of mass destruction before the eyes of the world. See George W. Christopher, Theodore J. Cieslak, Julie A. Pavlin, et al., "Biological Warfare: A Historical Perspective," *Journal of the American Medical Association*, Vol. 278, No. 5 (August 6, 1997), pp. 415–416.

14. For an overview of the Defense Counterproliferation Initiative, see Counterproliferation Program Review Committee (CPRC), *Report on Activities and Programs for Countering Proliferation* (Washington, D.C.: Department of Defense, May 1996).

Technological advances, particularly in individual protective gear and unit mobility, have dramatically reduced the vulnerability of sophisticated armies to chemical weapons, and the ability to target and destroy chemical delivery systems at long range has increased dramatically. Nonetheless, chemical weapons use (and credible threats of use) would force soldiers to wear cumbersome protective gear, reducing their effectiveness. Nuclear and biological weapons have the potential to be vastly more effective than chemical weapons on the battlefield, enabling an adversary to destroy or disable large troop concentrations in single attacks. A regional adversary might also seek to disable the U.S. war effort with a limited number of pinpoint attacks against a handful of key installations and logistical nodes, conducting high-tech sabotage, in effect. The most attractive targets would be strategically vital fixed installations such as ports, airports, command centers, air and ballistic missile defense networks, and communications nodes.[15] Destroying or permanently disabling facilities of this kind would probably require nuclear weapons or repeated biological attacks, although the operational effectiveness of many strategic facilities could be reduced by the contamination caused by a persistent chemical (or perhaps even radiological) weapon. If used early in the war, when U.S. military forces would be particularly vulnerable while surging into the theater, limited NBC attacks could cause "substantial, possibly crippling, political-military problems for the United States and its allies."[16] NBC weapons could also be

---

15. In the words of an authoritative 1997 Department of Defense study of the subject, "[U.S.] national security strategy is dependent upon [U.S.] capability to project power into areas of unrest in order to deter conflict or, failing that, to bring the conflict to an early successful conclusion. This study reveals vulnerabilities to our power projection system, especially through the asymmetrical application of chemical and biological weapons, which can disrupt and delay force deployment into the theater of operations.... An enemy using relatively small quantities of chemical and biological weapons could exploit these vulnerabilities.... Military operations conducted according to the tenets of power projection were executable only on delayed and disrupted schedules when CONUS [continental United States] deployment facilities, prepositioned material, or key reception sites in the area of responsibility (AOR) were attacked with chemical or biological agents." U.S. Department of Defense, "Assessment of the Impact of Chemical and Biological Weapons on Joint Operations in 2010 (CB 2010 Study)," Summary Report, November 1997, p. 1.

16. The 1990–91 Gulf War illustrates the enormous logistical demands of deploying and sustaining U.S. troops in a regional war. About 94 percent of the cargo needed was delivered by sea through three ports in Saudi Arabia. Most of this

used against troops in the United States as they are preparing to travel to the theater of war. More generally, once the reality of the NBC threat had been demonstrated, the constant need to take NBC countermeasures would reduce the tactical effectiveness of U.S. and coalition forces.[17]

Nuclear, biological, or chemical weapons use would mark a major escalation in any conflict and would risk provoking strong retaliation, whether with conventional or nuclear weapons. The risk of provoking retaliation, rather than forcing retreat, would probably be greatest if troops were killed in large numbers. Thus, regional powers may feel an incentive to use NBC weapons early in a war against ports and other key infrastructure, both to demonstrate their weapons, and to limit the risk of retaliation by making it harder for an outside power to prosecute a war. Only nuclear weapons would permanently damage a port or airfield, preventing its use by outside forces. Persistent chemical agents could delay access, however, and biological or chemical attacks could kill personnel such as port laborers in potential host states, making the facilities harder to use.

In sum, regional powers could use nuclear, biological, and chemical weapons in war in a variety of ways. Not all would be equally effective, and all would entail considerable risk, but for a state that believed its only alternative was certain defeat in a conventional war, many of these options might seem appealing.

---

went through two ports on the Persian Gulf coast, within range of Iraqi Scud missiles. See James K. Matthews and Cora J. Holt, *So Many, So Much, So Far, So Fast: United States Transportation Command and Strategic Deployment for Operation Desert Shield/Desert Storm* (Washington, D.C.: Office of the Chairman of the Joint Chiefs of Staff and the United States Transportation Command, 1992); and William G. Pagonis and Jeffrey L. Cruikshank, *Moving Mountains: Lessons in Leadership and Logistics from the Gulf War* (Boston: Harvard Business School Press, 1992). The U.S. military has acknowledged that chemical or biological attacks against these ports could have seriously delayed the buildup of U.S. forces and slowed the tempo of the war. See also Joseph and Reichart, "Deterrence and Defense," p. 13.

17. According to one estimate, standard U.S. chemical weapons protective gear reduces individual performance by 50 percent or more. See "NBC Protection," FM3-4/FM 19-11, Headquarters, Department of the Army/Headquarters, U.S. Marine Corps, May 29, 1992, cited in Victor A. Utgoff, *Nuclear Weapons and the Deterrence of Biological and Chemical Warfare*, Occasional Paper No. 36 (Washington, D.C.: Henry L. Stimson Center, October 1997), pp. 5–6. See also Victor A. Utgoff, *The Challenge of Chemical Weapons: An American Perspective* (London: Macmillan, 1990), pp. 155–182.

NATIONAL DECAPITATION

Another possible motive for NBC aggression is national "decapitation" through a surprise strike on a state's leadership, perhaps as the opening salvo of a war. In its most extreme form, a nuclear blast on Capitol Hill during a State of the Union address would achieve this effect. So might a hidden aerosol sprayer in a van, dispensing a biological agent while driving through downtown Washington during a presidential inauguration. Either type of attack would result in the deaths of a significant number of the nation's elected leaders and senior government officials, as well as of many other civilians. The consequences of such an audacious strike against a state's government, although impossible to forecast with any precision, would surely be grave and might result in a period of nationwide panic and governmental paralysis.

Farfetched as this scenario may seem, the possibility of national decapitation is a long-standing concern among analysts and officials who have contemplated the threat of nuclear weapons. In the late 1970s and early 1980s, the vulnerability of the U.S. strategic nuclear command and control system to Soviet preemption became a central preoccupation of U.S. national security planning.[18] This effort — known as "Continuity of Government" (COG) — was motivated not by a belief that a preemptive Soviet nuclear strike was particularly likely, but by the recognition that the consequences of such a strike, should it occur, would be incalculably high; that the manifest vulnerability of the U.S. strategic command and control system was making such a strike marginally more likely by creating a situation in which a nuclear war might be "won" by one side; and that major investments in the modernization of strategic nuclear delivery systems were irrational if the deficiencies in the command and control system were left unremedied. Accordingly, both the Carter and Reagan administrations invested heavily in analyzing and reducing this vulnerability.[19]

---

18. See John D. Steinbruner, "Nuclear Decapitation," *Foreign Policy*, No. 45 (Winter 1981–82), p. 19; Ashton B. Carter, "Assessing Command System Vulnerability," in Ashton B. Carter, John D. Steinbruner, and Charles A. Zraket, eds., *Managing Nuclear Operations* (Washington, D.C.: Brookings, 1987), pp. 555–610; Paul J. Bracken, *The Command and Control of Nuclear Forces* (New Haven: Yale University Press, 1983), pp. 232–237; and Kurt Gottfried and Bruce G. Blair, eds., *Crisis Stability and Nuclear War* (New York: Oxford University Press, 1988).

19. For detailed discussions of this issue, see Paul Bracken, "Delegation of Nuclear Command Authority," in Carter, Steinbruner, and Zraket, eds., *Managing Nuclear Operations*, pp. 352–72; and Carter, "Assessing Command System Vulnerability."

The similarity between the threat of U.S.-Soviet strategic nuclear decapitation and post–Cold War nuclear or biological decapitation is, of course, superficial in some respects. A Soviet decapitating strike was seen as a possible opening salvo of a global thermonuclear war that would target the entire U.S. strategic chain of command, as well as the communications systems on which it relies; the primary objective would have been to degrade U.S. retaliatory capability, thereby limiting the damage an American counterstrike could inflict and possibly forcing the United States to capitulate on Soviet terms.[20] A covert nuclear or biological strike by a small power, in contrast, could realistically aim only to kill the individuals at the pinnacle of the national command authority, since the U.S. command and control system is probably robust and redundant enough to withstand all but an enormous attack against many locations. That these individuals are vulnerable to a potential covert nuclear or biological attack is not really in doubt: as one analyst noted during the debates over strategic nuclear decapitation, "normal operations in the U.S. government require that its constitutional leadership be exposed most of the time."[21] Thus, although a limited nuclear or biological weapons attack could not eliminate the U.S. *technical* capacity to conduct and coordinate complex military operations, the simultaneous deaths of the nation's highest leaders could have devastating psychological and political consequences, resulting in the temporary enfeeblement of the world's most powerful state.

National decapitation or paralysis through an NBC strike is as much an opportunity as a motive. In the case of a hypothetical Soviet strategic nuclear strike during the Cold War, the key motive would presumably have been the wish to limit damage in a war that had not yet begun but that appeared inevitable.[22] This motive is less plausible in the case of covert decapitation by a small power, because the hidden attacker could not expect to dictate surrender terms to the United States through the threat of a second, even more devastating strike against U.S. population centers, as the

---

20. Carter, "Assessing Command System Vulnerability," p. 557.

21. Steinbruner, "Nuclear Decapitation," p. 26.

22. "A pre-emptive attack on the U.S. command structure is a rational defensive act for the Soviets once they have judged that nuclear war can no longer be avoided." Ibid., p. 19.

Soviet Union might have.[23] Indeed, for a regional power without a strategic nuclear deterrent to launch a covert nuclear or biological attack on the U.S. leadership could well be a recipe for national suicide, because if it identified the attacker, the United States could easily retaliate with nuclear weapons. Thus, even if a military defeat by the United States were believed to be inevitable, an attempt to decapitate the U.S. leadership through a covert nuclear or biological attack would be likely only if the attacker's hatred or thirst for revenge led it to place its wish to harm the United States above the well-being of its own citizens. The important point, however, is that the U.S. leadership is highly vulnerable to a covert NBC attack, and that this poses an opportunity that some state may seek to exploit in a manner that might prove a complete surprise.

The leading role of the United States in supporting regional policies unpopular with some states (e.g., the U.S. effort to contain Iraqi and Iranian power in the Persian Gulf region, or U.S. support for Israel) could make Washington a tempting target for an audacious zealot. Even so, the United States is probably not the nation most at risk of nuclear or biological decapitation. Again, the principal reason for this is the massive retaliatory capabilities of the U.S. armed forces, which make any direct strike against the U.S. homeland an immensely risky undertaking. Strikes are more likely against regional adversaries with more modest retaliatory capabilities (e.g., Saudi Arabia, Turkey, South Korea, perhaps Israel). The decapitation of a regional adversary might serve the strategic purposes of the attacker as well as or better than killing some portion of the American leadership.[24]

Decapitation of the United States government in a nuclear or biological attack by a small power would not necessarily mark the end of the war. It would, at most, slow the ability of the United States to retaliate, while making it likely that any eventual retaliation would be severe. This kind of attack makes sense mainly if the attacker feels confident of escaping

---

23. "By eliminating central coordination, it sharply reduces the effectiveness of opposing strategic forces; second, it offers some small chance that complete decapitation will occur and no retaliation will follow." Ibid., p. 19. Given its vast size and high investment in national command and control survivability, decapitating strikes against the United States are less likely to succeed than they are against states with smaller, less secure, and more geographically concentrated command and control systems.

24. An illustrative incident is the 1983 North Korean attack against the South Korean cabinet in Rangoon, Burma, described in Box 9, Rangoon Decapitation Attack, p. 235.

retaliation by remaining unidentified. A leader motivated by great hatred, a desire for revenge, or dementia might also carry out such an attack despite the interests of his state. An attacker might also seek to mislead the target state into blaming, and retaliating against, a third party.

DESTABILIZING ANOTHER SOCIETY OR ECONOMY

Weapons of mass destruction can be used to destabilize the society or economy of a rival. A serious nuclear, biological, or chemical weapons incident within a country — mass casualties might not even be necessary — would have a profound psychological effect on the citizenry. The vivid possibility of civilian deaths on a scale that dwarfs conventional terrorism would inject an unprecedented level of fear into a population. Very large or repeated attacks might even lead to panic and flight from cities. In an effort to counter the NBC threat and to control the reactions of its own citizens, a government might impose martial law in a prolonged state of emergency, which might degrade the core values and principles of the nation. As Fred Iklé writes, terrorism with weapons of mass destruction "could force the incumbent government to abandon civil rights and constitutional principles, one by one, thus compelling the government to dismantle the foundation of its own legitimacy."[25] Anonymous urban strikes could also demonstrate that a state is vulnerable, making later efforts to deter it easier and discouraging forceful action in response. An adversary that recognized these possibilities could try to use them to its own advantage, hoping that the trauma of a series of domestic NBC incidents would force the state in question to turn its attention inward, distracting and undermining its leadership and weakening it on the international scene.

Weapons of mass destruction could also be used to cause other types of extreme distress. Some types of biological weapons, for instance, could be used against crops or livestock, causing economic damage rather than human casualties, options that might be attractive to an adversary that wished to sap the resources of an international rival. Nuclear, biological, or chemical weapons could be used selectively to disable parts of a nation's critical infrastructure. Attacks on crucial economic nodes, such as the New York Stock Exchange, could have an economic impact disproportionate to the number of people killed. Moreover, modern nations like the United States have grown highly dependent on a handful of technical infrastructures, such as the electrical grid, oil and gas pipelines, telecommunications

---

25. Fred C. Iklé, "The Next Lenin: On the Cusp of Truly Revolutionary Warfare," *The National Interest*, No. 47 (Spring 1997), p. 13.

Box 9
North Korea's Attempt to Decapitate South Korea: The 1983 Rangoon Bombing

On October 9, 1983, North Korean agents detonated a bomb at the Martyr's Mausoleum in Rangoon (now Yangon) in Burma (now Myanmar), in a rare example of an attempt by one state to "decapitate" another.[1] The purpose of the attack was to kill members of the South Korean cabinet, who were attending a wreath-laying ceremony. The explosion killed seventeen visiting South Korean officials, including four cabinet ministers, as well as four Burmese citizens. South Korean President Chun Doo-Hwan was absent only because his entourage was delayed by traffic.

Three days later, Burmese soldiers captured Captain Kang Min Chul, one member of the five-man North Korean bombing team, just south of Rangoon. As the soldiers closed in on Kang he exploded a hand grenade, killing three of the soldiers and severely wounding himself. Another suspect, Major Zin Mo, leader of the assassination squad, was also captured, and the two were later tried for murder. Kang confessed that he and the other members of the team were ordered by senior North Korean military officers to assassinate Chun during his state visit to Burma.

Authorities suspect that the North Korean agents had either infiltrated the 200-man South Korean security contingent in Burma, or arrived on a North Korean freighter, the *Tong Oae Gu Kho*, which had docked in Rangoon in September. As a result of the incident, Burma severed diplomatic relations with North Korea. North Korea has always denied that it was involved in the incident.

NOTE

1. This account is based on Sein Win, "Witnesses Tell of Bloody Capture of North Korean Commando," Associated Press, November 30, 1983; and Associated Press, "Burma Says Agents of North Korea Set Blast that Killed 21," *New York Times*, November 5, 1983, p. A1.

---

systems, and transportation networks — the destruction of which could cause havoc and economic loss far out of proportion to the initial destructive event. This possibility, which began to receive considerable official attention in the second Clinton administration,[26] is more often associated

---

26. On July 15, 1996, President Clinton established the President's Commission on Critical Infrastructure Protection to conduct a long-term comprehensive review of infrastructure protection issues and to recommend a national policy for assuring

with "info-warfare" threats, but key parts of these critical infrastructures are at least as vulnerable to physical destruction as to "cyber" attack. While nuclear weapons would be excessive for attacking most infrastructure nodes, persistent chemical agents (such as VX) and possibly even high-intensity radiological weapons could disable critical infrastructure, and ensure that it is not brought quickly back on line, by rendering specific areas unsafe for human occupation. Bringing down all of a large system, such as the national power grid, would probably require a large number of coordinated attacks. Smaller segments of such systems could be shut down more easily, however, as could all of a local subway system. Such attacks might even be carried out with few or zero casualties, simply to cause economic damage.

REVENGE

A national leader might use nuclear, biological, or chemical weapons out of a desire for revenge. Although not an altogether rational motive, a thirst for vengeance can overpower detached calculation, especially for those who feel wronged, injured, or humiliated. The United States has no shortage of enemies — Saddam Hussein and Muammar Qadhafi come to mind — who could conceivably be motivated to launch a covert nuclear, biological, or chemical attack out of a desire to avenge an American affront. Indeed, Saddam Hussein attempted to avenge his defeat in the 1990–91 Persian Gulf War by trying to assassinate former President George Bush, and it has been alleged that the bombing of the World Trade Center was also an act of Iraqi retribution.[27]

More generally, some radical Islamic movements in the Middle East hold the United States responsible for the political and economic ills that beset their people, sometimes seeing an American-Zionist conspiracy to impose U.S. cultural and political hegemony on the Muslim world. Iran is the state that comes closest to embodying this messianic anti-Americanism, which, were it to combine with the humiliation of a military defeat on some future battlefield, might produce a determination to punish the United

their continued operation. This initiative emerged out of deliberations over Presidential Decision Directive (PDD) 39, which established U.S. policy on terrorist threats to the United States. See John Schwartz, "Retired General's Mission: Making Cyberspace Secure," *Washington Post*, January 31, 1997, p. A19; and Graeme Browning, "Counting Down," *National Journal*, April 19, 1997, pp. 746–749.

27. See Laurie Mylroie, "The World Trade Center Bomb: Who is Ramzi Yousef? And Why it Matters," *The National Interest*, No. 42 (Winter 1995/96), pp. 3–15.

States at any price. Most moderate political systems inhibit national leaders from committing violent, willful, self-destructive acts, but a dictatorship or fundamentalist theocracy could face few if any significant checks on its ability to strike out against the doctrinal enemies of the state.

Motives for Covert Delivery

Once a state has decided to use NBC weapons to achieve some important national objective, it must decide which targets to attack, what weapons to use, and how to deliver them. A state can rely solely on traditional military delivery systems, such as long-range aircraft and missiles, or it can employ special operations units, paramilitary forces, or even terrorist surrogates, to deliver the weapons covertly. Which delivery technique the state chooses will depend on its objectives, capabilities, and strategic circumstances, but there is no *a priori* reason for potential NBC attackers to limit themselves to traditional military delivery systems. Sabotage and paramilitary operations have been a part of virtually all wars in history, and there are no grounds to believe that future conflicts involving weapons of mass destruction will be any different.

There are three key reasons not to assume that states that decide to use NBC weapons will always opt for traditional military means of delivery. First, the state in question may lack access to ballistic missiles, strike aircraft, or other delivery systems with sufficient range, payload, and accuracy, or it may have difficulty creating effective warheads for the systems it does have. Second, the state may wish to create doubt as to who is responsible for the attack, either to avoid retaliation or to provoke the victim to retaliate against a third party. And third, the attacker may conclude that covert means of delivery are best suited for achieving strategic or tactical surprise in war, or in a prelude to war.

LACK OF EFFECTIVE ALTERNATIVE MEANS OF DELIVERY
A state that wishes to attack U.S. territory, military forces, or allies with nuclear, biological, or chemical weapons could be driven to covert means of delivery by a lack of viable alternative options. As far as direct attacks against the American homeland are concerned, only a handful of states possess the technical capacity to deliver NBC weapons over intercontinental ranges with ballistic missiles, bombers, or cruise missiles. All plausibly hostile powers that might attack the United States directly — including Iran, Iraq, Libya, and North Korea — presently have only covert means of

intercontinental delivery at their disposal. This fact is unlikely to change in the near future.

Most potential regional opponents of the United States are likely to have a greater range of tactical delivery systems at their disposal. These may include short-range ballistic missiles (including the ubiquitous Scud), fighter-bombers, attack helicopters, and basic cruise missiles. With a modest technological investment, any of these delivery systems can be adapted to deliver weapons of mass destruction, although this could be difficult with heavy, first-generation nuclear weapons.[28] Moreover, if the NBC threat emerges out of a regional crisis (rather than as a "bolt-from-the-blue" attack), then U.S. armed forces should be able to bring a formidable array of defensive systems to bear. Revolutionary technological advances have given the U.S. armed forces an unprecedented "situational awareness," dramatically improving their ability to identify and destroy specific targets at long range, especially if the target is airborne and hence distinct from the background clutter of the earth's surface.[29] No regional power is likely to pose a significant challenge to U.S. air superiority for at least another decade, a fact that severely limits the utility of fixed-wing and rotary aircraft as NBC delivery systems.[30] Missiles present a more serious

---

28. A simple gun-type weapon, similar to one of the first nuclear weapons developed by the United States, would weigh about 4,000 kg. Most ballistic missiles possessed by potential proliferators have a maximum payload between 1,000 and 1,500 kg. See Li Bin, "Nuclear Missile Delivery Capabilities in Emerging Nuclear States," *Science and Global Security*, Vol. 6, No. 3 (1997), pp. 311–331.

29. See William J. Perry, "Desert Storm and Deterrence," *Foreign Affairs*, Vol. 70, No. 4 (Fall 1991), pp. 66–82; Joseph S. Nye, Jr., and William A. Owens, "America's Information Edge," *Foreign Affairs*, Vol. 75, No. 2 (March/April 1996), pp. 20–36; and Eliot A. Cohen, "A Revolution in Warfare," *Foreign Affairs*, Vol. 75, No. 2 (March/April 1996), pp. 37–54. For an interesting debate on the interaction between technology and technique in warfare, calling into question elements of the case for the revolution, see Stephen Biddle, "Victory Misunderstood: What the Gulf War Tells Us about the Future of Conflict," *International Security*, Vol. 12, No. 2 (Fall 1996), pp. 139–179; the three critiques it provoked in the same journal a year later, *International Security*, Vol. 13, No. 2 (Fall 1997), pp. 137–162; and Biddle's response, ibid., pp. 163–174.

30. For a detailed examination of American air superiority in the Gulf War, including discussion of the technological factors that contributed to it, see Eliot A. Cohen and Thomas A. Keaney, *Gulf War Air Power Survey: Summary Report* (Washington D.C.: U.S. Government Printing Office [U.S. GPO], 1993), pp. 223–251.

defensive problem, but the U.S. armed forces are making major strides in their ability to identify, track, and shoot down incoming ballistic and cruise missiles. It is entirely possible that a regional adversary will judge its own military means of NBC delivery to be ineffective against U.S. defenses, and will opt instead for covert means of delivery. Of course, as noted in Chapter 2, the covert delivery of nuclear, biological, or chemical weapons against an area that is at a heightened state of readiness and internal security — as it likely would be in the prelude to, or during, a military confrontation — is no simple matter, and success is far from guaranteed. But the prospects for success with traditional military means of delivery may be even worse.

AMBIGUOUS ATTRIBUTION

Anonymity can be a significant advantage of covert means of delivery. Covert delivery holds the possibility that the attacking state can avoid being identified as the perpetrator of the attack; traditional means do not. If successful, a covert NBC attack should leave only minimal forensic evidence behind, forcing the target state to conduct a lengthy and possibly fruitless investigation into who was responsible. Since an act of nuclear, biological, or chemical aggression carries enormous risks of retaliation, the responsible party stands to benefit from any delay or ambiguity in the attribution of the attack.

There are, however, significant limitations on the extent to which a state can be sure of remaining anonymous after committing a covert NBC attack. The attack plan may be penetrated, detected, and defeated by the law enforcement or national security agencies of the intended victim, or post-attack investigation may quickly uncover incriminating evidence. Even more important, the more closely connected the attack is to some clear conflict, the less likely it is that the victim will be uncertain who is responsible. There would be little doubt about responsibility for a covert NBC attack designed to achieve military advantage in a regional war. Likewise, determining who is responsible for NBC use that is intended to deter the United States from getting involved in a regional conflict, or to disrupt a U.S.-led coalition by threatening geographically essential regional allies, should be a fairly simple matter, since the adversarial powers in the conflict will be known. In all cases of NBC attack by states, the range of candidates could be narrowed down to a handful of states currently experiencing troubled relations with the victim state, although it might be impossible to exclude the uncomfortable possibility that a completely independent non-state actor, or a third state hostile to both parties, was responsible for the act. The states most likely to be drawn to covert means of delivery by the possibilities of ambiguous attribution are likely to be the ones motivated primarily by a wish to decapitate a national leadership, destabilize the society or economy of an adversary, or take revenge for some past wrong, since these motives can be more readily divorced from known political conflicts than can the motives of deterrence and warfighting.

SURPRISE

Finally, covert means of NBC delivery are ideally suited to achieving surprise. This can be useful for delivering a devastating blow before the opponent has the opportunity to put up its guard, and can be important for the physical or psychological effectiveness of certain kinds of attacks. Surprise is particularly important if the objective of the attack is to destroy a high-value target that is small or mobile, or that can be defended effectively in situations of heightened readiness.[31] All traditional military means of NBC delivery can be detected at long range by warning systems, reducing their ability to destroy these high-value targets unless the weapons are fired in a massive salvo, or can evade defenses. Thus, if the objective of the NBC attack is to wipe out a nation's leadership or to destroy a key logistical node or mobile command post, covert means of delivery are likely to be preferred to traditional military means because of the higher likelihood of taking the target by surprise.[32]

Surprise is especially important for attacks involving biological weapons. The reason for this is that it is possible to limit the lethality of most biological attacks through appropriate prophylaxis or medical treatment if it is known that the attack is coming or has recently occurred.[33]

---

31. If the intended victim has received prior warning of the attack, the target's higher state of readiness is likely to complicate most forms of covert and overt NBC delivery that during peacetime pose only minimal operational and technical challenges.

32. Indeed, in its discussions of the "paramilitary/covert and terrorist WMD threat," the principal threat scenarios envisaged by the U.S. Department of Defense appeared to be attacks against "military and civilian personnel, facilities, and logistical/mobilization nodes." Counterproliferation Policy Review Committee, *Report on Nonproliferation and Counterproliferation Activities and Programs* (Washington, D.C.: Department of Defense, May 1995), p. 5.

33. Timely warning would make it possible for a prepared population to avoid biological casualties almost entirely. One study indicates that a mask similar to a simple surgical mask with a cost under $5 could reduce the effectiveness of BW agents by a factor of 10,000. See Karl Lowe, Graham Pearson, and Victor Utgoff,

The arrival of an overt means of delivery, such as a ballistic missile or cruise missile that releases an aerosol instead of exploding, is likely to arouse the suspicion of the victims, possibly providing time for a damage-limiting response. This consideration, combined with the difficulty of delivering biological warfare agents in a military environment, suggests that there are particularly strong reasons why biological weapons, if they are ever used effectively, are likely to be used in a covert mode.[34]

Covert Delivery: At Least as Likely as Ballistic Missile Attack

Ballistic missiles are widely regarded as the delivery vehicle of choice for nuclear, biological, and chemical weapons.[35] Indeed, the U.S. Department of Defense even defines ballistic missiles themselves as "weapons of mass destruction," regardless of the warheads they carry. During the Cold War, the Soviet Union's Strategic Rocket Forces were regarded as one of the central threats to U.S. national security, prompting hundreds of billions of dollars of defense investment over a period of decades.[36] In the post–Cold War period, the ballistic missile threat remains a powerful focus of attention in U.S. national security planning, although emphasis has shifted from the ballistic missile threat against the United States itself to the theater ballistic missile threat.[37] Accordingly, in the mid-1990s, U.S. spending on a variety of different ballistic missile defense (BMD) systems totaled approximately

---

Potential Values of a Simple BW Protective Mask, Institute for Defense Analyses Paper No. P-3077 (Alexandria, Va.: Institute for Defense Analyses, September 1995), prepared for the Office of the Undersecretary of Defense for Policy.

34. For a concise discussion of the difficulty of delivering biological weapons by ballistic missile, see U.S. Congress, Office of Technology Assessment (OTA), *Technologies Underlying Weapons of Mass Destruction* (Washington, D.C.: U.S. GPO, December 1993), pp. 98–99.

35. "The majority of NBC proliferators appear to view missiles, and specifically ballistic missiles, as the delivery system of choice." Joseph and Reichart, "Deterrence and Defense," p. 7.

36. One study estimates that the United States has spent approximately $4 trillion on nuclear weapons and related infrastructure. See Stephen I. Schwartz, ed., *Atomic Audit: The Costs and Consequences of U.S. Nuclear Weapons Since 1940* (Washington, D.C.: Brookings, 1998).

37. See Richard A. Falkenrath, "Theatre Missile Defence and the Anti–Ballistic Missile Treaty," *Survival*, Vol. 36, No. 4 (Winter 1994–95), pp. 140–160.

$3–4 billion per year — an amount that is at least an order of magnitude greater than U.S. spending designed specifically to reduce U.S. vulnerability to covert NBC threats.[38]

We argue in this section that the differences between the ballistic missile threat and the covert NBC threat are not sufficient to merit an order of magnitude difference in resource allocation. Just as there are no known post–World War II cases in which a state has conducted a nuclear, biological, or chemical attack by covert means, there is no history of NBC-armed ballistic missiles being fired in anger. One must therefore look at factors other than the historical record to assess and compare the ballistic missile and covert NBC threats to U.S. territory, military forces, and allies.

To make this argument, we compare ballistic missiles and covert means of NBC weapons delivery across seven parameters: (1) number of potential attackers; (2) ease of attacker identification and likelihood of deterrence; (3) tactical offensive utility; (4) likelihood of achieving surprise; (5) defenses, including the U.S. ability to locate and preempt; (6) financial cost and technical difficulty; and (7) warhead effects and shock value. This analysis considers threats to American cities as well as regional threats to U.S. military forces and allies. However, we believe that the highest interest threatened should be the primary point of reference in a comparative threat assessment: the security of American cities must be regarded as a higher U.S. national security interest than the security of foreign cities.

Based on this detailed comparison, we conclude that the covert NBC threat is at least equal to the ballistic missile threat, and that national efforts and expenditures to reduce the covert NBC threat should reflect this equivalence. There are many relevant differences between the ballistic missile threat and the covert NBC threat, but there is no sound basis on which to judge the ballistic missile threat more serious than the covert NBC threat. Whether this conclusion implies that the emphasis on the ballistic

---

38. For an overview of the U.S. ballistic missile defense program, see William J. Perry, *Annual Report to the President and the Congress* (Washington, D.C.: U.S. Department of Defense, March 1996), pp. 219–224; Prepared Statement of Paul G. Kaminski, Undersecretary of Defense for Acquisition and Technology, to the Senate Armed Services Committee, March 6, 1997, available as "DoD's Ballistic Missile Defense Strategy," *Defense Issues*, Vol. 11, No. 25 (no date given), at <www.defenselink.mil:80/pubs/di_1996.html>; and Prepared Statement of Paul G. Kaminski to the Military Research and Development Subcommittee, House National Security Committee, March 6, 1997, available as "DoD's Ballistic Missile Defense Programs," *Defense Issues*, Vol. 12, No. 14 (no date), at <www.defenselink. mil:80/pubs/di_index.html>.

missile threat should be reduced, or that the priority afforded to the covert NBC threat should be increased, hinges on judgments about the appropriate level of security and the marginal contributions of alternative security-related expenditures.[39]

NUMBER OF POTENTIAL ATTACKERS

In 1998, four states possess unambiguously the technical capacity to strike U.S. territory by ballistic missile: Great Britain, France, China, and Russia. How fast this number will grow is a subject of great controversy: a November 1995 National Intelligence Estimate (NIE) concluded that "no country, other than the major declared nuclear powers, will develop or otherwise acquire a ballistic missile in the next 15 years that could threaten the contiguous 48 states or Canada."[40] This conclusion was hotly contested by national missile defense proponents, who foresee a larger threat emerging sooner. Even without resolving the argument over the number of potential ballistic missile attackers, however, it is clear that the number of potential covert NBC attackers is very much larger. Indeed, the former is a subset of the latter and always will be, due to the high cost and technical sophistication of long-range ballistic missiles. The technical potential to deliver a limited number of weapons covertly against the United States is nearly omnipresent in the international system. All states that might be regarded as hostile to the United States have the potential capacity to attack U.S. cities by covert means, should they choose to do so. Likewise, as argued in Chapter 3, countless non-state actors possess the minimal organizational capacity needed to carry out covert attacks, and some of these are capable of building improvised NBC weapons.

ATTRIBUTABILITY AND THE LIKELIHOOD OF DETERRENCE

Ballistic missile attacks are as easy to deter as almost any other conceivable warlike act, since tracing them to their source makes the attacker simple to identify. When ballistic missiles are fired, their boosters burn large amounts of rocket fuel in a very short period of time, which releases heat. The infrared signature of a missile plume can be detected by U.S. early warning

---

39. This larger set of issues is discussed further in Chapters 5 and 6.

40. A leaked copy of the "President's Summary" of the NIE was reprinted in "Do We Need a Missile Defense System?" *Washington Times*, May 14, 1996, p. 15.

satellites, pinpointing the launch site.[41] In addition, after the boost phase, ballistic missiles follow free-fall flight paths to their targets, and radar data can be used to trace the missiles' paths back to their launch points. Thus, even if the United States has no way to defend against incoming ballistic missiles, it will still know with complete certainty from whose territory they were fired, and thus precisely whom to retaliate against.[42] An attacker will be aware of this fact, and this awareness, coupled with the expectation of retaliation, forms the essence of deterrence. There can be little doubt that American retaliatory capabilities — both nuclear and conventional — would exercise a strong cautionary effect on any state that contemplated firing a ballistic missile at the United States.

The covert NBC threat is dramatically different. In a successful covert NBC attack against the United States, the U.S. government might remain completely ignorant of the identity of the attacker. Neither the weapon used nor the delivery means would necessarily identify the attacker, and the lower cost and lesser technical difficulty of smuggled NBC weapons make the pool of possible attackers much larger. Thus, even if the attack were foiled and the perpetrators apprehended, the United States might still not know who was behind the attack, whether it was a state, a non-state group acting independently, or a state-sponsored or state-directed group. If a biological weapon were used, the government might not even know that the attack had taken place until several days afterward. An investigation would have to be undertaken to determine whom to blame, possibly in the midst of unprecedented human casualties, panic, environmental contamination, and consequence management activities. If the attack occurred during a military crisis with a hostile state, that state might well become the primary suspect, but translating suspicion into proof might be difficult. The investigation could drag on for weeks or months, and even then might reach conclusions too tentative to support the decision to retaliate against a suspected attacker.

---

41. See "Report to the American Physical Society of the Study Group on Science and Technology of Directed Energy Weapons," *Reviews of Modern Physics*, Vol. 59, No. 3, Part 2 (July 1987), pp. S146–S147.

42. Deterrence, of course, would not be relevant in an instance of accidental or unauthorized launch. Although an accidental or unauthorized missile launch from China or Russia is highly unlikely, the consequences would be grave, and this concern is sometimes cited as a justification for U.S. post–Cold War expenditures on national missile defense. See William Safire, "Defenseless America," *New York Times*, May 9, 1997, p. 27.

Ambiguity in attribution poses a serious problem for deterrence. If the attacker believes that it can escape retaliation altogether by escaping blame, then deterrence fails. Of course, no potential attacker in a covert NBC scenario is likely to be completely confident of avoiding detection or identification: some risk is inevitable, and the United States has a strong record of identifying and tracking down the perpetrators of major terrorist attacks. Nonetheless, deterrence of covert NBC attacks must be regarded as significantly less reliable than deterrence of ballistic missile attacks.[43]

TACTICAL MILITARY UTILITY

Tactical military utility — a function of promptness, accuracy, repeatability, survivability, controllability, and payload — differs starkly for ballistic missiles and covert means of NBC delivery. Ballistic missiles have a clear advantage in being extremely prompt, flying hundreds of miles in only a matter of minutes; covert attack plans, in contrast, are likely to require long preparation, and may take days or weeks to carry out. Ballistic missiles can be fired in salvos, whereas only a few covert attack operations can be sustained simultaneously. A covert attack can probably be more accurate than a primitive ballistic missile like the Scud, but the total payload that can be delivered in a covert operation is probably lower than can be delivered in a ballistic missile salvo.[44] Ballistic missile strikes can be repeated until the launchers are destroyed or the missile inventory exhausted; covert attack plans would probably be difficult to repeat because of the victim's countermeasures. Covert delivery is likely to be less controllable and possibly less reliable than a ballistic missile strike, because it will involve either a covert operation or the unattended shipment of weapons by mail, freight, or other means.

Thus, except in certain special military situations, such as attacks on headquarters, warning systems, or logistical nodes, covert means of delivering NBC weapons will generally have a lower tactical military utility

---

43. Another interesting possibility is that a covert attacker might be able to create the impression that a third party had carried out the attack, provoking U.S. retaliation against that state.

44. This is more of a limitation on chemical attacks than on nuclear or biological attacks. A chemical attack designed to kill tens of thousands of people would require many tons of agent and many separate dissemination points, and a correspondingly large operation to carry it out. Sophisticated biological weapons or reasonably compact nuclear weapons could kill large numbers of people in a single attack, making the delivery operation less detectable.

than NBC-armed ballistic missiles.[45] If military commanders have alternative means of delivery at their disposal, they will have relatively little use for covert NBC delivery plans. To the extent that these commanders influence the national security strategies of their countries, covert NBC delivery is not likely to figure prominently, and priority is likely to be given to the acquisition of effective conventional means of NBC delivery. Yet it is important to remember that not all militaries have conventional means of NBC delivery at their disposal; that military commanders may play only a small role in setting their state's national security strategy; and that the attractiveness of covert NBC attacks is best measured primarily in strategic and political, not tactical, terms.

LIKELIHOOD OF ACHIEVING SURPRISE

Both ballistic missiles and covert means of delivery offer reasonably good chances of surprising the victims, catching them unaware and unprepared, and hence most vulnerable to the effects of the warhead. The degree to which surprise is important depends strongly on whether the victim has any defenses against the attack, and on the extent to which the efficacy of these defenses depends on warning; these issues are discussed under warhead effects, below.

Ballistic missile launches can be detected by U.S. early warning satellites virtually everywhere in the world, but because the missiles travel at such high speeds — up to 7 kilometers per second (Mach 18) for an ICBM — surprise, in the sense of catching people at the target site unprepared, is still possible. Whether satellite-warning information is relayed to the individuals in the target zone in time for them to take defensive precautions depends on many factors, including the speed and efficiency of the U.S. communications system, the flight time of the missile, and the readiness of the people in the target zone. That even personnel at a high state of readiness can be caught unaware by ballistic missiles was demonstrated on February 15, 1991 — nearly six weeks after the initiation of hostilities —

---

45. Another interesting question in this regard, however, is how the tactical military utility of ballistic missiles in regional wars compares to that of other overt means of delivery, such as strike aircraft, cruise missiles, and artillery. See John R. Harvey, "Regional Ballistic Missiles and Advanced Strike Aircraft: Comparing Military Effectiveness," *International Security*, Vol. 17, No. 2 (Fall 1992), pp. 41–83; and Steve Fetter, "Ballistic Missiles and Weapons of Mass Destruction: What is the Threat and What Should be Done?" *International Security*, Vol. 16, No. 1 (Summer 1991), pp. 5–42.

when an Iraqi Scud missile destroyed a U.S. barracks in Dhahran, Saudi Arabia, killing 28 and wounding more than 100. Missiles fired over longer ranges offer greater warning time and, consequently, a reduced probability of surprising the victim. An intercontinental ballistic missile fired at the continental United States from Eurasia would have a flight time of approximately 30 minutes,[46] giving the U.S. government the option of alerting people in the target area.[47] Such tactical warning would usually make it possible to protect key political leaders from a single nuclear weapon, or from a larger chemical or biological strike, either by removing them from the area or by sheltering them. It would, however, have limited impact on civilian casualties from nuclear and chemical attacks on unprepared urban areas. In the absence of an effective civil defense program, it actually might increase casualties by causing panic. Tactical warning of a biological aerosol attack would not help an unprepared population avoid exposure, but would allow medical treatment to commence early, saving many lives.

Covert delivery, by its very nature, depends on surprise. A successful covert NBC attack is likely to achieve total surprise. Subsequent attacks would face diminishing probabilities of achieving surprise (as is also the case for ballistic missiles), but the chance of surprise will remain greater than zero until the defender acquires some way to detect specific attacks before they are carried out. Covert delivery is thus likely to be the preferred method for attacking targets that can be defended effectively on the basis of tactical warning.

DEFENSES

Defenses against ballistic missiles and covert means of delivery are highly dissimilar. Shooting down a ballistic missile in flight is physically possible but extremely demanding due to the missile's small size and high velocity, as well as to the fact that ballistic missiles spend part of their trajectory outside the atmosphere. To be effective, a ballistic missile defense (BMD) system must seamlessly coordinate an array of highly sophisticated sensors, interceptors, and fire control software. The difficulty of successfully defending against ballistic missiles grows roughly in proportion to the size

---

46. An ICBM such as the U.S. MX missile with a range of 11,000 kilometers has a flight time of about 30 minutes. See Harvey, "Regional Ballistic Missiles and Advanced Strike Aircraft," p. 44, Table 1.

47. A missile fired at a range of six hundred kilometers would have a flight time of about 7 minutes. Ibid., p. 44, Table 1, and p. 64.

of the area being defended and the range of the missile being defended against. Moreover, ballistic missiles can be fitted with inexpensive but highly effective countermeasures, or "penetration aids," designed to confuse and defeat a defensive system. In general, the offense has the advantage in an encounter between a ballistic missile defense system and a ballistic missile, and this advantage is likely to be decisive and ultimately insurmountable if the adversary is adaptive and intelligent. The defender will only be able to sustain a lead if the adversary is constrained by very limited technical capacity and funding, and even then the cost to the defender would be considerable.

The United States is the world's leader in ballistic missile defense technology — and in the political emphasis placed on developing it — but despite decades of effort and tens of billions of dollars of expenditure, the deployment of an effective ballistic missile defense system has so far proved elusive. At the national level, the United States currently has no defense against ballistic missile attacks: in a missile attack against the United States, the incoming missiles would be detected by U.S. satellites and early warning radars but could not be intercepted before they struck their targets. This clear vulnerability has provided much of the political impetus behind the movement to develop and deploy a national missile defense (NMD) system beyond that permitted by the 1972 Anti–Ballistic Missile (ABM) Treaty. Yet it is not at all clear that an effective NMD system lies within the technological reach of the United States, much less that it would come at an acceptable cost.

Greater progress has been made with tactical and theater ballistic missile defense (TMD) systems, of which the United States has deployed several and is developing more.[48] The technical challenges of missile defense operations are more tractable when the goal is to defend smaller areas (such as military bases, ports, or cities) against the slower, shorter-range missiles generally used by the likely regional adversaries of the United States (such as the Scud missile, with a range of 300–800 kilometers).[49] Even so, the flawed performance of the Patriot missile-defense

---

48. See the chapter entitled "Department of Defense Response," in Department of Defense, *Proliferation: Threat and Response 1997* (Washington, D.C.: U.S. Department of Defense, 1997), available at <www.defenselink.mil/pubs/prolif97/secii.html>.

49. The Scud missile and its derivatives have ranges between 300 and 800 kilometers. See Lora Lumpe, Lisbeth Gronlund, and David C. Wright, "Third World Missiles Fall Short," *Bulletin of the Atomic Scientists*, Vol. 48, No. 2 (March 1992), pp. 30–37.

system against Iraqi Scuds in the 1990–91 Gulf War revealed just how challenging even tactical missile defense can be.[50] The next generation of U.S. tactical and theater missile defenses will significantly improve on the Patriot's effectiveness, but the advantage will still lie with the offense in a ballistic missile engagement, and the protection offered by whatever TMD systems the United States ultimately deploys is certain to remain imperfect.

If they are detected in advance, covert attacks are relatively easy to defend against: a ship with a nuclear weapon in the hold can be boarded, turned around, or sunk; a civilian aircraft with nuclear, biological, or chemical weapons on board can be shot down; a van with a biological aerosol sprayer in the back can be stopped, disarmed, and quarantined; a nerve gas canister in an building's air duct can be isolated and contained, and the building evacuated; a terrorist with an improvised nerve gas dispenser in his backpack can be apprehended or shot. The problem, of course, is that there is no guarantee that the United States will be able to acquire the sort of detailed intelligence and specific warning needed to carry out these defensive measures in advance of a covert NBC attack. Even so, however, ballistic missiles are significantly harder to defend against than covert means of delivery.

Preemption can be a form of defense against an imminent attack. If a state believes that a nuclear, biological, or chemical attack is about to be launched against it, it will have a powerful motive to strike first against the attacking force as part of a damage-limiting strategy. Much Cold War anxiety resulted from the possibility that a thermonuclear war could arise out of the superpowers' mutual incentives to preempt each other's strategic nuclear forces in a crisis. Similar incentives will also exist in any future WMD crisis. Successful preemption depends on two variables: first, an ability to locate and identify the delivery system; and second, a capacity to destroy or disrupt it. Covert means of attack are relatively easy to destroy or disrupt if they can be detected and identified in advance, but because of their very nature, detection and identification are highly uncertain propositions. On the other hand, ballistic missiles can often be detected in advance and can almost always be identified, but — at least if they are mobile — can be destroyed only with considerable difficulty and risk. During the Gulf War, the coalition's air forces had great difficulty destroying Iraq's Scud missile launchers, which reinforced the lesson that

---

50. For a critique of the Patriot's performance, see Theodore A. Postol, "Lessons of the Gulf War Experience with Patriot," *International Security*, Vol. 16, No. 3 (Winter 1991/92), pp. 119–171.

conventional preemption of mobile ballistic missiles is a significant military challenge.[51] However, the success rate would be considerably higher if the targeted ballistic missiles were stationary (as they are more likely to be if they have intercontinental range); or if the United States were willing to use nuclear weapons in its preemptive strikes, as it might if it believed that the consequence of not doing so would be a nuclear detonation in an American city.

FINANCIAL COST AND TECHNICAL DIFFICULTY

The financial costs and technical difficulty of delivering NBC weapons over intercontinental ranges by ballistic missile are vastly higher than for covert means of delivery. So far, only the five declared nuclear powers have developed any sort of intercontinental ballistic missile capability (including submarine-launched ballistic missiles, SLBMs), and doing so required extensive research and development programs, as well as great expense — probably no less than $100 million per ICBM or SLBM when all development and infrastructure costs are taken into account.[52] Short and intermediate-range ballistic missiles can sometimes be purchased on the international arms market, so the technical difficulty of acquisition may not be an issue, but even primitive ballistic missiles are expensive: one 1988 report estimated the price of a Scud missile at $1 million per unit, with

---

51. See *Gulf War Air Power Survey*, Vol. II: *Operations and Effects and Effectiveness* (Washington D.C.: U.S. GPO, 1993), Part II, pp. 265–266, 330–340.

52. The experiences of Great Britain, France, and China demonstrate the cost, difficulty, and time involved in acquiring indigenous ICBM and SLBM capability. Britain, frustrated by its attempts to keep up with rapid developments in missile technology, ended up purchasing SLBMs from the United States and building four submarines to carry them, at a total cost of approximately £345 million at 1964 prices (equivalent to something like $4 billion in 1997 prices). This figure is considerably lower than the cost of indigenous development. Although France had some American assistance and had tested nuclear weapons as early as 1960, it did not deploy intermediate range ballistic missiles (IRBMs) until 1971, nor SLBMs until 1972. China, which tested a nuclear weapon in 1964, did not deploy a true ICBM until 1981. See Robert S. Norris, Andrew S. Burrows, and Richard W. Fieldhouse, *Nuclear Weapons Databook*, Vol. 5: *British, French and Chinese Nuclear Weapons* (Boulder, Colo.: Westview, 1994), pp. 100, 194–196, 363.

longer-range missiles approaching $20 million each.[53] In addition to acquisition costs, maintaining a viable ballistic missile capability also requires steady expenditures on training, operations, launchers, infrastructure, targeting data, and maintenance — all on top of whatever costs are associated with developing, testing, and deploying usable nuclear, biological, or chemical warheads. While these costs and difficulties can be surmounted by a determined, wealthy, industrialized state, they are substantial enough to force any government to pause before embarking on a ballistic missile program intended to threaten targets on the other side of the planet.

It is hard to imagine a covert NBC delivery means that could approach the cost and technical difficulty of an intercontinental ballistic missile. At the low end, clandestine delivery could be very cheap and almost trivially simple. Once a nuclear weapon is on hand, how much does it cost and how hard is it to put it into a cargo container and onto a ship bound for New York? More imaginative and complex covert delivery systems, such as a GPS-guided civilian aircraft (a "poor man's cruise missile"), a hidden biological aerosol sprayer on a van, or improvised nerve gas dispensers, are much cheaper and easier to make than ballistic missiles, especially intercontinental ones. The contrast with short-range ballistic missiles is somewhat less stark, but short- and even intermediate-range missiles cannot threaten the United States itself, making them less important to U.S. threat assessments. In sum, as between ballistic missiles and covert means of delivery, there can be no doubt that covert means are far cheaper and easier.

WARHEAD EFFECTS AND SHOCK VALUE

Under most circumstances, the effect of the means of delivery on the damage and shock value of a nuclear weapon attack is likely to be minor, holding accuracy and other factors constant. A limited number of nuclear detonations in a U.S. city would have comparable effects regardless of whether the weapons were delivered by ballistic missile or covert means. In a larger attack, however, ballistic missiles would have an advantage in that they could be fired in a barrage, compounding the damage caused by individual warheads. The number of NBC weapons that can be simulta-

---

53. Steven Zaloga, "Ballistic Missiles in the Third World," *International Defense Review*, Vol. 11 (1998), p. 1425, cited in Harvey, "Regional Ballistic Missiles and Advanced Strike Aircraft," p. 65, n. 35.

neously delivered by covert means is limited, which makes covert delivery unsuitable for large preemptive strikes.

Covert means of delivery may, however, be preferable to ballistic missiles for limited chemical and biological attacks. This is largely because surprise matters more for biological and chemical attacks than it does for nuclear attacks; short-notice preparations can reduce the casualties caused by a biological or chemical attack to a much greater extent than they can the casualties caused by a nuclear attack. In a nuclear attack, individuals near ground zero can do very little to avoid being killed by blast, heat, radiation, and secondary fires. People further away may benefit from taking shelter (particularly in a specially designed bomb shelter) or from staying indoors to avoid radioactive fallout, but only strategic warning, allowing evacuation, can prevent significant numbers of people from dying.

In the case of chemical attacks, however, civilian casualties can be significantly reduced if the target population dons gas masks and retreats into well-sealed shelters.[54] Taking full advantage of this possibility requires both strategic warning, to allow gas masks to be distributed and defensive preparations to be made, and tactical warning, to allow time to take shelter. Ballistic missile attacks would provide the latter, but not the former. Since covert chemical weapons attacks would cause maximum casualties if used against crowded, enclosed targets, strategic warning on its own makes it possible to reduce the danger by closing or increasing security at the most vulnerable potential targets, such as subways and sports arenas.

Surprise is most important to the effects of biological attacks. With both strategic and tactical warning, the lethality of most biological weapons can be reduced more than a thousandfold if the members of the target population simply put on $5 respiratory masks for the duration of the attack.[55] This fact alone suggests that ballistic missiles are not the best delivery vehicles for repeated attacks with biological weapons, since after a few attacks the target population will begin to carry filter masks as a matter of course. While tactical warning of attack with a biological weapon would not enable an unprepared population to avoid exposure, it would

---

54. However, even simple civil defense measures can backfire when implemented by an inadequately prepared population. During the Gulf War, the Israeli government distributed gas masks and nerve agent antidotes to the general population. During Iraqi Scud missile attacks, several Israelis suffocated in their gas masks. Others became extremely ill by injecting themselves with atropine in response to what they wrongly thought was a chemical attack in progress.

55. See Lowe, Pearson, and Utgoff, *Potential Values of a Simple BW Protective Mask.*

give the target state an opportunity to save many of the victims by initiating medical treatment immediately, a crucial factor in determining the course of some biological warfare illnesses. Thus, ballistic missiles carrying biological weapons, by announcing their arrival, would enable states with strong medical infrastructures to greatly reduce the consequences of the attack. As a result, covert means have significant advantages over ballistic missiles for biological weapons delivery.

Whether the target state is surprised or not, the number of people killed in an NBC attack will depend in part on its level of preparedness and the effectiveness of its response efforts. The United States is presently only minimally prepared, and there are significant opportunities for low-cost measures to reduce U.S. vulnerability, particularly to biological weapons. Our recommendations in this area are discussed in Chapter 5.

Independent of the effects of surprise, biological weapons are hard to deliver effectively via ballistic missile. It is difficult to achieve efficient, wide area dissemination from a hypersonic projectile with a steep reentry angle. Furthermore, because ballistic missiles generate intense heat when they reenter the atmosphere, biological weapons being delivered by ballistic missile must be carefully insulated and protected — not an impossible task, but one that increases the level of sophistication necessary to carry out the attack and further increases the attractiveness of covert means of delivery relative to ballistic missiles.

The "shock value" of a nuclear, biological, or chemical weapon attack is likely to be similar whether missiles or covert means of delivery are used. Populations are likely to be no less terrorized by attacks from within their midst than by attacks from the sky. If anything, the shock and terror of a covert NBC attack could be worse, since uncertainty as to the identity and whereabouts of the attacker would leave open the possibility that the attacks might continue, and that retaliation and damage-limiting counter-strikes might be impossible to carry out.

Conclusion

The risk that an international adversary of the United States will carry out covert NBC attacks against U.S. territory, military forces, or allies cannot be discounted. Historical infrequency aside, there are reasons why a state might use nuclear, biological, or chemical weapons against U.S. interests. Many of these reasons have to do with the asymmetrical power relations that presently exist between the United States and all its potential opponents. Moreover, once an adversary decides to employ weapons of mass destruction, it is entirely possible that it will also decide to deliver the weapon by covert means, emulating the techniques of a terrorist organization. This threat is at least as serious as the threat of attack with NBC-armed ballistic missiles. But unlike ballistic missile defense, which holds a privileged position in U.S. defense planning (and spending), countering the covert NBC threat has fallen through the cracks of American national security strategy. The remaining chapters of this book describe how the U.S. response to the covert NBC threat can be strengthened to match the U.S. national interests at stake.

Box 10
Iraqi NBC Programs

Since the mid-1970s, Iraq has pursued a variety of programs aimed at developing chemical, biological, and nuclear weapons and the delivery systems needed to make them militarily useful. Its chemical weapons program contributed heavily to its war against Iran during the 1980s, and constituted a serious and well-recognized threat to coalition forces in the 1990–91 Persian Gulf War. Iraq had also initiated an extensive biological weapons program in 1974, which had produced usable biological weapons before the Gulf War. The quality of these weapons was unknown, but they were considered a serious threat to coalition forces, enough to prompt the United States to make explicit threats to deter their use by Iraq.[1] The nuclear program had not produced a weapon by the time of the war, and probably would not have succeeded in doing so for at least another three years. Nevertheless, Iraq had a surprising range of undetected nuclear facilities, and had made more progress in its nuclear efforts than other states realized before the war.[2]

Some of Iraq's nuclear, biological, and chemical weapons infrastructure was destroyed during the Gulf War. However, significant parts of the nuclear and biological infrastructure, unknown to the intelligence agencies of Iraq's opponents, survived. Large questions remained about the extent of the programs, and about the survival of weapons and facilities not destroyed in the war that might allow Iraq to maintain or reconstitute the capability to use weapons of mass destruction. As a condition to its cease-fire with coalition forces in 1991, Iraq was ordered by the United Nations Security Council (UNSC) to cease its chemical, biological, nuclear, and ballistic missile weapons programs. UNSC Resolution 687 authorized the creation of the United Nations Special Commission (UNSCOM) to oversee the destruction of all prohibited materials and weapons in Iraq. After initial Iraqi non-cooperation with UNSCOM, the Security Council adopted Resolution 707 which demanded that Iraq "provide full, final and complete disclosure ... of all aspects of its programmes to develop weapons of mass destruction ... and all holdings of such weapons."[3] Next, in anticipation of the possible cessation of full-scale UNSCOM inspections, the UN Security Council adopted Resolution 715, which provides for ongoing monitoring in Iraq, and of Iraqi imports, to ensure that the country does not re-establish covert weapons programs.[4]

Postwar inspections conducted by UNSCOM, and by the International Atomic Energy Agency (IAEA) for nuclear matters, have revealed a huge amount of information about Iraq's weapons programs, and have overseen the destruction of much of Iraq's infrastructure for producing nuclear, biological, and chemical weapons and ballistic missiles.[5] These inspections

Box 10, Iraqi NBC Programs, *cont.*

have been carried out in the face of ongoing intensive efforts by Iraq to harass, intimidate, and deceive inspectors; to hide records, equipment, and supplies; and generally to preserve as much as possible of its arsenal and its options for future production of prohibited weapons.[6] There is particular concern that Iraq may retain stocks of chemical and biological weapons, a few ballistic missiles, chemical and biological warheads for missiles, and substantial chemical and biological agents. Furthermore, Iraq has attempted to import banned weapons-related equipment, including missile guidance components from Russia.[7]

The Iraqi chemical weapons program, whose existence was known from the earlier Iran-Iraq War, was a surprise to international inspectors in its magnitude and sophistication. According to one CIA analyst, Iraq had a stockpile of 150 tons of sarin and 411 tons of mustard gas, and had sufficient precursors to manufacture nearly 500 tons of VX.[8] Among the chemical agents that Iraq managed to produce and weaponize were mustard gas, VX, sarin, tabun, and quantities of equipment and materials needed to produce soman.[9] Delivery systems included bombs, artillery shells, and missile warheads. Under the supervision of UNSCOM inspectors, the Iraqis destroyed 28,000 chemical munitions, 480,000 liters of chemical agents, and approximately 1,800,000 kilograms of precursor agents.[10] Specialized production facilities and equipment were also destroyed. Iraq is suspected, however, of hiding significant equipment for production of chemical agents, possibly including for large-scale production of VX.[11] Iraq is also suspected of having hidden smaller quantities of chemical weapons or precursors that would enable it to make weapons suitable for at least limited attacks.

Although the U.S. government suspected before the 1991 war that Iraq had some sort of biological weapons program, the extent of this program was unknown to UN inspectors and the U.S. government, and indeed remains mysterious and controversial. The details of the program only began to emerge in 1995, four years into the inspections.[12] Until 1995, Iraq lied continuously about the extent of the program, claiming that it had conducted some research, but had not weaponized any agents.[13] However, following the defection of General Hussein Kamel, a top Iraqi official who had overseen the biological weapons program, the Iraqi government admitted producing almost 10,000 liters of concentrated botulinum toxin, 8,400 liters of anthrax, and 340 liters of concentrated *Clostridium perfringens,* the causative agent of gas gangrene.[14] Iraq also produced rockets, artillery shells, gravity bombs, and ballistic missile warheads to deliver these biological warfare agents, as well as an aerial spraying system capable of delivering 2,000 liters of agent over a target.[15] Iraq claims to have destroyed these weapon systems in mid-1991 (in violation of its cease-fire commitment), but has provided UNSCOM with no solid evidence to support this claim. It is

Box 10, Iraqi NBC Programs, *cont.*

believed that Iraq's wish to retain this biological weapons capability caused it to step up its campaign against the UNSCOM inspectors in 1997, and to declare a number of "presidential" and other sensitive sites off-limits to inspectors — the issue that nearly led to U.S. military strikes against Iraq in February 1998.

Iraq was also suspected of having a nuclear weapons program before the Gulf War, but the program was thought to be much smaller and less advanced than it turned out to be. The United States and other outside observers were also completely unaware that Iraq was pursuing electromagnetic separation technology for uranium enrichment.[16] Iraq may originally have intended to pursue a weapons program based on plutonium,[17] but after Israel bombed the Osiraq reactor in 1981, Iraq's clandestine nuclear weapons program focused primarily on uranium enrichment using gaseous diffusion, electromagnetic separation, and gas centrifuges.[18] After its invasion of Kuwait, Iraq sought a shortcut to building a single nuclear weapon, planning to divert the tens of kilograms of highly enriched uranium research reactor fuel in its possession to weapons use.[19]

It is widely agreed that Iraq would eventually have succeeded in building nuclear weapons, but opinions differ on when. Some estimates suggest that Iraq would have been able to deploy a single nuclear device by the end of 1991,[20] but others argue that five years is a more reasonable estimate.[21] Although Iraq's nuclear weapons complex has largely been destroyed, much of the specialized expertise needed for a nuclear weapons effort is still in place, and it is likely that Iraq would quickly seek to reconstitute its nuclear program in the absence of UN inspections.

Among the many lessons of the Iraq experience, four are particularly worth noting. First, UNSCOM's postwar experience with Iraq demonstrates the difficulty even a highly intrusive inspection regime faces when confronted with a state determined to conceal its NBC programs. Second, the ambivalence and inability of the international community to compel Saddam to live up to his disarmament commitments and allow full access for UNSCOM has seriously undermined the inspection regime, and makes it unlikely that any system of long-term monitoring will work in Iraq. That Russia, China, and to a lesser extent France are unwilling to give strong support to the uprooting of Iraq's weapons of mass destruction programs also suggests that the international community will be reluctant to enforce arms control measures in future cases, which are nearly certain to be even less clear-cut. Third, the fact that large-scale weapons facilities, including biological agent production and calutron enrichment plants, were not detected or located by intelligence in advance of the war is a disheartening reminder of the difficulty of detecting clandestine NBC programs by external means; this is especially so because small facilities appropriate for producing

Box 10, Iraqi NBC Programs, *cont.*

chemical or biological weapons for covert use, or for weaponizing black-market nuclear material, would be even harder to detect. Fourth, Iraq's impressive spending before the war, and its far more expensive intransigence in the face of the postwar inspections and sanctions, demonstrate that some states may be willing to pay extraordinarily high economic, political, and military costs in the search for weapons of mass destruction. Iraq is estimated to have spent more than $10 billion over a decade on its nuclear program before the war, and has foregone some $120 billion over the more than six years that economic sanctions have been in force — sanctions it could largely have avoided by declaring all of its nuclear, biological, and chemical activities.[22] Iraq or another similarly motivated and well-funded proliferator might reasonably decide that even at a price as high as $100 million to $1 billion, the quicker and more certain route to a small nuclear arsenal provided by the illegal purchase or theft of 100 kg of HEU would be well worth the money and risk. For a state capable of building implosion weapons, that amount of material would be enough for several warheads.

NOTES

1. See Lawrence Freedman and Efraim Karsh, *The Gulf Conflict, 1990–1991* (Princeton, N.J.: Princeton University Press, 1993), p. 257. On the biological weapons program in particular, see Jonathan B. Tucker, "Lessons of Iraq's Biological Warfare Programme," *Arms Control*, Vol. 14, No. 3 (December 1993), pp. 236–246.

2. For a published pre-war assessment of Iraq's nuclear activities, see Leonard S. Spector, *Nuclear Ambitions: The Spread of Nuclear Weapons, 1989–1990* (Boulder, Colo.: Westview, 1990), pp. 186–202. For postwar analyses of Iraq's progress, see David Albright and Robert Kelley, "Has Iraq Come Clean at Last?" *Bulletin of the Atomic Scientists*, Vol. 51, No. 6 (November/December 1995), pp. 53–64; David Albright and Mark Hibbs, "Iraq's Shop-Till-You-Drop Nuclear Program," *Bulletin of the Atomic Scientists*, Vol. 48, No. 3 (April 1992), pp. 27–37; David Albright and Mark Hibbs, "Iraq's Quest for the Nuclear Grail: What Can We Learn?" *Arms Control Today*, July–August 1992, pp. 5–8; and David Albright and Mark Hibbs, "Iraq's Bomb: Blueprints and Artifacts," *Bulletin of the Atomic Scientists*, Vol. 48, No. 1 (January/February 1992), pp. 30–40.

3. UN Security Council Resolution 707, S/RES/707 (1991), August 15, 1991, Paragraph 3, Section (i).

4. UN Security Council Resolution 715, S/RES/715 (1991), October 11, 1991.

5. Useful overviews of the UNSCOM/IAEA inspection effort can be found in the Stockholm International Peace Research Institute annual publication, *SIPRI Yearbook* (New York: Oxford University Press, various years).

Box 10, Iraqi NBC Programs, *cont.*

6. "Iraqis Still Defying Arms Ban, Departing U.N. Official Says," *New York Times,* June 25, 1997, p. 1.

7. See testimony of Ambassador Rolf Ekeus, executive chairman of UNSCOM, in U.S. Congress, *Global Proliferation of Weapons of Mass Destruction,* Part II, Hearings before the Permanent Subcommittee on Investigations of the Committee on Governmental Affairs, U.S. Senate, 104th Cong., 2nd Sess. (Washington, D.C.: U.S. Government Printing Office, March 20, 1996), pp. 90–104; and Report by the Executive Chairman of the Special Commission, U.N. Security Council Document S/1997/301, April 11, 1997, pp. 12–13.

8. See testimony by Gordon C. Oehler, Director of the Nonproliferation Center, Central Intelligence Agency, S. Hrgs. 104-422, *Global Proliferation of Weapons of Mass Destruction,* Part I, Hearing before the Permanent Subcommittee on Investigations, Committee on Governmental Affairs, U.S. Senate, 104th Cong., 1st Sess. (Washington, D.C.: U.S. GPO, November 1, 1995), pp. 211–212.

9. See David A. Kay, "Lessons from Our Iraqi Experience," briefing with slides presented on April 16, 1997; Burck and Flowerree, *International Handbook on Chemical Weapons Proliferation,* pp. 41, 47; Stockholm International Peace Research Institute, *SIPRI Yearbook 1996: Armaments, Disarmament, and International Security* (New York: Oxford University Press, 1996), p. 697; and Robert W. Chandler, *Tomorrow's War, Today's Decisions: Iraqi Weapons of Mass Destruction and the Implications of WMD-Armed Adversaries for Future U.S. Military Strategy* (McLean, Va.: American Committee on Developmental Affairs, 1996), pp. 90–99.

10. *SIPRI Yearbook 1996,* p. 697.

11. Report by the Executive Chairman of the Special Commission, UN Security Council Document S/1997/301, April 11, 1997, p. 18.

12. William J. Broad and Judith Miller, "Iraq's Deadliest Arms: Puzzles Breed Fears," *New York Times,* February 26, 1998, pp. A1, A10–A11.

13. A good account of the results of the biological warfare elements of UNSCOM's inspections up to 1993 can be found in Tucker, "Lessons of Iraq's Biological Weapons Program," pp. 229–271.

14. Oehler Senate Testimony, pp. 211–212.

15. See Kay, "Lessons from Our Iraqi Experience," p. 3.

16. Electromagnetic isotope separation uses simple mass spectrometers called calutrons. The technology was developed by the United States for the Manhattan Project, and was used to enrich uranium for the Hiroshima bomb. It was quickly abandoned by the United States due to its high power consumption and other problems, however. The method was considered so undesirable that intelligence efforts and export controls did not treat it as a possible proliferation route, one reason Iraq's effort escaped early detection. See Albright and Hibbs, "Iraq's Shop-Till-You-Drop Nuclear Program," p. 36.

Box 10, Iraqi NBC Programs, *cont.*

17. Spector, *Nuclear Ambitions*, pp. 186–187.

18. See Albright and Hibbs, "Iraq's Bomb: Blueprints and Artifacts," pp. 30–40; and David Albright and Robert Kelley, "Massive Programs, Meager Results," *Bulletin of the Atomic Scientists*, Vol. 51, No. 6 (November/December 1995), pp. 56–60.

19. "IAEA Says Iraq Planned Short Cut to Nuclear Device," Reuters, August 29, 1995; and "IAEA Says Iraq Nuclear Clampdown Successful," Reuters, September 11, 1995. Iraq's plan called for further enriching the fuel before use. See Albright and Kelley, "Has Iraq Come Clean at Last?" pp. 53–54.

20. See testimony by former IAEA inspector David A. Kay, Senior Vice President, Hicks & Associates, *Global Proliferation of Weapons of Mass Destruction*, Part II, Hearings before the Permanent Subcommittee on Investigations of the Committee on Governmental Affairs, U.S. Senate, 104th Cong., 2nd Sess. (Washington, D.C.: U.S. GPO, March 20, 1996), pp. 105–107.

21. On the technical challenges facing Iraq, see Albright and Kelley, "Has Iraq Come Clean at Last?" pp. 53–64. Albright and Kelly suggest that "Iraq could have produced enough highly enriched uranium for a small nuclear arsenal by 1996, if the calutron program had eventually worked or if gas centrifuges had been deployed somewhat earlier than planned." Ibid., p. 64.

22. David Kay estimates Iraq spent more than $10 billion over a decade on its nuclear weapons program before it was cut short by the Gulf War and the postwar inspections that led to the destruction of much of Iraq's nuclear infrastructure. David A. Kay, "Denial and Deception Practices of WMD Proliferators: Iraq and Beyond," *Washington Quarterly*, Vol. 18, No. 1 (Winter 1994), p. 85. According to David Albright and Robert Kelley, a 1987 document recovered by the UN inspections shows that Iraq let a $110 million contract for the construction of about 20 major buildings at Taramiya, one of the sites of its electromagnetic isotope separation (EMIS) program, and that associated chemical recovery and electrical power infrastructure were to cost another $55 million. Albright and Kelley, "Massive Programs, Meager Results," p. 56. The construction cost would have been only part of the total cost of the EMIS program; staffing the facilities, equipping them with calutrons, and running them to produce HEU would have added considerable costs.

Chapter 5

Recommendations

An Agenda for the American Government

Writing on nuclear weapons in April 1945, Secretary of War Henry Stimson told President Harry Truman that: "The future may see a time when such a weapon may be constructed in secret and used suddenly and effectively with devastating power by a willful nation or group against an unsuspecting nation or group of much greater size and material power. With its aid even a very powerful unsuspecting nation might be conquered within a very few days by a very much smaller one."[1] Sheltering the home front from devastation must rank among the highest national interests of a government and its military forces. One would thus expect a determined, systematic U.S. effort both to minimize the likelihood of covert NBC aggression and to close off all avenues of NBC attack.

But in its actions and policies the U.S. government does not treat the danger of covert NBC aggression as a first-order national security challenge, occasional rhetoric aside. There are critical deficiencies in the current U.S. capacity to cope with the covert NBC threat. Important high-leverage policy areas currently receive insufficient attention and funding. An array of federal, state, and local government agencies possess capabilities that are relevant to countering the covert NBC threat, but there is no overarching strategy, and no coherent organizational structure, for pulling these disparate capabilities together to meet the challenge posed by the possible covert use of weapons of mass destruction. Despite a few commendable initiatives, such as the 1996 Nunn-Lugar-Domenici amendment (see Box 11, Nunn-Lugar-Domenici, p. 262), the overall U.S. policy response to the problem of NBC terrorism and covert attack has been inadequate in comparison to the importance of the American interests at stake and the severity of the threat.

There is, of course, no technical "fix" that can end U.S. vulnerability to covert NBC attack. Potential policy responses to the covert NBC threat are scattered across diverse thematic areas and multiple jurisdictions, and many

---

1. "Memorandum Discussed with the President," April 25, 1945, reproduced in part in Henry L. Stimson and McGeorge Bundy, *On Active Service in Peace and War* (New York: Octagon Books, 1971), pp. 635–636.

Box 11
The Nunn-Lugar-Domenici Amendment

In July 1996, the Senate passed the Defense against Weapons of Mass Destruction Act of 1996, an amendment to the defense authorization act, by a vote of 97–0.[1] The act is better known as the Nunn-Lugar-Domenici amendment, after its main sponsors, Senator Sam Nunn (Democrat from Georgia, retired from the Senate in 1997), Senator Richard Lugar (Republican from Indiana), and Senator Pete Domenici (Republican from New Mexico). The amendment resulted from a series of hearings held by Senators Nunn and Lugar in 1995–96, which focused on the threat to the United States from weapons of mass destruction, and placed particular emphasis on the problem of NBC terrorism and the meager level of domestic preparedness against this threat.

The Nunn-Lugar-Domenici amendment had three main parts. The first was a set of measures designed to increase U.S. domestic preparedness for NBC terrorism. The most innovative aspect of this legislation was that it assigned responsibility for the nation's domestic preparedness against domestic NBC incidents to the Department of Defense. The law directed the president to take immediate action "to enhance the capability of the Federal Government to prevent and respond to terrorist incidents involving weapons of mass destruction," and "to provide enhanced support to improve the capabilities of State and local emergency response agencies to prevent and respond to such incidents at both the national and the local level."[2]

To begin meeting this objective, Congress provided approximately $50 million in supplemental funding to the Department of Defense in fiscal year 1997. It was allocated as follows: $16.4 million to establish a training program for state and local first responders; $6.6 million to assist the Public Health Service in establishing Metro Medical Strike Teams in major U.S. cities; $9.8 million to establish a national domestic terrorism rapid response team; and $9.8 million to begin a long-term program of exercises to test federal, state, and local capabilities. The U.S. Army's Chemical and Biological Defense Command (CBDCOM) was made responsible for the first-responder training program. The Department of Defense intends to hand this program over to the Federal Emergency Management Agency in fiscal year 1999.

The second set of initiatives was a package of increases to the administration's funding requests for a select set of programs aimed at reducing the risk of fissile material theft and diversion in the former Soviet Union. Most of this funding was directed toward the Department of Energy's nuclear cooperation programs in the former Soviet Union, several of which originated in the Department of Defense's Cooperative Threat Reduction program (the original Nunn-Lugar program). Congress increased funding of the Department of Energy's material protection, control, and accounting

Box 11, Nunn-Lugar-Domenici, *cont.*

(MPC&A) program to $112.5 million; its nuclear smuggling program to $8.6 million; its plutonium disposition program to $10 million; and the joint Energy-Defense plutonium-production reactor core conversion program to $13.5 million. The Customs Service was given $9 million to enhance its international cooperation program for detecting nuclear smuggling.

Finally, in response to what the Congress saw as inadequate Executive Branch coordination of the nation's nonproliferation and counterterrorism policies, the Nunn-Lugar-Domenici act mandated the establishment of a "National Coordinator for Nonproliferation Matters." This was intended to be an intermediate position between the national security advisor and the senior directors on the NSC staff, with authority analogous to that of the national drug policy coordinator (the "drug czar"). The Clinton administration resisted this congressional intervention into White House staff arrangements, and simply designated the deputy national security advisor as the national coordinator without enacting the reforms sought by Congress.

The Nunn-Lugar-Domenici amendment was a vital first step in the U.S. effort to address the problem of domestic or terrorist NBC attack, but further efforts will be needed if the United States is to reduce its vulnerability to weapons of mass destruction. In particular, the funding base of the domestic preparedness programs is insufficient to achieve the objectives sought by Congress, and the Department of Defense is not fully committed to this mission. The nuclear security programs funded by the Nunn-Lugar-Domenici amendment have a more secure financial base, but even these are periodically challenged by legislators opposed to "aid to Russia," especially in the House. Unless the White House becomes more engaged, Congressional efforts to improve the quality of national nonproliferation and counterterrorism coordination are unlikely to have a major effect.

NOTES

1. See Public Law 104-201, National Defense Authorization Act for Fiscal Year 1997, Title XIV: Defense Against Weapons of Mass Destruction, available in "Conference Report on H.R. 3230, National Defense Authorization Act for Fiscal Year 1997," *Congressional Record*, Vol. 142, No. 114, Part II (July 30, 1996), pp. H9073–H9078.

2. Similarly, the law directed the secretary of defense to "carry out a program to provide civilian personnel of Federal, State, and Local agencies with training and expert advice regarding emergency responses to a use or threatened use of a weapon of mass destruction or related materials." See "Conference Report on H.R. 3230," p. H9074.

of them are technically, operationally, and legally complex. But there are many measures that, singly or in combination, can make U.S. citizens and interests substantially less vulnerable. This chapter outlines a program of action that would, if implemented, greatly enhance the U.S. capacity to prevent and withstand NBC terrorism and covert attack.

The recommendations expressed in this chapter reflect our conclusions about the policy measures and initiatives that deserve highest priority. We applied two basic criteria to make these judgments. First, how important is the policy or capability in the nation's broad effort to reduce the NBC threat or a specific vulnerability to covert NBC attack? Second, how great a return could one expert from additional investment in that particular aspect of the overall U.S. response to the covert NBC threat? Thus our recommendations omit not only unimportant policy areas, but also important ones that currently receive adequate attention from the U.S. government.[2] We give preference to policy initiatives that are independently valuable, that is, to things the United States should do even if it were uninterested in reducing its vulnerability to NBC terrorism and cover attack.[3]

There are five key areas in which increased funding and effort can substantially improve the ability of the United States to contain and respond to the unconventional NBC threat: (1) national strategy, planning, and coordination; (2) intelligence and threat identification; (3) operational preparedness for crisis and consequence management; (4) fissile material security; and (5) declaratory policy and law. We outline them briefly here, and then discuss each in detail below.

The first key area is national strategy, planning, and coordination. The United States has no coherent national strategy for dealing with the covert nuclear, biological, and chemical threat. No agency in the U.S. government is currently required or equipped to conduct the strategic planning across multiple jurisdictional boundaries that is necessary to reduce U.S.

---

2. For example, we pay little attention to diplomatic efforts by the United States to dissuade other states from acquiring NBC weapons in the first place, to arms control, or to the military capabilities needed to retaliate against state aggressors. All three are important aspects of the overall U.S. program against the NBC problem, but none suffers from a sorely deficient U.S. policy response.

3. Examples of recommendations in this category include improving the effectiveness of the intelligence community, enhancing the quality of global surveillance and response to infectious disease, and increasing the rate at which U.S. military forces receive the training and equipment necessary for them to operate effectively in NBC environments.

vulnerability to covert NBC aggression. No powerful federal official is responsible for, or has a strong interest in, arguing in the federal budget process for non-traditional national security expenditures, such as training and equipping first responders at the state and local levels. Instead, what the United States has is a hodgepodge of disparate policies and operational capabilities — some quite formidable, others wholly inadequate — of haphazard origin and uncertain future. This incoherence of national planning and coordination is a key constraint on the ability of the United States to reduce its vulnerability to NBC terrorism and covert attack. Because the covert NBC threat crosses important jurisdictional lines, most importantly the one between law enforcement and national security, the impetus for national planning and coordination must come from the White House, which must work in close partnership with all relevant agencies. The impetus for such an effort can only come from the president or vice president, and must have the genuine support of influential Cabinet members to be implemented. This issue, however, is not presently a high-level priority of the U.S. government, and it is likely to become one only if a domestic NBC attack occurs.

The second key area concerns intelligence and threat identification. As an operational matter, a nation's ability to defend itself from a real threat of covert NBC attack will depend most critically on the quality and timeliness of its intelligence. Specific conspiracies are relatively easy to defeat if the authorities learn of their existence with adequate lead time and in sufficient detail to investigate and take action. Even generic early warning, without knowledge of the specifics of the attack plan, can allow a nation to undertake important damage-limiting preparations. Complete ignorance, on the other hand, cedes all advantages to the attacker, whose success or failure then hinges only on its own competence and luck. Acquiring good intelligence on the full range of potential NBC threats — state and non-state, foreign and domestic, covert and military — is a profoundly difficult task, but it must be emphasized because of its importance to a nation's ability to defend itself from existing and potential threats. The U.S. intelligence community already devotes considerable resources to this mission, but specific improvements are needed in its ability to acquire early warning of emerging NBC threats, especially by watching for the most likely indicators of small-scale, improvised NBC acquisition programs, abroad and at home;[4]

---

4. "Intelligence" is usually used to refer only to foreign intelligence, since U.S. intelligence agencies are largely prohibited from domestic spying. Improved intelligence on internal threats is needed, however, to respond effectively to covert

to improve the use of public health capabilities, particularly epidemiological surveillance, to detect medical evidence of NBC weapons programs and biological weapons attacks, and to identify those responsible for NBC attacks after an incident has occurred. Shortcomings in these areas are symptomatic both of the difficulty the U.S. intelligence community has had in adapting to the security challenges of the post–Cold War era, and of its failure to make use of state-of-the-art information processing technology. Since the disappearance of the Soviet threat, the shortcomings of U.S. intelligence have been commented upon and studied at length, by experts inside and outside the government, but the incremental pace of current reform efforts does not reflect an appreciation of the community's fundamental problems, or the political will to address these problems with the necessary boldness.

The third key area concerns operational preparedness for crisis and consequence management. Once a government detects or receives warning of a covert NBC attack, resources and capabilities from an exceptionally diverse array of local, state, and federal agencies can be mobilized to help resolve the crisis or limit its consequences. The first responders in a no-warning incident are likely to be local police, paramedics, fire fighters, and disaster management personnel. These first responders will eventually be reinforced by state and federal agencies with greater resources and more specialized capabilities. On the whole, however, the United States is very poorly prepared to conduct an effective operational response to covert NBC attacks at home or abroad. Four specific problems require urgent corrective action. First, the local public servants most likely to arrive on the scene in the critical early hours of a domestic NBC incident lack the training, equipment, and resources necessary to mount even the first stage of an effective damage-limiting response. Second, the specialized capabilities for responding to NBC incidents currently possessed by the federal government, including those of the military, are insufficient in scope and resources to respond to significant attacks on cities, key strategic facilities, or U.S. forces deployed abroad. Third, the specialized response capabilities and NBC defense resources that the federal government does possess reside largely in the Department of Defense, and are focused primarily on foreign military missions, not on responding to domestic NBC incidents. Fourth,

---

NBC threats. Information of this kind will have to be gathered by U.S. law enforcement agencies, which have the legal authority to conduct domestic investigations. Once it is available, however, experts from the intelligence community should contribute to its analysis.

existing national plans for integrating the response capabilities of multiple local, state, and federal agencies during the course of an NBC incident are not thoroughly practiced and hence not highly reliable. The U.S. government has recently taken a few tentative steps to address these problems, but serious deficiencies remain.

The fourth key area is that of fissile material security. No measure to limit the risk of nuclear terrorism is more important than ensuring that all stockpiles of fissile material (especially highly enriched uranium) and nuclear weapons themselves are properly accounted for and guarded. The former Soviet Union is the source of the most serious risks of fissile material diversion. A number of U.S. programs designed to improve the nuclear security standards of the former Soviet Union are already underway, but these efforts deserve greater political emphasis and funding because of their direct impact on the threat of nuclear terrorism.

The fifth key area concerns issues of declaratory policy and law. The infrequency of NBC violence in the past cannot be explained solely, or even principally, by the technical difficulty of obtaining or using weapons of mass destruction. NBC weapons have been within reach for many states, some non-state actors, and perhaps even a few individuals, but only a handful have taken the fateful steps of acquiring or using such weapons. The environment in which acquisition and use decisions are made is at least partially affected by U.S. law and declaratory policy, by international law, and by the norms that occasionally take hold in the international community, all of which can reinforce or undermine deterrence to some degree. Thus, in its law, declaratory policy, and behavior, the U.S. government should take care to maintain and strengthen those aspects of its own policies and the international environment that tend to discourage NBC acquisition and use, and to avoid actions that have the potential to aggravate existing threats or generate new ones. The U.S. government should also support a multilateral effort to make the possession and use of biological weapons a crime under international law.

The next five sections of this chapter address these five broad categories of recommendations in detail: national planning and coordination; intelligence; operational preparedness; fissile material security; and declaratory policy and law. In each section, we briefly describe the specific tasks involved, review the degree of success with which these tasks are currently being addressed by the U.S. government, assess the potential for improvement in each area, and make concrete recommendations.

National Strategy, Planning, and Coordination

A consistent theme in virtually all independent, executive-branch, and congressional evaluations of the U.S. policy response to proliferation of weapons of mass destruction and U.S. preparedness against NBC terrorism is that the quality of interagency coordination and long-range planning has been poor.[5] A vast number of different government actors are involved, but because of the multi-jurisdictional nature of the problem, no one except the president can be in charge of them all (see Figure 4). In this respect, U.S. policy and preparedness against covert NBC threats is like many other complex issues that do not obey national borders or bureaucratic boundaries. Problems like this can only be addressed by many agencies acting in concert. Although it is impossible to establish a unitary authority or command with responsibility for all aspects of prevention, preparedness, and response to covert NBC threats, the interagency planning and coordination that goes into these efforts is in urgent need of improvement. Without such improvement, the whole of the U.S. response will remain less than the sum of its parts, with the inevitable result being the waste of the limited resources that can be devoted to this problem, and unnecessary damage should an attack occur.

To a certain extent, this problem has been recognized within the Executive Branch, which conducted a major review of U.S. counterterrorism

---

5. The most important of these studies were the hearings on the global proliferation of weapons of mass destruction held by Senator Sam Nunn in 1995–96, and the 1996 Aspin-Brown report on the state of U.S. intelligence. The Aspin-Brown commission recommended the creation of a Global Crime Committee of the National Security Council, chaired by the national security advisor and including the secretaries of state and defense, the attorney general, and the director of central intelligence. Although established by law and executive order, the Global Crime Committee has never met, and the proposal has effectively been ignored by the Cabinet-level officials to whom it was directed. Commission on the Roles and Capabilities of the United States Intelligence Community, *Preparing for the 21st Century: An Appraisal of U.S. Intelligence* (Washington, D.C.: U.S. Government Printing Office [U.S. GPO], 1996), Chapter 4, available at <www.access.gpo.gov/int/pdf/report.html>. In 1995–97, there were also several classified studies of the quality of interagency coordination and long-range planning against NBC proliferation, terrorism, and other transnational threats. For an unclassified study, see General Accounting Office (GAO) Report No. GAO/NSIAD-98-39, *Combating Terrorism: Spending on Governmentwide Programs Requires Better Management and Coordination* (Washington, D.C.: U.S. GAO, December 1997).

policy in 1995, resulting in the signing of Presidential Decision Directive 39.[6] PDD-39 specified that the Federal Bureau of Investigation (FBI) would be the lead federal agency for the management of all terrorist crises, including those involving NBC weapons, that occur in the United States or that break U.S. law. The lead federal agency for managing the consequences of mass-casualty terrorist attacks, including NBC attacks, would be the Federal Emergency Management Agency (FEMA). PDD-39 also directed FEMA, the FBI, and other relevant agencies to review the adequacy of their counter-NBC response plans.[7]

PDD-39 was a constructive document, but problems remain. Most fundamentally, PDD-39 does not provide a blueprint for how the United States should improve its capabilities for responding to a covert NBC crisis, and fails to specify that preparing the nation for NBC attacks is a responsibility of the federal government, not of the states. Instead, its main contribution is to specify how federal agencies are to divide operational responsibilities among themselves in exercises and incidents. A clear allocation of operational responsibility is an important part of the nation's overall response to the covert NBC threat, but it is far from sufficient. The nation also needs to be able to conduct a strategic planning process across multiple jurisdictional boundaries, to determine which new capabilities are needed, where they should be located, when and how they should be acquired, and how they can best be integrated with existing capabilities. Similarly, PDD-39 does not give any agency the responsibility or the incentive to advocate non-traditional national security expenditures, such as enhanced epidemiological surveillance, or training and equipping first responders at the state and local levels. These capabilities are needed in the overall national response to the covert NBC threat, but lie outside the

---

6. This problem has also been recognized by the Congress, which mandated the establishment of a "National Coordinator for Nonproliferation Matters" in the 1996 Nunn-Lugar-Domenici amendment, a directive that the administration has avoided implementing (see Box 11, Nunn-Lugar-Domenici, p. 262).

7. The full text of PDD-39 is classified and has not been seen by the authors. This discussion is based on the unclassified version of the document released by the White House, and conversations with officials familiar with it. See "Unclassified FEMA Abstract on PDD-39," in U.S. Congress, *Global Proliferation of Weapons of Mass Destruction*, Part III, Hearings before the Permanent Subcommittee on Investigations of the Committee on Governmental Affairs, U.S. Senate, 104th Cong., 1st Sess. (Washington, D.C.: U.S. GPO, 1996), pp. 151–154.

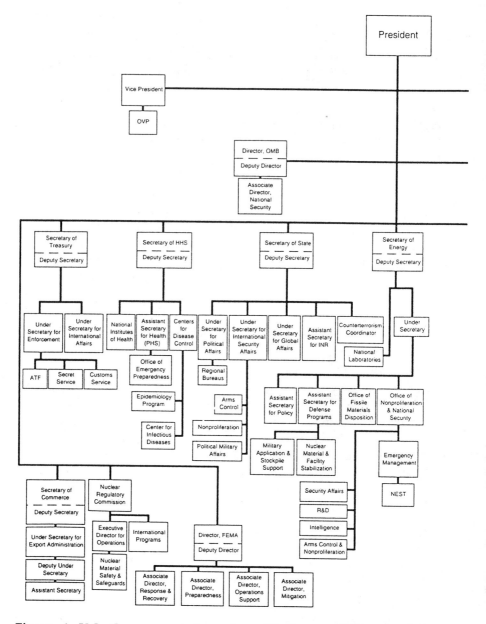

Figure 4. U.S. Government Agencies with Responsibility for NBC Defense.

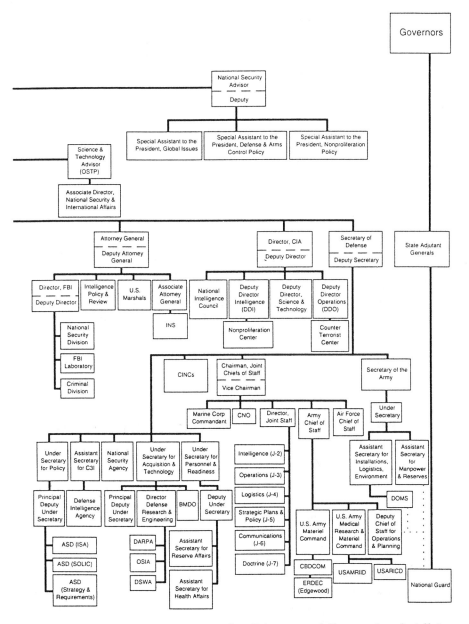

Prepared for the Belfer Center for Science and International Affairs, Harvard University, by Ted Lantaff.

normal institutional interests of established agencies. On the contrary, PDD-39 states: "Agencies will bear the costs of the participation in terrorist incidents and counterterrorist operations, unless otherwise directed."[8] This directive means that any efforts to prepare an effective response capability will be in direct competition with other agency programs for scarce funds. Without high-level backing, interagency programs tend to lose when fighting on these terms. In short, while the directive provides clear guidance on who is in charge during the course of a terrorist crisis, its language about what should be done in advance of an actual incident is too weak and non-binding to make effective advance planning likely.

Second, PDD-39 gives too much authority over NBC crises to the FBI, an agency for whom weapons of mass destruction have never been a core competency. The FBI has always had responsibility for protecting national security in addition to enforcing U.S. law, but its national security mission has been predominantly one of counterintelligence, that is, identifying and prosecuting foreign spies within U.S. national security agencies like the Central Intelligence Agency and Department of Defense.[9] Although counterintelligence is governed by a unique legal structure, it is similar to the FBI's core mission of investigating crimes and organized criminal networks. The FBI has substantially less experience in preparing for or conducting large-scale, multi-agency operations, as would be required in an operational response to a domestic NBC incident.

The key issue is not whether the FBI will perform well enough in the management of a real NBC crisis, although past exercises give some reason for concern here as well.[10] Rather, it is whether the FBI can realistically be

---

8. Ibid.

9. For a description of the FBI's mission and organization, see <www.fbi.gov>. The FBI's long-standing counterintelligence mission may also contribute to mistrust between the Bureau and the national security agencies (and officials) it polices.

10. For example, in the 1994 exercise Mirage Gold, which simulated a nuclear terrorist crisis, the FBI agent in charge of the interagency response force was unwilling to share information with other participating federal, state, and local agencies. There was also a fundamental policy conflict over whether or not to take important damage-limiting steps at the risk of alerting the terrorists to the investigation. The FBI later modified its policy of placing a local agent with general training in charge of NBC crises, in favor of specially trained agents deployed from FBI headquarters. Mirage Gold is not the only instance of this kind of counterproductive non-communication. In April 1995, when a nerve gas threat was made against Disneyland, the local fire chief was not told of the threat for five days,

expected to lead an effective long-term federal effort to reduce the vulnerability of the nation to covert NBC attack. The FBI is very effective at investigating crimes, but it has little proficiency at building capability in multiple bureaucratic and substantive domains. Not only is the FBI's basic mode of operation essentially reactive — it responds to actual or intended violations of the law — but the FBI is also a highly self-contained bureaucracy, and is notoriously reluctant to share information with other government agencies. And the FBI's attention is elsewhere; as one senior FBI official has noted, "unlike the military, who when not at war are training, law enforcement is continually engaged in real-time operations."[11] All these factors combine to make the FBI poorly suited for the role of planning and implementing a broad-based U.S. program for combating the full range of possible covert NBC threats. The basic weakness of PDD-39 is that while it settles an important tactical issue — operational responsibility in NBC crises — it gives responsibility for managing the important task of improving U.S. response capabilities to the wrong agency.

The Federal Emergency Management Agency, the lead federal agency for consequence management in NBC incidents, also presents problems under the PDD-39 framework. FEMA is a disaster relief agency, and it has a core competency in coordinating and conducting advance planning for complex, multi-agency operations. Its main vehicle for doing this is the Federal Response Plan, which lays out in detail precisely which agencies are responsible for which aspects of an integrated response to natural disasters. Since floods, forest fires, earthquakes, and hurricanes occur with some frequency, the effectiveness of the Federal Response Plan can be continually evaluated and improved by FEMA, which has become significantly more efficient as an institution since the late 1980s.[12] Recently, the interagency

---

until the day of the threatened attack. According to an analysis of the response effort, "despite the involvement of several local, federal and military agencies, little unified coordination was underway." *Strengthening the Fire and Emergency Response to Terrorism*, Report on a Conference organized by the International Association of Fire Chiefs and the Federal Emergency Management Agency, November 6–9, 1995, p. 10.

11. Robert M. Blitzer, Section Chief, Domestic Terrorism/Counterterrorism, FBI, "Supplemental Questions for the Record," in U.S. Congress, *Global Proliferation of Weapons of Mass Destruction*, Part III, p. 333.

12. For a detailed look at federal disaster plans, see Federal Emergency Management Agency (FEMA), *Federal Response Plan* (Washington, D.C.: FEMA, 1992) and its more recent amendments. For specific information on agency roles in

process has completed a terrorism annex to the Federal Response Plan, and FEMA has generally been an active proponent of improving U.S. capabilities for responding to domestic NBC incidents. FEMA works by harnessing the capabilities of other agencies at the local, state, and federal levels, and is an appropriate lead federal agency for NBC consequence management. Likewise, FEMA's ability to plan complex multi-agency operations is an important component of the nation's overall preparedness against covert NBC attacks. However, FEMA acting alone lacks the political power and financial resources needed to ensure that other agencies will make the necessary improvements in capabilities. FEMA thus cannot be expected to orchestrate or implement a major improvement in the nation's capacity to mitigate the effects of a domestic NBC attack.[13]

Finally, PDD-39 and other federal attempts to improve the coordination of NBC preparedness and response are flawed by their failure to delineate clearly and consistently the responsibilities of the different levels of government: federal, state, and local. While the federal government provides significant support to states affected by major disasters, the states have primary responsibility for building and maintaining emergency response assets. The first responders to any domestic NBC incident are very likely to come from state and local agencies, and their ability to recognize and react appropriately to an NBC incident is critical. Individual states, however, lack the resources and competencies needed to prepare adequately for the consequences of NBC attacks. The risk of such attacks is

---

responding to terrorism incidents, see the *Terrorism Incident Annex*, Amendment 11b to the *Federal Response Plan*. These documents are available at <www.fema.gov/home/fema/fed1.htm>.

13. FEMA's FY 1998 budget request was $4.7 billion, of which only a small part is available for building response capacity. Of the total, $2.1 billion goes to the Disaster Relief Fund, which provides financial aid to individuals and communities affected by disasters, an effort that is politically very popular, and $258 million goes to the National Flood Insurance Fund. Considerable resources are devoted to assisting localities in disaster preparedness in certain areas; the National Fire Academy, for example, receives $100 million. Budget figures are from a FEMA fact sheet, "1998 Request to Congress," February 13, 1997, <www.fema.gov/home/nwx97/budget98.htm>. Outside of FEMA's established programs, however, funds are very limited. In FY 1997, for example, FEMA was able to provide $1 million in grants to state and local governments to improve planning for response to terrorist attacks, and $1.3 million in training grants. See "Preparing for the Consequences of Terrorism," speech by FEMA Associate Director Kay C. Goss before the NATO Civil Emergency Preparedness Symposium, Moscow, April 22, 1997.

in any case best handled as a national security issue, and ensuring adequate preparedness is thus properly a federal responsibility. PDD-39 should be revised to reflect this, by specifying that it is the responsibility of the federal government to ensure — by providing resources, expertise, training, and equipment — that an adequate capacity to respond to the first phase of an NBC incident exists at the state and local level. The federal government should not, however, attempt to supplant the role of local responders, since this would require creating a widespread and expensive federal structure alongside the existing emergency response resources of states and localities.

For an issue as complex as the covert NBC threat, the only real option for improving the quality of national planning and coordination is to work with, not against, the existing "community-based" approach. No single office can be expected to coordinate all aspects of a society's response to covert NBC threats. Thus, the first step in an effort to reduce U.S. vulnerability to covert NBC attack is to augment the existing coordination mechanism in three critical areas: strategic planning; battling for budget dollars; and securing an appropriate level of engagement from both law enforcement and national security agencies. Failure to do this will make improvements in all other areas more difficult, and will limit the coherence of the overall effort. The impetus for enhanced coordination in the Executive Branch can only come from the president, vice president, or an influential Cabinet member.

We believe that strategic planning and programmatic oversight should be carried out by a new interagency "NBC Response Center," modeled after the existing Counterterrorist Center (CTC). The CTC is a part of the Directorate of Operations of the Central Intelligence Agency, but it has permanent staff representation from many different agencies, including the FBI, Department of State, and Department of Defense. The CTC combines the analysis of terrorist threats and coordination of some aspects of counterterrorist operations into a single body, and it is one of the U.S. government's most effective organizations for coordinating the work of several different agencies on an issue that crosses multiple jurisdictional boundaries. The national NBC Response Center that we propose should have a multi-agency staff of about fifty, and should be collocated and integrated with the CTC, with the two organizations sharing physical space and personnel. This new national resource should consolidate the related capabilities that have been developed by the FBI, FEMA, the Department

---

Recommendation 1:
Establish an NBC Response Center

The president should, by executive order, establish a new interagency federal NBC Response Center alongside the existing Counterterrorist Center.

The new center should have a staff of about 50 experts, drawn from all relevant agencies and consolidating existing dispersed capabilities.

It should provide:

- strategic planning and oversight of national efforts to respond to NBC threats;

- integration of foreign and domestic intelligence;

- a 24-hour-a-day point of contact for federal, state, and local officials with information on potential NBC threats;

- real-time NBC threat assessment; and

- direction of initial response efforts.

The president should create a new director-level position on the NSC staff to enhance the White House staff's ability to oversee the capability enhancements of all relevant federal, state, and local agencies. This person would report to the senior director for global issues and multilateral affairs.

---

of Health and Human Services, the Environmental Protection Agency, the U.S. Marine Corps, the Chemical and Biological Defense Command, and the Department of Energy.

In addition to establishing this new NBC Response Center, the National Security Council staff should be slightly augmented with a new director-level official responsible for policy development, oversight, and coordination. The FBI should continue to develop its own internal expertise in NBC matters, but should become increasingly engaged with the other agencies involved, in part through the NBC Response Center. The Department of Defense, and under it the Army National Guard, should be made responsible for the implementation of a long-term federal program for reducing U.S. vulnerability to covert NBC attack. The White House should direct the Department of Defense to prepare response capabilities adequate to significantly assist civilian consequence management efforts in realistic NBC attack scenarios. With high-level leadership, these initiatives could significantly enhance the quality of U.S. strategy, planning, and coordination for dealing with covert threats.

Recommendation 2:
Rationalize Departmental Responsibilities and Government Organization for NBC Response

The president should, by executive order:

- declare that the federal government, not the states, has responsibility for ensuring that the United States has adequate capabilities for managing the consequences of domestic NBC attacks;

- designate the Department of Defense as the agency responsible for leading a long-term interagency effort to build U.S. capability against covert NBC threats;

- direct the Department of Defense to seek funding for the Nunn-Lugar-Domenici program of not less than $500 million per year; and

- direct other departments (including the Departments of State, Energy, Justice, and Health and Human Services, the Federal Bureau of Investigation, and the Federal Emergency Management Agency) to support this Defense-led program, and to fund necessary programs within their own agencies.

The president and the Congress should require the FBI, the Department of Defense, and FEMA to generate an annual "Joint Report on Activities and Programs for Countering Domestic Use of NBC Weapons," along the lines of the counterproliferation report issued annually by the Department of Defense. This report should be made public, with classified annexes as necessary.

Intelligence: Detecting Clandestine Programs and Specific Threats

Intelligence is the first and most important line of defense against covert NBC threats. Any effort to reduce a nation's vulnerability to covert NBC attack must, therefore, seek to improve the quality of intelligence collection, analysis, and dissemination on the full range of extant and potential nuclear, biological, and chemical weapons threats, abroad and at home. Intelligence faces two critical, related tasks in its attempt to cope with covert NBC threats. The first is to detect clandestine NBC weapons programs of any size, anywhere in the world. The second is to acquire early warning of planned covert NBC attacks, identify any such attacks as they happen, and quickly convey this information to relevant decision-makers and operators. Both tasks are enormously difficult, the latter even more than the former, but both are vital.

Detecting clandestine NBC weapons programs is a long-standing priority for the U.S. intelligence community. States and non-state actors that decide to acquire nuclear, biological, and chemical weapons will generally seek to do so in secret.[14] Knowing who has NBC capabilities is of central importance to a state's ability to deter and defend against these NBC threats. Without advance detection of clandestine NBC weapons programs, the United States and the international community will lack critical information about the aims and capabilities of its state and non-state adversaries. There will be no opportunity to discourage, pressure, sanction, or take countermeasures against states and non-state actors seeking NBC weapons. Strategic warning of future NBC threats will be absent, and attribution will be even more difficult should a covert NBC attack occur.

The difficulty of detecting clandestine NBC programs results from the fact that the externally observable features of NBC weapons programs can often be disguised as legitimate industrial activity or research, and can always be minimized by keeping the program small. Despite its unparalleled technical capacity to collect intelligence (especially through satellite imaging and signals interception),[15] the U.S. intelligence community faces a profound technical and operational challenge in attempting to detect clandestine NBC activity, made worse by the low level of international intelligence cooperation on many of these issues, as well by as the extreme difficulty of developing high-quality human intelligence sources in violent transnational organizations. Evidence of this fact can be found in the 1980s controversy over the Soviet biological weapons program,[16] the well-publicized failure to accurately assess the Iraqi NBC programs prior to the

---

14. This penchant for secrecy is a consequence not only of the success of the international community in establishing international norms against proliferation, but also of the potential proliferator's fear of international or internal response. For a discussion of the value of secrecy or opacity in a nuclear weapons program, see Avner Cohen and Benjamin Frankel, "Opaque Nuclear Proliferation," *The Journal of Strategic Studies*, Vol. 13, No. 3 (September 1990), pp. 14–44.

15. For a description of these capabilities, see Desmond Ball, *Pine Gap: Australia and the U.S. Geostationary Signals Intelligence Program* (Sydney: Allen & Unwin Australia, 1988); William E. Burrows, *Deep Black: Space Espionage and National Security* (New York: Random House, 1987); Jeffrey T. Richelson, *The U.S. Intelligence Community*, 3rd ed. (Boulder, Colo.: Westview, 1995); and Curtis Peebles, *Guardians: Strategic Reconnaissance Satellites* (Novato, Calif.: Presidio Press, 1987).

16. See Box 3, Soviet BW Program, p. 68.

1990–91 Gulf War,[17] and the ongoing controversy with America's European allies over whether Iran has a secret nuclear weapons program.[18]

Detecting a non-state actor's clandestine NBC acquisition is an even greater challenge than detecting that of a state. The NBC weapons programs of terrorist organizations are likely to be smaller and more improvised than the military-scale programs on which intelligence gathering has historically focused. Non-state programs can also be located anywhere: in unfriendly states, in friendly states whose domestic affairs are not normally the object of intensive U.S. intelligence gathering, and even in the United States itself, where the law prevents most forms of domestic spying.[19] A good illustration of this problem is the failure, apparently on the part of every intelligence service in the world, to detect Aum Shinrikyo's nerve gas production facility in the Japanese countryside.

Detecting a specific covert NBC attack, whether planned or in progress, is another major intelligence challenge, particularly if the attack originates from a previously undetected weapon program. Effective action against a covert NBC threat will be impossible if warning is vague or arrives only hours or minutes before the attack. On the other hand, if the warning is both timely and highly precise, and provides accurate details of the attack plan, then the authorities will have a chance to defeat the attack through the use of force.[20] The reason for this is that covert NBC attacks are susceptible to

---

17. See Box 10, Iraqi NBC Programs, p. 255.

18. See Richard A. Falkenrath, "The United States, Europe, and Weapons of Mass Destruction," in Robert D. Blackwill and Michael Stürmer, eds., *Allies Divided: Transatlantic Policies for the Greater Middle East*, CSIA Studies in International Security (Cambridge, Mass.: MIT Press, 1997), pp. 203–230.

19. Suspicious activity at home can be investigated by U.S. law enforcement officials, but only if there is reason to believe that a crime has been or is going to be committed.

20. There is also a significant difference between an advance warning provided by the attacker, and independently acquired intelligence of an impending attack. If the attacker provides warning of an impending attack (perhaps in the context of a coercive demand), the information supplied by the warning is unlikely to be sufficiently precise — especially in terms of the time, place, and method of attack — to allow the targeted government to take effective countermeasures against that specific threat. (The warning might, however, assist the government in figuring out who is responsible for the attack.) On the other hand, if the government learns of an attack about to be launched or already underway through its own sources and methods, then the attack should be easier to disrupt, since the attacker can be taken

active countermeasures, and depend for success primarily on remaining secret.[21] An improvised nuclear weapon can be disarmed or disabled, or the truck transporting it can be stopped by a roadblock; a van equipped with a hidden aerosol sprayer can be destroyed or captured; a cargo ship with an improvised nuclear weapon in its hold can be stopped at sea. With over 17,000 local, state, and federal law enforcement agencies and well over a million military personnel, the United States has numerous trained, armed units that can be called upon to perform these missions, with or without special training and equipment. However, the success of such an operation depends crucially on the quality of intelligence available on the specific attack plan.[22]

Fundamentally, covert NBC attacks are difficult to detect and identify because the process of delivering the weapon can be disguised to make it outwardly indistinguishable from the background of lawful civilian activity. In some sense, a society's vulnerability to covert NBC attacks inevitably increases with the pace and complexity of its economy and the freedom of its civic life. There is an unavoidable tradeoff between maintaining the values and strengths of a free nation and taking certain steps that could significantly increase the odds of gaining advance detection of a terrorist or covert NBC attack. Only a police state, and one with very limited economic flexibility, could attempt to keep track of an entire society's movements, commerce, and private affairs. For a society of personal freedom and limited government, full-scale social monitoring is an impossibility, and even more selective surveillance measures encounter opposition because of their costs in privacy and civil liberties. Foreign intelligence collection efforts against terrorist threats, which are not bound by these restrictions, are also exceptionally difficult. According to John Deutch, then the director of central intelligence, the intelligence community strives "to provide

---

by surprise. Since almost all threats of nuclear, biological, or chemical terrorism have been hoaxes, it should also be easier to tell whether a threat is genuine or not when warning is acquired independently.

21. This is in marked contrast to overt military delivery methods, such as ballistic missile strikes, which are relatively easy to identify but quite difficult to defend against.

22. Counterterrorism exercises sometimes assume unrealistically good intelligence. This may sometimes be necessary to make it possible to exercise particular capabilities, such as predeployment of response assets. However, it also makes exercise objectives much easier to achieve, and makes it harder to assess and fix problems with no-warning response capabilities.

warning against all attacks before they occur, but this is an enormously difficult task. This type of tactical information depends upon access to dedicated terrorist groups who are well financed, skillful, and determined to commit atrocities. Such individuals have learned to keep their planning secret and confined to small cells."[23]

No agency has principal responsibility for detecting or identifying terrorist or unconventional NBC attacks: the threat is too diffuse and the task of combating it too esoteric to merit a dedicated agency. Success requires the collection of information on an attacker's activities from human sources, signals, or other technical intelligence sources; prompt, accurate analysis; and immediate distribution to relevant decision-makers. In the United States, many different bureaucracies have potential roles to play in detecting covert NBC threats: the intelligence community identifies and monitors specific threats abroad; the FBI has primary responsibility for coping with domestic terrorist activities, including those involving weapons of mass destruction, and for investigating terrorist attacks against U.S. citizens and installations abroad; the Secret Service (a unit of the Treasury Department) protects national leaders; the Customs Service enforces U.S. border laws and tries to prevent illegal or dangerous cargoes from entering the country; the State Department and the Immigration and Naturalization Service authorize the entry of individuals into the country, and monitor their exit; the Federal Aviation Administration and the Department of Defense protect U.S. airspace; the Coast Guard patrols U.S. territorial waters; and the Departments of Defense and State protect U.S. installations abroad. While any one of these federal agencies might detect a covert NBC attack against a U.S. target, state and local law enforcement personnel are equally likely to discover planned attacks before they occur. Indeed, the widespread presence of local officials in U.S. society makes them the most likely to stumble upon a covert attack in progress.

Despite the difficulties, the ability of the U.S. intelligence community to detect clandestine NBC weapons programs and identify discrete threats can be improved. Some of the needed improvements are specific to weapons of mass destruction, but others are generic. It is clear, for example, that the quality of intelligence on any particular issue will depend on the vitality and efficiency of the intelligence community as a whole. In effect, the covert NBC threat is one more reason why the United States should reform, reinvigorate, and modernize its intelligence community for the

---

23. John Deutch, "Fighting Foreign Terrorism," text of remarks, Georgetown University, September 5, 1996, p. 5.

Recommendation 3:
Reform and Reinvigorate the
U.S. Intelligence Community

The administration and the Congress should undertake a serious effort to reform, reinvigorate, and modernize the U.S. intelligence community for the challenges of the post–Cold War era.

The intelligence community should continue to improve the quality of human intelligence collection against transnational threats.

The intelligence community should adopt state-of-the-art information technologies to reform and enhance the community's current outdated information management systems.

challenges of the post–Cold War era. Similarly, improved intelligence cooperation with international partners is relevant to a range of national security issues, not least the covert NBC threat. Among intelligence reforms specific to the covert NBC threat, three are particularly important: enhancing the collection and analysis of intelligence on small-scale or improvised NBC programs conducted by states or non-state actors, both abroad and at home; improving the use of public health capabilities, particularly epidemiological surveillance, to detect medical evidence of NBC weapons programs and biological weapons attacks; and developing the technical capacity to perform forensic analysis of NBC weapons and materials in order to increase the U.S. ability to determine who is responsible for a particular incident.

REFORM, REINVIGORATE, AND MODERNIZE U.S. INTELLIGENCE
High-quality intelligence capabilities are essential to many of the most important national security tasks facing the United States in the post–Cold War era. Since the collapse of the Soviet Union, however, the performance and even the relevance of the U.S. intelligence community, which has an annual budget of roughly $30 billion, has been increasingly questioned by outside critics and some Congressional leaders. Intense criticism was further encouraged by the CIA's most damaging security failure ever, the Aldrich Ames case uncovered in February 1994; revelations of a lack of fiscal accountability, including the profligacy of the National Reconnaissance Office; and reports of past illegal or unethical practices, such as the support of right-wing death squads in Guatemala. The intelligence community has been censured before — in the 1970s for serious

abuses in domestic spying and covert operations, and in the 1980s for a rash of security lapses and the Iran-Contra scandal — but the threatening environment of the Cold War meant that the *raison d'être* of the intelligence community was never seriously questioned. With the passing of the Soviet threat, however, the critiques of U.S. intelligence have become more fundamental: that it has become insufficiently responsive to the needs of policymakers; that its collection and analysis practices have not been adjusted to reflect post–Cold War priorities; and that it is being hobbled by obsolete information processing systems and excessive secrecy.

A full review of why and how the U.S. intelligence community should adapt to its post–Cold War circumstances is beyond the scope of this study. The general issue of intelligence reform has been addressed elsewhere by numerous studies and commissions since the 1940s, and with increasing frequency and openness since the 1970s.[24] The latest review was produced by the Aspin-Brown Commission, a Congressionally chartered panel chaired by Les Aspin and Harold Brown, both former secretaries of defense, which contains an extensive analysis of the problems faced by the intelligence community and many worthy recommendations.[25] For present purposes, it is important to emphasize that reforming and reinvigorating the intelligence community as whole is an important precondition to improving its ability to deliver accurate, timely information on covert NBC threats. Specific improvements are needed in two key aspects of the intelligence process. The first is in the way that the intelligence community goes about collecting information on contemporary threats to U.S. national interests, particularly those with a transnational character. The United States currently has a vast technical infrastructure for collecting intelligence information, but reforms are needed to enhance the quality of human intelligence on transnational threats and to ensure that collection priorities reflect policy needs and national strategy.

The second set of reforms needed in the intelligence community is more important but more difficult, and has to do with how collected information is processed, analyzed, and conveyed to decision-makers. There have been rapid advances in the quantity and quality of raw data collected from

---

24. For a useful overview of these studies, see Commission on the Roles and Capabilities of the United States Intelligence Community, *Preparing for the 21st Century*, Appendix A.

25. See ibid. Another important study is Council on Foreign Relations, *Making Intelligence Smarter: The Future of U.S. Intelligence* (New York: Council on Foreign Relations, 1996).

technical sources, especially from signals and imagery. However, the intelligence community's techniques for analyzing this information have lagged, with the dominant mode of information processing still being individuals or small groups of analysts operating within a hierarchically structured system. Information often becomes "stove-piped," meaning it flows primarily up and down within the analysis hierarchy, and is not shared adequately between different groups of analysts working with different databases and perhaps looking for different patterns. The routine exchange of information is impeded by the lack of efficient technical systems for data sharing, and by security rules, bureaucratic barriers, and legal restrictions, including the privacy rights of U.S. citizens, which limit the use of intelligence in law enforcement. As a result, the intelligence community wastes resources in redundant analytical efforts, and is less effective than it could be at drawing correct, timely conclusions from information widely distributed across classified and open sources.

The inefficiency of information management in the U.S. intelligence community is becoming increasingly evident as advances in computer technologies are improving the ability of businesses to process, analyze, and manipulate very large, heterogeneous multi-source databases, such as those used for targeted direct marketing and the management of telecommunications networks. U.S. intelligence practices now lag behind the best commercial practices in information management, the exact opposite of what was true at the beginning of the digital age, when the intelligence community had access to the most advanced computers in the world. Correcting this problem will require nothing short of a revolution in the information management of the full intelligence community, demanding a near total overhaul of its technological systems and security rules, new institutional structures, and a new generation of analysts and information managers with very different skills.[26] While an extraordinarily difficult challenge, successfully realigning the intelligence community in this way could significantly improve its ability to meet the intelligence challenges of the twenty-first century, including that of NBC terrorism and covert attack.

---

26. For a discussion of these issues, see Defense Science Board 1997 Summer Study Task Force, *DoD Responses to Transnational Threats*, Vol. 1 (Washington, D.C.: Office of the Undersecretary of Defense for Acquisition and Technology, December 1997), pp. 37–40.

Recommendation 4:
Improve International Intelligence Cooperation

The U.S. intelligence community should increase its level of international cooperation against shared transnational threats.

The State Department should place particular emphasis on building a cooperative international system for monitoring cross-border traffic.

PROMOTE INTERNATIONAL INTELLIGENCE COOPERATION

The intelligence process benefits from sharing information not only among agencies, but also among nations. Intelligence sharing could increase the odds of acquiring advance warning of covert NBC threats, and also of gaining multilateral support for political, economic, or military countermeasures. The United States has the most technically sophisticated intelligence apparatus in the world, but it is far from perfect, and most other developed nations maintain some capability to gather and analyze information from beyond their borders. Several of the most serious post–Cold War threats — including those involving weapons of mass destruction — are fundamentally transnational in character, crossing state borders freely, gravitating toward lower risk settings, and endangering the interests of many nations, not just the United States. Against threats of this kind, international intelligence cooperation can make a significant difference.

The advantages of international intelligence cooperation against shared threats have long been recognized, and the U.S. intelligence community has exchanged intelligence information with a large number of states — friendly, ambivalent, and hostile. The United States has also engaged in regular, structured intelligence exchanges within the North Atlantic Treaty Organization (NATO). For the most part, however, international intelligence cooperation is done on an *ad hoc* basis, in response to specific threats and crises, and is limited to "finished products" rather than raw data and source information. Intelligence agencies are inherently secretive, a tendency that originates with the need to protect vulnerable sources and methods and that is reinforced by law, security regulations, and institutional mentality. If it is difficult to share information between agencies of the same government, sharing between nations is an even greater challenge. Moreover, from the U.S. perspective, full intelligence sharing could easily become a highly one-sided exercise, given the American dominance in many collection disciplines. Yet to increase its ability to acquire accurate, timely intelligence on major transnational threats, including NBC threats, the United States must be in a position to receive information possessed by similarly interested countries on a regular basis. To do this, Washington must be prepared to reciprocate, which will require a major effort to reduce the bureaucratic and security obstacles to comprehensive and routine intelligence sharing with key friends and allies.

One particularly important area of increased international intelligence cooperation is in the monitoring of border crossings. International borders offer unique opportunities for tracking transnational threats: passports are checked, virtually all travelers at regular border crossings are subject to at least cursory examination, and many are also required to go through a visa-application process in advance. Illegal entry into countries is always possible, but it is often difficult and risky. The standards of border control vary greatly from country to country, and there is no international effort to use border controls to deal with shared transnational threats. The United States is gradually modernizing its border control systems, and like many states keeps careful track of the numbers of stolen passports. The passport numbers and names of most people entering the United States are now electronically compared with central U.S. databases of passports reported stolen and individuals believed to be criminals, terrorists, or foreign agents. This system allows U.S. law enforcement personnel at the borders to detain or monitor suspect individuals. At the international level, however, there is no coherent, effective system for using the information gathered at border crossing points to identify individuals traveling on stolen passports or believed to be wanted for crimes or associated with violent organizations; these useful tasks could be performed very efficiently using modern information technologies.

The importance of sharing information on border crossing was made clear by an act of Middle Eastern terrorism that nearly succeeded. In September 1995, Hussein Mohammed Hussein Mikhad, a Lebanese Shi'ite, was recruited by the Hezbollah to conduct a terrorist bombing in Israel.[27] After training in the Bekaa Valley, Mikhad assumed the identity of a British accountant, Andrew Newman. Newman's passport had been stolen three years earlier in Paris, and Mikhad's picture was inserted into Newman's passport by expert forgers at the Iranian embassy in Beirut. Mikhad then went by car to Damascus, flew to Vienna, and took a train to Zurich. On April 4, 1996, he took a Swissair flight to Ben-Gurion International Airport,

---

27. This account, based on the interrogation of Mikhad by Israeli security personnel, is taken from Douglas Frantz and Catherine Collins, "The Accountant Is a Terrorist," *New York Times Magazine*, November 10, 1996, pp. 45–49.

Recommendation 5:
Improve Detection of
Small-scale NBC Weapons Programs

U.S. intelligence gathering efforts against clandestine NBC weapons programs should be augmented and reoriented to detect small-scale improvised programs producing weapons suitable for covert use.

Working through the federal NBC Response Center, the intelligence and law enforcement communities should jointly develop and implement a system for gathering information on potential NBC threats through the self-policing efforts of commercial suppliers of dual-use equipment and materials.

---

and entered Israel as Andrew Newman. On April 12, he was severely injured in his East Jerusalem hotel room when he accidentally detonated a quantity of C-4 plastic explosive that he was inserting into a clock radio that had been modified to conceal and detonate the explosive.[28] The lesson of this episode is clear: if the British, Austrian, Swiss, and Israeli governments had had a system for sharing information about stolen passports, Mikhad could have been identified as a security risk and apprehended. Instead, he slipped through some of the tightest border security in the world. A variety of technical systems, not unlike existing credit card verification networks, could remedy this situation, forcing terrorists and covert operatives to adopt more elaborate and difficult methods of international movement. The United States should take the lead in designing low-cost systems of this kind, and in creating the international political will needed to implement them quickly and widely.

ENHANCE COLLECTION AND ANALYSIS ON SMALL-SCALE OR IMPROVISED NBC PROGRAMS

The U.S. intelligence community is fully aware of the importance of detecting and acquiring detailed information on clandestine weapons of mass destruction programs run by states that may have hostile intentions. The record of success in this area is imperfect, but it is a vitally important mission that deserves the continued strong support of the U.S. government. There is, however, something of a gap with respect to the detection of small-scale or improvised programs, especially those conducted by non-state

---

28. Mikhad acquired the modified clock radio from his Hezbollah contact in Zurich. Where he acquired the C-4 is unknown or has not been revealed.

actors located in friendly states or in the United States itself. This gap results not from a judgment that the possibility of a small-scale NBC program presents no threat to the United States, but from the fact that the collection and analysis systems of the intelligence community were designed principally to target industrial-scale military NBC programs, particularly those in Soviet Union. These systems now need to be augmented and reoriented to detect smaller, lower-technology programs for weapons below the threshold of military utility but suitable for covert use.

One way to improve detection of small weapons-acquisition efforts is to expand and institutionalize the self-policing of commercial suppliers of dual-use equipment and materials. The sale of certain biological pathogens within the United States is now subject to modest regulation, and the recipients of these organisms are required to be centrally registered.[29] Chemical suppliers for laboratories and industry already exercise a certain amount of diligence about their customers, in many cases requiring new customers to provide information on their organizations. But much more could be done to encourage legitimate companies to gather and report information that might point to a clandestine NBC program. These steps would not require changing the rules that govern when and how U.S. citizens may be investigated by law enforcement agencies.

To improve its ability to detect small-scale clandestine weapons programs, the U.S. government should do three basic things in the broad area of industrial self-policing. The first is to study the proliferation pathways most likely to be used by non-state actors and states seeking only a limited, improvised NBC weapons capability, with the objective of providing clear guidance to all legitimate suppliers on the types of materials, equipment, and expertise that should arouse suspicion when sought for no apparent legitimate purpose. With respect to biological weapons, for example, manufacturers of aerosol generators should be asked to be cautious of customers interested in biological aerosolization, especially in certain particle size ranges.[30] Since the technical requirements for small-

---

29. For an overview of the new regulations, and of legislation aimed at preventing biological terrorism, see James R. Ferguson, "Biological Weapons and U.S. Law," *Journal of the American Medical Association (JAMA)*, Vol. 278, No. 5 (August 6, 1997), pp. 359–360.

30. The potential utility of commercial spray equipment for biological weapons use is illustrated by Iraq's acquisition of "several hundred modern Italian-made pesticide dispersal systems that were fitted with sprayer nozzles capable of generating aerosols of the 1–5 micron size optimal for biological warfare." Raymond

scale programs are different from those of large-scale military programs (see Box 6, Terrorist vs. Military Weapons, p. 100), this list of critical items is likely to have some significant differences from the lists that guide national export control laws and policy. Specialized production and processing equipment for bacteria might be worth watching, for example, even when it is too small to be useful in a military-scale program. Biological weapons acquisition is still possible without such high-performance equipment, but the indicator is still worth watching because would-be biological terrorists might try to follow the easier route of using commercial equipment optimized for the tasks at hand. Efforts to improve detection of low-technology proliferation programs depend on having a good understanding of the various possible acquisition pathways. If the necessary analysis of these pathways has not already been done by the intelligence community, it should be.

The second step is to distribute lists of critical items to all potential suppliers, and to ensure that these suppliers have strong incentives to notice and report suspicious purchases. For example, legitimate chemical suppliers should be asked to report inquiries about or purchases of particular combinations of chemical weapons precursor chemicals, as well as the purchase of certain key chemicals by people with no apparent technical reason to need them. With respect to exports, the reporting system should utilize the existing export control system, augmented where necessary by requiring additional declarations on sales of sensitive items below the normal quantity thresholds.[31] This self-policing system should be set up in consultation with existing regulatory agencies and the appropriate trade associations, which should also be engaged in its implementation. The United States should encourage other states to adopt similar measures, and to coordinate their efforts with the United States. To the extent possible, the enforcement of this reporting should remain voluntary, based on the normal commercial practice of exercising due diligence. However, if voluntary compliance appears ineffective, the reporting requirements should be

---

A. Zilinskas, "Iraq's Biological Weapons: The Past as Future?" *JAMA*, Vol. 278, No. 5 (August 6, 1997), p. 420.

31. For discussions of this issue, see Chapter 2, pp. 104–105; and American Bar Association (ABA) Standing Committee on Law and National Security, Task Force on Nonproliferation of Weapons of Mass Destruction, *Beyond CoCom — A Comparative Study of Export Controls: Germany, United Kingdom, France, Italy, and Japan and the European Union Export Control Regulation* (Washington, D.C.: ABA Standing Committee on Law and National Security, September 1994).

imposed in law or administrative regulation, possibly even by making companies liable under criminal or civil law for damage that results from their failure to exercise due diligence over the sale of items that directly contribute to a weapons program.[32]

Third, the U.S. government will need to establish a central point of contact to which companies can direct their reports of information that may point to a clandestine weapons program. This point of contact should be the new federal NBC Response Center affiliated with the Counterterrorist Center, proposed above. This center will need to be staffed with trained experts from both the intelligence and law enforcement communities, since the prohibition on domestic spying makes it necessary to handle purely domestic reports through law enforcement channels. The center should be prepared to receive and integrate information obtained from a variety of sources in order to perform real-time threat assessment, and should have the authority to call on additional information-gathering or operational response assets as needed.

Fourth, the United States and its international partners should actively encourage whistle blowers and defectors to come forward with information relating to covert nuclear, biological, and chemical weapons programs that they may be involved in or aware of. The United States currently has a standing offer to pay up to $500,000 in reward for information on espionage activities against the United States.[33] Similar awards, better advertised and in substantially greater sums, should be offered for information leading to the detection of clandestine weapons programs and threats involving weapons of mass destruction, and should be bolstered with the promise of protection and asylum if necessary.[34]

---

32. Jonathan Tucker makes a similar proposal in "Chemical/Biological Terrorism: Coping with a New Threat," *Politics and Life Sciences*, Vol. 15, No. 2 (September 1996), p. 180.

33. Title 18 of the U.S. Code, Section 3071, authorizes the attorney general to make payment of up to $500,000 to any person who provides information on espionage activity that leads to the arrest and conviction of a person committing an act of espionage against the United States, or conspiring or attempting to do so, or that leads to the prevention or frustration of an act of espionage against the United States. See <www.fbi.gov/ansir/ansir.htm>.

34. This idea is also suggested in Philip B. Heymann, *Terrorism and America: A Common Sense Strategy for a Democratic Society*, BCSIA Studies in International Security (Cambridge, Mass.: MIT Press, 1998).

Recommendation 6:
Enhance Epidemiological Surveillance

The president should direct the Centers for Disease Control to improve their existing systems of medical monitoring and epidemiological surveillance, in cooperation with the federal NBC Response Center, in ways that increase the speed and accuracy with which medical evidence of potential NBC weapons programs can be gathered and covert biological weapons attacks can be identified.

Congress should provide funding for these efforts, and for increased multinational efforts to improve the quality of epidemiological surveillance worldwide.

These initiatives would increase the ability of the U.S. government to detect small-scale clandestine weapons programs both abroad and at home. This would be a significant achievement, even if the resulting detection abilities remained far from perfect. Not only would it improve the chances of timely warning, it would also reduce aspiring proliferators' confidence in escaping detection, thus increasing the odds that they will opt against NBC acquisition and, if that fails, making their NBC acquisition efforts harder and more complex. Even if some routes to NBC acquisition remain open, closing off the easiest ones is still extremely important, since doing so raises the costs, risks, and visibility of clandestine weapons programs.

IMPROVE MEDICAL MONITORING AND EPIDEMIOLOGICAL SURVEILLANCE

Public health systems offer a separate a set of opportunities for the early detection of clandestine NBC programs and biological weapons attacks. To date, these opportunities have been largely ignored by the national security and intelligence agencies concerned with threats from weapon of mass destruction. Detection through medical monitoring relies on the fact that all weapons programs are vulnerable to accidents, particularly when conducted with minimal safety equipment by individuals with modest training. Accidents in a nuclear, biological, or chemical weapons program are likely to produce distinctive medical symptoms in exposed personnel, and possibly even in innocent bystanders. Examples of such medical indicators include cutaneous or respiratory anthrax, a disease that almost never affects humans in the United States, but that might result from a laboratory accident or weapon test involving anthrax; pneumonic plague, very rare in the United States, and a possible indicator of similar work with plague; radiation sickness; and organophosphorous nerve-agent poisoning, which ordinarily would appear only among workers exposed to certain pesticides. Any case of a disease or poisoning syndrome that matches the signature of exposure to NBC weapons should be treated as potential evidence of a clandestine NBC acquisition effort. This is one of the few sources of leverage available to the intelligence community. Detailed lists of suspicious symptoms should be widely distributed to medical personnel throughout the United States and abroad. Reporting requirements should be established within existing public health monitoring systems to ensure that information relating to possible NBC exposure is promptly conveyed to a central point of contact for analysis and investigation.

Medical monitoring is also important for early detection of biological attacks. As explained in Chapter 2, most biological weapons do not cause immediate ill effects, and can be invisible and odorless. Thus, unless the agent dispersal device is noticed, biological attacks could easily go unnoticed until the public health system detects a suspicious disease outbreak in a specific population. The symptoms of many biological warfare diseases initially resemble a bad cold or the flu, so the detection of a biological attack could easily take several days, by which time many victims might be beyond the reach of treatment. Early detection, however, increases the time available to treat victims, which should result in fewer casualties if an appropriate medical response can be mounted quickly (see Table 6, p. 155).[35]

The process of detecting and characterizing disease outbreaks is known as epidemiological surveillance. In the United States, responsibility for this task at the federal level lies with the Centers for Disease Control (CDC) in Atlanta, Georgia, and at local levels with state and local health

---

35. If advance warning of a biological attack is available, simple preventive measures could substantially reduce its impact. The equipment and materials for individual protection against known biological threats can be quite inexpensive: most important are snug filter masks and rudimentary decontamination capabilities, such as sodium hypochlorite solution (bleach), and soap and water. Masks, however, will prevent exposure to a biological aerosol only if worn, making them ineffective in the absence of warning. See Karl Lowe, Graham Pearson, and Victor Utgoff, *Potential Values of a Simple BW Protective Mask*, IDA Paper P-3077 (Washington, D.C.: Institute for Defense Analyses, September 1995); and David R. Franz, "Physical and Medical Countermeasures to Biological Weapons," in Kathleen C. Bailey, ed., *Director's Series on Proliferation*, No. 4 (Livermore, Calif.: Lawrence Livermore National Laboratory, 1994), pp. 55–65.

departments.[36] An essential component of all effective national and global public health systems, epidemiological surveillance focuses mainly on naturally occurring infectious diseases. It is an exceptionally cost-effective public policy instrument, saving annually tens if not hundreds of thousands of lives, and literally billions of dollars in medical costs and lost productivity due to illness. The expertise and infrastructure needed to detect and characterize natural outbreaks is virtually identical to that required to detect deliberately caused outbreaks.[37] The existing systems of epidemiological surveillance should, therefore, be used to accelerate the detection of covert biological weapons attacks, and should be augmented and refined in a variety of ways to help achieve this objective. This potential partnership between the national security and public health communities should be supported by both sides, since both stand to gain.[38] In particular, American and global epidemiological surveillance capabilities, which were allowed to decline in the 1980s, now require significant reinvestment to cope with new infectious diseases (such as Ebola, AIDS, Lyme disease, Legionnaires' disease, and hantavirus), the massive resurgence of familiar diseases (such as cholera, malaria, yellow fever, diphtheria, and tuberculosis), and increasing bacterial resistance to antibiotics. According to a White House study: "Our earlier successes in controlling infections have bred complacency. Consequently, the component of the public health system that protects the public from infectious microbes has been neglected,

---

36. The CDC is an agency of the U.S. Department of Health and Human Services. See <www.cdc.gov>.

37. See Peter Barss, "Epidemic Field Investigation as Applied to Allegations of Chemical, Biological, or Toxin Warfare," *Politics and the Life Sciences*, Vol. 11, No. 1 (February 1992), pp. 5–22; Mark L. Wheelis, "The Role of Epidemiology in Strengthening the Biological Weapons Convention," in Erhard Geissler and Robert H. Haynes, eds., *Prevention of a Biological and Toxin Arms Race and the Responsibility of Scientists* (Berlin: Akademie Verlag, 1991), pp. 277–283; and John P. Woodall, "Review of WHO Health and Epidemic Information as a Basis for Verification Activities Under the Biological Weapons Convention," in J.S. Lundin, ed., *Views on Possible Verification Measures for the Biological Weapons Convention* (London: Oxford University Press, 1991), pp. 59–70.

38. See Stephen S. Morse, "Epidemiological Surveillance for Investigating Chemical or Biological Warfare and for Improving Human Health," *Politics and the Life Sciences*, Vol. 11, No. 1 (February 1992), pp. 28–29; and Mark L. Wheelis, "Strengthening Biological Weapons Control through Global Epidemiological Surveillance," *Politics and the Life Sciences*, Vol. 11, No. 2 (August 1992), p. 183.

both here and abroad, and its focus has narrowed."[39] To date, however, there has been only moderate political support for increasing U.S. epidemiological surveillance budgets, and almost none for increased support of international organizations like the World Health Organization. With the active support of the national security community, it may be possible to ease the budget constraints faced by epidemiological surveillance programs.

The United States has a reasonably effective system of epidemiological surveillance, which is maintained by the CDC in cooperation with the Council of State and Territorial Epidemiologists.[40] Improving the speed and accuracy with which this system can detect domestic biological attack is, therefore, primarily a task of making it work faster and better, though a few specific improvements would increase its capacity to cope with man-made disease outbreaks.[41] First, medical practitioners should be better educated to recognize the symptoms of likely biological warfare diseases, and must be required by law to report all cases to the CDC immediately. Major medical centers and hospitals should also be required to maintain a supply of portable medical test kits for key biological warfare agents to speed disease identification. Second, the CDC and other public health centers that receive epidemiological intelligence should bolster their capacity to carry out the testing and analysis needed for very rapid determinations of the

---

39. National Science and Technology Council, Committee on International Science, Engineering, and Technology (CISET), Working Group on Emerging and Re-emerging Infectious Diseases, *Global Microbial Threats in the 1990s* (Washington, D.C.: The White House, 1996), p. 2. This document is available at <www.whitehouse.gov/WH/EOP/OSTP/CISET/html/ciset.html>.

40. The CDC maintains an annually updated list of about 50 "notifiable diseases," which are defined as diseases "for which regular, frequent, and timely information regarding individual cases is considered necessary for the prevention and control of the disease." Medical personnel, doctors, and public health officials are required by state law and various medical regulations to report incidents of notifiable diseases. See Centers for Disease Control, Epidemiology Program Office, *Summary of National Notifiable Diseases, United States, 1995*; available at <www.cdc.gov/epo>. Anthrax is on the 1995 list, but numerous other biological warfare diseases are not.

41. See Wheelis, "Strengthening Biological Weapons Control," pp. 179–189; Wheelis, "The Role of Epidemiology in Strengthening the Biological Weapons Convention,"; and Woodall, "Review of WHO Health and Epidemic Information as a Basis for Verification Activities Under the Biological Weapons Convention."

nature and possible extent of emerging disease outbreaks.[42] Their initial judgments must be quickly conveyed to the federal interagency NBC Response Center, where the information can be integrated with intelligence from other sources. In situations of heightened risk but before an attack has been conclusively identified, the existing system of public health alerts should be used to highlight particular symptoms that medical personnel should watch for, and to increase the monitoring of patients with weakened immune systems, who will generally become symptomatic before healthy patients.[43] Third, the CDC should enhance the ability of its Epidemic Intelligence Service (EIS), a rapid-response investigative unit, to diagnose and respond to possible biological weapons attacks.[44]

The quality of epidemiological surveillance in much of the developing world is substantially below that in the United States. Since microbes do not recognize national borders, and the Third World is a reservoir for many lethal diseases, effective epidemiological surveillance must be global in scope. Likewise, biological weapons attacks or production accidents can occur anywhere in the world, and the United States has an interest in knowing about all of them. Therefore, the U.S. government should increase its investment not only in its own public health infrastructure, but also in

---

42. For a detailed set of recommendations on how this should be done, see National Science and Technology Council, *Global Microbial Threats in the 1990s*, Section VI.

43. The CDC or other agencies should also have the capacity to deploy real-time biological weapons sensors when they become available. These sensors are currently under development by the Department of Defense.

44. The Epidemic Intelligence Service was originally established in 1951, during the Korean War, to deal with biological warfare threats. It has since evolved to focus on naturally occurring disease outbreaks, and has not played a major role in the investigations of allegations of chemical, biological, or toxin weapons use, such as the "Yellow Rain" controversy or the Gulf War syndrome. On the EIS, see Alexander D. Langmuir, "The Potentialities of Biological Warfare Against Man: An Epidemiological Approach," *Public Health Reports*, Vol. 66 (1951), pp. 387–399; Alexander D. Langmuir and J.M. Andrews, "Biological Warfare Defense: 2. The Epidemic Intelligence Services of the Communicable Disease Center," *American Journal of Public Health*, Vol. 42 (1952), pp. 235–238; Alexander D. Langmuir, "The Epidemic Intelligence Service of the Centers for Disease Control," *Public Health Reports*, Vol. 95 (1980), pp. 470–477; Fitzhugh Mullan, *Plagues and Politics: The Story of the United States Public Health Service* (New York: Basic Books, 1989), pp. 139–140; and Barss, "Epidemic Field Investigation," p. 15.

Recommendation 7:
Improve Capability for Post-attack Attribution

A new executive order should rescind the decision that major acts of terrorism involving NBC weapons, directed against U.S. military forces, or potentially involving foreign powers, will always be investigated under FBI leadership. The lead agency should be chosen based on the circumstances of the particular case, and other appropriate agencies should be tasked to assist as needed.

To improve the chances of timely and accurate post-attack attribution, the U.S. government should improve its technical infrastructure for nuclear, biological, and chemical forensics at the FBI Laboratory, the national laboratories, and the U.S. Army Medical Research Institute for Infectious Diseases (USAMRIID).

Working through the Centers for Disease Control and the U.S. Agency·for International Development (USAID), the U.S. government should initiative a systematic, worldwide effort to produce a comprehensive genetic map of human pathogen strains.

---

that which monitors the global appearance and spread of infectious diseases.

It is worth noting that the utility of an epidemiological surveillance system in reducing a society's vulnerability to biological weapons attack depends on the medical system's ability to mount an effective medical response without advance warning. As discussed below, medical response to a biological weapons attack requires an adequate supply of appropriate medicines, trained personnel to deliver them, and a high-readiness mobilization system. While the U.S. medical system has a very high general level of capability, important gaps exist in stocks of key equipment and supplies needed to care for large numbers of biological casualties. This situation should be remedied by government action, and can be remedied at reasonable cost.

POST-ATTACK ATTRIBUTION

Finally, the United States needs improved forensic capabilities to help determine who is responsible for anonymous nuclear, biological, and chemical weapons incidents. A state or non-state actor which has carried out one NBC attack may be able to carry out more, making the identification and neutralization of unknown NBC attackers imperative.

Moreover, public opinion is likely to demand retribution for a mass-casualty terrorist incident, and a consistent record of forceful retaliation against previous attackers is necessary to deter future ones. Indeed, the *perception* that the United States (or the international community) has excellent NBC forensic capabilities is critically important for deterrence, since it will tend to erode the confidence of potential NBC aggressors in their ability to escape reprisal by remaining anonymous.

In the absence of conclusive evidence, the attribution of responsibility for an NBC attack to a particular state or non-state actor is likely to be a political decision made at high levels, since the potential consequences of retaliation are serious. To inform any such post-attack attribution decisions, a state needs both professional investigators and technical experts with specialized knowledge of the materials and equipment used in weapons of mass destruction. While the U.S. government's conventional investigative capabilities are very good, its organization and technical infrastructure for attributing covert or terrorist NBC attacks to a specific actor are less well developed.

According to PDD-39, the FBI has lead responsibility for investigating acts of terrorism where U.S. law is involved. This organizational arrangement is appropriate for investigating acts of conventional domestic terrorism, such as the Oklahoma City bombing, which are properly construed as law enforcement matters. The FBI's ability to conduct investigations of this kind is unparalleled in the United States. But it is less clear that the FBI is the appropriate lead federal agency for conducting investigations of terrorist acts that may have been committed by foreign powers (states or non-state actors), or that involved unconventional weaponry. The investigation of the bombing of the Khobar Towers in Saudi Arabia, for instance, has been conducted not by the Departments of State or Defense or the intelligence community, but by the FBI, which has no particular understanding of Saudi society or the geopolitics of the Persian Gulf.[45] Thus the apolitical FBI was inserted into the delicate U.S.-Saudi relationship, on which the U.S. military presence in the Gulf largely depends. The FBI was in effect given responsibility for making a determination that could have serious national security implications, since a finding that Iran was behind the bombing could lead to war. This

---

45. This is a change from the past. After the bombing of Pan Am Flight 103 over Lockerbie, Scotland, which may have been state-sponsored, the U.S. interagency investigation was led by the Department of State, with the Department of Justice and the FBI in supporting roles.

situation would almost certainly become untenable if the attack being investigated had killed not nineteen U.S. soldiers, but hundreds or thousands. The FBI is quite effective in the black-and-white world of domestic law enforcement, but national security consists mainly of shades of gray. Because attacks with international overtones may have a variety of vital military, diplomatic, and intelligence implications, the president should reconsider the decision always to put the FBI in charge. Instead, the lead agency should be chosen on a case-by-case basis, and agencies not in the lead, including in some cases the FBI, should assist as required.

The U.S. technical infrastructure for conducting forensic investigations into NBC incidents is also limited. These weaknesses are least acute with respect to nuclear weapons and materials, where the U.S. national laboratories, particularly Los Alamos and Lawrence Livermore, possess extraordinary analytical capabilities, as well as some ability to recover evidence from the field (mainly through the Nuclear Emergency Search Team). But there are few comparable resources for chemical or biological weapons. The U.S. Army's Technical Escort Unit (TEU) is trained and equipped to disable and transport chemical and biological munitions (including improvised ones), but is not an evidence recovery team. The CDC and the U.S. Army Medical Research Institute for Infectious Diseases (USAMRIID) are two of the world's leading centers for analyzing infectious diseases. Both are able to conduct field epidemiological studies, but the field operations of both have been directed against natural disease outbreaks, not those caused by deliberate human action. The FBI Laboratory is the nation's leading institution for criminal forensics, but historically it has not been a major center for expertise on weapons of mass destruction. After being strongly criticized for mismanagement and lax scientific standards,[46] the FBI Laboratory is now being substantially upgraded, and is moving to a new $130 million facility at the FBI Academy in Quantico, Virginia. According to the FBI, a major focus of the renewed laboratory will be hazardous materials, including nuclear, biological, and chemical weapons and materials. A new Hazardous Materials Response Unit, specially trained in NBC evidence recovery, was established by the FBI in 1996. Although the FBI is not starting from a position of great expertise in these matters, its apparent institutional commitment is a promising sign, as was the appointment of Donald Kerr, a nuclear-weapons scientist, as director of the

---

46. See David Johnston, "Conducting One Inquiry, The Subject of Another: U.S. Lab Toils Amid Pressure from All Sides," *New York Times*, August 3, 1996, p. 24.

FBI Laboratory in October 1997.[47] With these new capabilities, the FBI will have the necessary capacity to collect and analyze many kinds of evidence relevant to covert NBC attacks, should they occur.

Perhaps the most important aspect of preparing for the forensic analysis of any future NBC incident is to gather and catalog in advance samples of as many different nuclear, biological, and chemical materials as possible. With nuclear materials, it is sometimes possible to determine the age and geographic origin of the material through isotopic and chemical analysis.[48] This will generally require some knowledge of the different nuclear material production and handling practices of different countries, and even of individual facilities within countries, at different times. Intelligence on these matters could and should be improved, but it is already surprisingly good, as demonstrated by Germany's ability to pinpoint the origins of several nuclear material caches that were stolen in the former Soviet Union and recovered.[49] Far less, however, is known about the chemical fingerprints of chemical weapons precursor materials and the genetic and other biological fingerprints of biological warfare agents. Chemical agents carry trace impurities that may make it possible to learn

---

47. Donald Kerr is the former director of Los Alamos National Laboratory, and a long-time employee of the Department of Energy, with extensive experience in weapons of mass destruction issues. According to Louis Freeh, Kerr's "background will be invaluable as the FBI carries out its priority efforts to prevent terrorists from using nuclear, biological, or chemical weapons in the United States." Louis J. Freeh, "Statement at News Conference on Appointment of New Director of FBI Laboratory," Washington, D.C., October 21, 1997; the document is available at <www.fbi.gov/pressrel/lab/introker.htm>.

48. A discussion of the related problem of retrospective determination of reactor operating history and of uranium enrichment activities can be found in Steve Fetter, "Nuclear Archeology: Verifying Declarations of Fissile Material Production," *Science and Global Security*, Vol. 3, Nos. 3–4 (1993), pp. 237–259.

49. For instance, it is now known that the 383 grams of plutonium seized by German police in Munich on a Lufthansa flight from Moscow in August 1994 had been stolen from the Obninsk nuclear research facilities outside of Moscow. Initial analysis of the plutonium done by the Europeans indicated the material probably came from Obninsk. The Russian government was able to confirm this suspicion after it was supplied with a sample of the material, though Moscow's public posture on the matter remains ambiguous. See Mark Hibbs, "Primakov Confirms to Germany: Munich Plutonium from Obninsk," *Nucleonics Week*, Vol. 37, No. 7 (February 15, 1996), p. 1.

certain details of the process by which they were produced, and perhaps about the origin of the precursor chemicals used.[50] With respect to biological agents, the natural process of mutation within the pathogen means that specific strains of the agent tend to be associated with specific times and geographic areas.[51] At present, with little knowledge of the necessary data, investigators are more likely to miss or misinterpret important clues. Information on the geographic distribution of disease strains can only be gathered through extensive sampling and analysis, but if it were available it would provide valuable clues to determining the origin of agents causing suspicious disease outbreaks. It should therefore be gathered on a systematic, global basis as part of a U.S.-led program to improve the quality of worldwide epidemiological surveillance. Indeed, the public health benefits of a comprehensive genetic map of human pathogens are likely to be substantially larger than the biological-defense benefits.

Finally, the NBC forensic capabilities of the U.S. government should be kept secret, especially as they are being enhanced. As a matter of policy, the government should subtly exaggerate its true capabilities, with the objective of strengthening deterrence by making potential attackers feel less confidence in their ability to escape attribution and thus retribution.

Operational Preparedness for Crisis and Consequence Management

Operational preparedness refers to a society's capacity to manage NBC crises while they are in progress, and to mitigate the consequences of attacks that occur. Dozens of federal, state, and local agencies possess capabilities that could become involved in an operational response to a covert attack with NBC weapons. With a few exceptions, however, these capabilities are not robust enough to be very effective once NBC weapons have been used. Moreover, these capabilities are generally not knitted together as well as they should be. As a result, a covert NBC attack against an American target could easily overwhelm response capabilities, resulting

---

50. It is theoretically possible to make chemical signatures easier to analyze by adding "taggants" — trace chemicals intended to provide detectable evidence of the source — to potential precursor materials. U.S. law requires chemical taggants to be added to plastic explosives sold in the United States, but cost and technical barriers appear to make similar measures for precursor chemicals infeasible.

51. Wheelis, "Strengthening Biological Weapons Control," p. 181.

in unnecessary casualties and more severe political repercussions over the long term.

The United States should aim for a substantially higher level of domestic operational preparedness against NBC contingencies. In an ideal world, the entire U.S. first-responder community — the police officers, firefighters, paramedics, and other public servants who are on duty at all times and in most populated areas — should have enough training to recognize the possible signs of an NBC threat, and should have immediate access to a single point of contact at the federal level (e.g., to the NBC Response Center we propose). This national center should be able to assess the available information quickly, determine whether the incident is serious, and advise the on-scene first responders of the prudent course of action. Specific units from the immediate first-responder community with more advanced training and some specialized equipment would assume operational command, endeavoring to prevent the NBC attack if possible or, should it occur, to preserve themselves, contain the situation, and prepare to limit its consequences. Based on a quick decision at the national level, designated units from a wide range of state and federal agencies — up to and including the active military — would be mobilized according to the appropriateness of their capabilities, their readiness, and their proximity to the scene. These reinforcements would integrate quickly with local operators according to joint operational plans that would have become familiar through realistic training exercises. Specially trained national experts would communicate with the media, providing information to maximize public safety and minimize the risk of mass panic.

There is infinite variation and complexity in how an NBC crisis could progress, but it is clear that U.S. response capabilities are deficient in each of the discrete steps just described. Four particular weaknesses deserve urgent attention. First, the community of first responders across the United States is almost totally unprepared to cope with the operational demands of an attack involving a weapon of mass destruction. Second, the specialized resources that the federal government can quickly mobilize in response to a covert NBC attack are inadequate in number, geographic dispersal, and level of capability. Third, because domestic NBC preparedness is not a core mission of the Department of Defense, the bulk of the nation's specialized capabilities for dealing with NBC incidents are not optimized for missions at home, and there is little impetus from the most powerful national security agency for improvements in domestic preparedness. And fourth, the existing U.S. plans for integrating the response capabilities of local, state, and federal agencies during the course

---

Recommendation 8:
Build State and Local Capabilities

The Nunn-Lugar-Domenici domestic preparedness program should be made a permanent program in the Department of Defense, with its budget increased to at least $500 million per year.

The National Guard should be made responsible for the day-to-day implementation of the Defense Department's programs for improving NBC preparedness at the state and local level.

Each adjutant general of the National Guard should be held accountable for the level of operational preparedness of cities and counties in his or her state. Preparedness levels should be subject to regular review by national inspection teams.

All state and local response personnel (police, fire, emergency medical, inspectors) should receive basic NBC awareness training, initially as part of a federally sponsored remedial training program, and later as an integral part of their professional education.

Specialized first-responder units (HAZMAT, bomb squad, SWAT teams, and local emergency managers) should receive more intensive training in NBC crisis and consequence management, and should be provided with necessary equipment by the federal government.

Funds from the expanded Nunn-Lugar-Domenici program should be used to expand the existing Metro Medical Strike Teams (MMST) in the 100 largest U.S. cities.

A system of stockpiles of medicines and medical equipment for treating biological and chemical weapons casualties should be established to eliminate existing shortfalls.

---

of an NBC incident are unreliable because they are not supported by a sufficient national program of field exercises. Addressing these four weaknesses in U.S. operational preparedness would significantly improve the ability of the United States to respond to a covert NBC attack.

ENHANCE LOCAL AND STATE AGENCY PREPAREDNESS

The immediate community of first responders in a given city or region consists of its police force, its fire departments, and its emergency medical personnel (mobile as well as those in hospitals). It is they who are most likely to be the first at the scene of a domestic NBC incident. In most major cities, this initial response can usually be augmented in an hour or less by additional units with more specialized capabilities, such as the fire department's hazardous materials (HAZMAT) teams, the police department's bomb squads and special weapons and tactics (SWAT) teams, and public health and disaster relief workers from the city, county, state, and possibly even federal governments. With time, more specialized capabilities — including those from the Army, the Marine Corps, and the National Guard — can be brought into the area by the state and federal governments. But, in a real incident, the first responders will generally have to manage on their own during the critically important first hours of the crisis. They are currently unprepared for this task.

The greatest opportunities to limit the damage of covert NBC attacks, or prevent them entirely, exist during the first phases of the incident. It is important, therefore, that police and fire departments, disaster management agencies, and emergency medical personnel be trained to identify the signs of potential or actual incidents, and to react appropriately once the weapon type has been characterized. With nuclear weapons, the opportunity to limit damage largely disappears when the weapon is detonated. With chemical weapons, the opportunity can last for hours. With biological weapons, in contrast, the opportunity to save lives through medical treatment can last for days or even weeks. In general, with no-warning chemical and biological weapons attacks, non-specialist emergency and medical personnel would bear primary responsibility for identifying the nature of the incident, for treating the initial wave of casualties, and for implementing the first stage of any large-scale emergency response plan. Because of this, the United States should work hardest to improve state and local preparedness for biological and chemical disaster response.

Local first responders in almost all U.S. jurisdictions presently lack the protective equipment, decontamination capacity, medical supplies, and training needed to mount an effective, immediate operational response to a chemical attack. An effective response to a chemical weapons attack will require a local rapid response unit equipped with personal protective equipment, with chemical agent detection devices, with decontamination facilities for victims and for emergency personnel, and with pharmaceuticals for treating chemical agent exposure. This unit will also need training to use the equipment properly, and will need to be organized so that people and equipment can be brought to the site of an emergency in a fast, efficient manner. Hospitals will need to be able to ensure that they do not become contaminated by walk-in patients. Supplies of atropine and other nerve-gas antidotes will be necessary. Almost all of these capabilities and resources are missing or inadequate in almost all American cities.

If a biological attack is the cause of a disease outbreak, that fact may go unrecognized by the public health system for days after the agent is first released. A suspicious pattern will probably be recognized only when large numbers of patients begin to show symptoms. Awareness training for police and fire personnel, teaching them to be suspicious of unexplained machines generating fogs or smokes, could improve the chance that an official at the scene would recognize a possible agent release, but this form of detection would still be unlikely. Even after being detected, the outbreak could easily overwhelm local medical systems. When an attack is detected, the ability of the public health system to determine where and when it occurred, and to find the victims and bring them in for treatment, would heavily influence the death rate from most lethal biological agents.[52] Immediate access to adequate stocks of medicines and vaccines will be essential to an effective medical response. Supplies of these essential medicines should be monitored by the federal NBC Response Center to ensure that regional and national stocks are sufficient to respond to a major biological weapons incident.

Of course, one cannot expect all potential first responders in the United States to have a deep understanding of nuclear, biological, and chemical weapons. But the United States should establish a system of layered capabilities to respond to domestic NBC attacks. As the first layer, emergency and medical officials at the federal, state, and local levels should have a basic awareness of the potential for domestic acts of NBC terrorism, should be trained to be attentive to suspicious activity or equipment suggesting a possible NBC threat, and should know exactly whom to contact for more expert advice and assistance.[53] This awareness training should become an integral component of the professional education of all

---

52. The cost, difficulty, and effectiveness of medical treatment for victims exposed to biological warfare agents depend heavily on early detection and timely action. Victims of many of the more easily available agents (presumably those most likely to be used in a covert attack) can be treated effectively with standard pharmaceuticals. Early treatment can prevent many victims exposed to bacteria or botulism toxin from becoming sick, and can sharply reduce the fatalities from an attack. See Chapter 2, pp. 151–155 (especially Table 6). Note, however, that the illnesses caused by some agents, including viral agents, certain toxins, and possibly genetically manipulated bacteria, could be partially or completely untreatable.

53. Furthermore, if a low-cost individual protective mask or hood can be developed, this too should be made available to as many first-responder personnel as possible.

law enforcement, fire, and emergency medical personnel, Customs agents, and environmental, health, and safety inspectors. The federal government should provide course materials, expert instructors, and distance-learning opportunities to all relevant training institutions.

The second layer of defense against a domestic NBC weapons incident should be provided by the specialized response units that already exist in most major cities — the HAZMAT teams of the fire department, the police department's bomb squads and SWAT teams, and the emergency management officials of the city or state. These units can generally arrive at the scene of an incident in less than an hour, sometimes even in a matter of minutes. It is reasonable to expect personnel from these units to have a relatively detailed knowledge of possible NBC threats. With federal assistance, all such teams should be trained to respond appropriately to NBC incidents, including how to work as part of an operation under federal command. They should be able to use, and have ready access to, the basic equipment needed to make an effective first response to a domestic biological or chemical incident, including portable detection equipment and sensors, individual and group protective gear, and some decontamination capability. Bomb squads should receive basic training and equipment for rendering chemical and biological weapons safe. Establishing this level of capability will be more expensive than creating broad-based NBC awareness, since it will involve more intensive and specialized training, as well as the provision of necessary equipment.

The third layer of domestic defense against NBC attack should be provided by a new system of specialized local medical response units capable of organizing an effective operational response to a large-scale chemical or biological weapons attack. The Public Health Service has already created units of this kind, called Metro Medical Strike Teams, in Washington, D.C., and Atlanta, and seeks to establish them in the nation's 100 largest cities by the year 2003. The Metro Medical Strike Teams draw their personnel from local emergency agencies, and provide them with the training they need to respond to chemical and biological attacks. Each team is tailored to the unique circumstances of the city in which it is located, integrated into its emergency response system, and given supplies of appropriate protective equipment, pharmaceuticals, communication systems, and decontamination gear.[54] Their purpose is to provide large

---

54. For a description of the Metropolitan Medical Strike Team concept, see testimony of Admiral Frank Young, U.S. Public Health Service, in U.S. Congress, *Global Proliferation of Weapons of Mass Destruction*, Part I, Hearings before the

population centers with a chemical and biological consequence management capability that can be made available in 30–60 minutes — a critical need in the nation's overall defense against weapons of mass destruction. The Nunn-Lugar-Domenici amendment allocated $6.6 million from the defense budget in fiscal year 1997 to assist the Public Health Service in establishing a planned first set of twenty-seven Metro Medical Strike Teams, but the Clinton administration requested no additional funding for this activity in its fiscal year 1998 budget request.[55] This program should be fully funded under an expanded Nunn-Lugar-Domenici account within the Department of Defense.

In 1997, the federal government began to provide basic biological and chemical awareness training to some state and local first responders under the Nunn-Lugar-Domenici program, but this effort will have little long-term impact unless the level of resources devoted to it is increased and the program is established as a permanent, high-priority mission of the Department of Defense. The Army's Chemical and Biological Defense Command (CBDCOM) is in charge of the training program. The CBDCOM program has suffered from three key problems in its design and implementation. First, it was designed primarily to provide "train-the-trainer" instruction at the local level, but so far the training provided to these would-be trainers is insufficient for them to train others. Second, the program does not provide the equipment and supplies necessary to assemble a working response capability. And third, it has not succeeded in establishing a coherent model for how local emergency responders should work together under the unique stresses of a chemical or biological incident. Instead, it allows the interagency politics of the local areas' emergency response systems to dictate allocations of roles and responsibilities, even where these conflict with operational needs created by the realities of biological and chemical weapons effects. Unless the funding base of this program is significantly increased, and the Department of Defense begins to take its implementation seriously, the Nunn-Lugar-Domenici program

---

Permanent Subcommittee on Investigations of the Committee on Governmental Affairs, U.S. Senate, 104th Cong., 2nd Sess. (Washington, D.C.: U.S. GPO, 1996), pp. 248–254.

55. "DoD intends to provide no funding to support these DHHS teams beyond FY 1997." Department of Defense, *Report to Congress: Domestic Preparedness Program in the Defense against Weapons of Mass Destruction* (Washington, D.C.: U.S. Department of Defense, May 1, 1997), pp. 18–19.

will not make significant progress in enhancing local biological and chemical preparedness.

In sum, any comprehensive attempt to improve overall U.S. preparedness against covert biological and chemical attacks will involve a highly unusual federal program to train and equip personnel in the state and local first-responder community. The federal government cannot issue an unfunded mandate to state and local agencies requiring them to prepare for biological and chemical incidents. Instead, the federal government can and should offer the resources and direction necessary to ensure that all regions of the country have some capacity to respond to biological and chemical incidents. Because of the Nunn-Lugar-Domenici amendment, some progress has already begun to be made in this direction, but the reluctance of many in Congress and the administration to sustain the effort and to fill the many gaps that remain suggests that these initial efforts are likely to have only a minor impact. The Nunn-Lugar-Domenici domestic preparedness program should be permanently established within the Department of Defense, and its resources increased by at least an order of magnitude, from about $50 million to $500 million. To develop a more regular and firmly institutionalized relationship between the federal government and the relevant responder groups at the state and local level, the National Guard should be given principal responsibility for organizing and implementing the necessary program of state and local capability enhancements for biological and chemical defense, and individual Guard commanders should be held accountable for preparedness deficiencies in their regions (for reasons we explain below).

INCREASE THE BREADTH AND DEPTH OF SPECIALIZED FEDERAL RESOURCES
Federal agencies have unique capabilities for responding to NBC incidents that cannot be duplicated at the local level. When they can be brought to bear in a timely fashion, these federal resources can make the difference between success and failure in NBC crisis-management and consequence-management contingencies. The federal government also has special responsibilities for dealing with acts of domestic and international terrorism, as well as for incidents involving weapons of mass destruction. According to PDD-39, the FBI is the lead federal agency for domestic NBC crisis management, while FEMA is the lead federal agency for domestic NBC consequence management.[56] In an NBC incident, these lead agencies

---

56. See "Unclassified FEMA Abstract on PDD-39," in U.S. Congress, *Global Proliferation of Weapons of Mass Destruction*, Part III, pp. 151–154.

Recommendation 9:
Enhance Specialized Federal Response Resources

The FBI should continue to develop its Critical Incident Response Group of special agents trained for NBC crises, as well as its Hazardous Materials Response Unit.

U.S. Special Forces should continue to develop operational techniques and technologies for resolving NBC crises.

The Department of Energy should continue to support the Nuclear Emergency Search Team, and should increase its funding of advanced wide-area search technologies and weapons disablement techniques.

The Department of Defense should exempt the Army's Technical Escort Unit, the Marine Corps' Chemical and Biological Incident Response Force, and the U.S. Army Medical Research Institute for Infectious Diseases from further across-the-board budget cuts, and the resources devoted to these functions should be increased.

The Federal Emergency Management Agency (FEMA) should expand and accelerate its program of field exercises for managing the consequences of NBC attacks.

The federal government should continue to fund the research and development of technologies suitable for reducing domestic vulnerability to covert NBC threats through the Technical Support Working Group.

would have the authority to draw from the full range of federal government resources, including an array of elite units and specialized capabilities relevant for solving unique NBC-related problems.[57] Although these federal capabilities form a strong foundation on which to build a response capacity, the existing resources are inadequate in several respects.

First, the federal government does not have a single, well-advertised point of contact for officials who have acquired information indicating a possible NBC threat or incident.[58] Under the current system, reporting

---

57. Emergency management capabilities at the state level are also, for the most part, integrated into federal disaster response plans.

58. Current Department of Defense plans under the Nunn-Lugar-Domenici program call for the creation of a "hot line" for state and local officials to seek information and expert advice on NBC crises, but this service was not yet operational in 1997. Furthermore, it is not clear that the hot line will provide access to all federal resources relevant to mounting an effective response to an NBC incident, nor is it clear which agency will maintain the service after the Department

procedures vary from agency to agency and weapon type to weapon type, and depend heavily on the first responders' initial assumptions about the nature of the incident. Given the critical importance of time in an unfolding NBC incident, it is vital that potential indicators of an NBC threat be reported immediately to the 24-hour federal NBC Response Center, proposed above, which could provide real-time expert threat assessment and prompt advice to on-scene personnel. The existence and purpose of this center should be emphasized in the basic NBC awareness training that all first responders should receive. The experts at this center would also be responsible for mobilizing appropriate resources according to established response plans.

The proposed NBC Response Center could call on a variety of federal resources, including a number of elite units with specialized capabilities relevant to the management of an NBC crisis.[59] For example, the FBI, after a run of embarrassing exercises and Congressional criticism, established a Critical Incident Response Group, consisting of special agents trained in the management of NBC and other major crises, and is significantly enhancing its ability to investigate and analyze forensic evidence from NBC incidents.[60] U.S. Special Forces can provide teams that are trained and equipped to defeat specific terrorist threats, including those that involve weapons of mass destruction.[61] The Department of Energy's Nuclear Emergency Search Team (NEST) has specialized instruments and expertise for detecting nuclear weapons, determining their design features, and

---

of Defense transfers the Nunn-Lugar-Domenici program to FEMA or some other agency in fiscal year 1999.

59. For a survey of these capabilities, see Department of Defense and Department of Energy, *Joint Report to Congress: Preparedness and Response to a Nuclear, Radiological, Biological, or Chemical Terrorist Attack* (Washington, D.C.: U.S. Department of Defense and U.S. Department of Energy, April 18, 1996).

60. After the Oklahoma City bombing, Congress increased the FBI's budget by $77.1 million in 1995, $158.8 million in 1996, and $133.9 million in 1997. These funds have been used for a variety of purposes, but among them has been the enhancement of the FBI's internal capabilities for investigating and responding to nuclear, biological, and chemical weapons incidents. See Louis J. Freeh, "Counter-terrorism," Statement before the Senate Appropriations Committee, U.S. Senate, May 13, 1997, available at <www.fbi.gov/congress/counter/terror.htm>.

61. William S. Cohen, *Annual Report to the President and the Congress* (Washington, D.C.: U.S. Department of Defense, April 1997), p. 195.

disarming or disabling them, as well as for modeling the weapons effects and fallout patterns likely to result if a weapon detonates.[62] The Technical Escort Unit (TEU), an Army unit specializing in chemical weapons transport and emergencies, has two high-readiness teams that are trained to disable chemical and biological weapons, and that possess equipment for individual protection, agent detection and identification, and decontamination.[63] The Marine Corps' Chemical and Biological Incident Response Force (CBIRF) is trained and equipped to operate in environments that have been contaminated by chemical and biological weapons, and to provide medical care to up to a few hundred victims.[64] But because there are only a few teams with these capabilities, stationed in only a handful of locations around the country, there will be substantial delays before they can respond to a surprise attack like the Tokyo subway attack; this means that the critical first phase of any response will still have to be carried out by non-specialist local responders. These capabilities can, however, be pre-deployed to high-risk events and locations to good effect, as was done during the 1996 Atlanta Olympics and the June 1997 Denver G-8 meeting.[65]

Second, the U.S. emergency medical system has only the most limited ability to cope with the effects of large-scale biological or chemical weapons attacks. There is no strong U.S. system for rapidly detecting and characterizing the deliberate (or accidental) release of biological warfare agents, and reliable real-time biological weapons sensors do not yet exist.

---

62. On NEST, see Mahlon E. Gates, "The Nuclear Emergency Search Team," in Paul Leventhal and Yonah Alexander, eds., *Preventing Nuclear Terrorism* (Lexington, Mass.: Lexington Books, 1987), pp. 397–402; and "Secretive Unit Awaits Call to Battle Nuclear Terrorism," *San Diego Union-Tribune*, December 12, 1993, p. A1.

63. Total strength of the unit is about 150 personnel. Technical Escort Unit briefing slides, "Technical Escort Unit: Command Brief," 1996; and *U.S. Army Technical Escort Unit: First On Scene*, fact sheet, no date, distributed by the Technical Escort Unit.

64. The CBIRF includes a rapid response force with 120 personnel, able to deploy on four hours notice. This force includes 22 decontamination personnel and 39 casualty-clearing and medical-stabilization personnel. Briefing slides, "Chemical and Biological Incident Response Force: America's Consequence Management Force," presentation for MARFORLANT Capability Exercise, no date.

65. See Jonathan B. Tucker, "National Health and Medical Services Response to Incidents of Chemical and Biological Terrorism," *JAMA*, Vol. 278, No. 5 (August 6, 1997), p. 365; and Chris Seiple, "Consequence Management: Domestic Response to Weapons of Mass Destruction," *Parameters*, Vol. 27, No. 3 (Autumn 1997), pp. 119–134.

Most chemical attacks will be easier to detect, since they will tend to announce themselves by producing immediate casualties. A large biological or chemical attack could completely overwhelm available medical resources, as exposed or merely frightened citizens surge into hospitals seeking treatment. In most locales, there are serious deficiencies in the availability of key antidotes, antitoxins, antibiotics, vaccines, and equipment needed to treat the victims of biological or chemical attacks.[66] The expansion of the Metro Medical Strike Team program described above would address some of these deficiencies, and the remainder of the problem should be addressed by establishing a national medical stockpile system to assure adequate supplies of crucial medicines and equipment in case of a large attack.

Even if appropriate supplies are available, however, local medical services could easily be overwhelmed after a large attack, and there would still be a need to mobilize federal medical response assets to supplement them. The Federal Response Plan managed by FEMA assigns responsibility for emergency medical functions to the Department of Health and Human Services (DHHS), which maintains the National Disaster Medical System (NDMS). Dozens of special medical teams distributed around the nation are prepared to provide emergency medical services in the event of natural or man-made disasters, and can be deployed with 12–24 hours notice.[67] They do not, however, possess sufficient resources to respond to an incident involving thousands or tens of thousands of victims, especially if many of them are acutely ill. The military possesses more extensive emergency medical response capabilities, but these units are generally not structured to deploy on short notice to domestic incidents in concert with multiple

---

66. Some of the key medicines, such as certain antibiotics, are also used to fight more common illnesses, so adequate stocks may already exist. But botulism antitoxin, anthrax vaccine (which is needed to treat the disease, not just prevent it), and equipment such as mechanical ventilators are not available in the quantities needed. On the inadequacy of local and regional stocks of pharmaceuticals, see U.S. Department of Health and Human Services, *Health and Medical Services Support Plan for the Federal Response to Acts of Chemical/Biological (C/B) Terrorism* (Washington, D.C.: U.S. Department of Health and Human Services, June 21, 1996), cited in Tucker, "National Health and Medical Services Response to Incidents of Chemical and Biological Terrorism," p. 365.

67. These units are known as Disaster Medical Assistance Teams (DMATs). Three of the DMATs — those stationed in Winston-Salem, Denver, and Los Angeles — have enhanced capabilities for NBC incidents.

other federal, state, and local civilian agencies. The high-readiness Aeromedical Isolation Team at USAMRIID can be deployed worldwide on 12-hour notice, but its sophisticated mobile treatment facility can only accommodate two patients at a time.[68] Improving the capabilities of the NDMS, and restructuring some military units to allow them to be called up quickly in a domestic emergency, would substantially improve federal response capabilities.

Third, the federal government has been insufficiently aggressive in developing and disseminating new technologies relevant to improving U.S. operational preparedness against covert NBC threats.[69] Since 1987, the Technical Support Working Group (TSWG, an interagency body chaired by the Departments of Defense and Energy) has sought with some success to accelerate the fielding of technologies for combating terrorism.[70] But the government's R&D programs have not yet provided all of the technologies needed. Several key technological deficiencies, such as real-time biological agent sensors,[71] wide-area search capabilities, and advanced NBC weapons disablement techniques, are high current priorities. But the technology requirements defined at the national level have tended to emphasize the specialized needs of the military and of federal counterterrorism units, not those of a broad-based domestic program for improving preparedness against covert NBC attack. As a result, most of the advanced technologies being developed are too expensive or too technically demanding for widespread dissemination among non-specialized agencies. In other cases, however, state and local response assets could benefit from equipment that

---

68. Department of Defense and Department of Energy, *Joint Report to Congress: Preparedness and Response to a Nuclear, Radiological, Biological, or Chemical Terrorist Attack*, p. 21.

69. For an overview of several key technological possibilities, see Donald D. Cobb and Walter L. Kirchner, "Reducing the Threat of Nuclear, Biological, and Chemical Proliferation and Terrorism," Los Alamos National Laboratory, written testimony provided to the Permanent Subcommittee on Investigations of the Committee on Governmental Affairs, U.S. Senate, March 13, 1996; and Counterproliferation Program Review Committee (CPRC), *Report on Activities and Programs for Countering Proliferation* (Washington, D.C.: Department of Defense, May 1996).

70. The Technical Support Working Group also has international cooperation agreements with Israel, the United Kingdom, and Canada.

71. The development of a real-time biological weapons detection system is one of the top technology priorities of the Defense Counterproliferation Initiative.

has already been developed to meet military or other federal needs, but funding constraints are prohibitive. The federal government should give more attention to ensuring that those with primary responsibility for coping with domestic NBC incidents benefit from the full potential of technologies that already exist or that are under development, and Congress should provide funds in an expanded Nunn-Lugar-Domenici program to meet this need.

In addition to these capability improvements, the federal government has a role to play in identifying specific buildings and public places that are particularly vulnerable to mass-casualty terrorist attacks, or that present unusually high risks of being the targets of a covert NBC attack.[72] Once identified, expert guidance and resources should be made available to "harden" these targets — that is, to make them less vulnerable to attack. These measures can be as simple as posting extra guards or making ventilation intakes inaccessible, or as complex as installing chemical and biological agent alarms.[73] After the Oklahoma City bombing, for example, the federal government began a program of reducing the vulnerability of federal office buildings to large conventional explosions with structural reinforcements and physical impediments to movement (such as the closing of Pennsylvania Avenue at the White House). These programs should be continued, and expanded to include measures specifically relevant to the chemical and biological weapons threat.[74]

MAKE DOMESTIC NBC PREPAREDNESS A CORE MISSION OF THE U.S. ARMED FORCES

The U.S. military has most of the nation's technical and operational capacity to counter specific NBC threats, including most of its capacity to operate in a chemically or biologically contaminated environment; to decontaminate casualties, equipment, and facilities; and to treat large numbers of chemical and biological warfare victims.

---

72. Because crowded, enclosed spaces greatly increase the effectiveness of small quantities of chemical and biological weapons, attackers seeking to kill large numbers of civilians would probably seek out subways, indoor sports arenas, theaters, or other similar targets.

73. Changing building codes to require that the air intakes of large new buildings be placed high above ground is one low-cost measure that could, over time, help to reduce vulnerability.

74. Target security measures are basically irrelevant against nuclear weapons, unless they are so extensive as to exclude the weapon from the entire target area.

Recommendation 10:
Make Response to Domestic NBC Attacks a
Core U.S. Military Mission

The Department of Defense should expand and accelerate its efforts to train and equip U.S. military forces for operations against NBC-armed adversaries.

Civilian leaders in the Department of Defense, the White House, and the Congress should direct the uniformed military to assume permanent responsibility for ensuring that the United States has an adequate operational capacity to respond to covert NBC attacks, particularly to manage their consequences.

The Army National Guard should adopt the reforms of the Defense Department's Counterproliferation Initiative, placing particular emphasis on preparing for domestic chemical and biological weapons attack.

The Army National Guard should acquire the equipment and training necessary to assist in short-notice operational response to large-scale biological and chemical attacks. This equipment should include protective suits, detection systems, and decontamination gear.

It is virtually certain that military assets would be mobilized to respond to any major domestic NBC incident. Yet the Department of Defense does not maintain a dedicated operational ability, parallel to the Department of Energy's NEST program in the nuclear area, to support domestic crisis or consequence management activities against chemical and biological threats. Instead, the military has a handful of high-readiness units with very specialized capabilities that can be deployed on short notice for military and civilian contingencies alike, and a wide range of general-purpose forces, including mobile medical units, that have some training and equipment necessary to operate in an NBC environment, but that are usually occupied with other missions or that take days or weeks to mobilize.

The Defense Department has a well-established system for providing military support to civil authorities (MSCA) in the case of major domestic emergencies. This function is carried out under the Federal Response Plan, and is coordinated by the Director of Military Support (DOMS) within the Department of the Army. In principle, virtually any military resource could be made available in a domestic crisis through the MSCA system, but in practice the system is not prepared to provide the short-notice and large-scale deployment of appropriately trained military assets that might be needed in a domestic NBC crisis. DOMS would administer the available military assistance, but has no responsibility for building the new capabilities that might be needed, nor for assuring the ability of military units to operate with their civilian counterparts.

As a general matter, the Department of Defense does not consider the defense of the American homeland against covert NBC attacks a core mission. Such attacks fall under the heading of terrorism, the response to which the Defense Department sees as a law enforcement responsibility, which the military will support if ordered and when possible. Like the war on drugs, the armed forces see the domestic response to terrorism, including NBC incidents, as a diversion from their primary mission of projecting American power abroad, and a misuse of defense dollars better spent on hardware or operations and maintenance. This view is shared by most members of the Congressional committees that oversee the Department of Defense. The Department is reluctant to allow its resources to be earmarked for non-military purposes, since doing so can undermine the readiness of military units. The Pentagon did not want the domestic NBC training program for first responders mandated by the Nunn-Lugar-Domenici amendment, and current plans call for its transfer to FEMA in fiscal year 1999. The Reconstruction-era law known as *Posse Comitatus*, which prohibits the military from making arrests, is often cited as the reason for the military's ambivalence toward the domestic NBC problem,[75] but the real reasons have to do with resources and the incentive structures of individual military leaders. As far as terrorism is concerned, the highest priority of the Department of Defense is protecting U.S. forces deployed

---

75. On the law of *Posse Comitatus* and its implications for the military role in civil disasters, see Thomas R. Lujan, "Legal Aspects of Domestic Employment of the Army," *Parameters*, Vol. 27, No. 3 (Autumn 1997), pp. 82–97. Lujan's account of the use of military forces in past civil disaster relief efforts makes it clear that under existing legal exceptions, the law of *Posse Comitatus* does not prevent use of military resources in such emergencies. He also notes that military and National Guard personnel sometimes believe the law is more restrictive than it actually is. See also Peter M. Sanchez, "The 'Drug War': The U.S. Military and National Security," *Air Force Law Review*, Vol. 34 (1991), pp. 109–152; and Roger B. Hohnsbeen, "Fourth Amendment and Posse Comitatus Act Restrictions on Military Involvement in Civil Law Enforcement," *George Washington Law Review*, Vol. 54, Nos. 2–3 (January–March 1986), pp. 404–433.

abroad from terrorist attack, a mission that was strongly emphasized in the aftermath of the Khobar Towers bombing.[76]

The Department of Defense attaches some priority to improving the capacity of the U.S. armed forces to fight in nuclear, biological, and chemical warfare environments, and much is already being done under the Defense Counterproliferation Initiative. This initiative has tended to emphasize the capabilities that are most important to regional warfighting, such as ballistic missile and cruise missile defense, passive defense, strategic and tactical intelligence, battlefield surveillance, hard-target and mobile-target kill technologies, and force protection. Most of these reforms are only indirectly related to defending against covert NBC attacks on domestic targets. The Counterproliferation Policy Review Committee has identified "Defend against Paramilitary, Covert Delivery, and Terrorist WMD Threats" as a key area for capability enhancement,[77] but it ranked this goal 13th of 15 priorities, followed only by supporting U.S. export controls and arms control inspections. The low ranking reflects the assumption that, in situations of active hostilities against an NBC-armed regional adversary, covert delivery will present a relatively modest threat compared to traditional forms of military delivery, such as artillery, aircraft, and

---

76. On the response to the Khobar Towers attack, see the testimony of Secretary of Defense William J. Perry, General John M. Shalikashvili, and General J.H. Binford Peay III, in Senate Hearings 104-832, *Bomb Attack in Saudi Arabia*, Hearings before the Committee on Armed Services, United States Senate, July 9 and September 18, 1996 (Washington, D.C.: U.S. GPO, 1997), pp. 4–34. The achievements and limitations in the Defense Department's response are examined in some detail in General Accounting Office, *Combating Terrorism: Status of DOD Efforts to Protect Its Forces Overseas*, Report No. GAO/NSIAD-97-207 (Washington, D.C.: U.S. GAO, July 1997). The Defense Department's effort is primarily focused on reducing the risk of casualties from high-explosive attacks, not from possible chemical or biological attack.

77. The military is improving the support, training, and equipment provided to the specialized military units responsible for detecting, neutralizing, and rendering NBC weapons safe in permissive and non-permissive environments; developing new technologies useful for coping with covert NBC threats; pre-positioning specialized equipment for NBC response teams abroad; and improving the physical security of high-risk Department of Defense facilities. See CPRC, *Report on Activities and Programs for Countering Proliferation*, pp. 58–63; and Jason Sherman, "New Team of Experts to Scrutinize Army Force Projection Capabilities," *Inside the Army*, December 2, 1996, p. 1.

missiles.[78] However, while it may be true that covert delivery will pose only a modest threat to U.S. troops, it remains the principal NBC threat to the U.S. homeland.

The military's own need to protect its forces on the battlefield against chemical and biological attacks, through attack detection and protective equipment, and to treat the large numbers of biological warfare casualties that could result from a surprise biological attack on the battlefield, have substantial overlaps with civilian consequence management tasks. Protection of overseas military bases from covert attack with chemical, biological, or nuclear weapons is another important military mission, and one that demands solutions to many of the same problems the United States faces domestically, including the challenge of detecting a silent biological attack in peacetime.[79] Military capabilities that address the warfighting needs of the regional commanders in chief — including rear-area defense, security of key logistical nodes and command posts, and the protection of allied populations — can also be deployed against domestic NBC threats. Medical capabilities for treating victims of biological and chemical attacks, and stocks of the relevant medicines, are directly applicable to U.S. domestic consequence-management needs. With these capabilities, the military has the potential to be a key source of aid in an NBC crisis. It should be directed to take on a greater role in this area.

There is little doubt that the U.S. military would be ordered to participate in the response to any serious NBC incident at home, and would willingly do so. The question for the nation is how best to permanently engage the formidable resources of the Department of Defense in a steady,

---

78. The May 1996 report of the Counterproliferation Policy Review Committee noted that "in view of the growing recognition of WMD terrorism as a significant national security threat, the CPRC believes that the current ACE (Area for Capability Enhancement) priority 13, 'Defend Against Paramilitary, Covert Delivery, and Terrorist WMD Threats,' should be elevated in priority when the ACE priority list is revised." CPRC, *Report on Activities and Programs for Countering Proliferation*, p. ES-11.

79. Several of the research and development programs being run under the auspices of the Defense Counterproliferation Initiative seek to improve the ability of the U.S. military to protect high-value fixed sites from covert attacks involving weapons of mass destruction, particularly biological weapons. See Department of Defense, *Proliferation: Threat and Response* (Washington, D.C.: U.S. Department of Defense, 1997), chapter 5; available at <www.defenselink.mil/pubs/prolif97>.

systematic program of preparation to reduce U.S. vulnerability to covert NBC attack. The question has three main answers.

First, the Department of Defense should expand and accelerate its on-going effort to train and equip U.S. forces for operations against NBC-armed adversaries. To date, the Counterproliferation Initiative has achieved much in the area of technology research and development, but it has been considerably less successful in enhancing the quality of training and equipment in combat units. Many of the key deficiencies in chemical and biological defense identified during the 1990–91 Gulf War still existed in 1998.[80] The military's gradual incorporation of counterproliferation into its training, tactics, and mindset is creating a much stronger knowledge base for more specialized capability enhancements. One of the keys to improving U.S. operational preparedness against domestic NBC threats is to ensure that the enhancements in the armed forces' overall capacity to fight in proliferated regional environments also enhance society's capacity to cope with domestic NBC attacks. Further efforts are needed, as indicated by the recommendation of the Defense Department's Quadrennial Defense Review that the counterproliferation procurement budget be boosted by $1 billion over the five-year defense plan, a proposal accepted by Secretary of Defense William Cohen.

Second, civilian leaders in the Department of Defense, the White House, and the Congress should direct the uniformed military to assume permanent responsibility for ensuring that the United States has an adequate operational capacity to respond to covert NBC attacks, particularly in the management of their consequences. The Defense Department has already been obliged by Nunn-Lugar-Domenici to provide NBC training to first responders, but the Pentagon has not accepted the permanence of this mission, and intends to transfer the training program from CBDCOM to FEMA by 1999.

Third, the National Guard should assume day-to-day control over the implementation of the Defense Department program for improving

---

80. See U.S. Congress, GAO, *Chemical and Biological Defense: Emphasis Remains Insufficient to Resolve Continuing Problems*, GAO/NSIAD-96-103 (Washington, D.C.: U.S. GAO, March 1996); ibid., *Testimony*, GAO/T-NSIAD-96-123 (Washington, D.C.: U.S. GAO, March 1996); Department of Defense, *Proliferation: Threat and Response*; and U.S. Department of Defense, Counterproliferation Chemical Biological Defense Network, *Nuclear, Biological, and Chemical Defense: Annual Report to Congress* (Washington, D.C.: U.S. Department of Defense, 1997), <www.acq.osd.mil/cp/nbc97.htm>.

domestic NBC preparedness.[81] The Guard, drawing on the expertise of the entire Department of Defense and other federal agencies, should assume responsibility for providing state and local first responders with appropriate levels of NBC training and equipment in the context of an expanded Nunn-Lugar-Domenici program. Each state's Adjutant General should be held accountable for the level of operational preparedness in cities and counties of his or her own state, which should be subject to regular review by the national inspection teams. The Guard should also acquire key equipment necessary to launch an effective operational response to a large-scale NBC attack, such as protective suits, detection systems, and decontamination gear. Individual Guard units should become fully qualified in the use of this equipment. The Guard should not displace the FBI or FEMA as the lead federal agency of domestic NBC response, but it should become the principal agent for building domestic capabilities for mounting an effective response to an NBC incident. If implemented, these reforms would not only dramatically improve the quality of U.S. operational preparedness for domestic NBC incidents; they would also enhance the value of the National Guard for task-specific foreign deployment in wartime.

There are four basic reasons for giving this mission to the National Guard. First, National Guard units are stationed throughout the United States, in close proximity to virtually all possible domestic targets of an NBC attack. Second, the Guard has both military and civilian functions: it can be mobilized not only by the president, for deployments as a military unit, but also by state governors, for disaster relief missions (e.g., floods,

---

81. In its 1997 summer study on transnational threats, the Defense Science Board (DSB) also recommended that the Army National Guard "provide a national consequence management capability ... to increase DOD support to state and local agency responses to domestic incidents of all types, but with particular emphasis on chemical or biological incidents." Defense Science Board, *DoD Responses to Transnational Threats*, p. 29. This recommendation appears to have been accepted by Secretary of Defense William Cohen, who has created a task force to develop a plan for giving the Army National Guard the capabilities needed to implement this mission. See Elaine M. Grossman, "DOD Creates 'Tiger Team' to Plan Reservists' Role in U.S. Crisis Response," *Inside the Pentagon*, November 27, 1997, p. 1. The National Defense Panel made a similar recommendation in its report *Transforming Defense: National Security in the 21st Century* (Washington, D.C.: U.S. Department of Defense, 1997), p. 55. For a slightly different approach, see also Charles L. Mercier, Jr., "Terrorists, WMD, and the U.S. Army Reserve," *Parameters*, Vol. 27, No. 3 (Autumn 1997), pp. 98–118.

Recommendation 11:
Improve Federal, State, and Local
Cooperation for NBC Response

FEMA, the FBI, and the Department of Defense should jointly develop a national program of field and tabletop exercises to prepare and test federal, state, and local preparedness for domestic NBC incidents. Funding for this program should be drawn from the federal agency budgets and, for state and local agencies, from the Nunn-Lugar-Domenici budget.

In cooperation with the National Governors' Association, the U.S. Conference of Mayors, and the National League of Cities, the White House should establish an intergovernmental council to assist in the development and implementation of systematic domestic preparedness enhancements at the state and local level.

hurricanes) as well as law enforcement functions (e.g., riot control). As a part of the U.S. armed forces, the Guard is mission-oriented, and can be relied upon to implement a long-term program of action, but as an agency of state government, the Guard is able to develop close working ties with the full range of first responders. Third, like the active military, the National Guard is slowly adopting the reforms of the Defense Department's Counterproliferation Initiative, with enhancements in the quality of its training and equipment for operations in NBC-contaminated environments. These reforms should be expanded and accelerated, and should place particular emphasis on domestic NBC response and civilian preparedness. Finally, despite its relatively modest role in U.S. national security strategy, the National Guard has always enjoyed strong political support in the Congress, which appreciates the close connection between Guard units and local constituents. As a result, it is likely to be easier to build political support for making domestic NBC preparedness a new mission of the National Guard, requiring new resources, than to do so for the active services. This combination of factors makes the National Guard the proper bureaucratic home for the mission of preparing the nation to respond effectively to a covert NBC attack.

INTEGRATION OF MULTIPLE LOCAL, STATE, AND FEDERAL AGENCIES

Investing in new capabilities across many different agencies can improve the U.S. ability to manage NBC crises and their consequences, but an effective response will also depend on the ability of these diverse agencies to work together effectively. Experience from exercises and crises illustrates a number of interrelated problems that can undermine the effectiveness of a multi-agency response to a demanding incident: lack of appropriate training can leave individual agency representatives ill-equipped to play a constructive role; poor advance planning and coordination leave roles, goals, and missions to be sorted out under crisis conditions, resulting in confusion, delays, and errors; ignorance about established roles and goals adds to these problems; interagency and intergovernmental rivalries impede cooperation, as well as the advance planning that could ease cooperation; and genuine conflicts between goals (such as whether to try to save lives by evacuating a city at the cost of tipping off an attacker that its plan is compromised) have not been sorted out at the national level, and result in conflicts between agencies and levels of government that have differing priorities.

The inadequacy of the federal government's preparation for domestic NBC incidents was revealed in an October 1994 full-field exercise called Mirage Gold, which simulated a nuclear terrorist threat in New Orleans.[82] The after-action reports from this exercise document the "inherent conflict between the law enforcement and the emergency assistance missions,"[83] as well as an array of serious deficiencies in the involved agencies' preparation for actual NBC incidents, particularly on the part of the FBI. These interagency coordination problems were highlighted by an influential set of hearings held by Senator Sam Nunn in March 1996, at which all of the relevant agencies testified that they were actively working to overcome the coordination problems disclosed during Mirage Gold.[84]

---

82. According to the FBI, "Mirage Gold became a focal point for changes which were needed by all agencies." Blitzer, "Supplemental Questions for the Record," p. 332.

83. Major General Joseph Kinzer, Deputy Commanding General for the 5th U.S. Army, Memorandum for Commanding General, FORSCOM, Ft. McPherson, Ga., Subject: Exercise Mirage Gold After Action Report, November 15, 1994, Annex E, pt. 3.a.(1); reprinted in U.S. Congress, *Global Proliferation of Weapons of Mass Destruction*, Part III, p. 416.

84. See *Global Proliferation of Weapons of Mass Destruction*, Part III. For discussion of the problems highlighted by Mirage Gold, see *Exercise Mirage Gold: After Action Report* (Washington, D.C.: Federal Emergency Management Agency, April 1995); and *The Mile Shakedown Series of Exercises: A Compilation of Comments and Critiques*, partial document (declassified, with deletions) (Las Vegas, Nev.: U.S. Department of Energy, Nevada Operations Office, February 18, 1995).

The single most important technique for identifying interagency conflicts and improving interagency coordination is to conduct regular full-field exercises in realistic, challenging NBC scenarios, with independent observers to help record and analyze the results. Several federal agencies, notably FEMA and the FBI, became more active in exercising their NBC response capabilities in the mid-1990s, often in cooperation with other agencies. Because the interagency operational challenges are so severe, however, the federal government should require and pay for at least two joint full-field NBC crisis and consequence management exercises every year, which would include all relevant federal, state, and local agencies. Many more smaller scale exercises, involving a more limited range of participants, should also be held each year. This program of more frequent and extensive field exercises will grow even more vital as new agencies become involved (e.g., the National Guard), and as new counter-NBC capabilities are built at the federal, state, and local levels.

Frequent exercises are an extremely important tool for improving the ability of disparate agencies at the federal, state, and local levels to cooperate effectively, but other measures are important as well. A nationwide program of NBC capability enhancements can only succeed if the relevant agencies from the different levels of government share a strong sense of common purpose and mission. To help achieve this largely political objective, the White House should establish an intergovernmental domestic preparedness council in cooperation with the National Governors' Association, the U.S. Conference of Mayors, and the National League of Cities. The purpose of this new body would be to organize and motivate state and local leaders to support the program of NBC capability enhancements, and to enhance the quality of state and local cooperation with federal efforts. The president should convene this group at the level of interested governors and mayors once per year, and working-level meetings should be held two or three times per year. Staff support for the effort should be provided by the federal NBC Response Center.

Nuclear Weapons and Fissile Material Security

Insecure fissile material raises the risk of nuclear terrorism, as explained in Chapter 2. Nuclear terrorism would not be a serious threat if all stockpiles of nuclear weapons and direct-use fissile material were held under secure conditions. However, the degradation of the Soviet nuclear custodial system

Recommendation 12:
Secure Nuclear Weapons and Fissile Material

The Departments of Defense and Energy should continue to provide full funding to nuclear security projects in Russia (particularly fissile material protection and accounting), and they and the Congress should shelter these programs from budget cuts.

The U.S. government should expand and accelerate its purchase of Russian highly-enriched uranium (HEU) through the existing U.S.-Russian HEU purchase agreement, including through the direct purchase of undiluted and partially diluted HEU. These improved commercial terms should be linked to the completion of bilateral agreements on nuclear stockpile data exchanges, verified warhead dismantlement, the reciprocal monitoring of excess fissile material, and the accelerated implementation of nuclear security measures in Russia.

The U.S. government should encourage Russia to dilute its excess weapons-grade HEU to less than 20 percent enrichment as rapidly as possible, by offering advance payments under the U.S.-Russian HEU purchase agreement.

The U.S. Department of Energy should accelerate its technical assistance programs aimed at helping the Russian government to convert its three plutonium-production reactors so that they will no longer produce weapons-grade plutonium.

The United States and Russia should promptly begin the permanent disposition of their excess weapons plutonium stocks through parallel programs of reactor burn-up and vitrification. These programs should be conducted on a reciprocal, cooperative basis.

To reduce the incentives for former Russian weapons scientists to emigrate, the U.S. government should expand programs, such as the Department of Energy's Initiatives for Proliferation Prevention (IPP) program, which assist Russia in redirecting military-industrial establishments and weapon scientists into productive commercial enterprises and scientific research. These programs should focus most strongly on Russia's three largest plutonium cities — Chelyabinsk-65, Tomsk-7, and Krasnoyarsk-26 — as well as the Russian chemical and biological weapons complex.

has heightened the risk of nuclear terrorism by rendering vast quantities of fissile material more accessible than at any other time in history. The U.S. government has been fairly active in attempting to address this issue, but the problem is of such a scale that it will require vigorous, sustained effort for many years before the risk of nuclear leakage is fully contained.

Other studies have already analyzed this problem in detail, presenting a range of prescriptions. The recommendations presented here include the most important ideas that have emerged from this large literature.[85] Taken together, these measures constitute the best insurance policy against the risk of nuclear terrorism; it is a far more cost-effective agenda than boosting the capabilities of the federal nuclear crisis management capabilities, for instance. Safeguarding nuclear weapons or fissile material in proper facilities is a much simpler task than locating and recovering stolen fissile material, preventing its weaponization, or defending against an improvised nuclear weapon used in a covert attack.

Declaratory Policy and Law

Finally, it is worth recalling that the infrequency of NBC violence in the past cannot be explained solely, or even principally, by the technical difficulty of obtaining or using weapons of mass destruction. Many states, some non-state actors, and perhaps even a few individuals have had NBC weapons within their reach. Only a handful, however, have taken the fateful steps of acquisition and use. The reasons for this are primarily pragmatic in

---

85. See Graham T. Allison, Owen R. Coté, Jr., Richard A. Falkenrath, and Steven E. Miller, *Avoiding Nuclear Anarchy: Containing the Threat of Loose Russian Nuclear Weapons and Fissile Material*, CSIA Studies in International Security (Cambridge, Mass.: MIT Press, 1996); Richard A. Falkenrath, "The HEU Deal," ibid., Appendix III; Matthew Bunn and John P. Holdren, "Managing Military Uranium and Plutonium in the United States and the Former Soviet Union," *Annual Review of Energy and Environment*, No. 22 (1997), pp. 402–486; John P. Holdren, "Reducing the Threat of Nuclear Theft in the Former Soviet Union," *Arms Control Today*, March 1996, pp. 14–20; Committee on International Security and Arms Control, National Academy of Sciences (NAS), *Management and Disposition of Excess Weapons Plutonium* (Washington, D.C.: National Academy Press, January 1994); James L. Ford and C. Richard Schuller, *Controlling Threats to Nuclear Security: A Holistic Model* (Washington, D.C.: National Defense University Press, 1997); Oleg Bukharin, "Nuclear Safeguards and Security in the Former Soviet Union," *Survival*, Vol. 36, No. 4 (Winter 1994–95); Frank von Hippel, "Fissile Material Security in the Post–Cold War World," *Physics Today*, June 1995, pp. 26–31; Frank von Hippel, Marvin Miller, Harold Feiveson, Anatoli Diakov, and Frans Berkhout, "Eliminating Nuclear Warheads," *Scientific American*, August 1993, pp. 43–49; William Potter, "Exports and Experts: Proliferation Risks from the New Commonwealth," *Arms Control Today*, January/February 1992, pp. 32–37; and Guy B. Roberts, *Five Minutes Past Midnight: The Clear and Present Danger of Nuclear Weapons Usable Fissile Materials*, U.S. Air Force Institute for National Security Studies, Occasional Paper No. 8, February 8, 1996.

Recommendation 13:
Strengthen Declaratory Policy and Law

The United States should continue to support broad multilateral arms control agreements that delegitimize NBC weapons possession and use, especially the Chemical Weapons Convention and the Biological Weapons Convention.

The United States should strongly condemn all cases of NBC weapons use.

The United States should maintain its current policy on international terrorism, including the extraterritorial jurisdiction of U.S. law.

The U.S. government should support an international initiative to negotiate and sign a convention that would define biological weapons possession and use as crimes under international law.

---

character, as argued in Chapter 1. Potential aggressors undertake some sort of risk calculation when they consider using weapons of mass destruction. They may weigh the value of the objective they wish to achieve, the extent to which the use of NBC weapons will contribute to this goal, and the likely responses of their adversaries — in particular, the expected damage from retaliatory action. The rarity of NBC violence in the past is best explained in reference to these calculations. Simply put, aggressors capable of NBC weapons use have not often judged the benefits of use to outweigh the costs. The risk of retaliation in kind — that is, of a reciprocal or escalatory exchange of NBC weapons — has weighed heavily, perhaps decisively, in many decisions against NBC use.

The United States has some capacity to affect the calculations of its potential adversaries, including those that may conduct covert NBC attacks. Historically, much of this effort has fallen under the rubric of deterrence. During the Cold War, the United States sought to deter Soviet aggression (both strategic nuclear attack and, more dubiously, conventional aggression in distant regions) by threatening nuclear escalation or retaliation. To make this threat credible, and hence to enhance the quality of deterrence, the United States invested heavily in its strategic nuclear capabilities, and American leaders, in their actions and statements, constantly sought to maintain the Soviet perception that the United States was prepared to initiate the use of nuclear weapons if necessary, and certainly to carry out retaliatory strikes. This was essentially a strategy of deterrence by the threat of punishment. It is, however, also possible to deter an adversary by denial — that is, by undertaking defensive preparations designed to lower the adversary's confidence in its ability to achieve its objectives by force.[86] This distinction is quite important in considering how the United States can deter covert NBC attacks.

Any state or non-state actor that considers attacking U.S. citizens, forces, or allies with NBC weapons faces enormous risks of punishment. The United States has an unrivaled capacity to punish its international adversaries through the use of force, up to and including nuclear bombardment. Even non-state actors, which usually cannot be directly attacked by military means, face very severe risks, including relentless pursuit by U.S. and allied intelligence and law enforcement agencies. Any group or government competent enough to carry out an NBC attack against the United States is probably intelligent enough to understand that doing so will bring the full weight of the world's only superpower down upon it — assuming, of course, that the United States learns the identity of the attacker. This suggests that if deterrence of an NBC attack fails, it is likely to have failed not because the attacker underestimated the cost of conducting the attack, but because it (a) felt it could escape detection; (b) felt that all alternative courses of action were worse; or (c) for reasons of fanatical motivation or dementia did not care about the prospect of punishment.

The United States should work to maintain the perception that any government or group that used NBC weapons against American interests would suffer enormously. Fortunately, there is little reason to believe that this perception is in jeopardy — at least insofar as it concerns the U.S. willingness and ability to use overwhelming force. There are certain self-imposed constraints on U.S. action, such as the illegality of assassination, the non-use of chemical and biological weapons, and the general principle that individuals should be punished through the judicial process. But even within these constraints — which might not remain sacrosanct in the immediate aftermath of an NBC attack — the United States still has numerous options for conventional and nuclear punishment, and the prospect of criminal prosecution in the United States for mass murder is likely to be regarded by international terrorists as high punishment. U.S. leaders should occasionally state in public that the United States could and would retaliate forcefully against any NBC attacker, but the point is rather obvious. What is not obvious, however, is that the United States would be

---

86. This distinction was made in Glenn H. Snyder, *Deterrence and Defense: Toward a Theory of National Security* (Princeton, N.J.: Princeton University Press, 1961), pp. 14–16.

able to identify the party responsible for a covert NBC attack with sufficient confidence to trigger the effective use of force. This is the issue of attribution, discussed earlier, which is primarily a function of the quality of U.S. intelligence, investigative, and forensic capabilities. U.S. leaders should periodically state in public — perhaps even with some deliberate exaggeration — that the United States has these capabilities and is constantly improving them.

The other aspect of deterrence of covert NBC threats that needs work falls into the category of deterrence by denial. As noted throughout this volume, the United States is acutely vulnerable to covert NBC attacks, due to the difficulty of detecting these attacks in the first place, and due to its limited ability to mitigate the consequences of attacks that do occur. The recommendations made earlier in this chapter are aimed at correcting these deficiencies. This effort should be motivated in part by the desire to decrease the confidence of potential attackers in their own ability to carry out successful, massively destructive attacks against U.S. targets. As the quality of American preparedness for covert NBC attacks begins to improve, this progress should be subtly advertised, and perhaps even exaggerated, by the U.S. government.

Practical considerations probably dominate the decisions of potential NBC aggressors to use or refrain from using their weapons, but decision-makers do not rely exclusively on strategic or pragmatic calculation to determine what they should do; most are also influenced by what they, and those around them, believe is right and wrong.[87] U.S. policy should use this

---

87.   In practice, it is rarely possible to know the relative influence of normative and pragmatic factors in any individual decision. Indeed, decision-makers may themselves be unable to disaggregate their own thought processes. It is fairly clear that Saddam Hussein's decision not to attack Israel with chemical weapons was made for pragmatic rather than moral reasons, since he had previously used these weapons against Iran and his own Kurdish nationals, but this case is unusual for its simplicity. Hitler's decision not to use nerve gas on the battlefield during World War II is more typical, since it probably resulted from a combination of practical concerns, such as logistical difficulties and the possibility of in-kind retaliation, and normative ones, since Hitler and many of his generals had themselves seen the horrible effects of poison gas in the trenches of the Great War. The relative weightings of these concerns cannot be readily assayed. But the impact of normative considerations should not be ignored simply because it cannot be measured. For a discussion of related issues, see Richard M. Price, *The Chemical Weapons Taboo* (Ithaca, N.Y.: Cornell University Press, 1997); and Richard Price and Nina Tannenwald, "Norms and Deterrence: The Nuclear and Chemical Weapons

fact to advantage by strengthening international norms against all forms of NBC acquisition and use, and by trying to avoid actions that appear hypocritical or that otherwise weaken these norms.

Some people argue that any explicit discussion of norms in defense policy is counterproductive or even dangerous, since it breeds complacency and undercuts political support for real capability enhancements. This may represent an unfortunate political reality in the Congress or elsewhere, but it is no reason for U.S. policy to ignore the role of normative considerations in international decision-making. It is also sometimes said that norms against NBC acquisition and use are simply irrelevant, since the individuals most likely to present real NBC threats are already beyond the bounds of moral behavior. This assertion represents a more fundamental error. U.S. policy does not and should not rely solely on norms to influence the behavior of specific bad actors, such as Saddam Hussein; non-normative policy instruments are available for this purpose. But the existence of a norm, or a law, can contribute to the objectives of U.S. policy by facilitating the formation of international coalitions against these actors. Norms against NBC weapons may also add moral disapprobation to the list of considerations that have discouraged the vast majority of national and non-state leaders from using, and a substantial majority from acquiring, weapons of mass destruction. Moreover, even if individual leaders are unaffected by these normative considerations, the broad delegitimization of NBC weapons may make a state's own citizens, or even the members of a terrorist organization, more inclined to reveal a secret procurement effort to the outside world.[88]

There is no inconsistency between an aggressive program to prepare for the likelihood that state and non-state adversaries will acquire and use NBC weapons, on the one hand, and the delegitimization of these activities, on the other. In fact, the two efforts are strongly reinforcing. Norms work best when they are fortified with self-interest. An active U.S. program of preparing for covert NBC aggression, such as that outlined in this chapter, should reduce the utility of this form of attack for potential perpetrators.

Taboos," in Peter J. Katzenstein, ed., *The Culture of National Security: Norms and Identity in World Politics* (New York: Columbia University Press, 1996), pp. 114–152.

88. Even a marginal increase in the number of people willing to expose NBC weapons programs can have an important effect on the ability of states or groups to keep them secret, and on their interest in beginning such a program. While this effect is far from reliable, loss of ideological faith in a state or political movement has been the source of some of the most important intelligence coups in history.

Individual analysts often disagree on the relative weighting that norms and capabilities should have in a state's overall response to the NBC threat, but there is no doubt that both are desirable. A sensible policy should seek to strengthen the norms against NBC acquisition and use as much as possible; to convince those who violate this norm that they will suffer grave consequences and fail to achieve their aims; and to hold to a minimum the damage that even a persistent aggressor is able to cause with NBC weapons.

Together with its international partners, the United States has made significant contributions to the strengthening of global norms against NBC weapons acquisition and use over the past decades. The United States could do still more, however. These norms are generally embodied in formal international legal agreements, most of which the United States has played an active role in negotiating. Among the most important of these normative agreements are the 1925 Geneva Protocol, which bans the use of chemical weapons in warfare; the 1968 Nuclear Non-Proliferation Treaty (NPT), which permits only five member states to possess nuclear weapons; the 1972 Biological Weapons Convention (BWC), which bans biological weapons programs; and the 1993 Chemical Weapons Convention (CWC), which bans chemical weapons possession and requires the destruction of existing chemical weapons stockpiles. The existence of these agreements has helped establish the principle that the possession and use of chemical and biological weapons is beyond the bounds of civilized behavior, as is the possession of nuclear weapons by states that have voluntarily forsworn this option. The Geneva Protocol and the BWC — neither of which contains effective enforcement or verification provisions — and the NPT have been violated repeatedly,[89] but the level of NBC activity in the international system over the past decades would almost certainly have been higher if there had been no treaties or principles to violate.

Declaratory policy is another instrument that can be used to strengthen international norms against NBC acquisition and use, as well as the perceived disincentives to NBC use, better known as deterrence. U.S. national leaders can and do articulate the arguments — both moral and pragmatic — against NBC weapons. Iraq and North Korea, for example, were strongly condemned in the early 1990s for their violations of their own

---

89. The CWC entered into force in April 1997; it remains to be seen whether it too will be violated. Its stringent verification provisions make it quite different from the Geneva Protocol and the BWC. Its ambitious timetable for destroying existing chemical weapons stockpiles is unlikely to be met by several states, including Russia.

nonproliferation commitments, as was Iran for its clandestine NBC programs. Ukraine, Belarus, and Kazakstan were persuaded to relinquish the nuclear weapons they inherited from the Soviet Union with a combination of pragmatic and ethical arguments. In general, however, the United States has difficulty making compelling ethical arguments against other states' possession of weapons of mass destruction, since it has never condemned its own massive weapons programs of either the past or present. We argue that the United States should strongly condemn all cases of NBC weapons use, and encourage others to do the same. It has missed opportunities to do so in the past. The Reagan administration, for example, issued only a mild statement against Iraq's use of chemical weapons against Iran and against Iraq's own Kurdish population during the 1980s. Far stronger language, and action, were called for, especially considering that, at the time, the United States was supporting the Iraqi regime.[90]

With respect to terrorist groups and other violent non-state actors, U.S. declaratory policy is clear and sound.[91] First, the United States says that it does not make concessions to terrorist demands, an assertion that has usually (but not always) been true. Second, terrorists have always been strongly condemned by the United States, treated as criminals, and pursued relentlessly. U.S. law allows international terrorists who attack American citizens or property to be prosecuted in the United States even if they committed their crimes abroad, and were captured in a foreign country (even in a country not cooperating in the investigation) and brought forcibly to the United States.[92] Since the mid-1980s, U.S. agencies have had a number

---

90. The United States was not alone in this failure. "In the face of incontrovertible evidence that Iraq had violated the 1925 Geneva Protocol by resorting to the use of chemical weapons in its war with Iran, there was nevertheless a widespread reluctance among nations, including the moderate Arab states, to see Iran emerge the victor. Thus, the penalties imposed on Iraq — a call by the Security Council to cease and desist and the imposition of some export controls on a few chemicals — had little impact on that country's subsequent behavior." Gordon M. Burck and Charles C. Flowerree, *International Handbook on Chemical Weapons Proliferation* (New York: Greenwood Press, 1991), pp. 537–538.

91. For a summary of U.S. counterterrorism policy, see "Special Briefing by Ambassador Philip C. Wilcox, U.S. Coordinator for Counterterrorism," U.S. Department of State Daily Press Briefing, April 30, 1996.

92. For information on the state of U.S. law in this area, and for some examples of the policy debate, see U.S. Department of Justice, Office of Legal Counsel, "Memorandum for Dick Thornburgh, Attorney General, Re: Authority of the

of major successes in arresting international terrorists abroad for trial in the United States, the most spectacular of which was the capture of Ramzi Yousef, the World Trade Center bomber, in Pakistan on February 7, 1995.[93] And third, the United States has a policy of punishing the state sponsors of international terrorism by unilateral and multilateral means, using political pressure, economic sanctions, and sometimes military action. The United States also offers technical assistance to states that are trying to combat terrorism, and consistently raises the issue of terrorism in international meetings. Behind these policies is a basic philosophy that states should have a monopoly on the use of force.

Third, by its own behavior, the United States sets an example for the rest of the world; its example has in many cases strengthened the norms against NBC acquisition and use, but in a few cases has not. The United States renounced its offensive biological weapons program in 1969, clearing the way for the 1972 Biological Weapons Convention. In 1991, the United States similarly agreed, reciprocally with the Soviet Union, to eliminate its chemical weapons stockpile, leading to the signing of the CWC in 1993. Under the terms of the Nuclear Non-Proliferation Treaty, which was extended indefinitely in 1995, non–nuclear weapon states voluntarily forswore the acquisition of nuclear weapons, and accepted the application of international verification measures on their civilian nuclear activities. In

---

Federal Bureau of Investigation to Override Customary or other International Law in the Course of Extraterritorial Law Enforcement Activities," June 21, 1989; Jeanne M. Woods, "Presidential Legislating in the Post–Cold War Era: A Critique of the Barr Opinion on Extraterritorial Arrests," *Boston University International Law Journal*, Vol. 14, No. 1 (Spring 1996), pp. 1–53; Catherine Collier Fisher, "U.S. Legislation to Prosecute Terrorists: Antiterrorism or Legalized Kidnaping?" *Vanderbilt Journal of International Law*, Vol. 18, No. 4 (Fall 1985), pp. 915–959; Adam W. Wegner, "Extraterritorial Jurisdiction Under International Law: The *Yunis* Decision as a Model for the Prosecution of Terrorists in U.S. Courts," *Law and Policy in International Business*, Vol. 22, No. 2 (Spring 1991), pp. 409–440; and Jimmy Gurulé, "Terrorism, Territorial Sovereignty, and the Forcible Apprehension of International Criminals Abroad," *Hastings International and Comparative Law Review*, Vol. 17, No. 3 (Spring 1994), pp. 457–495.

93. See "U.S. Jury Convicts 3 in a Conspiracy to Bomb Airliners," *New York Times*, September 6, 1996, p. A1. Mir Amal Kansi, the man responsible for a fatal shooting at the gates of the Central Intelligence Agency, was apprehended in Afghanistan or Pakistan in June 1997; "U.S. Seizes Suspect in Killing of 2 CIA Officers," *New York Times*, June 18, 1997, p. A1. See also Christopher S. Wren, "Long Arm Of U.S. Law Gets Longer," *New York Times*, July 7, 1996, Section 4, p. 4.

return, the five treaty parties that possess nuclear weapons, including the United States, pledged peaceful nuclear cooperation and reductions in their nuclear arsenals, with the goal of the eventual elimination of nuclear weapons. While the United States has reaffirmed its commitment to work toward nuclear disarmament, all indications are that the required international negotiations will be slow, and the nuclear weapon states will retain their nuclear weapons for the near future, albeit in reduced numbers. U.S. policy on peaceful nuclear cooperation has been criticized by some other nations for being unduly discriminatory and for imposing restrictions that were not envisioned in the original NPT bargain. For example, the United States has strongly opposed nuclear cooperation with states that have complied with International Atomic Energy Agency (IAEA) safeguards but that are believed by U.S. intelligence to have clandestine nuclear weapons programs. This situation is clearest in the case of Iran. The United States maintains, correctly in our view, that the NPT does not require nuclear cooperation when there is good evidence to believe that the state in question is seeking nuclear weapons, in violation of the most fundamental purpose of the treaty. With respect to disarmament, the United States and Russia (following the initiatives of the Soviet Union) have made massive reductions in their levels of deployed tactical and strategic nuclear weapons since the late 1980s, and are in the process of dismantling thousands of excess nuclear warheads. The two states should go further still, and should dismantle the thousands of functional detached warheads that both currently intend to keep as a "strategic reserve,"[94] but the non–nuclear weapon parties to the NPT can no longer argue that the two nuclear superpowers have disregarded their Article IV commitment to deep and meaningful reductions.[95]

In general, we believe the United States has an appropriate policy posture toward the acquisition and use of weapons of mass destruction by states and non-state actors, and has worked constructively to delegitimize these weapons in the eyes of the world. Where there are deficiencies in this effort, they usually result from recognized policy trade-offs. The United

---

94. On the importance of reducing the size of the U.S. and Russian strategic nuclear reserves, see National Academy of Sciences, *The Future of U.S. Nuclear Weapons Policy* (Washington, D.C.: National Academy Press, 1997).

95. Indeed, the United States seeks a new strategic arms reduction treaty with Russia (START III) that would codify even greater reductions in the two sides' nuclear arsenals. The Russian Duma must ratify START II, however, before the U.S. government will begin serious negotiations on START III.

States could, for example, strengthen the norm against nuclear weapons by renouncing and destroying its own nuclear arsenal, but such a step would be precipitous given the existence of large nuclear arsenals in other states, and many would argue that the diffuse benefits of such a step are unlikely to compensate for the specific military and psychological consequences of losing an ultimate deterrent. Likewise, in its nuclear weapons doctrine, the United States, and its NATO allies, have rejected the principle of "no first use" of nuclear weapons, at least against nuclear-armed adversaries, arguing that they must retain the option of initiating nuclear weapon use in order to maintain a strong deterrent. The United States has, however, extended no-first-use pledges to non–nuclear weapon states in a variety of contexts. Examples include the 1978 assurances offered by Secretary of State Cyrus Vance, in which the U.S. government pledged not to use nuclear weapons against non–nuclear weapon states party to the NPT that are not allied with nuclear weapon states; pledges embodied in the Latin American, South Pacific, and African nuclear-weapon-free-zone treaties; and the 1995 pledge that the United States, Britain, France, and Russia made to secure support for the indefinite extension of the Nuclear Non-Proliferation Treaty.[96]

There is an inherent tension between no-first-use pledges, which help strengthen the international norm against nuclear weapons, and the desire to use nuclear threats to deter regional adversaries, such as Iran or Iraq, from using chemical or biological weapons.[97] A degree of ambiguity has already entered into this aspect of U.S. declaratory policy: in 1991, George

---

96. An account of U.S. non-use pledges, and an argument against creating new exceptions that would allow nuclear retaliation for chemical and biological weapons use, can be found in George Bunn, "Expanding Nuclear Options: Is the U.S. Negating Its Non-Use Pledges?" *Arms Control Today*, May/June 1996, pp. 7–10.

97. For the debate over the use of nuclear threats to deter chemical and biological weapons use, see Victor A. Utgoff, *Nuclear Weapons and the Deterrence of Biological and Chemical Warfare*, Occasional Paper No. 36 (Washington, D.C.: Henry L. Stimson Center, October 1997), pp. 5–6; David Gompert, Kenneth Watman, and Dean Wilkening, "Nuclear First Use Revisited," *Survival*, Vol. 37, No. 3 (Autumn 1995), pp. 27–44; Stuart E. Johnson, *The Niche Threat: Deterring the Use of Chemical and Biological Weapons* (Washington, D.C.: National Defense University Press, 1997); "Viewpoint: Nuclear Deterrence Won't Stop Unorthodox Weapons," *Aviation Week and Space Technology*, September 9, 1996, p. 94; Frank J. Lebeda, "Deterrence of Biological and Chemical Warfare: A Review of Policy Options," *Military Medicine*, Vol. 162, No. 3 (March 1997), pp. 156–161; and Bunn, "Expanding Nuclear Options."

Bush told Saddam Hussein that he and the Iraqi people would "pay a terrible price" if Iraq used chemical or biological weapons, a statement that was widely interpreted as a veiled nuclear threat.[98] This degree of ambiguity is justified by the needs of regional deterrence, and avoids most of the harm that explicitly abandoning past no-first-use pledges would do to the moral authority of the United States in multilateral nonproliferation diplomacy.

The U.S. government is, however, missing a unique opportunity to strengthen the global norm against weapons of mass destruction, and that is to negotiate a new multilateral convention that would make the production, stockpiling, and use of biological weapons crimes under international law.[99] Such an agreement would make individual participants in a biological weapons program subject to prosecution in other nations or international courts. The existing international legal agreements that ban the production and use of biological weapons apply only to states, while individuals are subject to the laws of the states that have jurisdiction over them. Many, but not all, states have national laws that make the acquisition and use of biological weapons criminal offenses; some that do have such laws lack the ability to enforce them. A powerful state like the United States can assert extra-territorial jurisdiction over individuals that violate U.S. law outside of U.S. borders, but the legitimacy of this position under international law is open to question.[100] Making the possession and use of

---

98. "Statement by Press Secretary Fitzwater on President Bush's Letter to President Saddam Hussein of Iraq," January 12, 1991, in *Public Papers of George Bush*, Book 1: *January 1 to June 30, 1991*. However, Bush had reportedly already decided against the use of nuclear weapons in the Gulf. See William M. Arkin, "Calculated Ambiguity: Nuclear Weapons and the Gulf War," *Washington Quarterly*, Vol. 19, No. 4 (Autumn 1996), pp. 3–18; and James A. Baker III with Thomas M. DeFrank, *The Politics of Diplomacy* (New York: G.P. Putnam's Sons, 1995), p. 359.

99. We are indebted to Matthew Meselson for suggesting this idea. See Matthew Meselson, "Strengthening the BWC and Criminalizing Biological Weapons Under International Law," commissioned paper presented at the 47th Pugwash Conference on Science and World Affairs, Lillehammer, Norway, August 1–7, 1997.

100. Examples of existing crimes under international law include war crimes, genocide, slavery, torture, piracy, hijacking, kidnaping of diplomats, theft of archeological treasures, and interference with submarine cables. Not all of these, however, are universally recognized. For an overview of the limited and rather incoherent scope of international criminal law, see M. Cherif Bassiouni, "The Penal Characteristics of Conventional International Criminal Law," *Case Western Reserve*

biological weapons a crime under international law would have two positive effects and virtually no costs. First, the existence of a convention of this kind, if its enforcement seemed credible, might add to the list of pragmatic reasons weighing against a decision to acquire or use biological weapons, since the long-term risks of such an effort might seem greater to the individuals involved. Second, this convention could reinforce the strong position of the international community that the use of disease as a weapon, by anyone and for any purpose, is a basic moral wrong.

Conclusion

There is much that can be done to reduce the vulnerability of the United States to covert NBC attack. The recommendations outlined above represent our judgments about the areas where current capabilities are most deficient, or where additional effort offers the highest leverage against the problem. It is not a tidy agenda. There are no simple, technical solutions to the national security threats posed by the potential for covert nuclear, biological, or chemical attack. The vulnerability cannot be eliminated or substantially reduced in the same way as some military threats, with specific technical or operational countermeasures developed to meet particular offensive systems. This is a major difference between the covert NBC threat and traditional military NBC threats, such as ballistic missiles: the appropriate response to the latter tends to be relatively straightforward, if technologically complex, while the former requires responses scattered across diverse policy areas and multiple jurisdictions. Reducing vulnerability to covert attack requires a very broad range of responses, as well as leadership and strategic coordination.

Although we have not attempted to estimate the costs of the measures we propose, implementing this agenda would not be cheap. Nevertheless, the total cost would be small compared to other national security programs. Strong progress could be achieved with spending on the order of $1 billion per year, which we would allocate to national coordination (5 percent), intelligence (25 percent), operational preparedness (40 percent), and fissile

---

Journal of International Law, Vol. 15 (1983), pp. 27–37. A collection of the major international conventions that create and govern international criminal law, and of some of the key draft conventions that have failed to draw sufficient support for adoption, can be found in Christine van den Wyngaert and Guy Stessens, eds., *International Criminal Law: A Collection of International and European Instruments* (The Hague: Kluwer Law International, 1996).

material security (30 percent). The cost of the investments proposed here seems reasonable, compared to the total U.S. federal budget, the defense budget (about $250 billion), or even just the ballistic missile defense budget (about $3 billion). A central contention of this book is that any U.S. government willing to spend $1 billion per year on national missile defense research and development projects should be willing to spend a comparable sum to reduce U.S. vulnerability to covert NBC aggression, since the number of potential covert attackers is much greater than the number of states armed with long-range ballistic missiles, and because U.S. capabilities to identify and therefore deter covert attackers are so much less reliable than the U.S. ability to identify ballistic missile attackers.

We have avoided recommendations that would affect essential aspects of American society, such as freedom of movement and other constitutionally guaranteed rights. Some may object to our recommendations for a greater military role in what is currently a law enforcement matter, or for more systematic monitoring of commercial information on potentially NBC-related transactions, on the grounds that these measures may infringe on essential civil liberties. We believe, however, that these measures can be implemented in ways that do not dilute basic American rights, and require no changes in the rules that govern when and how the government may investigate its citizens. It should also be remembered that our recommendations are for measures to be taken in advance of any real incident. If a domestic NBC attack does actually take place, it is quite possible that the policy response of the U.S. government, shaped by the resulting climate of fear and anger, may do grievous harm to essential American liberties. Limited action in advance, taken in ways that do not conflict with essential U.S. values, can provide some insurance against a later overreaction.

Chapter 6

Conclusion

We have argued above that the United States is highly vulnerable to covert attack with nuclear, biological, and chemical weapons, and that there is reason to believe that the threat of such attacks is significant and growing. We have also proposed a broad program of action to reduce U.S. vulnerability and contain the threat. Taking action now is a hedge against a low-probability, high-consequence threat. It is an act of prudence, like an insurance policy. The probability of a covert NBC attack against U.S. territory, forces, or allies is higher than commonly assumed, and the priorities of U.S. national security strategy should be adjusted to reflect this fact. Focusing on covert and terrorist means of NBC delivery is also an act of logic, like locking the back door as well as the front door of a house.[1] Strong investments in defense against ballistic missiles and other military NBC threats should be balanced with comparable investments in denying access to NBC weapons and preparing to counter non-military or transnational NBC threats. Prudence and logic, however, are not the only factors that influence U.S. national security policy, and are probably not even dominant.

There are several political obstacles to vigorous, balanced action against the covert NBC threat. One is public and official ignorance about the nature of the threat and what can be done to reduce it. This book has tried to address this problem, but it is clear that other studies, conveyed by different people in different ways to different audiences, will be needed to shift the conventional wisdom of the U.S. national security community. U.S. analysts and officials need to stop dismissing NBC weapons in general, and covert delivery in particular, as the stuff of farfetched, nightmarish scenarios. The

---

1. As Fred Iklé has put it, opponents of national missile defense "point out — correctly — that nuclear weapons and other mass destruction weapons could be smuggled into the United States or delivered by aircraft. This argument is like saying we should not lock the front door because a thief could come in through the back door we also left open. Of course, the several routes of attack must be defended against; and of course, such defenses can never be guaranteed to be perfect." Fred C. Iklé, "Do We Need a Missile Defense?" *Wall Street Journal*, June 20, 1996, p. 18.

risk is real, and ranks among the most serious challenges to vital U.S. national interests in the post–Cold War era. Similarly, it is important to understand that it is possible to reduce U.S. vulnerability to covert NBC attack substantially, without compromising core American values or civil liberties.

A second political challenge is that responding to the covert NBC threat does not strongly support any high-priority objective of U.S. foreign or domestic policy. It does not directly promote democracy or free trade, increase stability to Europe or Asia, or bring peace to troubled regions. Indeed, if improperly conceived it may even collide with the basic constitutional priorities of preserving civil liberties and protecting the citizenry from the arbitrary power of the state. Implementing the agenda we lay out in Chapter 5 would yield significant collateral benefits in the areas of disaster management, public health, and intelligence capabilities, but these are not high-priority issues for the nation's political leaders. Perhaps the only exception to this is the protection of U.S. forces deployed abroad, particularly in the Persian Gulf, where reduced vulnerability to covert NBC attack could translate into increased staying power. The indirect benefits of an improved response could prove significant, saving lives at home and helping to preserve America's ability to lead internationally. But such benefits are hard to recognize in advance.

Moreover, the measures needed to reduce U.S. vulnerability to covert NBC threats generally command little support in the bureaucratic and electoral politics that lie behind the U.S. defense budget. Many of these measures require expenditures in domains that have traditionally had little if anything to do with the military, such as first-responder preparedness and epidemiological surveillance. The Congressional committees concerned with national security are protective of the defense budget, and many legislators (and generals and admirals) are reflexively opposed to using the defense budget for purposes outside of traditional military missions. The jurisdictional divide between law enforcement and national security is particularly strong, and creates serious obstacles to the conception and implementation of an appropriate package of initiatives. All sides of the debate have ready excuses for why their particular organizations cannot or should not bear the cost of implementing the measures needed. Moreover, despite relaxation of Washington's climate of fiscal austerity in the late 1990s, politicians still struggle more to preserve existing projects that benefit their constituents than to find new ones that necessitate compensatory offsets in the federal budget.

Many of these obstacles would disappear if the United States suffered an NBC attack at home. In the atmosphere of national emergency that would follow a successful NBC attack, or even a credible threat of NBC use, the political will and funding necessary to implement a vigorous response to the covert NBC threat would become considerably easier to generate, but there would also be a very real risk of political overreaction. Unwise and wasteful measures — both offensive and defensive — might be taken reflexively, with costs measured not only in dollars, but in liberties, lives, and strategic position. In the aftermath of a mass-destruction attack, the national leaders who were uninterested in hedging against an uncertain threat might find themselves being held accountable for the nation's failed preventive efforts and low level of preparedness. The excuses given for not having done more beforehand will ring hollow. By far the best thing U.S. policymakers can do to avoid having to make these excuses is to focus on the threat before it reaches emergency proportions, and to begin implementing a balanced agenda of preventive and preparedness measures, such as that laid out in Chapter 5. Doing this before the first attack will require uncommon foresight and leadership.

No state can make itself invulnerable to all forms of internal and external aggression, and trying to do so is certain to waste resources. The question, therefore, is when a nation should stop investing in any particular national security activity. This question has no single "right" answer: individuals see threats differently, place different values on their own security, and may change their minds as their external environment changes. The answers rely on subjective judgments about how likely an uncertain event is, how severe its consequences would be, and the extent to which a proposed policy initiative would make a difference. Thus, in addition to the various political obstacles to taking more vigorous action against the covert NBC threat in advance of an actual emergency, there is also the intellectual problem of not being able to specify exactly how much is enough. The limits of prudence are not obvious.

We have argued that the United States should devote substantially greater resources to preventing the emergence of covert NBC threats and reducing its vulnerability to those that do emerge. We have described a broad prescriptive agenda for achieving these objectives. We have not tried to put a price tag on the measures we propose, since we recognize that such figures are essentially irrelevant in the political process that determines how the federal budget is spent. However, the level of U.S. spending on ballistic missile defense suggests the order of magnitude at which the United States is prepared to invest in defending its territory and forces from one particular means of NBC delivery. There is no reason to believe that the threat of covert delivery is less serious than the threat of ballistic missiles delivery, so it is not unreasonable to conclude that the United States should be prepared to spend about $1 billion per year against the covert NBC threat, with corresponding increases in the level of high-level attention and bureaucratic commitment.

To justify this level of proposed new effort, we have provided an assessment of the covert NBC threat that examines technical vulnerabilities as well as the possible motivations of potential state and non-state adversaries. We have tried to make this threat assessment as convincing as possible, but not at the price of overstating our case. There are vast uncertainties surrounding the covert NBC threat, particularly regarding the likelihood of future attacks. No one knows enough to justify a national crusade against the problem, or the surrender of core American values and civil liberties. But the United States does know enough to justify becoming significantly more focused on precautions against the threat, and to begin a systematic, balanced program of action aimed at reducing U.S. vulnerability to this deadly form of attack.

✢ ✢ ✢ ✢ ✢

In Homer's epic, Achilles was killed only after he had defeated his greatest opponent, Hector, the champion of the Trojans. In a fit of rage, the arrogant Achilles desecrated the body of his slain foe. This angered the god Apollo, who knew of Achilles' hidden vulnerability. Later, as Achilles battled a lesser adversary, Apollo guided an arrow to Achilles' heel, mortally wounding the warrior who had believed he was invincible. The heel was the hero's vulnerability, but hubris proved his greatest weakness.

Acronyms

ANC	African National Congress
ANO	Abu Nidal Organization
AOR	Area of Responsibility
ASD (ISA)	Assistant Secretary of Defense for International Security Affairs
ASD (SOLIC)	Assistant Secretary of Defense for Special Operations and Low-Intensity Conflict
ATCC	American Type Culture Collection
ATF	Bureau of Alcohol, Tobacco, and Firearms
BMD	Ballistic Missile Defense
BMDO	Ballistic Missile Defense Organization
BW	Biological Weapons
BWC	Biological Weapons Convention
C^3I	Command, Control, Communications, and Intelligence
CBDCOM	U.S. Army Chemical and Biological Defense Command
CBIRF	Chemical and Biological Incident Response Force (U.S. Marine Corps)
CBW	Chemical and biological weapons
CDC	Centers for Disease Control
CIA	Central Intelligence Agency
CINC	Commander in Chief
CNN	Cable News Network
CNO	Chief of Naval Operations
CoCom	Coordinating Committee
CPRC	Counterproliferation Program Review Committee
CTC	Counterterrorist Center
CW	Chemical Weapons
CWC	Chemical Weapons Convention
DARPA	Defense Advanced Research Projects Agency

DDI	Deputy Director of Intelligence (CIA)
DHHS	Department of Health and Human Services
DDO	Deputy Director of Operations (CIA)
DOD	U.S. Department of Defense
DOMS	Director of Office of Military Support
DSWA	Defense Special Weapons Agency
EIS	Epidemiological Intelligence Service
EMIS	Electromagnetic Isotope Separation
ERDEC	Edgewood Research, Development, and Engineering Center
FARC	Revolutionary Armed Forces of Colombia
FBI	Federal Bureau of Investigation
FEMA	Federal Emergency Management Agency
FORSCOM	U.S. Forces Command
GIA	Armed Islamic Group (Algeria)
GPS	Global Positioning System
HAZMAT	Hazardous Materials
HEU	Highly Enriched Uranium
HHS	Department of Health and Human Services
IAEA	International Atomic Energy Agency
ICBM	Inter-Continental Ballistic Missile
INS	Immigration and Naturalization Service
IPP	Initiative for Proliferation Prevention
IRA	Irish Republican Army
IRBM	Intermediate-Range Ballistic Missile
MMST	Metropolitan Medical Strike Team
MPC&A	Materials Protection, Control, and Accounting
MRTA	Tupac Amaru Revolutionary Movement
MSCA	Military Support to Civil Authorities
NBC	Nuclear, Biological, and Chemical
NEST	Nuclear Emergency Search Team
NDMS	National Disaster Medical System
NIE	National Intelligence Estimate
NMD	National Missile Defense

NPT	Nuclear Non-Proliferation Treaty
NSC	National Security Council
OMB	Office of Management and Budget
OSD	Office of the Secretary of Defense
OSIA	On-Site Inspection Agency
OSTP	Office of Science and Technology Policy
OTA	Office of Technology Assessment
OVP	Office of the Vice President
PDD	Presidential Decision Directive
PHS	Public Health Service
PKK	Kurdish Workers' Party
PLO	Palestine Liberation Organization
R&D	Research and Development
RAF	Red Army Faction (Germany)
SLBM	Submarine-Launched Ballistic Missile
TEU	Technical Escort Unit
TMD	Tactical Missile Defense
TSWG	Technical Support Working Group
UNSC	United Nations Security Council
UNSCOM	United Nations Special Commission on Iraq
USARICD	U.S. Army Research Institute for Chemical Defense
USAMRIID	U.S. Army Medical Research Institute for Infectious Diseases
WMD	Weapons of Mass Destruction

Index

accidents: detection of clandestine NBC program due to, 57, 109, 110, 124–125, 291, 295, 310; in Aum Shinrikyo chemical weapons program, 20, 22, 24; in Soviet biological weapons program, 68–69, 124, 151; Sverdlovsk anthrax accident, 68–71

acquisition of NBC weapons: 62, 87, 210; indigenous production of biological weapons, 116–117; indigenous production of chemical weapons, by Iraq, 226–227, by North Korea, 72, by Syria, 72; indigenous production of fissile material or nuclear weapon, xviii, 18, 86, 88, 99, 127, 129–131, 258, 262; indigenous production of missiles, 250n; smuggling of nuclear material across borders, 41, 43, 127, 137, 140; smuggling of nuclear weapon across borders, 21, 27, 140, 141, 244, 264, 337; see also under accidents

aerosolization: aerosol biological weapons use by Aum Shinrikyo, 20, 22, 31, 151; defined, 15, 107; detection and warning, 280, 288, 292; of biological warfare agents, 16, 112–114, 119, 120–121, 151, 152–153, 171, 231, 241, 247, 249; of chemical warfare agents, 17, 107–108; production of, 87, 99, 175

Algeria: interest in nuclear program, 64, 65; religious terrorism in, 182, 184, 201; violence in, 46, 47, 51, 55, 56, 180

amateur terrorism, rise in: 181, 196, 199–200

American Type Culture Collection (ATCC): 40, 41, 116

anonymity, advantage of to covert attacker: 113, 193, 223, 234, 239, 296–297; see also attribution of responsibility for attack

anthrax: 117, 118-119, 124, 142, 152-153, 154, 155, 171, 291, 294, 311; possession or use, by Aum Shinrikyo, 20, 24–25, 31, by Germany, 36, by Iraq, 87, 256, by Japan, 76, by South Africa, 78, Soviet Union, 68-70, 124, 151n; threat by German biologist, 43; see also Larry Wayne Harris

area attacks: possible use of NBC weapons in, 139; biological weapons in, 99, 119, 120n, 121, 122n, 143, 144, 151, 152–153, 228, 236; chemical weapons in, 17, 143, 149, 150, 236; nuclear and radiological weapons in, 5–6, 14, 15, 112, 155–158

The Robert and Renée Belfer Center for Science and International Affairs

Graham T. Allison, Director
John F. Kennedy School of Government, Harvard University
79 JFK Street, Cambridge MA 02138
(617) 495-1400

The Belfer Center for Science and International Affairs (BCSIA) is the hub of research, teaching, and training in international security affairs, environmental and resource issues, and science and technology policy at Harvard's John F. Kennedy School of Government. The Center's mission is to provide leadership in advancing policy-relevant knowledge about the most important challenges of international security and other critical issues where science, technology, and international affairs intersect.

BCSIA's leadership begins with the recognition of science and technology as driving forces transforming international affairs. The Center integrates insights of social scientists, natural scientists, technologists, and practitioners with experience in government, diplomacy, the military, and business to address these challenges. The Center pursues its mission in four complementary research programs:

- The International Security Program (ISP) addresses the most pressing threats to U.S. national interests and international security.

- The Environment and Natural Resources Program (ENRP) is the locus of Harvard's interdisciplinary research on resource and environmental programs and policy responses.

- The Science, Technology, and Public Policy (STPP) program analyzes ways in which science and technology policy influence international security, resources, environment, and development, and such cross-cutting issues as technological innovation and information infrastructure.

- The Strengthening Democratic Institutions (SDI) project catalyzes support for three great transformations in Russia, Ukraine, and other republics of the former Soviet Union — to sustainable democracies, free market economies, and cooperative international relations.

The heart of the Center is its resident research community of more than one hundred scholars: Harvard faculty, analysts, practitioners, and each year a new, interdisciplinary group of research fellows. BCSIA sponsors frequent seminars, workshops, and conferences, many open to the public; maintains a substantial specialized library; and publishes books, monographs, and discussion papers. The Center's International Security Program, directed by Steven E. Miller, publishes the BCSIA Studies in International Security, and sponsors and edits the quarterly journal *International Security*.

The Center is supported by an endowment established with funds from Robert and Renée Belfer, the Ford Foundation, and Harvard University, by foundation grants, by individual gifts, and by occasional government contracts.